BIAFRA
THE MAKING OF A NATION

BIAFRA
THE MAKING OF A NATION

BY

ARTHUR AGWUNCHA NWANKWO

AND

SAMUEL UDOCHUKWU IFEJIKA

PRAEGER PUBLISHERS
New York · Washington

BOOKS THAT MATTER

Published in the United States of America in 1970
by Praeger Publishers, Inc., 111 Fourth Avenue,
New York, N.Y. 10003

© 1969 in London, England, by Arthur A. Nwankwo
and Samuel U. Ifejika

Library of Congress Catalog Card Number: 70-108559

Printed in Great Britain

TO HIS EXCELLENCY
GENERAL C. ODUMEGWU OJUKWU
SYMBOL OF THE BIAFRAN REVOLUTION

THE AUTHORS

ARTHUR AGWUNCHA NWANKWO was born on August 19, 1942, in Ajalli, Awka Province, Biafra. He attended St. Cyprian's School (primary), Port Harcourt, and County Grammar School, Ikwere-Etche. In summer 1963, he was at Lincoln University, Pennsylvania, USA, and in summer 1965 at Howard University, Washington DC. He graduated BA in history and political science in June 1966 at Eastern Mennonite College, Harrisonburgh, Virginia, where he was a college scholar. Later he attended graduate school at Howard University, and took a graduate fellowship and teaching assistantship at Duquesne University, Pittsburgh, where he graduated MA in political science (African Affairs) in June 1967.

Immediately after his graduation in 1967, he returned to his home-land, and was for a time employed in the Ministry of Information.

SAMUEL UDOCHUKWU IFEJIKA was born on April 12, 1942, a native of Achi, in Oji River Province. After elementary school, he attended Dennis Memorial Grammar School, Onitsha, secondary and higher schools. He then attended the University of Lagos, Nigeria, which he left on account of the crisis there in 1965; he subsequently graduated in law at the University of Biafra, Nsukka, in June 1967. While at the University of Lagos, he engaged in active student leadership and led the students during the University crisis of 1965. At the University of Biafra he was Vice-President of the Law Society, and was elected Orator and Vice-President of the graduating class, 1967.

Samuel Ifejika has long been active in the youth and student affairs of Nigeria and Biafra; he has contributed to the press, radio and television at home and abroad, and is a local correspondent of the Institute of International Youth Affairs, New York. He has served in the various war-time Committees of Biafra such as the Armed Forces Education Committee. He was for a time senior staff editor of *Biafra Time*.

ACKNOWLEDGMENTS

Writing under the strains and stresses of the Biafra–Nigeria war, amidst the rattle and rumble of machine guns and shells, the whizzing and roaring of Nigerian jet bombers and fighters – pouring down demolition and incendiary bombs, and spouting and spraying cannon bullets on Biafran civilian populations – the staccato of defiant Biafran anti-aircraft guns, the authors have not found the production of this book an easy task. Often, with our scripts under our arms, we have had to dive for cover from raids from the Anglo-Soviet-supported Nigerian Air Force. On one occasion cannon bullets have whistled into our study, shattering window-panes and missing us by inches. Naturally, the speed of our work fluctuated with every turn of the war.

It is impossible to mention all those who have, by their kind co-operation, made possible the successful completion of this book. There are, however, a few to whom we feel compelled to express openly our gratitude.

First and foremost, we acknowledge our gratitude to His Excellency General Chukwuemeka Odumegwu Ojukwu, whose magnificent leadership of the Biafran cause has inspired the writing of this book.

We must also express our indebtedness to Mr. Victor Nwankwo, of the Engineering Faculty, University of Biafra, for his many months of intensive research, to the fruits of which this book owes heavily.

Our particular thanks go to Dr. Okechukwu Ikejiani for his untiring support, constant encouragement, searching criticisms and most helpful advice, and to Mr. H. A. Obu for his invaluable and selfless patronage.

We are also indebted to the late Major Chukwuma Kaduna Nzeogwu for a precious hour of free, frank and revealing interview, Professor B. O. Nwabueze and Mr. Cyprian Ekwensi for their patience in going through the manuscripts and making valuable suggestions, Mr. Hope Obinya, Barrister B. S. C. Nzenwa, Barrister Eze Ozobu and Mr. Ben Chukwura for their help in a variety of ways.

A*

We are grateful to Mr. Patrick Amah for his efficiency in typing and retyping the manuscripts.

We have tried to document and acknowledge any borrowings from the works of others. To these and others whom we may have inadvertently overlooked we are grateful

For obvious reasons, we did not have access to as much materials as we would have liked. This is particularly so in the chapters which dealt with the role of the Army in the Nigerian politics. However, whatever shortcomings which arose from this have been nearly (if not completely) offset by hundreds of interviews with both military personnel and civilians who were prominent actors in that theatre of Nigerian and Biafran history. To these kind people we are immensely grateful.

We must, however, state that we have no apologies whatsoever for our views in this book and bear full responsibility for them.

SAMUEL U. IFEJIKA
ARTHUR A. NWANKWO

CONTENTS

INTRODUCTION

The sovereign, independent Republic of Biafra came into existence on May 30, 1967. Before that date Biafra was part of the Federation of Nigeria and called Eastern Nigeria. As a territorial unit Biafra is almost rhomboid-shaped, with an area of 29,400 square miles, and demarcated to the south by the Bight of Biafra, to the west by the lower reaches of the River Niger and its Delta, to the east by the highlands of Oban and Ikom and Obudu plateau, and to the north by a boundary following, approximately, the 7° North Latitude.[1] Biafra is wholly located within the tropics. Its population is nearly 15 million. It has four main tribes – the Ibos, the Ibibio-Efiks, the Ijaws and the Ogojas. Detailed analysis of Biafran society belongs to a book on anthropology or sociology. This book is concerned with the social, economic and political factors which culminated in Biafra's independence.

To understand these factors, we have to look into Nigerian history – especially its political history. The Federation of Nigeria, which became independent on October 1, 1960 – almost a hundred years after Lagos was ceded to the British Crown by King Dosunmu – was about 373,000 square miles in area and had an estimated population of about 34 million at the time of her independence, making her easily the most populous country in Africa, the fourth in the British Commonwealth and the thirteenth in the world. Because of her size and population, Nigeria was expected to play a leading role in Africa.

Paradoxically, Nigeria's size and her population, so vast and heterogeneous, contributed to the utter lack of internal peace and harmony which was her post-independence experience. Like other Federations created by Britain, and in the quest for economic and imperial gains in foreign lands, totally dissimilar or diverse peoples – diverse in culture, religion, ethnic and tribal groupings – were brought together under one political umbrella. By the grace of the British Government, Northern Nigeria, one of the three regions of pre-independence Nigeria, had a size and population larger than those of all the other regions put together, and by the grace of the British Colonial policy the control of the Nigerian central government became permanently stuck into the hands of conservative Northerners who were more amenable to British influence than their progressive, virile Southern neighbours. A common experience of colonial tutelage became an additional factor of divergence rather than a basis of unity. Even Nigeria's experiment in 'unity in diversity' was not supported by geography or natural factors. Thus Nigeria was throughout a disunited country. Without internal unity and power, she could play no important role in Africa.

In the first two years of her Independence, Nigeria was given somewhat more than her deserved respect in the international scene. But as her internal stresses and crises became more explosive, the attitude of other African nations soon became that of contempt. Gradually but steadily, she lost the opportunity of leading Africa.

But the tragedy of Nigeria is the crassness of the misconception of her true circumstances on an international level. A false picture of her greatness was presented by certain European nations, who also portrayed her as Africa's showcase. These nations pretended not to be aware of Nigeria's social factors, nor of the fact that she was a boiling pot of unbridled corruption, irrational tribalism, vaunting ambition, pent-up resentment, suspicion, fear of ethnic domination, misguided ancestral glories, political intolerance, religious bigotry and administrative irresponsibility. According to Conor Cruise O'Brien,

> The Federation of Nigeria was for long presented to the American public (and the world at large) as the most hopeful and even 'stable' country in Africa; it was democratic and good and frequently contrasted with Ghana, which was authoritarian and bad.[2]

Working under this misguided estimation of Nigeria's posture and image, even as eminent a specialist in African Affairs as Joseph Palmer (once America's Ambassador in Nigeria; later Assistant Secretary of State, African Affairs) advised his government to pour aid into Nigeria. This false estimation must have been a contributory factor to the world's first natural reaction to Biafra's independence and the Biafra–Nigeria war being that Nigeria should remain one.

More descerning and sincere observers, however, knew that all was not well with Nigeria. Nigeria's explosive social and political factors portended grave danger to her unity. In the words of Otonti Nduka,

> A nation built on the foundation of bribery and corruption in high and low places, nepotism, political jobbery, and the baser elements of human nature, is heading for trouble, despite all appearances to the contrary.[3]

Very much like the equatorial jungle, Nigeria might have appeared calm and comfortable with green luxuriant foliage, but in reality it swarmed underneath with fiery, poisonous reptiles and hungry man-eaters. By the pertinent observation of O'Brien,

> In fact the old Federation (Nigeria) was only nominally democratic and it carried within it from the beginning, more explosive possibilities than any other African States.[4]

It was partly to rescue the country from her political and social iniquities – from the anarchy to which she was drifting and from the corruption and callousness of her politicians, and thereby salvage her international image – that Major Chukwuma Nzeogwu and four other nationalistic majors, with the aid of other soldiers, effected the January 15 military *coup d'état* in 1966. Nigeria's moral debasement and its exponents were vicious cankerworms which had eaten deep into the fabric of the Nigerian social and political structure. These factors had tossed the country from one crisis to another. Each crisis was marked by a callous disregard for the Constitution of the land and a deliberate rape of democratic principles. As each crisis brought the country close to a bloody disintegration, it was thought to be the last straw. In each case Nigeria only survived by unjust compromise and make-do solution-concessions. The country's ability to compromise fundamental issues became almost proverbial, and certainly an outstanding political characteristic, and this was so because it paid both the politicians who operated the corrupt political machine and the foreign economic overlords who acted behind the scene. The military men who executed the January 15 coup refused this kind of compromise.

As in any other society, the morals of Nigerian society reflected her dominant needs. If a society is morally bankrupt, it is doomed to stagnation, because moral debasements such as corruption can interfere seriously with all the advancements of a nation. Nigeria's ills demanded a painstaking diagnosis, which had to be followed by a fundamental cure. The coup of January 15 aimed at providing this cure.

However, as fate would have it, the Revolution which the 'five majors' started on January 15, 1966, was not theirs to continue and carry through. This part was entrusted to Major-General J. T. U. Aguiyi-Ironsi, as the General Officer Commanding the Nigerian Army. General Ironsi was neither one of the planners of this Revolution nor a believer in it. The game of politics was neither his ambition nor his calling. The fact that he came to head the National Military Government was purely accidental. Nevertheless, having been entrusted with this great responsibility, he resolved to do his duty and to serve his country selflessly and as he knew best. With an unusually wide national perspective, he made NIGERIAN UNITY the central purpose of his administration. Because of his exuberant goodwill, which he also attributed to others, he unduly trusted his aides, overlooked much, and failed to generate enough force and awe to back his desire for unity.

Taking advantage of this fact, the Northern soldiers, under the leadership of Lt.-Col. Gowon, organised and executed the July 29 massacre. Ironsi was kidnapped and murdered. The organisers of the second coup took over the Central Government. Instead of immediately undertaking the normal and basic functions of all civilised governments – that of protecting life and property – they intensified, with sadistic brutality, the pogrom which the North had initiated on May 30, 1966, against Easterners resident in the North, West and Lagos. 30,000 Easterners were killed, and many more thousands were wounded, maimed or disfigured. As insecurity to life and property mounted in Nigeria, Eastern Nigerians living in the North, West and Lagos – areas occupied by Northern troops – who had escaped death or torture at the hands of Northern soldiers and civilians, started to return to Eastern Nigeria in great numbers, not as voluntary immigrants, but as refugees, or displaced persons. Of these there were about two million.

The refugee question is very important because it played a leading role in Nigeria's ultimate efforts towards a peaceful settlement of her crises, and because Lagos was not prepared to approach the matter with realism it was one of the contributory factors of Biafra's independence. The story of the Moors expelled from Castile in 1502 or the Moriscos driven out in 1609, or still the Protestants expelled from various Catholic countries during the Counter-Reformation – all these were happier cases. Those involved were at least given some days to embark upon their journey and allowed to carry their personal property with them. Not so the Biafran refugees. They left under great danger and came home entirely destitute of all the wherewithal of life – a most shocking experience. The staggering figure of two million is the highest number of refugees known in a single exodus, and about equal to the total number being handled by the United Nations High Commissioner for Refugees (UNHCR), established in Geneva on January 1, 1951, as one of the international bodies for protection and settlement of refugees – victims of persecution in search of asylum. The Arab refugees who had to leave Palestine (now Israel) numbered only about 988,000. Apart from the fact that they were voluntary immigrants who suffered no torture, attack, massacre or political persecution of any kind at the hands of the Israelis, neither were their women raped or their property looted or plundered, and they were offered relief and protection by the United Nations Relief and Works Agency for Palestine Refugees. The 200,000 Southern Sudanese Christians who fled to Uganda under the alleged persecution of the Muslim majority in the North of Sudan had relief and help organised for them by the Government of Uganda from the United Nations Refugee Agency.

The case of the Eastern Nigerian refugees was entirely different. Nothing came from the World Body – the United Nations. Nigeria, under the leadership of Yakubu Gowon, regarded the refugee question not as a national issue which ought to be tackled with a sense of urgency and responsibility, but rather as a misfortune merited by them. Consequently, he did all he could to complicate the problem.

At the Aburi meeting of Nigeria's military leaders – a peace meeting held at Aburi, Ghana, at the initiative of Lord Brockway,[5] a true lover of the African people – it was decided, among other things, that the Federal Government should continue to pay the salaries of all refugees who had not found alternative employment until March 31, 1967. This agreement, like other decisions reached there, was not honoured by Lagos. Yet the Aburi agreements were reached before an international mediator. Moreover, Lt.-Col. Gowon steadily assumed the role of a dictator in Nigerian politics. On May 29, 1967, he staged a one-man coup against Nigeria by unilaterally dismissing the Supreme Military Council and announcing that he had divided Nigeria into twelve states without consulting the people directly concerned. At this stage, the people of Eastern Nigeria saw no other road to their survival and honourable existence than in the declaration of the independent, sovereign Republic of Biafra on May 30, 1967.

Gowon's reaction was to declare genocidal war on Biafra on July 6, 1967, first in the name of 'police action', and later 'total war' which, by definition, and as perfected by Nazi Germany under Hitler, meant a war of extermination. In the course of that war, Lagos has not only secured the assistance of the Soviet Union and the Harold Wilson Government of Britain, but has contemplated chemical and bacteriological warfare, has consistently bombed areas of civilian concentration like churches, schools, market places and hospitals, rather than military targets, thus providing weighty evidence that it is fighting a war of extermination. Gowon's troops have engaged in wanton destruction of public and historic buildings and private homes. Indeed, the story is very similar to that of Rome when the barbarians descended upon that city. Biafrans, having hardly any alternative, have resisted this Federal mad-cap rising and are fighting to win in order to survive. That Nigeria has not been able to defeat Biafra militarily, in spite of the fact that she had from time to time fixed dates for victory, bears out the words of Winston Churchill that those who play the aggressor should remember that 'there would not be a war if the other man did not think he also had a chance', no matter how sure they might be that they could easily win.

Biafra, as a political reality, has come to stay. On April 13, 1968, the progressive and confident people and Government of Julius Nyerere's Tanzania took the initiative in recognising Biafra officially as a sovereign, independent State. By the principle of *Micro-nationalism*, the authors hold that what makes a nation is not the size of its population but its potentialities, the homogeneity of its people and the possibilities of a synthesis of its components in all their aspects. A nation can thrive, no matter how small its territory or how sparse its population, provided there is among its peoples the consciousness of being, and the volition to be together in order to assure the success of the end of the nation-state, which end is the common good. Biafra, in size and population, is bigger than many nations. Her population is equal, for example, to the total number of people inhabiting the West African states of Togo, Dahomey, Ghana, Liberia, Sierra Leone and Gambia together,[6] and her population density of over 500 persons per square mile is the highest in the whole of Africa.

The corollary of the principle of micro-nationalism is that the nation is not an inflexible structure which is absolute, irrespective of prevailing circumstances, but an affirmative framework whose primary aim is the collective welfare of its peoples, and which should adjust itself with preponderating circumstances in order to maintain its ability to achieve its aim. When, therefore, new conditions arise which are a negation of the happiness and well-being of the people of a country, it is not only justifiable but imperative and obligatory that these people should establish for themselves a new nation which assures their welfare, and should set for themselves new territorial limits to correspond with this new nation. This is the choice, the decision, Biafra has made.

The American Declaration of Independence, adopted in Philadelphia on July 4, 1776, acknowledged that in the course of human events it may become necessary for 'one people to dissolve the political bonds which have connected them with another', and 'to assume among the powers of the earth the separate and equal station to which the Laws of Nature and of Nature's God entitle them'. The same Declaration also acknowledged that when any government 'becomes destructive of the ends of life, liberty and happiness, it is the right of the people to alter or to abolish it'. And when we remember that the American people suffered neither pogrom nor genocide, but 'taxation without representation', Biafra's case becomes more compelling.

As a nation, Biafra has the will and the potentialities to

shoulder the responsibilities of nationhood, and to make a concrete and positive drive towards her national goal. With reasonable probability of permanence and stability, she has fulfilled all the traditional requirements for her recognition by the civilised world. She occupies a defined territory, has an organised government with popular support, is independent of control by any other state, and has shown capability in observing the obligations and norms of international law. If the nations of the world have any moral conscience, if injustice should not direct the course of mankind, Biafra should be recognised by all nations. Even Nigeria is called upon to recognise Biafra in order to start with her economic association so essential to her survival. In spite of her initial insistence that America should renounce her independence, Britain did the same, as epitomised in the Treaty of Paris, September 3, 1783.

In the magnanimity of her leadership, and in the resourcefulness and intelligence of her people and their will to survive, Biafra is a great nation. In the words of the Biafran Head of State, Lt.-Col. C. Odumegwu Ojukwu:

> Indeed, we are braced to face and conquer the challenge of the future. We believe that the tomorrow we face or the battle for survival will not be won by bullets or by savagery but by brain-power, modern skills and the determination to live and succeed. We also believe that out of the carnage and wrecks of the past will emerge a new breed of men and women: resolute, powerful and prosperous.

With courage, determination and brain-power, we shall survive and succeed.

1

BRITAIN AND NIGERIAN UNITY

> Commerce took us [Britain] to Africa; Commerce keeps and
> will keep us in West Africa. . . . The day it ceases to be so,
> West Africa ceases to be of use to the Empire. It will become
> a costly play thing, and the British people are too essentially
> practical a people to care long for toys of that kind.
>
> MOREL

(i) THE CREATION OF NIGERIA

Nigeria and the concept of a Nigerian nation were an entirely
British creation. The name 'Nigeria' coined from the word
'Niger' (meaning 'black') was first suggested by Miss Flora
Shaw, one-time correspondent of the London *Times*, in an
article in *The Times* on January 8, 1897.[1] Miss Shaw later
became the wife of Lord Lugard, Nigeria's foremost colonial
administrator and the maker of modern Nigeria. Before 1897,
the area which came to be known as Nigeria, was variously
referred to by travellers and geographers as 'Niger Coast
Protectorate', 'Central Sudan', 'Houssa States' or 'Nigritia',
'Slave Coast', the 'Royal Niger Company territories', and such
general names. The name 'Nigeria' was first officially recognised in a House of Commons debate on the Royal Niger
Company in July, 1899, but there was no such official entity as
'Nigeria' until 1900, neither did Nigeria have a common ruler
before this date.

As Nwafor Orizu[2] pointed out:

> What really existed in that part of the Western Sudanese
> territory were a number of independent national states which
> were all politically and territorially separate, and in many
> cases linguistically and culturally different.

It will be wrong therefore, for any one to give the impression that
Nigeria, before the British, had a common political background
or heritage. Indeed, during the piecemeal acquisition of Nigeria

by the British, rulers in the various national states remained either unconcerned about or unaware of events happening in other territories which later came to be grouped together as Nigeria. Most of these nation states had existed for thousands of years before the British, and must be distinguished from tribes. According to Orizu, whereas *tribes* are 'large communities of peoples, generally with the same language, living in one geographical area and having fairly common customs and outlooks on life, but not politically united', such as the Ibos or Yorubas, *national states* are 'distinctly political areas, each under a different sovereign power, mutually independent of the other political states, even though such different states existed within the framework of a tribe, such as the Onitsha Kingdom, the Arochuku Kingdom and the Nnewi Kingdom – all members of the Ibo tribe.'[3]

The British came and brought under their control an aggregation of tribes and national states which had existed independent of one another, often as mutually hostile communities. They sought to impose a common nationality, a common government, to which all *peoples* enclosed within the borders of Nigeria would give obedience, allegiance and loyalty. As Margery Perham, a careful student of Nigerian affairs and the biographer of Lord Lugard, observed:

> European rule was imposed like a great steel grid over the amorphous cellular tissue of tribal Africa and the hundreds of independent and often hostile communities were held within its interstices in peace.[4]

But if there was peace, it was an uneasy peace which at all times contained enormous centrifugal forces. As Margery Perham herself admitted, this kind of imposition 'does not turn two hundred or more tribes into a nation' but can only, at best, make them 'recognise their affinity within large groups'.[5] She went on:

> Even the distant prospect of the removal of the steel framework which has held them firmly together in an imposed order and co-operation, at once gets each group reckoning up what natural strength it will have to protect itself or dominate its neighbours when all are left to find their own level of power.[6]

The experience of Nigeria after the British left, and the ultimate disintegration of that country, have amply borne out this statement.

The British acquisition of Nigeria forms part of the story of the scramble for Africa which was sanctioned at the Berlin Conference of 1884–5. The geographical units over which the imperial powers were to exercise their rule were in almost all cases 'essentially artificial creations' carved out of Africa, with hardly any considerations for ethnic and cultural homogeneity.[7] These boundaries were settled more on the basis of economic and political expediency than on historical and social considerations. Some Europeans who participated in or were connected with the scramble were even known to have made the question of Africa's new frontiers a matter for jokes across the drinking tables, at times using paper and pencil to delineate and delimit territories upon which they had never set their feet. Lord Salisbury, in 1890, declared that:

> We have been engaged in drawing lines upon maps where no white man's foot ever trod; we have been giving away mountains and rivers and lakes to each other, only hindered by the small impediment that we never knew exactly where the mountains and rivers and lakes were.[8]

Lord Salisbury was speaking at a Mansion House dinner a day after the Anglo-French declaration which settled the present boundaries between Nigeria, Dahomey, Niger and Chad.

Speaking in the same vein to the Royal Empire Society, a former Commissioner-General of Southern Nigeria humourously stated that:

> In those days we just took a blue pencil and a rule, and we put it down at Old Calabar, and drew that blue line up to Yola. . . . I recollect thinking when I was sitting having an audience with the Emir, surrounded by his tribe, that it was a very good thing that he did not know that I, with a blue pencil, had drawn a line through his territory.[9]

The Commissioner was telling his listeners how he participated in demarcating the boundaries of African territories.

The case of Nigeria, in particular, was an example *par excellence* of the callous indifference of an imperial power in building a territorial unit embracing a bewildering complexity of human and physical elements for economic motives, without much regard for the harmonious living of the peoples enclosed within such an area. Scholars and anthropologists have identified as many as four hundred ethnic groups or tribes in the former Nigeria.[10] Most of these have their own distinct languages, religions, traditions and institutions. These were indeed 'in the Nigerian context . . . really different nationalities, who united and established a political union in the form of a federation, as a result of historical circumstances.'[11] Their very existence constituted an 'anthropological phenomenon' which ought not to have been treated lightly. The colonial powers disregarded the reality of tribes as powerful cultural units. Inevitably, as a result of this attitude and the type of political union imposed upon the *peoples* of Nigeria, tribalism developed to become Nigeria's most basic, most baneful problem.

Apart from the human factors in the Nigerian case, there were also physical and natural factors, all of which had significant influence upon the history and development of the Nigerian peoples. Most areas of Southern Nigeria are closely hemmed in by forest and swamps (in the coastal belt); this produced a virile, highly individualistic and productive people. Northern Nigeria, on the other hand, is open savannah and semi-desert, except in the Middle-Belt area which has a difficult rocky terrain. This produced a conservative, less enterprising type of people, with strong indigenous traditions and centralised institutions. Thus, due to geography alone, the Nigerian people were different peoples, leading to differences in human ecology, way of life and outlook on life, and militating additionally against national unity. All the factors enumerated above combined to shape the whole development of Nigeria's political destiny.

Nor did the way that Nigeria was acquired by the British help to give the peoples of Nigeria a sense of common political destiny. The British administration of any part of Nigeria formally commenced in 1861, with the cession of Lagos to the British Crown. After the British Parliamentarians were persuaded to accept that 'legitimate trade', and not slave trade, should be the foundation of imperial prosperity[12] by abolishing the slave trade in 1807, European traders and merchants were constrained to adjust to the new trade in such commodities as palm oil, ivory, cotton and other tropical products, instead of human beings. The British Government did everything within its powers to see that the slave trade was stopped. Between 1819 and 1869 it kept permanently in West African waters a 'British West African Squadron', and was prepared to spend as much as £750,000 annually in this programme of abolition. Where there was local resistance by African chiefs who wanted the trade continued for their own advantage, force was used. Such a resistance was a part cause of the British interference in the politics and kingship struggle of Lagos between Kosoko and Akitoye.

It was alleged that Lagos was the greatest 'stronghold' for slave dealing and the slave trade, being a sea port to the Atlantic with a prosperous slave-dealing king. This state of affairs was openly offered as the only reason why the British decided to annex Lagos and bring it under the Union Jack. However, it is pertinent here to be reminded that the British Government foreign policy during the middle of the nineteenth century was that trade must go everywhere in the world, and that this must be effected by force where necessary. This policy, it must be admitted, did not enjoin territorial acquisition. In fact, the slogan then was 'commerce without territorial aggrandisement', the current view in Britain being that trade meant profit, whereas acquisition of overseas territories meant responsibility and expense.[13] The British Government, therefore, did not show much zeal in acquiring territories in Africa until about 1885. Even though the 'new imperialism' did not define itself as involving territorial acquisition, commercial expansionism inevitably and ultimately saddled Britain with territorial aggrandisement, especially where the British prestige was at issue. At that time Britain had a Foreign Secretary to whom this prestige meant much and to whom the idea of territorial acquisition for trade was not anathema. That Foreign Secretary was Lord Palmerston.[14] The guiding principles of his foreign policy were free trade, commercial expansion and the maintenance of Britain's national prestige.[15] His record shows clearly that he was always prepared to use force where necessary in order to ensure that his trade expansionist programmes were not impeded and that British prestige suffered no tarnishment. In fact, it was during his prime ministership that Lagos was annexed to the British Crown, and the whole business was attended all through by a show of force.

As the British trading interests along the coast grew, British merchants and traders there wanted some form of political support from their home government to protect these interests. The British Government, however, proceeded to meet this demand with caution. It tried to deal initially with West Africa unofficially by appointing or employing local volunteers, not professional civil servants, as its agents. In 1849, therefore, it appointed John Beecroft,[16] Governor of Fernando Po, as Consul for the Bights of Benin and Biafra. Beecroft and subsequent consuls, as men on the spot, were convinced that the only way to assure and protect British trading interests was to meddle in local politics, with a view to the ultimate annexation of the areas concerned.

These consuls, as their records show, forced or manoeuvred the local chiefs and rulers into treaties of trade, protection and cession of territory. They organised courts of law, such as the Court of Equity, and arrogated to themselves the right to depose, appoint and recognise chiefs, using the British Navy to harass and intimidate the local inhabitants. They did all this in spite of the fact that by the official definition of their functions as consuls they normally should have taken no part in the politics of the country or areas to which they were assigned, and could only have acted validly as diplomatic channels between Britain and the peoples of Nigeria. In spite of the non-authorisation of these excesses, the British Government under Lord Palmerston gave an unwritten warrant of governmental sanction and acquiescence to them.[17]

Beecroft was a stubborn believer in the acquisition of territory. As the first consul charged with supervising and protecting British trading activities in the Bights of Benin and Biafra, and supported by British super-cargoes, he immediately took upon himself powers which had not been conferred upon him. He developed and perfected the 'gun-boat technique'. In Lagos, using the slave trade issue as a pretext for intervention in local politics, he deposed Kosoko and installed his uncle, Akitoye, as king.[18]

Though Lagos did not become a British protectorate after the deposition of Kosoko, a decision had already been taken in

England that Lagos must be possessed permanently. Lord John Russell was then Foreign Secretary under Palmerston, and the British Government was only biding its time. Akitoye died in 1853 to be succeeded by his son Dosunmu, again with the help of a British Consul. In the same year a permanent British Consul was appointed for Lagos in the person of Benjamin Campbell, while Beecroft's jurisdiction was limited to the Bight of Biafra. The new king was not able to get the support of the local chiefs and his subjects. This situation presented Kosoko, in exile, with an opportunity to try to regain the Lagos throne. Consular diplomacy frustrated Kosoko's design and ultimately he was forced, as an alternative, to accept appointment as the ruler of the neighbouring territories of Lekki and Palma on the mainland. The ultimate aim of the Consul was to annex Lagos; to have total control over legitimate trade and to serve as a base for dealing with the situation in the interior where civil war was brewing between the various Yoruba states of Oyo, Ibadan, Ijebu-Ode, Abeokuta, Ijebu Remo, Ilesha, Ilorin and Ikorodu. All the British consuls in Lagos – Beecroft, Campbell, Brand and Foote, in that order – had consistently urged the British Government to take over Lagos. In June, 1861, the British Government gave its agreement and the acting consul was instructed to annex Lagos. The Consul completed his negotiations with the puppet king on July 30, 1861, and on that day Dosunmu signed a treaty of cession – ceding Lagos to the British Crown with a bribe of £1,030 a year, guaranteed him for the rest of his life.[19]

This deed heralded 'a new era of British policy in Nigeria . . . under the guise of humanitarian motives but, in reality, to ensure the development of her trade on this coast'.[20] The new state of affairs assured the British Government and its merchants virtual monopoly of the new trade in Lagos. It also ended finally the vocal assertion of local Nigerian traders that they had the right to trade with any European power of their choice and on their own terms. Penetration into the interior was the next logical step. Within four years after the annexation, Lagos, under the zealous exactions of Freeman, its first Governor, Lekki, Palma, Badagry and a number of Yoruba warring towns were either annexed to the British Crown or brought under British control. By 1896, Ibadan, Abeokuta, Oyo and other important Yoruba towns had been forced to sign treaties of protection and to accept British residents.

In the British penetration of the interior, the same gun-boat method which had been used in Lagos was employed. Consul Beecroft employed the method in one or two more places in Southern Nigeria before he died in 1854. Out of sheer hatred for King William Pepple, Beecroft took advantage of the factional strife in his kingdom of Bonny to secure his deposition in 1854, allegedly for misgovernment. Beecroft presided over the Court of Equity which decided that Pepple must be exiled and made sure that this decision was carried out in spite of the official view, as expressed by him, that Pepple was rejected by his people as represented by all Bonny chiefs. In his place he installed a puppet who would be agreeable to his programmes. As it turned out, however, the purported deposition came to be seen as a serious miscalculation, for Bonny was not to know peace or an acceptable legal ruler until Pepple was recalled to his throne in 1861, after eight years' exile in England. Pepple came back with full regal dignity and received £4,520 in compensation.

Beecroft also interfered, in 1851, with the internal politics of Old Calabar. He ended up there once more by presiding over a panel of kingmakers for the selection of a new king. By the time of his death, in 1854, it had become an established pattern for local coastal chiefs to seek British support for their continuance in office, and for British residents and representatives to use the same method as their predecessors to manipulate local politics in the way that best suited British interests. It was this technique which ultimately resulted in the extension of British 'protection' to the remaining areas of Nigeria.

It has been pointed out that, in spite of the recommendations of the Adderley Parliamentary Select Committee of 1865 that signing new treaties of protection would be inexpedient, the British pressed on with the design of building a third colonial empire in Africa. Apart from the enthusiasm of her consuls, one other factor responsible for this was the pressure of her traders and merchants. The response of the British Government to their demands in what came to be known as Nigeria bears out well J. S. Furnival's statement that 'the flag has usually followed trade',[21] instead of the other way round. Speaking in the same tone, Morel, a well-known West Africa merchant, had declared that 'commerce took us [Britain] to Africa; commerce keeps and will keep us in West Africa. . . . The day it ceases to be so, West Africa ceases to be of use to the Empire. It will become a costly plaything, and the British people are too essentially practical a people to care long for toys of that kind.'

The whole effort of the British Government to colonise and secure protectorate treaties over Nigerian territory represents an attempt to protect the investments and interests of British traders and merchants. It also shows an awareness of the potentialities of the African hinterland, for according to Mary Kingsley, these regions of great natural riches would be of immense 'advantages . . . to a manufacturing nation like ourselves. . . .' Taking palm oil alone (used for manufacturing soap and for lubricating the giant industrial machinery), whereas in 1806 the import of palm oil from the Oil Rivers to Liverpool amounted to 150 tons, in 1839 the figure stood at 13,600 tons, and by 1870 had exceeded 28,000 tons. In fact, as time went on, the British Government had to take a decision that the enormous and growing possibilities of the hinterland trade should no longer be left to the merchants and traders of Liverpool, London, Bristol and Glasgow alone. The trade must be government controlled and directed.

The barriers created by inland sovereign states had an effect on trade, as well as the inter-tribal wars in the interior, especially in Yorubaland. There was also the question of competition from local middlemen and from foreign powers like France and Germany. These would have to be dealt with and the only effective way of solving the problem was by securing protectorate treaties, for unless this was done the areas involved could not be said to be under British power either in fact or in law, though her traders and merchants were there. Because of the stiff resistance of some local rulers, punitive expeditions were undertaken in some cases, with a view to conquest and subjugation.

In what came to be known as Eastern Nigeria, King Jaja of Opobo championed opposition against European penetration to the interior. Born in Amaigbo in the heart of Iboland in 1821, he was later sold into slavery to Bonny where, in Anna Pepple's House, he became ultimately accepted as leader. Because of serious factional strife which broke out in 1867 and resulted in a civil war in 1869, Jaja severed connection completely and permanently with Bonny, and established a new kingdom in 1870 which he called Opobo. From there, he carried out a most effective blockade which cut off European traders from the hinterland trade, thereby causing them enormous loss of money. It was reported that Liverpool's trade with Bonny and Opobo fell to the sum of £500,000. The 'African Association' – a European trading association formed between 1880 and 1885 – complained bitterly and incessantly about Jaja's obstructionist policy. As a result, Jaja was forced to sign a Protectorate Treaty with Britain in 1884 under which, however, he managed to retain a good deal of commercial rights. Jaja's blockade and opposition, however, continued, but the British would not tolerate this under the new order of things. In September 1887, Harris Johnson, then vice-consul, went to Opobo with all the troops he could command and decoyed Jaja to Accra. There he was tried before Admiral Sir Hunt Grubble, who condemned him to five years deportation to the West Indies, with an annual allowance of £800. Jaja died in exile.

Jaja's case illustrates clearly that Britain's takeover of Nigeria was not a smooth process, in course of which they obtained the ready acquiescence of all the local rulers. There were instances of violent and prolonged resistance, even after 1900, as evidenced in the Aro Expedition of 1901–1902.

It was in the Niger Delta area that the British took a determined view that the policy of non-expansionism must end. This was seen as the only way to maintain the monopoly of British traders, so seriously threatened by their French and German counterparts. In 1872, because of the growing importance of the interior trade and the need to offer greater protection to the traders, the British Consulate at Fernando Po was transferred to Old Calabar on the mainland. In 1873, the 'Courts of Equity' were for the first time officially established by an Order-in Council, with the Consul, alone and personally, empowered to levy fines of up to £200, to impose imprisonment for up to twenty-one days and to banish for up to one year. This was a prelude to the declaration of a British protectorate over the area. This declaration was made after the Berlin Conference of 1885, when the British declared the Niger area the Oil Rivers

Protectorate. In 1893, this Protectorate was given the name of Niger Coast Protectorate after being extended into the interior. It was still to become the Protectorate of Southern Nigeria in 1900, after the Charter of the Royal Niger Company was revoked in 1899. Its control was transferred from the Foreign Office to the Colonial Office.

The extension of British power to Ilorin and other Fulani emirates of Northern Nigeria was the work of the Royal Niger Company created by Sir George Dashwood Taubman Goldie, who has been described as the 'Rhodes of Nigeria' and whom Hancock and Flint came later to refer to as the 'most mysterious of empire builders'. All through, since the acquisition of Lagos by the British, the British traders had been steadily pressing into the interior. In 1866, a consulate had been opened at Lokoja under J. M. Macleod, but because of local resistance and violence it was closed in 1869. However, Britain did not give up her interests in the hinterland trade. About that time the investments of her traders in the Delta area and along the banks of the Niger amounted to £1,000,000.

Taubman Goldie came to Nigeria principally to discover why a company owned by his nephew, Holland Jacques and Company, was not making profits. On his arrival in 1877, he found that, from the time of the abandonment of the Lokoja consulate in 1869, British trading interests had been neglected, that the trade monopoly could not be maintained, and British traders were engaged in cut-throat competition. In fact, the British were in grave danger of losing everything. Goldie concluded that, to establish the British monopoly, the British companies trading in the lower Niger – Messrs. Alexander Miller Brothers and Co. (Glasgow); James Pinnock and Co. (Liverpool); West African Co. (Manchester); and the Central African Trading Co. (London) – would have to be amalgamated. This was done in 1879 when the United African Company was inaugurated. Lord Aberdare, a former cabinet minister, became Chairman of the new venture, while Goldie, though undisputably the leading spirit, became Vice-Chairman. This was a fortunate strategy for British enterprise in Nigeria.

In 1881, Goldie applied to the British Government for a charter in the Company's name. Because of its small capital, this demand was refused, but within barely a year Goldie raised its capital from £125,000 to a million pounds, changing the company's name at the same time to National African Company. About 1884 he bought out two French companies (Compagnie Française de l'Afrique Equatoriale and the Compagnie du Sénégal), thereby eliminating their trade competition. The field was now cleared for planting British power in the Niger territories. Danger of further foreign competition drove Goldie to a hurried conclusion of treaties with local tribesmen and rulers of the areas between the Delta and the confluence of the Niger and Benue. The Foreign Office agreed to ratify them. Hewett, Consul for Bights of Benin and Biafra, also concluded protectorate treaties with local rulers of areas between Lagos and Rio del Rey. Ultimately the whole of the lower Niger and Benue were brought under British protection.

Meanwhile, as further competition between Germany, France, Britain, Belgium and some other European powers in Africa was developing into an open conflict, Bismarck, the Imperial German Chancellor, convoked an international conference in Berlin to discuss both the future of the Congo and the procedure for the partition of Africa. This conference lasted from November 1884 to February 1885. Britain was represented by Hewett and Goldie, and was able to claim there the mouth of the Niger and the whole of its lower course, as a result of the efforts of these two men. In June 1885, Britain issued formal notification of the declaration of a Protectorate over the Niger Districts, renamed Oil Rivers Protectorate. In July 1886, Goldie got his charter and changed the name of his company to the Royal Niger Company.

The Royal Niger Company was acting in dual capacity: administrator responsible to the British Government and a commercial concern responsible to its British stock-holders. Goldie set up a governing council, a supreme court, a central prison, a private army of one battalion, called the Royal Niger Constabulary, a hospital and botanical gardens. He made Asaba his administrative headquarters. In spite of all these, it soon became evident that he could not establish proper possession and consolidation of the interior until the British Government took a hand. In fact, the Company's authority hardly went beyond the range of the ship's gun, although Goldie dispatched his troops to Nupe and Ilorin when the activities of the natives of these areas were posing serious threat to the peaceful trade of the Company. But surely, by the time the British Government made up its mind to revoke the Charter of the Royal Niger Company in 1899, the boundaries of Nigeria were already marked out. On January 1, 1900, the Protectorate of Northern Nigeria was proclaimed with the British flag hoisted at Lokoja.[22] Sir Frederick Lugard, who had served in the West African Frontier Force,[23] was appointed the first High Commissioner or Governor.

Despite the declaration of a British Protectorate over Northern and Southern Nigeria in 1900, a lot had still to be done to bring the areas concerned under British control. The first step towards the unification of Nigeria was taken on May 1, 1906, when Lagos and Southern Nigeria, which had previously existed separately, were amalgamated to become 'the Colony and Protectorate of Southern Nigeria'. This achieved an economic purpose, for after this time the British were able not only to cover the cost of their administration of these areas but also to have a good surplus as profit. Moreover, this exercise virtually established the geographical extent of Nigeria as it came to be known and can be taken as marking the beginning of effective British administration in Nigeria.

In many areas of the interior, punitive expeditions had to be undertaken to force the people there to accept British rule and the British ideas of law and authority. The North, with its defiant and proud emirs, and the Ibo land in the South were ultimately to be brought under control, but with much difficulty. The most important military expedition undertaken in Southern Nigeria was the Aro expedition of 1901–1902, against the 'guardians' of the famous Arochukwu Oracle. In the North, Kano and Sokoto, for instance, were not subjugated until 1903. Control was established over Bornu in 1906, while some of the pagan tribes in the plateau areas and Benue valley remained beyond central control until the 1920s.

After the events of 1900, Nigeria had two separate administrations – northern and southern, with administrative headquarters in Kaduna and Lagos respectively, independent of each other and each directly responsible to the Colonial Office. A lieutenant-governor was appointed for each of the administrative areas. In June 1910, Lewis Harcourt, the

B

Secretary of State for the Colonies, made a proposal to the House of Commons for the amalgamation of the two separate administrations of Nigeria. He announced that he had recalled Sir Frederick Lugard from Hong Kong, where he was Governor, to assume new duties in Nigeria. Lugard, after his return to Nigeria, submitted a report to the Colonial Office in March 1913, calling for the amalgamation of the different administrations of Nigeria. This amalgamation was effected on January 1, 1914, with Lugard as Nigeria's first governor-general. Giving reasons for this amalgamation, Michael Crowder[24] stated that:

> The immediate reason for the decision . . . was economic expediency. The Northern Protectorate was running at a severe deficit, which was being met by a subsidy from the Southern Protectorate, and an Imperial Grant-in-Aid from Britain of about £300,000 a year. This conflicted with the age-old colonial policy that each territory should be self-subsisting . . . . It was also felt that the prosperous Southern Protectorate could subsidise its northern neighbour until such a time as it became self-supporting. Furthermore, there was the pressing need to co-ordinate railway policy, which at the time was practically non-existent.

Britain's overriding interest in Nigeria was economic, and the step taken to amalgamate was aimed at assuring profits and better exploitation of local resources. The two administrations in Nigeria before 1914 not only exhibited differences of aim and method, but were actually antagonistic to each other. In the field of transport, as in other fields of economic life, they ran rival systems. For instance, in 1912 – there were two competing railway systems – the Minna–Jebba–Lagos system and the Minna-Baro–Niger system.[25] All these had increased expenditure and led to administrative duplications.

The foregoing account has attempted to show the piecemeal acquisition of the territory which came to be known as Nigeria, and how the British came to concern themselves with the administration of that territory. Acting from Lagos under a colonial governor, Old Calabar under a Foreign Office consul and Lokoja under a chartered trading company, separate and unco-ordinated British forces and interests spread out to establish British presence and control over a vast area, which was christened Nigeria. Coleman points out that:

The fact that such acquisition was piecemeal and occurred in successive stages accounts in part for the extreme unevenness in the degree of social change and modernisation among the various groups and areas of Nigeria. This unevenness had added internal stress to already existing tensions.[26]

Taking the factors of tribe, culture, geography, and social and political history together – none of which in the Nigerian circumstance helped to cement the bonds of national unity – the failure of the British attempt ultimately to give Nigeria 'unity' is no matter for surprise. The new indigeneous leaders that emerged from the different parts of the country, following the current of nationalism, felt compelled to create a sense of national identity and unity within the existing frontiers. But deeper, natural factors could not be ameliorated by artificial political creations. Nor did the British, in their administration of Nigeria, make up for these shortcomings imposed by nature.

(ii) BRITAIN'S CONTRIBUTION TO NIGERIA'S DISUNITY

There are many nations in the world today that have been able to achieve *national unity* and consciousness in spite of the fact that they started as 'geographical expressions' in which were enclosed peoples of different backgrounds and culture. The United States provides a good example. At the time of its inception and for long afterwards it was made up of many tribes and races or people of various nationalities. Apart from the American Indians, there were the Dutch and the British who came in the seventeenth century to escape from the religious and economic persecution of their home governments. These were followed by Africans, Nordic and Mediterranean peoples, East European Jews, Asians and others.[27] Today, after years of constitutional metamorphosis, it is one united powerful nation, comprising a people of one nationality, one culture and one destiny. After the international boundaries of Nigeria were determined, the British started their experiment in 'unity in diversity'. Politically and economically, they aimed at creating a united Nigeria. But the actual experience of Nigeria was that the British, by the policies of their colonial administrators, only succeeded in furthering Nigeria's divisions and sectional loyalties, rather than encouraging national unity and consciousness.[28] It was with a full appreciation of this fact that Dr. Conor Cruise O'Brien, commenting on the Biafra–Nigeria situation in an article in *The New York Review*, declared that 'the nature of the colonial experience in Nigeria was therefore such that, far from narrowing the differences between the peoples who underwent it, it actually widened and deepened these'.[29] Perhaps, with a progressive policy of unified administration and government, it could have been possible for Nigerians to develop a feeling of common identity and national unity. That was how most other nations with situations similar to Nigeria's achieved true nationhood: the form and character of both the administration and government are of great relevance.

Starting from 1900, the territorial separateness and individuality of the component units of the country were encouraged. Each of the three separate colonial territories – the colony of Lagos and the protectorates of Southern and Northern Nigeria – was independently administered and directly responsible to the Colonial Office in Britain. These territories even had frontier controls. The administrators responsible for them maintained different policies and aims. This continued even after the amalgamation of Nigeria in 1914. The fact that in 1906 there was an attempt to impose a united colonial bureaucracy made no difference. If the amalgamation of Nigeria had a political purpose, the bond of political unity was only in the person of Sir Frederick Lugard, who became the first Governor-General of Nigeria.

Despite the event of 1914, Lagos, which was later to become the capital of Nigeria, was not divested of its unique status as a colony, but in fact retained this character until 1951, when the Macpherson Constitution came into force. The other territories of Nigeria remained protectorates. Thus, while the inhabitants of Lagos had the rights of British citizens and owed allegiance to the British sovereign, the same was not true of the other peoples of Nigeria,[30] at least by British constitutional law, although in international law there is practically no difference of any legal validity.

Nor did the native administration system introduced in Nigeria help in the complicated task of nation building. After Lugard had established British authority in the North, lack of sufficient funds and personnel drove him to inaugurate the now-famous system of *Indirect Rule* there. The North was authoritarian and hierarchically organised, and had traditional political institutions that could easily be adapted to serve the needs of local government under the general supervision and surveillance of colonial administrators. Though this system worked extremely well in the North, it succeeded in reinforcing already existing parochialism and conservatism, and achieved the preservation of traditional values. Indirect Rule was also attempted in the South but the idea was abandoned in 1950,[31] and in its place was introduced a local government system largely according to the English pattern. An essential part of this system was the local council, and in the Nigerian circumstance where tribalism was a fundamental factor in social living, each small group started asking for its own local council within its own tribe, thus influencing the fragmentation of the country and creating the focus of new loyalties.

Right from the inception of Nigeria, the North, encouraged by the British policy of separate development, wanted their own distinct and separate development, in which they would have nothing to do with the South. The Southerners who found themselves in the North, either as businessmen, traders, artisans or clerks in the Civil Service, were not treated as fellow Nigerians, but were looked upon as strangers or 'native foreigners' to be restricted to strangers' towns called *Sabon Garis*. Thus, despite the existence of a central government in Lagos, the South and North could not appreciate that they were under one common government. After 1861, there was a legislative council in Lagos, but the North did not participate in its deliberations until 1947; thus, before that date, there was no central legislative institution which could have fostered national unity.

For long the British administrators adopted a deliberate policy of excluding the educated élite from government and the Legislative Council. They preferred instead to deal with natural rulers. But the real life of these natural rulers centred around their particular communities. Most of them had never

travelled, and were most reluctant to leave their palaces –
either out of personal inclination or as a necessary attitude
imposed upon them by their traditional office. They could not,
therefore, develop a national outlook, nor, as a result, could
they attend Council meetings as required of them by the
British administrators. This remained a matter of concern to
Nigeria's colonial governors. For instance, in 1913 the Nigerian
Council was established as an advisory body, but the whole idea
was abandoned in 1922 because the six natural rulers appointed
to it would not attend its meetings. It was not until 1947, when
a more representative Council was established, that the educated
elements were given a better opportunity to participate in the
administration and government of their country. This led
immediately to the growth of nationalism. This is not surprising
as most of the educated Nigerians have had the chance to travel,
either in the process of acquiring education or in the quest for
gainful employment in the Civil Service, corporations, commercial houses, and other such places away from their birth-
places. This had given them the national outlook which
ultimately turned a good number of them into articulate
crusaders for national unity. These were the people the
colonial administrators could have exploited earlier to foster
the feeling of oneness and solidarity among all Nigerians.

Another important factor which resulted ultimately in
Nigeria's disunity was the British colonial policy in the field of
education and missionary evangelisation. This policy led to
differences in the timing and intensity of Western education
in different parts of Nigeria, and therefore to a differential
impact. The very wide gap in education and social thinking
between the North and the South came to militate against
national unity. When European missionaries came to Nigeria,
they showed zeal in evangelistic work and wanted to preach the
Gospel in all parts of the country, especially in the Islamised
North, where Muslim advance was most active. To break
through the North, the missionaries felt that concerted action
was necessary.[32] But they were soon to meet a stiff resistance
from the Northern emirs, who naturally opposed the infiltration
of Christian ideas into the North, which was already a Muslim
area. The British administrators exploited the opposition of
the emirs and supported them in their hostility to Christian

evangelisation and Western education, which the missionaries brought with them, because they felt this policy would help them in establishing Indirect Rule. Lugard, after the conquest of the North, had promised the emirs that the British would not tamper with their religion. Lugard saw in his opposition to Christian evangelism in the North a way of keeping this pledge, but in actual fact even a broad interpretation of his promise should not mean that the Gospels should not be preached in the North. Thus, 'under the formula of "indirect rule", Britain deliberately preserved the Muslim Middle Ages, deliberately impeding Christian missionary influence and modern education'.[33] Between 1900 and 1910 hardly any opportunity was given to missionaries to preach in the North. They could not preach or open mission schools in any area without the permission of the local emir. Thus in 1903 the Church Missionary Society could only open a school at Nupe with the permission of the Emir of Bida. The sanction and approval of the Emir of Zaria had to be obtained before Walter Miller could open a missionary school in Zaria in 1905. This procedure naturally made the progress of the missionaries more difficult and protracted, especially as the conservative and parochial Muslim emirs of the North would not allow Western ideas. The British administrators, rather than encourage the establishment of schools and missions in the North, actually killed the incentive for learning English by making Hausa the medium of intercourse with Northerners. British officials even learned Hausa.

In the South, a totally different approach was adopted. Not only did Southern Nigerians, being nearer to the coast, have greater opportunities for imbibing Western culture, because of their early contact with Europeans, but they were also very receptive to Western ideas. They listened to the Gospel, learned English in mission schools and acquired the necessary qualifications for employment in the colonial Civil Service as clerks, artisans and technicians, or as teachers and preachers in mission schools and churches. The new educated élite of the South found their way to the North and took up positions which Northerners could have occupied themselves had they been suitably qualified. Although the North alone was said to have about 54 per cent of the total population of Nigeria, it lagged far behind in education, especially at secondary school level. In about 1947, there were only 251 Northern students attending secondary schools, i.e. about 2·5 per cent of the total number of people then receiving secondary education in Nigeria.[34] Nor did the colonial government help to save the situation by building schools. About 1957 there was only one government secondary school throughout Northern Nigeria, and, after many decades of British administration of the region, it could still not produce sufficient educated personnel even to fill many of the minor clerical posts in the government departments and to participate intelligently in parliamentary democracy.

When, however, from about 1946, Nigeria started her march along the road of Constitutional development, the Islamic North started to feel its shortcomings. From the 1950s it made a deliberate effort to catch up with the South in education. Secondary schools started springing up. But it had lagged behind for too long to be able to compete with the South in social and political advancement. In 1957, when the Southern regions showed themselves prepared for self-government,[35] the North, aware of its unreadiness, spurned the idea. It had to wait for two more years before it could feel the confidence to take this kind of political plunge. About the time of Independence in 1960, the North, feeling jealous and apprehensive over Southern predominance in the Northern Civil Service, inaugurated the *northernisation* policy, by which an attempt was made to replace Southerners in the Service with either Northerners or expatriates. This became one of the root causes of Nigerian disunity.

About 1940, Nigeria was split up into four administrative units, made up of the Colony of Lagos and the Northern, Eastern and Western Provinces, the last two having the River Niger as boundaries. For reasons of economy, these administrative units were given a lot of powers, which were not taken away from them at the end of the war. As if to strengthen the separateness of these units Lord Milverton, otherwise known as Sir Arthur Richards, by his Constitution of 1946, inaugurated Nigeria's regionalism. This Constitution was made up of the proposals for constitutional reform by Governor Richards, presented to the Legislative Council in March 1945, at the end of the war. Contrary to the promises made in 1943

by Sir Bernard Bourdillon, before he relinquished the governor-
ship of Nigeria, that the people would be given adequate
opportunity to discuss the draft of their future Constitution,
the proposals of Arthur Richards were rushed through the
Legislative Council and hastily dispatched to the United
Kingdom.[36] Nationalist complaints against the Constitution
were ignored. Under the Constitution of 1946, three new regional
Houses of Assembly were created at Kaduna, Enugu and
Ibadan. The devolution of powers and functions which followed
this exercise strengthened already existing sectional loyalties
and inaugurated tribal or sub-nationalisms in Nigeria rather
than promoting Nigerian unity, for from that time on,
politicans started speaking and acting in terms of their particular
regions of origin. For instance, Dr. Azikiwe's attempt to maintain political power in the Western Region was resisted by
Western politicians with the lever of tribalism.[37] The desire
for more powers for the regions, which developed at once among
Nigerian politicians, resulted in yet greater autonomy being
granted to the regions in subsequent constitutional reforms –
viz., the Constitutions of 1951 and 1954. In 1957 the
individuality of the regions was further strengthened by the
appointment of regional premiers for the East and West.

From the period of regionalism, a good number of foreign
writers and commentators started expressing doubt as to the
ultimate existence of the Nigerian nation. Sir Arthur Richards
had argued that regionalism would provide a practical means
for achieving the objective of 'national unity in diversity'.
Sir Bernard Bourdillon, for his part, asserted that 'this measure
[regionalism] represents not the division of one unit into three,
but the beginning of the fusion of innumerable small units into
three and from these three into one. . . .' These observations
and hopes were not borne out by experience. More realistic
and prophetic observers were convinced that the attempt to
unite the peoples of Nigeria was doomed to failure. Thus, in
1954, Alan Burns was quite categorical in stating that 'there is
no Nigerian nation', and that the Nigerian regions were united
'only in so far as they are governed by a single power'. Burns'
opinion had the stamp of authority coming from a past colonial
administrator and a recognised historian. An American
sociologist, who carried out a survey of growth of separatist

B*

and tribal movements in Nigeria in 1947, reached the conclusion that 'the chances for a viable, united Nigerian nation are rather slim indeed'. Robin Hallet, putting his own observations in a layman's way, stated that the 'relations of the Regions one with another are hunted by fear and suspicion. The North, apprehensive of the South, hurries forward its policy of northernisation; the South is half-afraid, half-contemptuous and almost ignornt of the North. Then look how weak the Federal Government is. . . .' Even Lord Milverton saw the failure of his earlier prophesy when he admitted in 1955, that Nigeria 'is still more of a geographical expression than a nation'. Writing in *The Observer*, Colin Legum, Commonwealth correspondent, stated that Nigeria 'has not yet overcome the divisive forces which Lugard encountered when he went to West Africa at Joseph Chamberlain's behest in 1897'.[38]

Nor did Nigerian politicians themselves have faith in the continuance of the Federation. A special evidence of this fact was supplied by Mallam Abubakar Tafawa Balewa, the man who was later to become Nigeria's first prime minister, in a speech on the Appropriation Bill during the debates in the new Legislative Council, in April 1947. He said:

> Since the amalgamation of the Southern and Northern Provinces in 1914, Nigeria has existed as one country only on paper. It is still far from being united.[39]

He stated that the Nigerian people are historically different in their backgrounds and culture, and that 'Nigerian unity is only a British intention for the country'.[40] Continuing, he declared:

> We would like the world to know that in the Northern Provinces, we have got our leaders whom we have chosen ourselves, to be rulers and voices. *We do not want, Sir, our Southern neighbours to interfere in our development*. If the Southern people feel they are representatives for what they are agitating for and demanding, well they must know that the case of the Northern Provinces is different . . . but I should like to make it clear to you that if the British quitted Nigeria now at this stage, the Northern people would continue their interrupted conquest to the sea.[41]

Abubakar was replying to the opposition of the National Council of Nigeria and the Cameroons (NCNC), one of the country's political parties, to the Richards Constitution of 1946. The NCNC had maintained that it would divide rather than unite the country. The political party which the North formed in December 1949 was totally lacking in national outlook, and was called the Northern Peoples' Congress (NPC), providing another evidence that the North did not want to have anything to do with the rest of Nigeria. This political party was headed by the late Ahmadu Bello, the Sardauna of Sokoto, who became in 1959 the first Premier of the Northern Region.

In 1947, Obafemi Awolowo, one-time Premier of the Western Region, who later became Gowon's Commissioner for Finance had written that:

Nigeria is not a nation. It is a mere geographical expression. There are no 'Nigerians' in the same sense as there are 'English', 'Welsh', or 'French.' The word 'Nigerian' is merely a distinctive appellation to distinguish those who live within the boundaries of Nigeria from those who do not.[42]

Chief Awolowo was later to exploit tribal sentiment and prejudices to gain a political foothold in Western Nigeria,[43] and never gave any serious thought to the question of national unity until about 1959, when he contested the election to the Federal House of Representatives.

Lt.-Col. Yakubu Gowon, the military ruler of Nigeria from August 1, 1966, on his assumption of office on that date repeated the view already popular in the North that the basis of unity did not exist for the peoples of Nigeria. The Northern delegation to the Ad Hoc Conference which started on September 12, 1966, was later to advocate that 'the new Nigeria shall comprise a number of autonomous States. . . .' The inescapable conclusions from all this evidence, therefore, are: (i) that, despite more than fifty years of British rule, no true sense of national unity had developed among the peoples of Nigeria, and tribalism and sectionalism remained Nigeria's basic problem; (ii) that the ultimate collapse of the Nigerian Federation was the inevitable and natural consequence of British colonial policy in Nigeria. This policy, rather than achieve national unity, strengthened tribal loyalties and

Northern parochialism and produced for Nigeria, *sub-nationalism* in place of *nationalism*. The principal motive of the British in creating Nigeria was, of course, not to achieve the harmonious association and existence of the various peoples of Nigeria, but to serve an economic interest, and the internal boundaries of Nigeria were delimited out of administrative and financial expediency.

Apart from the British colonial policy in Nigeria, the creation of Nigeria into a federation by the British, which became settled after the Constitution of 1954, is a relevant issue for consideration. The actual experience of Nigeria has made even some of the exponents of federalism as the best form of government for peoples of multi-national states begin to doubt their conviction. It may well not be proper to rush to conclusions to the contrary, as far as the general theory is concerned, but by Nigeria's own circumstance it would appear that Britain did not weigh adequately some of the special aspects of Nigeria considered specifically as a federation: (i) The Federation was too big. Nigeria was the largest of Britain's colonial territories and was easily the most populous country in the continent of Africa.[44] Yet within its borders were enclosed various peoples and tribes characterised by extreme cultural and ethnic diversity. This fact made the achievement of unity very difficult, indeed impossible. Even when the nationalism that launched Nigeria to independence was very fervent, it found itself nevertheless in stiff battle with internal political re-groupings and subnationalism, and, by the time of independence, in spite of the enthusiasm and heightened expectations with which Nigeria's leaders accepted the new political status, any careful observer would have come to the conclusion that Nigeria was then still more of a 'geographical expression' than a nation, for it lacked most of the salient attributes of all true nations.

(ii) The internal boundaries and regional divisions of Nigeria helped to complicate matters and make the achievement of unity impossible. The country was, during the colonial period, slashed up into three regions – the Northern, Eastern and Western, each with its dominant ethnic group consisting of about two-thirds of the population of that region: the Fulani-Hausas of the North, the Ibos of the East and the Yorubas of the West. But what was peculiar in the association of these regions in a federal union was that the North alone had a size and population far larger than those of all the other regions combined: the North consisted of about three-quarters of the area of Nigeria and contained over half the total poulation of the whole country. This was a drastic departure from the recognised federal principle of not allowing any one of the states or regions to dominate others by sheer mass. The result, in the case of Nigeria, was to make fear of domination by the North very real and difficult to eliminate. The North was able to hold all the other regions to ransome merely because of its size and population. The NPC, its dominant political party, never bothered to contest elections in the South until 1964. Yet it was able to control the Federal Government till the military takeover in January 1966. For this reason, the North never really recognised people from other regions as equals and co-rulers in Nigeria.

In the Nigerian circumstance, because of the evils of tribalism and sectionalism, whichever region had control at the centre through its dominant political party would at once be in a position to determine the economic, if not the political, fate of all the other regions, for it could decide to use its position to favour or punish any particular region according to the requirements of its interests and political alignments. As a result of this state of affairs, the struggle for power at the centre became intense, and tribalism was fully exploited by Nigeria's politicians in the hope of achieving leadership and the dominating position at the centre. It is for this reason that the two censuses conducted in Nigeria between 1962 and 1964 turned out a huge failure. As we shall see, in the discussion of Nigeria's post-independence crises that will follow, the census, which ought to be a mere demographic exercise to help experts in economic planning, became instead a matter for political manoeuvre.

2

NIGERIA'S POST INDEPENDENCE CRISES: I

What experience and history teach is this – that people and
governments never have learned anything from it.

GEORG WILHELM HEGEL

Nigeria became an independent sovereign state on October 1,
1960. On that date, in a solemn and colourful ceremony, Princess Alexandra of Kent, on behalf of Her Majesty Queen
Elizabeth II of Great Britain, handed over to the late Nigerian
Prime Minister, Sir Abubakar Tafawa Balewa, the constitutional instrument of Nigeria's independence. By this act Nigeria
became the sixteenth African state to achieve nationhood in
1960. Because of her comparatively peaceful progress to independence and her large population and size, it was generally
hoped that she would play the role of a leader nation among the
emerging states of Africa, an examplar of a functioning democracy.

(i) TRIBALISM AND THE LEADERSHIP QUESTION

An ephemeral kind of unity had been created in the crucible of
the internecine and protracted struggle for independence. The
various nationalist fronts in the country had joined hands to
ensure the ending of colonial rule. Having succeeded in doing
so on October 1, 1960, it was assumed that the enthusiasm with
which the country was launched into nationhood would sustain
the Nigerian Federation and help her people to develop a sense
of common destiny and common nationality. The nationalists
who had engaged directly and actively in the independence
struggle had always insisted that independence would make a
lot of difference. Now that they had reclaimed power from outside agencies, the masses naturally expected a lot from them.
They expected the emergence of a new social order in which the
tension and oppression resulting from colonial rule would

cease, and in which their leaders, acting without the restraints and limitations of the colonial days, would usher in an era of prosperity and progress in all fields.

The leaders themselves, including the cadres of the nationalist parties, appeared, in the midst of this enthusiasm, to have braced themselves for selfless national service. They took time to warn the people that 'independence was not magic', but meant hard work, toil, sweat, self-sacrifice and self-reliance. The minds of those who thought that sovereignty meant the sharing of the 'national cake', or the end of social control, or the redistribution of wealth, were immediately disabused of these illusions, and the people of Nigeria responded to the call of duty with a preparedness to give the leaders of the country the necessary chance and goodwill to prove their mettle. Thus it was that for the first two years after independence Nigeria was in a mood of calm and serenity.

But events after this date were soon to prove that Nigeria's most vexing, most basic problems were those of tribalism, sectionalism – or subnationalism, and of leadership. Because there were no honourable and acceptable answers to these problems, Nigeria, during the period between 1962 and 1966, was to be launched into a series of stormy crises which brought the country to the brink of disintegration and ultimately led to the take-over of the Government by the Army on January 15, 1966. As a result of these crises, the hope of the Nigerian people for leadership in African politics and for maximisation of progress was frustrated. Indeed, Nigeria became the laughing-stock of the watching world.

Tribalism had always been a potent factor in Nigeria's history, but in 1951 it came to be actively exploited by Nigerian politicians in their political campaigns, and there started a campaign of hate and calumny against certain politicians who came from particular ethnic or tribal areas. As Nelson Ottah, former editor of the *Drum* magazine, put it:

One morning in 1951, the people of Nigeria were startled to hear of the formation of a political party with the gruff name of Action Group. . . . The Action Group was tribalistic. At the time, it was a Yoruba organisation which barred its doors to anyone who was by one jot less than a full-fledged son or daughter of *Oduduwa*. This terrible fact was noted and exploited by the NCNC.[45]

Tribalism is a concept based on tribe. A *tribe* can be said to be the largest social group in traditional societies made up of an aggregation of clans living in the same geographical area, sharing a common ancestry and language, and displaying a large measure of cultural identity and cohesion. Tribalism itself can be defined as a social illusion which is based on emotional attitudes of tribal groups. It is marked by stereotype prejudices, and it is essentially anti-national and anti-rational. Despite its illogicality, it provides for those who use it, especially in underdeveloped countries that are yet to attain political maturity, an effective weapon for social and political ends. Although education or literacy has often been said to broaden men's social outlook, the Nigerian experience was that the educated were often the most tribalistic, and their use of the weapon of tribalism against the illiterate masses drove a big wedge into the development of the feeling of unity in Nigeria, so much so that Nigeria's political history from the 'fifties became one long record of a people that lived in a turmoil of increasing hatred, treachery, suspicion and revenge. The political parties became based upon tribes and regions. Politicians became shamelessly mean and unscrupulous in their appeal to the baser loyalties of their tribesmen, and all considerations of principles and ideology were thrown to the winds. The whole political equilibrium became dislodged by centrifugal forces – not only tribalism, but nepotism, greed and political jobbery, signifying a sharp deviation from the ideals that make for nationhood.

Perhaps, with the right kind of leadership, Nigeria might have been saved from the nightmares and turbulence of her post-independence days. The lever of tribalism and sectionalism was used to deny the people of Nigeria the right kind of leadership. While Nigeria was at the threshold of independence, the question of *leadership* became a vexing problem for many well-meaning Nigerians, particularly the youth and intellectuals. Considering quality and character alone, the majority of people in Southern Nigeria felt that leadership should be conceded to Dr. Nnamdi Azikiwe, undisputably the father of Nigerian nationalism. Sincere and objective thinkers in Northern Nigeria were of the same opinion.

However, as political parties were based on regions, the NPC of Northern Nigeria won the 1959 General Elections, and took advantage of the population and size of Northern Nigeria. Sir Abubakar Tafawa Balewa, a vice-president of the NPC, was appointed Nigeria's Prime Minister by Sir James Robertson, the then Governor-General. Many Southerners were naturally suspicious and apprehensive, for was it not Balewa who in 1947 declared that 'Nigerian unity is only a British intention for the country' and that 'if the British quitted Nigeria now at this stage the Northern people would continue their interrupted conquest to the sea'.[46] This new nation seemed to have been called upon by fate to accept the leadership of a man who never truly believed in its nationhood, and who could still be nursing the idea of continuing the *jihad* down South according to the postulations of his ancestors and forbears.

Some Nigerian politicians reacted immediately to this prospect of domination in perpetuity by the conservative Muslim North. One of such politicians was Chief Obafemi Awolowo, the leader of the Action Group, the principal party in Western Nigeria. Chief Awolowo had contested the Federal General Elections along with others, and his party won 73 out of the total 313 seats. The NPC won 142 seats, all in Northern Nigeria, while the NCNC led by Dr. Azikiwe ('Zik') won 90 seats. Immediately the results were known Chief Awolowo declared a desire to form a coalition government of his party with the NCNC, in which leadership would be conceded to Azikiwe. Chief Awolowo emphatically expressed the view that he would rather have Azikiwe lead the country than Balewa.

However that might be, Awolowo's plans did not materialise. The NCNC could not accept his proposals, for it suspected Awolowo of duplicity. It was generally believed in the inner caucus of the party that while Chief Awolowo was pleading with the NCNC at Onitsha, Eastern Nigeria, his emissaries were at the same time making overtures to the NPC in Kaduna for the same purpose of forming a coalition government. The move by the Action Group leader was therefore emptied of all altruism.

Ultimately, the NPC and the NCNC – two parties with diametrically opposed ideologies – formed a coalition at the centre.

There were those who were optimistic enough to hope that this 'marriage of convenience' would manage somehow to plod through, and indeed produce a strong government at the Centre. Because it was a marriage of incompatibles, the going in fact turned out to be difficult. Balewa was appointed Prime Minister. One of the Nigerian nationalist newspapers reported that when, during the time the coalition was being negotiated, Balewa was asked whether he could concede leadership to 'Zik', he emphatically replied in his native Hausa dialect '*ba-bu*', meaning 'no'. 'Zik', to the surprise and dissatisfaction of many Southerners, ultimately became the Governor-General of the country on November 16, 1960 – his fifty-sixth birthday.

Azikiwe seemed to be satisfied with the fact that 'this is the second time that a person of African descent has been inducted into the office of Governor-General'.[47] In obvious reply to the dissatisfaction being expressed by some critics about his agreement to become Governor-General, he said:

In the view of certain observers, here and abroad, my decision to accept and assume the office of Governor-General has been surprising. They thought that since I was leader of a political party which contested the last federal elections, I should continue to fight in order to displace the present Head of our Government, instead of supporting the conclusion of a political truce and agreeing to become what one of them euphemistically described as 'a prisoner in a gilded cage'. Whilst I appreciate the good intentions of these critics, I should make it clear that one important reason why human society is unstable and full of conflicting emotions is because of the tendency to intensify rivalry beyond its normal course . . . in a team of many players all cannot be elected captains. . . .[48]

Azikiwe stated that he was 'satisfied with the present arrangements' and declared that 'my stiffest earthly assignment is ended and my major life's work is done. My country is now free, and I have been honoured to be its first indigenous Head of State.'[49] He asked: 'What more could one desire in life?' He called upon all Nigerians and all of Nigeria's leaders to join hands and give 'support and assistance' to Balewa's Government and the nation, and 'forget the wounds inflicted in the course of our internecine altercations'.[50]

Although for two years after independence it appeared as if this call was heeded, Nigeria could not for long suffer in silence under uninspiring and weak leadership. This leadership question is one of paramount importance in any new country, especially a country like Nigeria, torn by tribal divisions and hatred, and looked up to to play a decisive role in African politics. The leader of such a new nation must be a 'hero', like Nkrumah of Ghana, Sekou Touré of Guinea, Senghor of Senegal, Nasser of Egypt and Bourguiba of Tunisia – triumphant, evangelising, sure-footed and confident,[51] and charismatic in order to be able to lead the divided peoples of the country into true nationhood and prosperity in the difficult period immediately preceding independence. With such a leader at the helm of affairs, people will get to observe the calls and requirements of the nation out of feelings of loyalty and affection for the leader – feelings which they may not at first have for the nation.

Such qualities of leadership were clearly lacking in Balewa. Many Nigerians considered him excessively moderate, cautious, weak and uninspiring, and he came later to be regarded as a stooge of the colonial masters from whom Nigerian nationalists had wrested independence. With this kind of attitude towards him prevalent, some other Nigerian leaders did not see why they should co-operate with him. Indeed, their attitude towards him bordered on contempt. When Azikiwe lost the leadership of the country and agreed to become a Constitutional Head of State, the country lost the opportunity of virile and inspiring leadership. This was due to tribalism and sectionalism.

It is pertinent to observe here that, not long after Azikiwe entered the State House as Governor-General, his political stature and image began to diminish. His later warnings[52] to Nigerian politicians went unheeded when Nigeria became launched into her nightmares and crises. Indeed, Azikiwe was considered not only to be 'a prisoner in a gilded cage', but was accused by some of the youth and the intellectuals in the country of being in advantageous conspiracy with the feudal North in order to perpetuate Northern tyranny against the South. They felt that the once militant, dynamic and enterprising 'Zik', whom the masses regarded as something near a demi-god, had betrayed the aspirations and hopes of the youth.[53]

Whether these accusations were justified or not should perhaps be left to posterity to answer, but certainly Nigeria's lack of strong and charismatic leadership at the centre contributed to the political strifes and crises that bedevilled her after independence.

(ii) EMERGENCY IN WESTERN NIGERIA

After the British had left, the major motivation for unity – viz. the nationalist struggle against colonial rule – was gone. Nigerians now turned their attention inwards, to domestic problems. Ethnic, regional or other particular interests, which had temporarily held back their claims, started to reassert themselves. Gradually the sense of restraint disappeared among the country's leaders, and some of them, out of inexperience and over-zealousness, or even irresponsibility, began to manifest the 'infantile maladies of independence'. The prospect of continued peace in Nigeria became very gloomy.

On May 20, 1962, there occured a split in Chief Awolowo's Action Group. This crisis is most significant in Nigeria's history for, from the moment of its inception, Western Nigeria did not know peace again until the military coup of January 1966. In fact the continuation of the unrest, bitterness, rancour and bloodshed which it brought to Western Nigeria, and the apparently insincere, if not indifferent approach which the Federal Government adopted, was one of the major reasons for the Army takeover of government in Nigeria on January 15, 1966.

The Action Group's internal crisis started in a small way. But little did those who launched it realise what ills it would carry with it for the country. After the Action Group lost the Federal Election of 1959, Awolowo became leader of the opposition in the Federal legislature, while Chief Samuel Ladoke Akintola became Premier of Western Nigeria. According to Nelson Ottah, this was a 'fatal step' for Chief Awolowo, for he lost the base of his security and found that, without being the head of any of the governments in the Federation, he was like a man that has gone from 'the twilight into darkness'.[54] In September 1960, the Action Group leader, with some young intellectuals in the party, formulated and launched the ideology of democratic socialism, and it was adopted as the ideology of the Action Group. This ideology did not seem to have been favoured by Akintola and his clique supporters, and in fact he did everything to distort this ideology, working in collaboration with the party's extreme right wing. Akintola started also to collaborate with the NPC and therefore wanted the Action Group to stop all its political activities in Northern Nigeria. He also began to take a number of important steps about cocoa prices, taxes and school fees without consulting his party chief. When therefore, on May 20, the Action Group annual congress met in Jos, Northern Nigeria, Akintola was charged with planning to displace Chief Awolowo as the leader of the Action Group, with acting without consultation and with squandermania. Akintola himself replied that the insistence that he should consult party officials before taking any major decisions hampered his administration.

At the end of the congress the Action Group decided to remove Akintola as Premier of Western Nigeria. The knotty question was how to do this. Chief Akintola, not feeling surefooted, refused to advise the summoning of the Western House to test his popularity by a vote of confidence. In this event Chief Awolowo got the majority of members of the Western House to sign an affidavit stating that they had lost confidence in Chief Akintola as Premier. On the strength of this affidavit the then Governor of Western Nigeria, Sir Adesoji Aderemi, was asked to exercise his powers under the Constitution of Western Nigeria to remove Akintola as Premier.[55] Aderemi thereupon removed Akintola as Premier, and appointed Alhaji Dauda S. Adegbenro in his place. But Akintola refused to accept that he had been validly removed and refused to relinquish office, maintaining that his dismissal must be as a result of a vote obtained on the floor of the Western House. He also filed an action in the Ibadan High Court challenging his dismissal by the Governor. A situation arose, therefore, in which there were two claimants to the office of Premier, each angling for support from Lagos and from the Western legislators.

When ultimately the Western House met on May 25, 1962, to debate a motion of confidence in Chief Akintola, serious fighting broke out in the House between the two factions, and the police had to use tear gas to disperse the rioting legislators.

Following this disturbance and the tension that had developed in Ibadan as a result of the premiership tussle, the Federal Government came directly to intervene in the affairs of Western Nigeria by declaring a state of emergency throughout the region and taking over the regional government. This decision had been influenced largely by the NPC, with the support of the NCNC. Under the Emergency Powers Regulations of 1961, Dr. Moses Koye Majekodunmi, the Federal Minister of Health, was appointed Administrator over Western Nigeria, with extensive powers. After the clash in the Western House, Akintola was formally dismissed from the Action Group. But he thereupon formed the United People's Party (UPP). Many leading members of the Action Group resigned and joined the UPP. To stop further political activities in the region the new Administrator placed under detention or restriction many of the region's politicians.[56]

There was no doubt that a serious situation had developed in Western Nigeria, but there was no doubt that the NPC-dominated Federal Government of Lagos was eager to pull a political string against the Action Group. It was clear that Chief Akintola had the sympathy, if not the support, of the NPC, which saw in the Action Group crisis an opportunity of destroying that turbulent party completely and politically incapacitating its leader. The Action Group was seen in NPC circles as a threat to Northern domination for, during the Federal Elections of 1959, the Action Group dared to contest and win seats in Northern Nigeria. It has also to be pointed out that without the support of the NCNC, probably no state of emergency could have been declared over Western Nigeria. If the NCNC cabinet members had objected and resigned there would have been a serious crisis, and Balewa and the NPC could not have carried out their plans. The NCNC connived with the NPC and maintained a conspiracy of silence. The NCNC was also thinking in terms of a political advantage. As the party in opposition in the Western House, it felt that the destruction of the Action Group (which was running the government) would give it the opportunity to come into power in the West.

While the emergency was on, apparently to put the Action Group in utter disarray, a three-man Commission of Enquiry was set up by the Prime Minister under the chairmanship of Mr.

Justice G. B. A. Coker to inquire into the working and financial administration of six statutory corporations in Western Nigeria, more especially the National Bank and the National Investment and Property Company (NIPC). The aim was to discredit the Action Group and its leadership. After sitting about three months, it found that Chief Awolowo's conduct while he was a minister of the Crown in Western Nigeria fell short of the standard expected. In the words of the report:

> We are satisfied by and large that Chief Awolowo knew everything about this diversion of large sums of money both from the National Bank of Nigeria Limited and the National Investment and Property Company Limited into the coffers of the Action Group. His scheme was to build around him with money an empire financially formidable both in Nigeria and abroad, an empire in which dominance would be maintained by him by the power of the money which he had given out.

The Commission, of course, absolved Chief Akintola from blame – although the ordinary man in the street could still contend that Chief Akintola was a leading figure in the Action Group when all the irregularities that the Coker Commission turned up were committed. The reputation of the Action Group and its leaders was severely tarnished by the report of the Commission. The Action Group's funds were also frozen by a court order.

At the same period the Action Group leader, Chief Awolowo, and twenty-four others, including the leader of the Dynamic Party, Dr. Chike Obi, two well-known journalists, Bisi Onabanjo and Lateef Jakande, were charged with treasonable felony and conspiracy to overthrow the Federal Government by force. As a result of this charge S. G. Ikoku, General Secretary of the Action Group, Chief Anthony Enahoro, its second deputy national president, and two other leading Action Groupers, Ayo Adebanjo and James Aluko, who had earlier fled the country, became wanted persons by the Nigerian police. At the close of the case for the Crown, four of the accused, Chief Alfred Rewane (Chief Awolowo's political secretary), Dr. Chike Obi, Tunde Amuwo and Muri Badmus, were discharged and acquitted. After many months of trial, on September 11, 1963, Chief Awolowo was sentenced by Mr. Justice George Sodeinde Sowemimo to ten years imprisonment for treasonable felony, five for conspiracy and two for unlawful importation of arms. The sentences were to run concurrently.

Looking at the whole episode, the conclusion appears inescapable that the NPC-led Government of Lagos was interested in the fate of both the Action Group as a party and Chief Awolowo as the leader of that party. Awolowo was obsessed with the idea of his 'unalterable destiny' – to rule Nigeria at any cost. It was alleged at his trial that he was prepared to use callous unconstitutional means to get that power. If this was true, he stands condemned by all responsible opinion. But it is also true that the Federal Government, in its over-zealousness to seal the fate of Chief Awolowo, resorted to all sorts of excesses and unfair treatment. During his trial Chief Awolowo was refused the representation of his counsel from the United Kingdom by the Federal Minister of Internal Affairs. It was never really proved in court, except for the statements of Dr. S. Onabamiro, that Awolowo really planned a revolution by force. Onabamiro's statements could be regarded as those of a man anxious to save his own head. This is borne out from the fact that he was in the original list of those accused with planning to overthrow the Federal Government, but he later turned a Crown witness.

It is no wonder then that Chief Awolowo came to be regarded by the masses of Southern Nigeria as a martyr on the altar of Nigeria's selfish and sectional politics. Akintola was dubbed a stooge of the NPC in the South. A good number of people even came to doubt the wisdom of the declaration of a state of emergency in the first place. It must be remembered that the declaration of this emergency was as a result of a fight or 'riot' inside the Western House by members themselves. There was no disturbance outside the House anywhere in the Western Region. Secondly, it was not the Action Group which provoked the fight. It was, in fact, first started by Akintola's Party men, supported by the NCNC. The Federal Government knew what was to happen and was ready. As soon as it was informed it used the police and tear gas to disperse the parliamentarians – a very high-handed method indeed – and the Prime Minister and the NPC–NCNC-dominated Federal Parliament immediately invoked the Constitution and dissolved the Western House. They knew that Akintola could not win. Judged in the light of later events, the conclusion therefore appears to be that it was unwarranted, and that it was all politics. If the Federal Government could declare a state of emergency in 1962 following the internal crisis in the Action Group, why did the same Federal Government refuse to take a similar line of action in 1965, when wholesale arson, looting and murder were taking place in Western Nigeria following the fraudulent Western elections of October that year? It was the same Federal Government under Sir Abubakar Tafawa Balewa. Perhaps a declaration of an emergency in 1965 would have jeopardised the NPC design in Western Nigeria. We see, therefore, how the Federal Government came to take a tribal, sectional or self-interested approach in the affairs of the country, deepening rather than closing up Nigeria's divisions.

(iii) THE CENSUS CRISIS

In 1962 Nigeria had her first population census since Independence. The fact that it turned out to be a big fiasco shows how hard it is to establish the simplest facts when the result may have major political consequences. Nigerians had last been counted between 1952 and 1953, but that was under the British. According to the results, the Northern Region had a population of 17,573,000, the Eastern Region 7,497,000, the Western Region 6,408,000, while the Federal Territory of Lagos had 272,000. The total population of Nigeria, therefore, was given as 31,750,000.[57] The political significance of the 1952–3 Census was that it assured the dominance of the North in the Federal Government since seats in the Federal House of Parliament were then allocated on a population basis. Out of the 312 seats in the Federal House, the North received 174 seats, thus placing it in an absolute majority. Since in Nigeria the major political parties were based on regions, a population census that gave the North such a majority meant handing over the Federal Government in perpetuity to the NPC.

In 1962, the Nigerian Federal Government under Balewa announced that it was going to hold another population census. Among the reasons given for ordering the census was the need to obtain all essential data for development plans in all fields.

Mr. J. Warren, an expatriate civil servant, was to be in charge, under the general ministerial responsibility of the Hon. Minister of Economic Development, Alhaji Waziri Ibrahim, a Northerner.

The census day was May 13, 1962. Warren had recruited enumerators and supervisors and had devised a pilot scheme to facilitate the exercise. By about July the Lagos headquarters had received all the figures for the Northern and Eastern Regions. Because of the political unrest in the Western Region, the results from there came after those of the other regions. When all the results were examined, the North showed an average increase of 30 per cent in ten years, bringing the total population to 22·5 million. Both the East and the West showed a rise of more than 70 per cent. Warren, making his report on the preliminary census figures, declared that the Northern results were reasonable, while the figures for the Eastern region appeared to him to have been 'grossly inflated'. Under Warren's advice, the Federal Government decided to verify and check results in selected areas in the country. This involved sending all the enumeration books back to the regions. Although an attempt was made to get the consent of all the regional premiers, including Senator Majekodunmi, who was then administering Western Nigeria under the emergency, the Eastern Premier, Dr. Michael Okpara, revealed that according to the 1962 census, the East came out with a population of 12·3 million. He stated quite categorically that the East would stick to this total. Since Waziri was determined that the checks and verifications must be carried out, it became clear that a political storm was about to explode in the country.

Early in December 1962, when the Federal House of Parliament was summoned, Waziri Ibrahim read out parts of the Warren report on the census. He read out the portion of it which stated that the Northern figures were reasonable, and that the Eastern results were inflated, but failed to tell the Parliamentarians what the totals were for the various regions. Following this one-sided and mutilated statement, a tension developed between the NCNC and NPC members in the coalition Government, while throughout Southern Nigeria there was a general outcry against the census results. The NCNC and Action Group Members of Parliament walked out of the Federal

House and demanded that Warren should have no further part
to play in the census affairs, and also that he should leave the
country.

When Parliament reassembled on December 10, 1962, the
Prime Minister, Sir Abubakar Tafawa Balewa, had some comments to make on the statement made the previous Wednesday
by Waziri Ibrahim. He described 'the whole drama of both the
Minister's statement and walk-out by some members' as
'embarrassing and unfortunate'.[58] He stated that the Minister
'should have been more restrained',[59] and announced that the
census would now come under his personal responsibility. He
declared that, because of the public controversy that had
developed over the census affairs, he would review the position
with a view to removing doubt and re-establishing confidence.

Following this statesmanlike announcement, feelings were
calmed down and the nation waited to see what solution would
be forthcoming. The Government had proceeded on the veri-
fication checks, but at the end of it, while the figures for the
East and West remained as before, those of the Northern region
rose suddenly from 22·5 million to 31 million. This meant an
increase since 1952–3 of about 80 per cent. Certainly it would
have been the biggest joke of the year had the Federal Government published the Northern figures. But the Balewa Government, that had all along looked for a reason to cancel the census
count, now found one. The census was accordingly cancelled by
the Prime Minister. The £1·5 million that had been spent thus
went down the drain.

After the first census had failed, it was agreed between the
various governments in the Federation that there would be a
new and quick count lasting only four days. It was also agreed
that, in each region, the enumeration would be done not only
by enumerators from that region, but also by those from other
regions. In this way, it was hoped, fraudulent practices would
be checked. In a broadcast to the nation on November 2, 1963,
on the second population count, Balewa, giving reasons for the
count, stated that:

The life of the present Federal Parliament ends in 1964, and
it is my intention to have a general election as soon as possible.
The electoral register now in use does not reflect sufficiently

the changes in population over the years. It is therefore agreed by all the Governments that particulars of eligible voters obtained through the census will be used in compiling a new electoral register for the General Election next year.[60]

Innocently, perhaps, Balewa had again reminded the people of Nigeria of the political implications of the census.

The Prime Minister also announced that 'the census this year is being organised by a body of high government officials appointed by all the governments in the Republic' and that 'the manner in which the population count will be made has been approved by all the governments'.[61] He also stated that 'besides counting by eight, certain checks and tests . . . will be applied in order to ensure accurate figures of the population'.[62] He went on,

> These include statistical sampling checks based on inter-nationally accepted principles; demographic tests based on sex and age distribution; specially arranged pre-enumeration checks; and special devices to remove double counting.[63]

All these were intended to impress the people of Nigeria and the world about the fairness of the coming census. But the hopes then expressed were not borne out by the actual counting and manipulations that followed it.

The census took place on November 5–8, 1963. In the Prime Minister's own words, it was organised to last for only four days in order to ensure an accurate count of people at places where they live.[64] Over 180,000 enumerators and supervisors were recruited, as against 45,700 in the one of 1962. As in the previous census, enumerators went from house to house asking every individual his name, age, ethnic group or nationality, religion and occupation. On all travelling points and regional boundaries, there were enumerators, and anyone they counted at these points they stained with a special indelible ink-mark on the thumb to prevent double counting at the destination. Travellers were ready to suffer this inconvenience, and co-operated because 'the governments in the Republic [attached] the greater importance to this census'.

At the end of the returns, a delay of about two months fol-lowed during which period the figures were said to be undergoing 'exhaustive test'. The Census Board released the preliminary figures of the 1963 National Population Census on February 24, 1964, and the figures for the various regions were as follows:

NORTH ..	..	..	..	29,777,986
EAST ..	..	..	..	12,388,646
WEST ..	..	..	..	10,278,500
MID-WEST	..	..	..	2,533,337
LAGOS ..	..	..	..	675,352
			Total ..	55,653,821

It will be observed that whereas the figures for the North rose to 29,777,986, as against her 22·5 million in 1963, those of the East were the same as the original total on which the Eastern premier, Dr. Michael Okpara, had taken his stand the previous year. The same was about the case with the West, now separated into two regions, with a population rise in one decade of almost 100 per cent.

The overall increase of the total Nigerian population in one decade was about 74 per cent. The United Nations demographers regarded a 2 per cent increase per annum as normal in Africa. In ten years, if one relies on the opinions of these experts, there would be an increase of 20 per cent. In the Nigerian circumstances, granting that there was some under-counting in 1952–3 due to evasions, and allowing about 5 to 10 per cent for this under-count, and thus bringing the total rise of the Nigerian population to 25 or 30 per cent in a decade, it would appear, therefore, that the census of 1963 was 'grossly inflated'. The Premier of the new region of the Mid-West, Chief Dennis Osadebay, declared it to be 'the biggest joke of the year'.

The Eastern Premier, backed by the Mid-Western Premier, 'completely' rejected the preliminary census figures that had been published. He charged that although the census was the responsibility of all the regional premiers, the Prime Minister had published the figures 'without consultation'. He declared:

Since the preliminary report was received, I have said that we would check the figures and if accurate, would accept them, but if inflated, would reject them. *I REGRET THAT THE INFLATIONS DISCLOSED ARE OF SUCH ASTRONOMICAL PROPORTIONS THAT THE FIGURES OBTAINED, TAKEN AS A WHOLE, ARE WORSE THAN USELESS.*[65]

Dr. Okpara then went on to detail the reasons why he was rejecting the preliminary figures. He explained that the Census Board based its checks against inflation upon the sampling count carried out by two inspectors comprising one from the home region and one from outside in about one-thirtieth of each census district. The area to be sampled was not to be disclosed until just before the count, but, in the case of the North, the areas to be sampled were disclosed long before the census took place.[66] He quoted the Census Board statement admitting this lapse, which statement read as follows:

We wish also to point out that it is the feeling of one or two members that the timing of the release of information regarding the identity of enumeration areas to be sampled was unfortunate, in the sense that it could have afforded a great deal of opportunity for unfair practice to anyone who might be so inclined.

He also cited a list of other irregularities spotted by inspectors from Eastern Nigeria who were sent to the North. They were listed as follows:

   (i) Counting of Eastern inspectors against the decision of the Board;

   (ii) Double counting;

  (iii) Counting of travellers and passers-by without staining their thumbs – in contravention of the Board's decision;

  (iv) Posting of inspectors after commencement of count – thereby permitting incredible counts of 900–2,559 persons in one day;

   (v) Counting sampled areas without the Inspector;

  (vi) Counting in market places against the Board's decision;

 (vii) Refusal of entry into Purdah;

(viii) Counting after November 8, i.e. after the last day of the count;

(ix) Counting of persons not seen, contrary to the Census Board's decision;
 (x) Refusal to let the Inspector initial enumeration book;
(xi) Merging of two enumeration books from two different areas, one of which was not covered by inspector;
(xii) Removal of black completed labels, thereby facilitating the double counting of persons in the same household;
(xiii) Late return of enumeration books.[67]

These irregularities were documented and reported to the Census Board.

Dr. Okpara pointed out that all these irregularities were detected in the small sampled areas, and wondered what must have happened in the rest of Northern Nigeria where there were no sampling and checks. He stated that because of 'these alarming irregularities, the Northern figures could not pass the generally accepted demographic tests' and, as a result, out of 'a total of 175 Census Districts in the North, as many as 49 failed all tests', 76 failed some of the tests, while only 99 Census Districts passed the tests.[68] In the East, of the 73 constituencies, 53 passed while 20 (of which 5 failed all tests) failed. In the West, out of 47 constituencies, 20 passed, while 27 failed and 10 failed all tests. Of the 15 in the Mid-West, 8 passed, 3 failed all tests and there were 7 failures in all. The Census Board decided not to apply the tests to the 3 constituencies in Lagos. These irregularities and deficiencies led to a scale-down of the figures, reducing the grand total from 60·5 million to the 55 million which the people of Nigeria were ultimately asked to accept. Dr. Okpara still maintained that the figure of 55 million for Nigeria was ridiculous. To obtain this inflated figure, the country had spent £2·5 million.

On March 16, 1964, the Prime Minister, Alhaji Balewa, stated in the Federal House that the 'Census Board comprising duly appointed representatives of the Governments in the Republic', had completed its job, and had given him the preliminary figures of the 1963 National Population Census. He declared:

I am advised that my acceptance and publication of these figures is final.[69]

He stated that he would be holding a meeting with Regional Premiers to discuss 'other matters in connection with the Census'. This ambiguous statement deepened rather than closed the controversy.

Widespread public reaction on the census now began. Students from the Southern universities (the University of Lagos, in Lagos, the University of Ibadan in Western Nigeria, the University of Ife, then at Ibadan, and the University of Nigeria, Nsukka, now University of Biafra) staged demonstrations against the census results. More than 600 students from the University of Nigeria came all the way from the East to hand over their protest memorandum to the Prime Minister in Lagos. The position of Ahmadu Bello University, Zaria, in the North, was quite understandable; they maintained silence over the census issue. Major political parties like the Action Group, the NEPU and the Dynamic Party, also spoke out against the census figures. S. L. Akintola's UPP, which entered into coalition with the NCNC at the end of the emergency period to run the government of Western Nigeria, accepted the census figures,[70] and thus it came about that the Akintola Government was the only Southern Government to do so.

Apart from parties and governments, there were a number of other powerful or influential organisations that organised protests against the census, and these included the Labour Congress, the Lagos City Council, the Zikist Movement and Otegbeye's Socialist Party.

However, in the face of the overwhelming dissatisfaction over the preliminary census figures, the Premier of Northern Nigeria and President of the NPC, Sir Ahmadu Bello, the Sardauna of Sokoto, announced that he had accepted the preliminary census figures, and that 'it is the intention of the Government of Northern Nigeria to proceed to work with them for the purposes of planning'.[71] He declared that 'the census was fairly conducted and the staff did their best at all levels'. He then proceeded to reply to the charges made against the North under some eighteen heads. To the charge that sample areas were disclosed to the Northern Region, he answered that this, being a criminal offence, 'should have been reported to the police for investigation'. On the allegation that 900 to 2,559 people were counted in a single day by one enumerator in the

North, he stated that 'there is no iota of truth in it' but that, to the best of his knowledge, 'the highest count was 958 people in four days and not in one day'. He asserted that the 'trick' of double counting did not take place in the North, neither was there any 'shred of evidence' that counting continued in the North after November 8. He stated that it was most unfair for anyone to accuse the Prime Minister of not consulting the Premiers before releasing the figures, as there was no decision to that effect. The Sardauna warned that 'my Government and my Party are fully prepared at any hour of the day, in any eventuality to meet any challenge'. Nigeria had thus reached a stage where a headlong clash between the various governments of the Federation was inevitable. Two governments (East and Mid-West) had rejected the census; another two (North and West) had accepted it, and these two opposing camps would want to remain stubborn in their stands. Nor was there a chance of a third census for Nigeria in this kind of muddle.

However, the East, convinced of the justice of its case, instituted actions in the Federal Supreme Court against the Governments of the Federation under Section 114 (1) of the Nigerian Constitution.[72] The Attorneys-General of these two governments were made nominal parties in two actions which were later consolidated with the consent of the parties. In each of the actions, the Eastern Government asked for a declaration that the Federal Government, its servants or agents, were not entitled to accept or act on the 1963 census figures. In the second action the Eastern Government alleged that the manner in which the census was conducted was unconstitutional, *ultra vires* and illegal, and therefore null and void, on the grounds of a wrong assumption of jurisdiction by the Prime Minister. The Eastern Government also alleged that the census was further vitiated on the ground of irrelevant considerations and bad faith and, to substantiate these allegations, it attached to its Statement of Claim particulars of irregularities. The Federal Government, in its turn, filed a motion in each case asking the court to dismiss the actions on the ground that no cause of action was disclosed, that the court had no jurisdiction to entertain the claim and that the action was frivolous and vexatious.

The Eastern Government was unsuccessful in its action.

C

The court in its holding stated that the Eastern Government had failed to prove that it had any legal right which could be enforced by the Court. It also held that, since the Premier of Eastern Region concurred in the setting up of a Census Board responsible to the Prime Minister, the Eastern Premier could not then contend that the creation of the Board was a contravention of a statutory provision – he could not approbate and reprobate at the same time.[73]

Now that the issue was finally determined by the Court, for any government believing in the rule of law the matter was as good as closed. The Eastern Government, though still smarting under a sense of palpable injustice, finally dropped the matter and accepted the conclusion of a political truce whose effect was to keep the North in its preponderance.

Nor was there any doubt as to the fact that it was this preponderance that mattered most to the North. After the census results were released by the Census Board on February 24, 1964, the Northern House soon entered into its Budget Session of March 1964. This offered the Northern legislators an opportunity to express their views on the preliminary census figures that had just been released. Thus on March 4, 1964, the Parliamentary Secretary to the Minister of Information, Alhaji M. Kokori Abdul, declared in the House:

> I have no doubt whatever and without fear that the Northern People's Congress has come to stay and to continue to stay and is *going to rule the Federation of Nigeria for ever*, as said by the Honourable Premier.[74]

At the same time, because of the controversy that followed the results of the census, this session of the House was used by the legislators to release their outbursts of feelings against the people of Eastern Nigeria. They demanded that those Easterners in the North 'should pack and go back' to the East. One of them (Alhaji Usman Liman) declared: 'Mr. Chairman, North is for Northerners, East for Easterners, West for Westerners and the Federation is for all.'[75] Whatever must have prompted these extremities, and whether the North maintained its dominance or not, the fact remains that the Nigerians, under Balewa, could not count themselves, and the true size of the Nigerian population will probably never be known.

(iv) THE UNIVERSITY OF LAGOS CRISIS, 1965

Not even the Nigerian Universities – these 'halls of learning', whose normal posture should have been that of neutrality in politics, and whose principal function – that of searching for the truth, teaching and proclaiming the truth without fear or favour, and preserving the truth – could escape the whirlwind of sectional politics and tribalism. The five-month crisis which in 1965 engulfed the University of Lagos, one of the five universities in the country, over the appointment of its vice-chancellor, was one of Nigeria's most shocking post-independence experiences, and shows how callous and petty some of Nigeria's politicians could be when their actions were being motivated by tribal and political considerations. It also illustrates the grave danger of subjecting universities to political and sectional interference, and highlights the whole issue of academic freedom and university autonomy.

Before Nigeria's General Elections of December 1964,[76] the NNDP (the party controlling the Government of Western Nigeria) had reached a top-level political agreement with the NPC (in control in the North), with which it was in a political alliance called the NNA for the purpose of contesting the elections, that if the NNA won the Federal Elections, the Vice-Chancellors of the Universities of Lagos and of Ibadan, who were Ibos from Eastern Nigeria, would be replaced by NNDP nominees. Dr. Samuel A. Aluko, a Yoruba lecturer and a well-known Nigerian economist, pointed this out in the *Nigerian Tribune* in an article entitled 'The Choice before the Nation, Universities and the Alliance'.[77] He warned that:

> If the NNA wins the Federal elections, it is going to interfere more and more with the academic rights of the universities. The NNDP has not hidden its determination to appoint Vice-Chancellors of universities on the basis of tribe; it made a public statement challenging the rights of the Ibos to the Vice-Chancellorships of the Ibadan and Lagos universities. It has lined up puppets to replace one or both of these illustrious Nigerians, should the NNDP win.

After the Federal elections and the crisis and bitterness that followed it, the NNDP did not waste time in working out a strategy for putting its intentions into reality. It decided to deal first with the University of Lagos as the term of office of the then Vice-Chancellor, Professor Eni Njoku, was due to expire on May 31, 1965, a few months later. The plan was simple. The intentions of the NNDP would be carried out through the ten-member Provisional Council of the University of Lagos made up of a Yoruba chairman, six other Yorubas, one Hausa, one Rivers man, and an expatriate. There was no Ibo man in the Council, and an Ibo Vice-Chancellor was going to be replaced. Anyone with any acquaintance with Nigeria's tribalism and past would recognise at once that this was a plan that could not fail, and not even the traditional commitments of the universities to the side of truth, justice and fair-play could influence certain members of Council when the issue of the Vice-Chancellor's appointment came to be decided by the Council. A daily newspaper in Western Nigeria, and an organ of the NNA, the *Daily Sketch*, wrote after the University of Lagos crisis became launched upon its stormy course, that 'Lagos was a Yoruba city and its University ought to be headed by a "son of the soil" '.[78] Professor Eni Njoku was replaced by Dr. Saburi O. Biobaku, and not all the protests of the University Deans, members of the academic and administrative staff, the students, and the general public could stop the NNPD from enforcing its decision that Njoku must go. The NNDP threw in everything and used the power of the Federal Government to see that its misguided intention, that holding of top offices in the universities should have a tribal and political tinge, was not jeopardised.

To put into perspective the crisis that was sparked off by the failure to reappoint Professor Njoku as Vice-Chancellor of the University of Lagos, it is necessary to give a brief account of the beginning and early development of the university. Soon after Nigeria became independent, the Federal Government appointed a Commission under the chairmanship of Sir Eric Ashby, Master of Clare College, Cambridge, to work out plans for Nigeria's post-School Certificate and higher education. The Ashby Commission recommended among other things the establishment of the University of Lagos,[79] which should be non-residential. The University should give special emphasis to commerce, business administration and economics. The Federal Government, in accepting the recommendations of the Commission,[80] felt it was entering upon an exciting and rewarding venture which would serve the special needs of Nigeria – an 'Investment in Education'.

In March 1962 the Federal Parliament passed the University of Lagos Act. A Provisional Council for the University was established in June, with Dr. E. N. O. Sodeinde as chairman. Professor Eni Njoku, one of the members of a UNESCO Commission set up by the Federal Government in June 1961 to advise on the creation and development of the University, and formerly Dean of the Faculty of Science and Professor of Botany in the University of Ibadan, was appointed first Vice-Chancellor. It was generally accepted at the time that the new University was lucky to have him, as an eminent academic, a man of rare capabilities and one with long experience in university and other kinds of administration.[81]

Professor Njoku was asked to create an unusual type of university – with no campus, though with good study and catering facilities. It was to have day and evening courses, according to the recommendations of the UNESCO Commission submitted to the Prime Minister in September 1961,[82] and accepted six months later by the Federal Government. Even though the University was to have a Medical School, the University of Lagos Act, 1962, stipulated that this should be 'an autonomous unit' of the University. Judged according to the history and tradition of British and African universities, these were innovations, the translation of which into practical reality involved a difficult and challenging task. However, Professor Njoku and the members of the academic and administrative staff immediately applied themselves to the task before them with courage and determination.

The first academic year began in late September 1962 in temporary premises at Idiaraba, Surulere, Lagos. Classes began while repairs and other improvements were still in progress. A small percentage of the students were quartered at the Baptist Academy (one of the Lagos Secondary Schools), while others lived either in hostels arranged for in the town by the University authority, or in private homes by their own arrangements. A fleet of mini-buses did shuttle services, conveying students from distant places to their places of study. In spite of these arrangements, designed to lessen difficulties, the myriad problems of running a non-residential university in an underdeveloped country like Nigeria soon became evident. These problems led students to organise protest demonstrations, calling upon the Federal Government to review its stand and give them a campus. (Professor Njoku, apart from his personal conviction that a campus was necessary, noted the students' protests and applied his weight and influence to persuade the Federal Government to listen to the students.) However, in spite of difficulties, by the end of the University's first session, it already held out great promise. The various faculties had worked out excellent syllabuses, lectures were going on, there were a good number of distinguished professors, deans and lecturers, and students were showing good response. The Federal Government therefore considered that the expenditure necessary to build a campus would not be unjustified, and so it was that, by the second academic year of 1963–4, the super-, structure of a permanent site started to rise in Yaba, Lagos under the strict supervision of the Vice-Chancellor. It was a beautiful site overlooking the Lagos Lagoon.

On January 18, 1964, the foundation stone of the new campus was laid by the Prime Minister, Tafawa Balewa. On that occasion, Professor Njoku openly criticised the concept of building a non-residential university. He said before the distinguished guests that came to witness the occasion:

We have been very fortunate in obtaining a site of such beauty and excellence as you all see today. When the idea of a University in Lagos was first mooted, it was suggested that it should have no campus at all. Some suggested that the University should consist of a skyscraper, occupying an acre or so of slum-clearance ground in central Lagos. This was the concept of a down-town University, 'like New York University', as I was told by one of the advocates of this proposal. Having since been to New York as guest of that famous University, and seen the great and costly efforts which have been made to buy up the surrounding property so as to create a campus, I am glad that the central Lagos proposal did not prevail.

Professor Njoku's idea at the time was not just to increase the percentage of residential students by having a campus, but to have a campus which would be able to accommodate as many students as wanted accommodation. A campus atmosphere is more conducive to serious study and many more students would be enabled to participate fully and meaningfully in university life.

Characteristically, however, Professor Njoku paid the greatest attention to academic matters. The UNESCO report of 1961 had asked for the maintenance of high academic standards in all courses offered in the University. He soon had around him a distinguished academic staff with long experience in the universities of Africa, Asia, Australia, Britain, Canada, Ireland, the United States and the West Indies. These academics came to join in 'the thrilling enterprise of establishing what would be a great university for an important nation in an Africa of great promise'.[83] The students, on their part, responded well and student-staff relations were good. Tribalism and politics played no part in the life of the University. Under the direction of Miss Elizabeth M. Moys a library was developed within two years. UNESCO, the Ford Foundation of America, the Trinity College of Durham, all made generous donations to the University and also seconded expatriate staff. The result was that the University made an excellent start and became recognised within less than three years of its existence as an institution of the first class. The UNESCO Report on the University noted this excellent start and the very high standard set. The staff published several text-books to adapt the University's own courses to the needs of the whole country, and represented the University at international conventions and seminars. It can then be imagined how shocking the news of the replacement of Professor Eni Njoku was to all those who knew and appreciated his exertions in building up the University and who were sincerely concerned about its orderly and uninterrupted progress.[84]

From a purely human or moral point of view, Njoku's replacement would attract objections for the following reasons. First, his replacement before June carried the implication that he would not personally pass out the first crop of the University of Lagos graduands. The University's first graduation ceremony or convocation would have taken place in June 1965. Secondly, it was being planned that students would move over to the permanent site of the University about the end of May 1965. Although it was he who had worked tirelessly to give the students a campus, he would not even see his students take over the new site.

Professor Njoku's term as head of one of Nigeria's universities was the shortest ever. Throughout the crisis period, the Provisional Council of the University could offer no reasons to the general public for the replacement other than that his term would expire on May 31, 1965, and therefore that he should be replaced. Neither corruption nor favouritism, and neither professional incompetence nor moral misconduct on the part of Eni Njoku was alleged. Very soon the issue had become a national crisis, and the people of Nigeria were demanding an explanation. In November 1964 the Provisional Council of the University had submitted to the Prime Minister the draft of a new Constitution for the University of Lagos, in which the name of Professor Eni Njoku was written as Vice-Chancellor. This Constitution was placed before the Federal Parliament. Had it not been for the dissolution of Parliament that soon followed for the purpose of contesting the Federal Elections of December 1964, and the crisis which resulted from these Elections, this Constitution would have been passed by Parliament before 1965. It was the same Provisional Council that wrote his name into the Constitution that was now trying to replace him.

About mid-February 1965 the Chairman of the Provisional Council, in contravention of section 6 (4) of the University of Lagos Act which demanded reference to the Council first in such matters, issued directives to the Senate asking it to submit nominations for the post of Vice-Chancellor. Members of the Council were also asked to send nominations. The Senate met and on February 18 submitted its report in which it recommended and urged strongly that Njoku should continue as Vice-Chancellor. The Chairman of the Council then decided on his own to summon for the following day, February 19, a meeting of the Council originally scheduled for February 26. Professor Njoku was not notified of the meeting of the 19th and this was a deliberate attempt to exclude him, even though the Standing Orders of the Council required that seven day's notice should be served to 'every member' before a meeting could be held. The main purpose of summoning the meeting for the 19th was, however, to exclude Professor L. C. B. Gower,

the representative of the Faculties of the University and the
Senate, from the Council meeting so as to deny the Senate and
the academic staff a voice in the Council on the question of
appointment of a new Vice-Chancellor. It was known to the
Council Chairman and A. Y. Eke, Secretary of the Council,
that Professor Gower would be leaving for Freetown, Sierra
Leone, on the 19th on urgent business which would keep him
away for about a week. Professor Gower had planned to be
back before the Council's meeting of February 29.

However, when Professor Njoku accidentally learnt of the
meeting of the 19th, he went straight to the meeting. In the
papers for the meeting,[85] members of the Council were asked
'to consider the following candidates for appointment to the
post of vice-chancellor with effect from June 1, 1965:

(i) E. Njoku (nominated by the Senate);

(ii) S. O. Biobaku (nominated by a member of the Council);

(iii) F. O. Dosekun (nominated by a member of the Council);

It was stated in the Council Paper that 'all the three are in-
terested in the post and are free and willing to accept an offer'.
Yet Dr. S. O. Biobaku had recently accepted an appointment
as Vice-Chancellor to the new University of Zambia,[86] while
Professor F. O. Dosekun of the Lagos University Medical
School had chaired the Senate meeting of February 18, which
had recommended that Eni Njoku should continue as Vice-
Chancellor. Secondly, whereas the Council had an up-to-date
curriculum vitae of each of these two men, what purported to be
Professor Njoku's *curriculum vitae* was 'cribbed from a Council
paper submitted for a different purpose in 1962, i.e. three years
ago"[87] This could not have been in his best interest. Because
of the lack of notice to him and the hurry in calling the Council's
meeting of February 19, he could not send his submissions in
time to the Council. This was contrary to both procedure and
natural justice. Eni Njoku, however, succeeded in securing the
adjournment of the meeting of February 19.

At the meeting eventually held on February 26, Dr. Biobaku
was selected as Vice-Chancellor. Voting was along tribal lines.
The seven Yoruba members of the Council voted for Biobaku,
while the three remaining members voted for Njoku. Earlier,

c*

Professor Dosekun had withdrawn his candidature for the obvious reason that the anti-Njoku members of the Council would not like their votes to be split between two candidates, possibly giving Eni Njoku an opportunity to retain his post. Thus the University Council became converted into an instrument of conspiracy to attain political and tribal objectives.[88]

Academic freedom demands that the University should be allowed to do its work without political, religious or tribal interference. A person nominated by the Senate was rejected by the Council, while another upon whom no report had been made by the Senate was appointed, and the Senate was not previously informed that the new appointee was a candidate for the post.[89] The better part of discretion and reason dictates that the Senate recommendations on the appointment should have prevailed, if the interests of the University were considered paramount. The Senate's views should be given priority in academic matters, being a body consisting of persons of academic distinction, mainly Professors and Heads of Faculties of the University, and as the highest academic authority in the University. The Council, on the other hand, is essentially a body of eminent laymen. By the University of Lagos Act, Section 6 (1), the Council was 'charged with the general control and superintendence of the property of the University . . .', while by Section 3 (2) the Senate had responsibility for academic matters and was empowered to 'give such directions as it thinks fit for the administration of the University'. The Council and the Senate are sovereign, each within its own sphere of authority and power. The ultimate decision on the appointment of a Vice-Chancellor was that of the Council, but by Section 6 (4) of the University of Lagos Act, this decision could only be made 'after consideration of a report by the Senate'. The object of this provision is to ensure that the academic qualifications of the proposed Vice-Chancellor are acceptable.[90] Academic conventions demand that the Senate report or recommendation should not be rejected by the Council without further consultation with the Senate, and that the Council's decision to reject must not be based on considerations other than ability and competence. To have a University at all, the Senate and the Council must work in harmony. It is unlikely that any Senate would co-operate with a Vice-

Chancellor appointed or selected by the Council without its over-riding consent.

Professor Biobaku's appointment would attract objection for another reason: that, from past evidence, he would appear not to believe in academic freedom and university autonomy. These demand that the university should be left free to conduct its own proper business without outside interference. Without these there would be spiritual despair or discouragement and the waning of intellectual enthusiasm, and the University could not serve as the 'conscience of society'. No self-respecting academic would care to belong to a University without academic freedom.

Before being appointed to the Lagos post, Dr. Biobaku was pro-Vice-Chancellor of the University of Ife, Western Nigeria. During his stay there, incessant squabbles and wrangles took place between the administration and members of the academic staff. These came to a head on December 19, 1963, when Dr. Biobaku enunciated his famous 'credo' outlining his views on the relationship between a university and the government. He declared that university lecturers must support the Government of Western Nigeria, and warned that anyone who would not comply must have the courage to resign his appointment forthwith, or be dismissed summarily by the administration. He went on:

> I wish to say most categorically, however, that the authorities of the university have only one policy and that is to support the government of the day to which the university looks up for sustenance.[91]

This statement summarises the attitude to academic freedom and university autonomy of the man who was to assume office as Vice-Chancellor of the University of Lagos on June 1, 1965. As Davidson Nicol has written, academic freedom 'does not involve disloyalty to the government or the country, but it should carry with it the implication that basically if members of the University do not feel that they should agree with the Government they should be able to say so without losing their posts'.[92] Commenting at the time upon Dr. Biobaku's policy statement, Professor E. O. Idowu of the Department of Religious Studies, University College, Ibadan, noted that 'a satanic principle' had been let loose upon 'this young country'. Professor H. A. Oluwasanmi accused Dr. Biobaku of bringing the entire academic community of Nigeria 'to the perilous brink of intellectual chaos'.

In the University of Ife itself, the statement sparked off a crisis which ultimately led to a mass exodus of staff, especially as Dr. Biobaku showed readiness to enforce his new policy. On February 3, 1964, a few weeks after his statement, he dismissed Professor V. A. Oyenuga, Dean of the Department of Agriculture, for not complying with his policy. In protest, four members of the academic staff, Dr. S. A. Aluko, Mr. M. E. D. Chambers, Dr. O. Odumosu and Dr. A. A. Fayemi, resigned their appointments. Shortly after, four others followed – Dr. O. Olunloyo, Dr. A. Babalola, Dr. O. L. Oke and Dr. T. O. Fayiga. To prevent a further exodus, a sudden mass promotion of staff followed.[93] But the University of Ife has never recovered from the damage. From the time Biobaku enunciated his 'credo' till he left the University, attempts to recruit suitably qualified staff for the University of Ife met with failure.[94] At the time of the University of Lagos crisis, the number of professors in the University of Lagos, which had only seven faculties, tripled the number at Ife, even though the latter had many more faculties and had been in existence longer.

For these reasons, widespread protests within the University of Lagos community followed the announcement on March 1 that Dr. Biobaku had been appointed Vice-Chancellor to that University. In the early morning of March 1, 1965, the Students' Congress passed a resolution[95] that until Professor Eni Njoku was reinstated as Vice-Chancellor, they 'on their part' would regard the University as closed. In furtherance of this decision, the students took over control of the main University premises at Ida-Araba and barricaded the main entrance to the University with classroom and dining-room chairs and tables. They also forwarded a protest letter to the Chairman of the Provisional Council of the University and to the Prime Minister of the Federation, Alhaji Balewa. Members of the Senate and senior members of the academic and administrative staff also joined the protest. The members of staff also sent protest letters to the Council.[96] From this, it was clear that virtually the whole University community was protesting against the Council's decision, and this unanimity continued till March 4, 1965. There were no lectures. In face of these protests, the Council resorted to intimidation and calumny, and the crisis escalated. From March 4 the NNDP identified itself openly with Dr. Biobaku, and NNDP politicians visited the campus with a view to breaking the solidarity of the students and staff. Their strategy consisted of inciting tribal hatred against Professor Eni Njoku, and deceiving the Yoruba students and staff into believing that the protests against Biobaku's appointment had tribal undertones. The Council, unable to control the situation, issued an order suspending the students and closing down the University indefinitely. Forced by the police power of the states, the staff and students were made to leave the university premises. The students immediately announced that they would challenge in court the Council's decision to suspend them.[97]

In spite of these high-handed and panic measures adopted by the Council, the crisis continued. Neither the students nor the staff would accept intimidation for an answer. Meanwhile, the Senate appointed on March 15, 1965, another member of staff, Professor T. B. H. McMurray, to the Council to replace Professor Gower, who had earlier resigned from the Council in protest against Njoku's dismissal. On March 22 the Provisional Council, instead of tackling objectively the crisis that was facing the University, offered Professor Njoku the post of Professor of Biology at a salary exceeding the normal salary for the post by £750 p. a.[98] Thinking that their new gesture would solve its problem, the Council announced that the University would reopen on April 5, 1965. It also announced that only those students would be readmitted who signed declarations of good behaviour.

However, as it turned out, the crisis was still continuing and indeed became more explosive. Students undertook tours to the various regions of Nigeria to explain their stand to heads of governments, to the other Nigerian universities and to the general public. The Students' Union gave eight reasons for the protests and these were embodied in leaflets and handbills it distributed to the general public. It read as follows:

(i) We protest against the inhuman and most irregular manner in which our present Vice-Chancellor, Dr. Eni

Njoku, is being removed for no just cause and contrary to the recommendation of the Senate – the highest academic body of the University – on whose advice the Provisional Council should act.

(ii) We protest against the manifest injustice and shabby treatment meted to Dr. Eni Njoku, who was strongly persuaded to relinquish his permanent and pensionable appointment as the Dean of the Department of Botany in the University of Ibadan so as to undertake the arduous pioneering task of establishing the University of Lagos.

(iii) We protest against the improper removal of Dr. Eni Njoku, whose expert co-ordination of the efforts of staff and students in building up the University has resulted in higher academic standards, close student–staff relation and satisfaction on the part of all. Besides, Professor Njoku's neutrality in politics has resulted in the insulation of the University from the vicissitudes of Nigerian politics.

(iv) We protest against the coming of Dr. Biobaku, whose declared political partisanship would deprive this University of its most cherished academic freedom. The vicissitudes of sectional politics which enveloped the University of Ife is (sic) still fresh in our memories.

(v) We protest against the coming of Dr. Biobaku since he already has a Vice-Chancellorship in Zambia, and it is only fair that he does not deprive Dr. Njoku of his post in the University of Lagos by holding on to the two posts.

(vi) We protest against the coming of Dr. Biobaku since this would give rise to such a great cleavage among the entire student and staff body. This would stifle academic progress in our young institution.

(vii) We are united in our purpose. Our struggle is not motivated by tribal or political considerations. This is a struggle against the two greatest national ills of this country, namely, tribalism and political bigotry.

(viii) We stand for JUSTICE and ACADEMIC FREEDOM and to keep Tribalism and Politics out of the University of Lagos.

It concluded:

> Our stand is clear!
> Our cause is just!

The Senate, in a meeting on March 29, passed four resolutions requesting the Council to state its reasons for its decision to replace the Vice-Chancellor; stating that the Senate no longer had confidence in the Council as then constituted; asking the Chairman of the Council to confirm or deny a press statement attributed to him that some senior members of staff were going to be disciplined by the Council; and pointing out that the requirement that students should sign a declaration to be of good behaviour was a usurpation by the Council of the disciplinary powers vested in the Senate. The Senate, acting under the powers given to it under Section 3 (2) of the University of Lagos Act, instructed students to disregard as *ultra vires* and void the direction issued to them by the Council. It further directed:

> That no lecturer or professor or other member of the academic staff of the University of Lagos, other than those in the Medical School, shall give or undertake to give lectures or tutorial or practical classes or otherwise undertake any instruction of students of the University of Lagos until this Senate has determined that conditions for the giving of such instruction are suitable and that the normal business of the University may proceed without the risk of disruption and in that atmosphere necessary for the imparting of knowledge to all legally-registered students.

This was an attempt on the part of the Senate to ensure that the right kind of atmosphere prevailed before lectures could be given. The Chairman of the Provisional Council described it as a strike action, and some members of the academic staff, notably Professor Gower and Mr. B. O. Nwabueze, were marked out for vilification. Professor Gower, in particular, became an object of a series of attacks by an NNDP Federal Minister, R. A. Akinjide.[99] These adversaries tended to forget that the members of the Senate, the majority of whom were expatriates, had no tribal or political axe to grind, but became members of staff, in Nigeria's circumstances, to 'help Nigeria build up a university of which they and Nigeria may be proud'.

For instance, Professor Gower, Dean of the Faculty of Law, had been head of the Department of Law in the London School of Economics and Political Science before coming to Nigeria in 1962. He was already an eminent world scholar with immense educational and administrative experience. When he arrived, Nigeria felt justly proud to have him. He was originally engaged as adviser to the newly established Council of Legal Education in Nigeria, but the Federal Government begged him also to accept an offer as head of the University of Lagos Faculty of Law. It is a paradox that because of the University of Lagos crisis, the very people who had invited him now showed such ingratitude. His crime was that he resisted the NNDP's replacement of Professor Eni Njoku on political and tribal grounds, and denounced a palpable injustice at meetings of both the Senate and the Council. His part in the matter all through was characterised by his known qualities of integrity, objectivity, fair play and fearlessness.

The unrealistic approach of intimidation and blackmail adopted by the Council did not stop the crisis. And so for five good months the students and staffs continued their protests. The period was also marked by extensive publishing in the press by the contending parties, explaining their various stands. The Senate members declared themselves to be acting under four principles:

(i) That there be reasonable security of tenure for academic and administrative staff. Where a member of the staff is on contract he should, on the expiration of his contract term, be reappointed if eligible and willing, unless there are compelling and expressly declared reasons to the contrary.

(ii) That such reasons must be based exclusively on academic and administrative ability and personal character, and political and tribal considerations must not be allowed to enter.

(iii) That the Council of a University must show proper respect for the legally constituted authority of the Senate – just as the Senate must show (as it always has) proper respect for that of the Council.

(iv) That the fact that a body has legal authority does not justify its exercise in an unethical and unjust manner in breach of all academic conventions. If adherence to truth, honesty and ethical behaviour cannot be upheld in a university it cannot be upheld anywhere.

There were also a number of legal tussles.[100] Because of the Senate resolution of March 29 stating that the University would not open on April 5 as decided by the Council, the Council, in a meeting on March 30, ordered the closure of the University until June 7. The Council also introduced a pass-system in the University – quite a novelty. However, when the new Vice-Chancellor tried to reopen the University on June 7, there were serious disturbances. The Vice-Chancellor himself was stabbed by a Yoruba second-year law student, T. K. Adams.[101] A number of arrests were made by the police, and a long trial followed, in which the NNDP showed keen interest.[102]

When all hopes were lost that the Provisional Council would retrace its steps and follow the path of reason, and when it decided instead on the expulsion of certain members of the academic staff, members of the academic and administrative staff, as well as students,decided on a mass resignation and withdrawal from the University. Six out of the seven faculty Deans of the University were either dismissed or resigned on their own. In 'an Open Letter[103] to the Nigerian People', fifty members of the University's academic staff, who had either given notice of resignation or been dismissed, mourned that 'now this has ended' – their efforts, their contributions to a 'growing great nation'. 'Our enterprise has failed, years of our lives have been wasted, our hopes . . . have been smashed.'

They pointed out:

No need to review the piles of memoranda, statements, press releases. No need to review the history of February's sudden chicanery and political manoeuvring. The issue was and is really quite simple. The University, as any worthy university, is governed according to law and should be run in accordance with ethical principles and universally recognised academic conventions. Only thus can it be free and achieve its purposes. The University's Provisional Council violated that law, and those ethical principles and academic conventions.

It violated these because of petty political reasons and tribalism. Thus the University was not given a chance to continue to gain international recognition – for, in the words of Ashby Commission report:

If a university is to enjoy international recognition (and it is a waste of money to have a university which does not set this standard for itself) it must be given freedom to run its own affairs on the standards of universities elsewhere.[104]

The open letter by the staff stated quite categorically:

The action of the Provisional Council, so clearly political and tribalistic, subjects the University to political and tribal domination. The only response of an academic man with a code of professional ethics is to object, and, if the objection is unsuccessful, to leave.

It concluded:

May God help Nigeria to protect academic freedom. God help its universities if they don't protect it.

The students on their part resolved as follows:

(i) That we have followed with great distress the series of blunders committed by the Provisional Council of the University of Lagos in the brazen attempt to impose a Vice-Chancellor on the University in contravention of justice and morality, academic conventions and, in fact, of all civilized ethics.

(ii) That we are fully in sympathy with the Senate of the University, and solemnly and whole-heartedly associate ourselves with their noble effort to salvage the University from political and tribal interference.

(iii) That by the most indiscreet act of expelling the Deans of the University, culminating in the mass exodus of the University's teaching and administrative staff, the Provisional Council has succeeded in destroying our institution, and the University of Lagos, that most promising seat of learning, is today no more.

(iv) That we the students, thus left with a debased institution where law, ethics and conventions, acclaimed and practised throughout the university world, have no place, and, therefore, whose degrees and diplomas will surely be received with spite and disdain outside the walls of this University, have been compelled to take the hard decision to withdraw from the University.[105]

Thus it came about that Nigeria's 'investment in education' yielded the dividend of a destructive crisis, all due to politics and tribalism. When the Lagos drama was concluded, with Dr. Biobaku remaining as the new Vice-Chancellor,[106] it was not long before the NNDP completed its avowed commitment to replace all non-Yorubas heading Nigeria's institutions of higher learning. A crisis of a less explosive nature was sooner or later launched in the University College of Ibadan. Had it not been for the early resignation[107] of Professor Kenneth Dike, Vice-Chancellor of that University, another man of Ibo origin, a crisis of equal magnitude could have taken place there.

3

NIGERIA'S POST INDEPENDENCE CRISES:
II. THE ELECTIONS

We may define a republic to be, or at least may bestow that
name on, a government which derives all its powers directly
or indirectly from the great body of the people, and is
administered by persons holding their offices during pleasure
for a limited period, or during good behaviour. It is
essential to such a government that it be derived from the
great body of society, not from an inconsiderable portion or a
favoured class of it.

The Federalist, No. 39

(i) THE FEDERAL ELECTIONS

After the Federal election of December 12, 1959, the Northern
People's Congress (NPC) formed a coalition government with
the National Council of Nigerian Citizens (NCNC). As stated
earlier, Alhaji Sir Abubakar Tafawa Balewa, deputy leader of
the NPC, became the first Prime Minister of an independent
Nigeria.[108] Dr. Nnamdi Azikiwe became President of the
Senate, and Chief Obafemi Awolowo's Action Group went into
a small but none the less vocal opposition. On November 16,
1960, Dr. Azikiwe was installed as Governor-General and Commander-in-Chief of the Federation of Nigeria.

On October 1, 1963, the Federation of Nigeria became a
Republic and Dr. Azikiwe was installed as President. In his
inaugural address he declared:

Instead of being restive, we have every reason to be
composed because our leaders have proved their mettle by
soberly guiding us safely through the crucible of political
apprenticeship during these three difficult years of transition
from monarchy to a republic.[109]

Surely the country was restive, but she need not have been if
her leaders had proved their mettle. Over the census issue of
March 1964, the country had a thorough bath in the lurid
stream of tribal sentiments which the issue generated. By April

1964 the political atmosphere of the country was again charged. Nigerians were getting ready for an election – the first post-independence Federal election. The period was marked by political manoeuvres and party realignments. Chief Akintola had earlier broken away from the AG, and formed the United People's Party (UPP). Soon after the emergency period he formed a coalition government with the NCNC, which has hitherto been in opposition.

This was not the end of Akintola's manoeuvres. As soon as the census rumpus ensued, he announced the death of the UPP and formed the Nigerian National Democratic Party (NNDP), pulling with him some NCNC party stalwarts. Notable among these was the ambitious Fani Kayode. Thus, the NCNC was once more in the opposition benches, but this time with the Action Group. The ground was now set for the Federal elections. Following the census issue mutual distrust had developed between the coalescing parties in the Federal Government. The NCNC naturally made an alliance with the Action Group for the purpose of the elections. Comparing the ideologies of the two parties, Dr. Michael Okpara, the NCNC leader, was later to declare:

The main differences between pragmatic African socialism (of the NCNC) and democratic socialism (of the AG) are: pragmatic African socialism is African in origin. Democratic socialism is essentially the socialism of Western Europe. Pragmatic African socialism therefore includes a revolt against foreign domination in thought. But the characteristic feature of democratic socialism is that in Western Europe it seeks to superimpose socialism on a society that has gone through the metamorphosis of an industrial revolution and installed capitalism. Pragmatic African socialism starts off with a society which has not yet gone through the changes of industrial revolution, and where capitalist control is yet relatively young and weak . . . we have discovered that the democratic socialism of the Action Group is practically indistinguishable from the pragmatic African socialism of the NCNC, since the economic picture has not been distorted by an industrial revolution and capitalism. This is the key to the coming together of progressive nationalists under United Progressive Grand Alliance (UPGA).[110]

The NNDP allied with the NPC under the name Nigerian
National Alliance (NNA). The NPC, of course, did not make any
pretences about its *'One North, One People'* ideology. The
party's name remained *Northern* People's Congress. The NPCers
made practically no attempt to contest elections in the South,
but concentrated all attention to winning all the seats in the
North – at all costs. One would wonder why, in spite of the
express parochialism of the NPC, the NNDP submitted to an
alliance with them. The answer lies in the fact that Chief
Akintola was a man who had no political ideology at all. He
stood for no principles but played the game of power politics
in a cold and ruthless way. If he was an unscrupulous schemer, it
is also true that he was clever and courageous. When he decided
on an intrigue he carried it out with boldness and without the
least compunction. There is no doubt that Akintola's
machiavellianism in politics contributed a great deal to the failure
of Nigeria.

As the year 1964 grew older, political parties were making
feverish preparations. Manifesto leaflets were fluttering from
campaign cars mounted with loud speakers. Old wounds were
reopened and that ugly destructive monster, tribalism, reared
its head once more. Political propaganda became more and more
defamatory and irresponsible. As sectional bitterness was inflamed, party organs of publicity became vehicles of tribal
sentiments.

It was certain that danger was looming not far ahead. On
May 6, the Head of State, Dr. Azikiwe, made a broadcast[111]
to the people of Nigeria in which he declared:

> In accordance with my Oath of office, I solemnly swore, on the
> assumption of my office as Head of State, to maintain and
> uphold the Constitution of the Federal Republic of Nigeria.
>   In view of recent events throughout our country, some
> citizens and inhabitants of Nigeria have been apprehensive
> about their fundamental rights which are entrenched in
> our Republican constitution. I am taking this opportunity to
> clarify the fundamental rights of the citizens as laid down in
> our constitution and also to appeal to all our law-
> enforcement agencies to perform their lawful duties and give
> protection to our citizens.

He reminded the nation of the fundamental rights of citizens entrenched in the Federal Constitution and appealed:

In the light of the above circumstances, I hereby call upon the citizens and inhabitants of the Federal Republic of Nigeria to desist henceforth from engaging in defamatory propaganda which entails the use of insulting words likely to cause public disorder, incite hatred among any segment of the people of Nigeria, calumniate any particular section of our country and thereby disturb the tranquility of our federal Republic.

Finally, he called on the law-enforcement agencies and warned that, 'in order to avoid a state of anarchy in Nigeria' they must protect the citizen 'from being impugned or violated by those who, through ignorance or impertinence, would flout the provisions of our laws and desecrate our constitution'. Unfortunately this appeal fell on deaf ears. To begin with, the Prime Minister refused to announce the date of elections until three weeks before the polling day. The Federal Electoral Commission had been given only six months to prepare and complete arrangements for the elections.

So it was evident from the beginning that the elections were going to be lawless and disturbed. The ruling party in the North gave instructions to natural rulers and the native authorities in the North to embark on massive arrests, intimidation and prosecution of opposing party members. Following this license, supporters of the United Progressive Grand Alliance (UPGA) were arrested on trumped-up charges; many without being informed of the offence they committed. Worse still, they were allowed neither bail nor permission to seek legal aid. The detainees were subjected to all sorts of cruel treatment, and were refused medical care. As would be expected, many died from their injuries, while others were starved to death. A team of lawyers sent by the UPGA to defend the legal interests of the UPGA supporters were arrested on charges of being more interested in politics than in law.[112] All weapons of the Northern Government were employed by the NPC to make life as miserable for these people as possible. The most notorious of these weapons were the native courts – *alkali* courts – and the native authority police, the *dandukas*. These two institutions were converted into party organs of coercion. The *dandukas* arbitrarily arrested political opponents of the ruling party in the North, and harassed them in their homes with search raids. In the *alkali* courts, the principle of presumption of innocence until guilt is established beyond reasonable doubt was completely unknown. The concept of justice depended entirely on the whims of the native magistrate. The testimony of a Muslim was considered to carry far greater weight than that of an 'unbeliever' – meaning Christians and all non-followers of Islam.

So glaring was this contemptuous abuse of human dignity that, on October 10, the Nigerian Bar Association appealed to all the Attorneys-General in the Federation to ensure that lawyers were allowed to discharge their professional duties without molestation, particularly in Northern Nigeria.

In the West, where Chief Akintola's NNDP was in power, the situation was no less gruesome. Local councils were instructed to impose curfews on their areas of jurisdiction, and road blocks were mounted against UPGA campaign teams. The principle of free and fair elections assumes that the people can vote intelligently if protected from external pressure. But of course, the people cannot vote intelligently if they are denied the chance of at least listening to those who seek their mandate. If, in the interest of peace and order, a curfew was considered necessary, justice would demand that any election within this period should be postponed.

In a society such as ours where, due to poverty and a low standard of literacy, other means of mass media such as radio, television and newspapers are ineffective, political campaigns provide the most effective means whereby political parties can have such personal contacts with the masses as are necessary for the latter to assess the former judiciously. It follows, therefore, that elections cannot be rightly and justly held when, for any reason, there is a ban on public meetings. 'Free elections and curfews don't mix'; so read the protest placard of a Western Nigerian demonstrator.[113]

In the North and West therefore, the instruments of power were boldly employed by those in power to repress and stifle opposition. Political opponents were victimised in all sorts of ways. Privations, beating up of political opponents, false arrests and detentions, denial of bail, prosecution on trumped-up charges – all these undemocratic acts were freely employed by remorseless politicians through the local authorities. As if these were not enough, every conceivable difficulty was placed in the way of the campaigning teams. They were refused accommodation in hotels and government-sponsored rest-houses. Nor were they even allowed to hold rallies, as there were always government-paid thugs to disperse crowds as soon as they had gathered.

On October 22 a meeting of leaders of the main political parties contesting the Federal elections was held in Lagos under the chairmanship of the Prime Minister, Sir Abubakar. The leaders reached a nine-point agreement to ensure free and fair election. Among other things it was decided that bans on public meetings be lifted, that permits for processions be granted, and that a peaceful atmosphere be maintained prior to and during the Federal Elections. These agreements were disregarded by the Nigerian National Alliance. Of this breach of faith, the *Nigerian Outlook* observed:

> The systematic violation and subsequent overthrow of the peace pact in Western Nigeria, agreed upon by political parties, has not come as a surprise, though it is very much regretted.[114]

Again on December 10, 1964, the voice of the Head of State, President Azikiwe, was heard over the network of the Nigerian Broadcasting Corporation. 'Having sworn to preserve and protect the Constitution,' he reiterated, 'it is my primary duty, as President of our beloved Republic, to guard jealously the cherished liberties of the citizens of Nigeria, by whose grace the politicians remain in office. Thus it is reasonable to expect that, during elections, the fundamental rights of the citizen must be protected and allowed to flourish in order to give the electorate a fair chance to assess the varying claims of opposing political parties. . . . The way and manner our electioneering campaign is being conducted leaves much to be desired. . . . It would appear that certain political parties are preventing their opponents from having the opportunity conveniently to explain their party policies and programmes. . . . The politicians in power. . . have no right to employ the instruments of power in order to perpetuate their stay in office. They are expected to give an account of their stewardship periodically, in an atmosphere that is devoid of violence and disorder, so that the voters should be in a position to assess their worth as faithful servants who are imbued with the principles of fair play and justice, and therefore worthy to be reappointed for another term.' He condemned denial of free expression and declared: 'Moreover, the fact that during the period of electioneering our governments had transferred the power of granting permits for meetings and processions and demonstrations from the police to the local authorities, has intensified the suspicion that the police power is being subverted for political ends, since the local authorities are constituted by politicians who have a stake in their survival as the party in power. . . . Instances have been cited of calculated deprivation of Nigerian citizens of their constitutional right to freedom of association in ten intimidatory instances, as follows:

"(i) The arrest of political opponents by local authority police because they were accused of holding private meetings in their homes to discuss political issues;

"(ii) The apprehension of political opponents before lay judges, who are not learned in the secular laws of the Republic;

"(iii) The remanding of political opponents in custody by local authority courts and refusing them bail, in spite of the bitterness of the charges levelled against them, and despite the willingness of accused persons to indemnify the state according to law;

"(iv) The accusation of political opponents of infringing unwritten law contrary to our Constitution;

"(v) The application of laws by lay judges on political opponents even though such laws are alien to the religious susceptibilities of accused persons;

"(vi) The conviction of political opponents for alleged infringement of written or unwritten law, without giving them the opportunity to be represented by learned counsel, especially where their individual liberty is involved;

"(vii) The deliberate hand-cuffing or chaining of accused

persons awaiting trial and marching them through the
streets as an ocular demonstration of the fate awaiting those who seek to preserve their fundamental
human rights;

"(viii) The passing of sentence of a term of imprisonment,
instead of fines, and at times including flogging of
political opponents, irrespective of the fact that they
are first offenders;

"(ix) The gaoling of political opponents in local authority
prisons whose standards in hygiene and sanitation
are said to be primitive and scandalous;

"(x) The virtual interference with the right of appeal of
political opponents by the employment of dilatory
tactics by incompetent local authority court officials
in preparing records of proceedings for a superior
court, in spite of the fact that the accused person
has already served his or her sentence whilst the record was being prepared. . . . Unless a free and fair
election is envisaged by the politicians, then the refusal to allow the electorate to attend public rallies
for the purpose of receiving the leaders of opposing
political parties, and hearing their views on national
issues, is a blatant invasion of the fundamental
rights of the citizen and a deliberate violation of our
Constitution. . . . The right of any person or party
to publish political pamphlets and air its views, and
also to criticise opponents, is guaranteed under our
constitution." '

The President observed that regrettably these allegations
of intolerance contained in his message were not only shame-
ful and embarrassing to a country professing liberal democracy
but also 'distort the image of our traditional hospitality as a
nation'. He also regretted the 'studied silence of the law enforcement agencies in the face of continued allegations of denial
and deprivation of fundamental rights to some citizens of this
country'.

Then came this prophetic note of warning:

. . . I have one advice to give to our politicians: if they have
decided to destroy our national unity, they should summon

a round table conference to decide how our national assets should be divided, . . . for it is better . . . that we should disintegrate in peace and not in pieces. Should the politicians fail to heed this warning, then I will venture the prediction that the experience of the Democratic Republic of the Congo will be a child's play, if it ever comes to our turn to play such a tragic role.

Tragically, though not surprisingly, this warning was ignored by those whose passion for power had blinded them and deafened their ears to all premonitions.

So the pillage continued: cars were burnt, houses set on fire, entrenched power arbitrarily brandished and the Constitution flouted. It seemed certain that the elections would be a farce.

To begin with, the voters' list was not available for sale to the public till December 17, two days before the closing date for nomination. Whereas the NPC had the voters' list, the UPGA members were forced to expose their nominators in an attempt to find out whether their names were in the voters' list. Thus their candidates and nominators were both made targets for arbitrary arrest, physical attack and even abduction in order to prevent them from being nominated.

Secondly, whereas in the East and the Mid-West all electors were supplied with nomination forms, many UPGA electors were denied this in the North and in the West.

Thirdly, even after succeeding in getting the nomination papers, the UPGA electors experienced great difficulty in submitting the filled forms because the electoral officers had decided to disappear. Polling booths were located in the most awkward positions such as in people's compounds. The Federal Electoral Commission had approved certain specifications for the construction of polling booths. Many booths were not built in accordance with these specifications.

Between December 20 and 22, the NNA announced that 66 of their candidates, including the Prime Minister, had been returned unopposed. This looked ridiculous, as the UPGA had nominated candidates for all the 167 seats in the North.

The UPGA announced that 15 had been returned unopposed. It was left to the chairman of the Federal Electoral Commission, Eyo E. Esua, to confirm these claims. On the 22nd, in an emergency broadcast to the nation, Mr. Esua admitted that there had been irregularities in the nomination of candidates. He cited four cases, one in Eastern Nigeria and three in Northern Nigeria, and observed that 'it is evident from what I have said that something is wrong with those cases'. He warned 'that the Commission has power under the Electoral Act of 1962 to postpone the election in a constituency where something has gone wrong'. He assured the nation that all the cases were being 'properly investigated' and promised that 'the result would obviously be made known by the Commission'.

But the nation waited in vain to hear from Mr. Esua. Meanwhile, the country entered upon what the Nigerian State House Diary later described as 'sixteen days of political crises'.

On December 23, Dr. Michael Okpara, Premier of Eastern Nigeria and leader of the UPGA, called for the Army to be invited to supervise the election. The next day, December 24, he led an UPGA delegation to the President and threatened that, unless the elections were postponed and irregularities righted, the UPGA would boycott them. On December 26, the President consulted with the Governors of Eastern, Western and Mid-Western Nigeria.[115] As a result of this meeting, the Prime Minister invited the four regional Premiers to a conference with him. He received no reply. On the same day, Dr. Okpara conferred with the President, who advised that, in the face of proven irregularities and threats of boycott and secession, the elections be postponed for six months to allow the United Nations to send experts to assist in conducting a free and fair election, as had been the case in 1959. The Prime Minister refused to agree to this. After 105 minutes of consultation, a laconic announcement informed the bewildered nation that the Prime Minister and the President had disagreed. The announcement added that it had been decided to summon all the regional Governors and Premiers to confer with both the President and the Prime Minister on their disagreement. The fear which gripped the nation as a result of the disagreement was to some extent mitigated by the hope that, when the regional governors and premiers met, good sense might prevail and a solution be found to a dangerous impasse. This hope was however shattered when, on the 29th, it became known that the regional Governors and Premiers of the West and North did not attend the meeting. Explaining his

absence, Alhaji Sir Ahmadu Bello said he did not attend because the meeting was called to discuss the secession of Eastern
Nigeria from the Federation. Chief Akintola, Premier of Western Nigeria, explained that he did not attend because the notice
was too short and he did not think the subject for discussion
fell within their competence.[116] The childishness of these reasons casts a great doubt on these leaders' understanding of the
seriousness of their responsibilities to the nation.

However, the President and Prime Minister went ahead to
confer with the Premiers and Governors of the Eastern and Mid-
Western regions. At the end of the meeting, they decided to call
the Federal Electoral Commission to adhere strictly to the Electoral Act of 1962, in the light of proven irregularities admitted
by the Chairman of the Commission himself. But this did not
solve the essential problem. Polling was less than eighteen hours
away. Meetings were held, decisions and resolutions were taken,
and agreements were reached, but the essential problem remained unsolved. The irregularities remained unstraightened.
Mr. Esua's silence since his broadcast of December 22 became
more ominous. It was obvious that the storm was coming and
nothing was really being done to avert it.

On the same day, December 29, the Joint Action Committee
of Nigerian Trade Unions called a strike in support of the
demand for the postponement of the election. This was immediately followed by the resignation of two members of the
Federal Electoral Commission, Mr. Akenzua and Mr. Aniagolu,
following disagreement with other members of the Commission
on the holding of the elections. All the time the State House
was busy receiving one delegation after another, some advising,
others threatening. It was at one of these conferences that the
Premier of Eastern Nigeria informed the President of the decision of the UPGA to boycott the elections because they had reason to believe that they would not be free and fair.

December 30 arrived and the disagreement between the Prime
Minister and President remained unresolved. The elections were
held in Northern Nigeria, in many parts of Western Nigeria and
in some parts of Mid-Western Nigeria. They were completely
boycotted in the East. The UPGA declared the elections a farce
and announced their determination not to accept any government formed on the basis of the elections.

Polling results showed a heavy win for NNA – 190 seats to UPGA's 40. On January 1, 1965, the President informed the Prime Minister that he would rather resign than appoint any person to form a government. He recorded a speech to be broadcast at 7.10 p.m. This was later cancelled by an instruction from the State House. A statement from the State House explained that efforts were being made to find a solution to the impasse. January 2 and 3, 1965, were marked by intensive political activities and manoeuvrings in both the State House and the Prime Minister's residence. The atmosphere continued to be sombre and uncertain until the evening of January 4 when, at 9 p.m., the President broadcast to the nation announcing that he had appointed Sir Abubakar to form a 'broad-based government'. A few minutes later, Sir Abubakar made a broadcast announcing the end of the crisis and his acceptance of the invitation to form 'a broad-based government'.[117]

This decision received a mixed greeting of praise and condemnation. *The Times* of London, *The New York Times* and the (Manchester) *Guardian* praised the President and the Prime Minister for preserving the unity of Nigeria. The *Nigerian Outlook*, condemning the settlement, declared; 'The President himself, on January 1, 1965, stated that "it would not be morally right to proceed with an election whose integrity was questionable". May we ask: Is it morally right to proceed with an election whose integrity was questionable? Or has the questionability of the election been corrected without a countrywide re-ballotting? Impossible.'[118]

There has been a great deal of debate on the justifiability of Dr. Azikiwe's role in this period of national crisis. There is no doubting that there was a great deal of activity behind the scenes in the State House, any attempt to recount which has been purposely avoided. This is because there have been conflicting versions about what happened. Some versions have given the impression that the President's last act in compromising his publicly proclaimed convictions was motivated by his apprehension for his personal safety and his material investments. Others suggest that Dr. Azikiwe so fears physical violence that he would go to any compromise to circumvent it. There are others, notable among which is the State House Diary, which have completely absolved Dr. Azikiwe of any blame, portraying him as the great nationalist whose every action was determined by his belief that violence cannot solve any problem, and also by his desire to preserve what he has helped to build. The State House Diary states that the President received legal advice from the Federal Attorney-General and Minister of Justice (Dr. T. O. Elias) and the Solicitor-General of Eastern Nigeria (D. O. Ibekwe), who were of the opinion that the President had no power under the Constitution to form an interim or provisional government, or to assume personally the powers of Parliament or the Cabinet. This is a strictly legal and constitutional view, and seems to derive its strength from the fact that the Nigerian Republican Constitution provides for a president invested with great powers, most of which are exercisable, not by him, but by others – notably the Council of Ministers. For example, he appoints members of the Cabinet and members of the Federal Electoral Commission, dissolves Parliament, and removes ministers in accordance with the advice of the Prime Minister.

Section 87, Sub-section (8) (a), of the Nigerian Republican Constitution states that:

'the office of Prime Minister shall become vacant when, after any dissolution of the House of Representatives, the Prime Minister is informed by the President that the President is about to reappoint him as Prime Minister or to appoint another person as Prime Minister.

Sub-section (2) of this same section states that:

'whenever the President has occasion to appoint a Prime Minister he shall appoint a member of the House of Representatives who *appears to him* likely to command the support of the majority of the members of the House.

Again Section 93, Sub-section (3), states that:

'where by this Constitution the President is required to act in accordance with the advice of any person or authority, the question whether he has in any case received, or acted in accordance with, such advice shall not be enquired into in any court of law.

In view of the above sections of the Constitution, it may be argued that the post of the Prime Minister was vacant the moment Dr. Azikiwe informed Sir Abubakar that he would not reappoint him to form a government. Therefore, he (Dr. Azikiwe) could have appointed someone else, as the Constitution leaves this exercise entirely to his discretion. But the point to note is that the President's discretion is not absolute. He must appoint somebody who appears to him *on reasonable grounds* likely to have majority support. It is a different thing if the President refuses to appoint a Prime Minister on the ground that, since the elections were not completed, there was no parliament by virtue of the existence of which the Prime Minister held office. But there is nothing in law which gives him the power to refuse to appoint a Prime Minister when it appears to him that the elections have not been properly carried out. It is for the Federal Electoral Commission, acting under the powers given to it by Section 156 (1) of the Electoral Act, to postpone elections in any constituencies where it is satisfied that there has been a substantial failure to comply with the requirements of this Act before the date 'fixed for holding the election in respect of nominations or otherwise however'. It is therefore very difficult to desist from blaming Eyo E. Esua, Chairman of the Federal Electoral Commission, and other numbers of the Commission for failing – due to whatever cause – to exercise this power. Messrs. Aniagolu and Akenzua are of course absolved from this blame since, having failed to convince other members of the Commission of the necessity to postpone the elections, they resigned.

In any case, the President was bound to act on the strength of returns sent to him by the Electoral Commission. The question arises: at what stage is the President to exercise his appointing powers? There is no parliament until the elections are completed (i.e. until all the returns have been made). Therefore, he cannot appoint a Prime Minister because a government cannot be based on a non-existent parliament. Of course, when the results of elections in two hundred out of a total of three hundred constituencies have been returned, it is obvious that a party which wins a hundred and seventy seats has clearly won a majority. The parliamentary leader of such a party may justly be asked to form a government. (This situation arose in 1959 when the then Governor-General of the Federation, Sir James

D

Robertson, appointed Sir Abubakar Prime Minister before all the returns were made.)

However, there is another angle to this. The Nigerian general elections of 1964 were completely boycotted in Eastern Nigeria. Could anybody therefore rightly and justly appoint a Prime Minister of a federation when no returns have been made from a component region of that federation? Secondly, could there be a parliament under a federal system when elections have not been held in one of the federating states? The question is even more fundamental in relation to the senate. If no senators were appointed from one part of the federation, could the parliament be said to be a lawful one? These are very pertinent questions which cannot be answered satisfactorily in the light of the Zik–Balewa compromise.

The Constitution is a living document. Therefore it should be elastic, flexible and expansive. Chief Justice John Marshall of the United States formulated and applied the principle of 'Implied powers' 'as a means of enhancing national power and constitutional flexibility'.[119] He declared:

'The sound construction of the Constitution must allow to the national legislator that discretion, with respect to the means by which the powers it confers are to be carried into execution, which will enable that body to perform the high duties assigned to it, *in the manner most beneficial to the people*. Let the end be legitimate, let it be within the scope of the Constitution, and all means which are appropriate, which are plainly adapted to that end, which are not prohibited, *but consist with the letter and spirit* of the Constitution are Constitutional. . . '[120]

The Nigerian situation was this: here was a constitutional Head on whom were vested great powers, which were exercisable by others – the ministers. If there were ministers all the time, everything would work harmoniously. But when there were no ministers, there was a complete standstill of government, and a fatal weakness of the Constitution came to light. Those who drew up the Constitution did not anticipate this situation, and there was therefore no provision for it. A broader view of this holds that the President is the guardian and custodian of the Constitution, acting in the interest of the people.

Upholding the Constitution means not only upholding it in the letter but also in practice and in spirit. In the Nigerian situation, the President was the only remaining person who could exercise those powers, even though the Constitution does not give him such a right. This is a situation that he should have approached with a deep sense of its importance, and a full realisation of his awesome responsibility to the people. That Dr. Azikiwe was fully convinced that the elections were a massive fraud is beyond doubt. The spirit of the Constitution envisages that he should appoint a Prime Minister who has been *fairly* elected. The law is meant for a living society. Therefore social philosophy must be applied in executing the law. This approach is outside the strict confines of the Constitution. But its end is legitimate, since it is within the scope of the Constitution. Thus, being the only appropriate measure to this end, and being consistent with the spirit of the Constitution, it is a constitutional approach.[121]

Of course, it is realised that a stand of this nature needs courage. Considering the risk of civil war that might have arisen out of this stand, it requires a President whose fortitude and conviction in achieving what is right for the people, and whose sense of duty to the spirit of his Oath, exceeds his fear of violence. On the other hand, it must be admitted that 'what is right for the people' is subject to determination. For the balance is yet to be struck between what is Nigeria's fate today and what would have been her fate if it had been thrown into a civil war then. Perhaps it would have emerged stronger, or perhaps disintegration would have come sooner; perhaps more, perhaps less blood would have been spilled in the process. There is no way of knowing now. Be it as it may, posterity, indeed every man of principle, would naturally ask; if the President was convinced that the elections were a farce, why did he not resign, rather than appear to condone fraud and political injustice by remaining in office? It is doubtful whether the 'settlement' really resolved the crisis. It was in the interest of the country that these irregularities should have been investigated and corrected once and for all. By so doing, the country might have been saved the shame and agony of facing the same problems again and again. *Drum* declared that Nigeria survived because her "sense of moderation and the spirit of compromise of her leaders prevailed to meet the sternest test our Federation has faced since independence'.[122] The truth is that Nigeria's brand of compromise was only a temporary measure that just succeeded in postponing the inevitable. When two people decide to live together, continued harmony requires concession from both sides. But when it is one side that makes the concession each time 'in the spirit of national unity', that unity will continue to be a fleeting shadow, as the time will surely and naturally come when the conceding side will run short of concessions. This has been the case with Nigeria, as will be seen later.

Late in January 1965, Isaac J. Boro and Jude K. Emezie, acting on behalf of the Students' Union of the University of Nigeria, Nsukka, filed a motion asking the Court to rule that the December 30 elections were unconstitutional and illegal and, therefore, should be declared null and void. The plaintiffs also requested the Court to order that the Federal Electoral Commission should conduct a free and fair general election throughout the Federation. Furthermore, they sought the Court's injunction to restrain the Clerk of Parliament, Mr. Adeigbo, from summoning the Parliament, contending that Sir Abubakar could not hold office as a result of the elections, and should therefore be restrained by the Court from continuing in office as Prime Minister of the Federation. Inimical as uncompromising doggedness may be to peaceful co-existence, improper concessions defeat its very purpose. Human nature being what it is, the love of having grows with having; and if concession must follow every demand, no matter how preposterous, the country's troubles become chronic. It was a defeat for the end of political justice to compromise a recurrent evil in the interest of peace. The best and most ethical approach would have been to eliminate the cause – the root cause. Any other approach perpetuates injustice and political fraud. Men do not cease to be dishonest merely because their dishonesty has been compounded. Nor are they likely to honour overtures of honest men unless they have a repentant heart. There cannot be a repentant heart unless there is religious conscience – a conscience sensitive to its own imperfections and faults and aware of its obligations towards others.[123]

(ii) WESTERN NIGERIAN ELECTIONS, 1965

The fraudulent manoeuvres of the Western Nigeria election of

1965 by the ruling Nigerian National Democratic Party led by Chief Samuel L. Akintola were a direct consequence of the total abortiveness of the Zik–Balewa compromise. At least, it is extremely difficult to think otherwise.

By the time the country emerged – or apparently emerged – from the nightmare of the Federal election crisis, she was already looking forward to the Western Nigeria election, which was due in October 1965. The strife-weary people of Western Nigeria hoped that this was their badly-needed opportunity to claim their right to a peaceful and unmolested life by throwing off, once and for all, the man whose introduction of intrigue, hatred and suspicion into their region in 1962 brought them nothing but anarchy and disorder. But Chief Akintola had a completely different view. He was determined to stay in office at all costs. It has been mentioned earlier in this chapter that, in Chief Akintola's reckless and inordinate ambition, the Northern Nigerian leaders found a useful tool. It will be recalled that, having discovered that the Northern People's Congress could not retain their dominant position in the Centre while remaining a strictly regional party, the Northerners sought to compromise the two desires by implanting Akintola's puppet regime in Western Nigeria. It will be interesting at this point to recall a man whose role in the history of Western Nigeria is startlingly analogous to Chief Akintola's. The *Are Ona-Kakanfo* is the Field-Marshal of Yoruba land. It is a title which is prestigious in itself, but the history of the exploits of those who have borne it has made the office one of very doubtful repute. The title of *Are Ona-Kakanfo* has always been conferred upon the most headstrong and venturesome among Yoruba soldiers, and most of the crises in the history of the Yorubas have been brought about by one Kakanfo or another. Notable among the Kakanfos is Afonja of Ilorin, the sixth Kakanfo of Yorubaland. Having by intrigue and intimidation forced Oba Aole, the Alafin of Oyo – the head of the Yoruba empire – to commit suicide, the inordinately ambitious Afonja embarked on a military campaign motivated by his desire to assert his independence of Oyo. This was in 1817,[124] by which date the Oyo Empire was showing signs of decline. To achieve his objective, Afonja enlisted the help of Hausa and Fulani mercenaries under an influential Fulani, Mallam Alimi. He succeeded, but the Muslims had their hearts in continuing their *Jihad* southwards into the Yoruba land.[125] By the time Alimi died his eldest son, Abdussalami, had established himself in Ilorin. Afonja realised this only too late, and when he tried to rid himself of his Muslim allies he was refused support by other Yoruba chiefs who had not forgotten his treachery. His army was defeated and he was killed, his body being publicly burnt in the market-place.[126] Thus the Yorubas lost Ilorin to the Muslims, and Abdussalami became the first Fulani emir of that Yoruba district.

When in 1964 the Government of Western Nigeria announced that the 'political and social resurgence of the Yoruba people of Western Nigeria is now becoming a reality with the installation of the Premier (Chief S. L. Akintola) as the (thirteenth) *Ore Ona-Kakanfo* of Yorubaland', many eyebrows were raised and many Nigerians speculated upon the significance of this move. Why did Akintola resuscitate this infamous title in spite of its association with perfidy, intrigue and bloodthirstiness, and in spite of the fact that the post had lain vacant for over fifty years? Was history repeating itself? Was Akintola going to be the twentieth-century Afonja who, in order to satiate his personal love for power, would sell his own fatherland to perpetual domination by the Hausa–Fulani oligarchy? In the light of available facts, the answer looks all too clear. The conclusion that Chief Akintola's megalomania had impawned the liberty and honour of his people to the whims of the regionalist Northerners is unavoidable.

The people of Western Nigeria, in any case, had arrived at this conclusion. From then on it became obvious that Chief Akintola was completely disaffected from his people. As with Kakanfo Afonja, reverence to royalty was for him a mere facade. If an Oba stood in his way, he dealt with him ruthlessly.[127] The twentieth-century Kakanfo, true to his nature, knew through his feelers that the discontent of his people was gaining in strength each day. Akintola's consequent feeling of insecurity drove him to the altar of tribalism. In the words of Dr. Ikejiani, 'tribalism is a creed, an emotional attitude and a symptom of insecurity'; as an ideology, it is a figment of imagination, but it is a weapon which has proved its efficiency when used in social and political conflicts.[128] He went on:

Crackpot tribalist propaganda aims at winning people to the open expression of tribalism by playing upon unconscious mechanisms rather than by presenting facts and arguments. Hence its personalised character, its consistent substitution of means for ends and the emphasis upon propaganda as an end to itself. It functions as a kind of wish-fulfilment. It attacks bogies rather than real opponents and systematically promotes an organised flight of ideas. Intended to provide gratification rather than enlightenment, tribalist political meetings and rallies have a ritualistic character, as shown by the fact that their contents are invariably the same. There is always tribal identification and glorification of the *status quo*.[129]

As soon as Alhaji Abubakar's broad-based government – which included the NNDP – was formed, Akintola got busy telling the Yorubas that now was the time for them to share in the 'national cake', to which they had hitherto been outdone by other tribes. That this sort of propaganda did the Yorubas more harm than good is shown by the rumpus that followed the replacement of Dr. Eni Njoku by Dr. Saburi Biobaku as the Vice-Chancellor of the University of Lagos.

On October 11, 1965, Western Nigerians went to the polls. The fraud of the 1964 Federal Election was repeated without the least dissimulation and on the grandest scale in the history of rigged elections. On the election day over 500,000 ballot papers were recovered from both the NNDP leaders and the NNDP electoral officers when they tried to dump them into the ballot boxes. Some 'pregnant' NNDP women were caught with ballot papers bulbously wrapped over their stomachs, while NNDP men were arrested with bundles of ballot papers conveniently hidden in the spacious depths of their *agbadas*, the Yoruba native dress. Ballot boxes already filled with ballot papers were recovered before polling began. The police also recovered lists of election results which the NNDP had prepared long before the polling day.

The NNDP had announced that sixteen of their candidates were returned unopposed. The electoral officers in the constituencies of these candidates were conveniently kidnapped and sent into hiding in Northern Nigeria to make certain that they did not receive nomination papers from the UPGA candidates. Some electoral officers who received nomination papers from, and issued certificates of validity to members of the UPGA were summarily dismissed, and replaced with new electoral officers who refused to recognise the certificates of validity issued by the dismissed officers.

It has already been stated that a fictitious list of successful NNDP candidates was recovered by the police. This did not in any way upset Chief Akintola's strategy. NNDP candidates were declared elected, in spite of the fact that they had not polled majorities of votes. The returning officers refused to announce results at the polling stations, but forwarded false results to the broadcasting stations for radio announcement. Unfortunately, the NBC and the Western Nigeria Broadcasting Service (WNBS) faithfully relayed these falsities to the public. Earlier, the UPGA leaders, apprehensive of the NNDP methods of running the election, had sent delegations to the Controller of the NBC, Lagos, and the Federal Prime Minister, requesting that a stop be put to the misuse of public information media, and that a network of NBC broadcasting stations be set up, so that reports be made directly from the counting stations instead of through the Ministry of Information. These requests were turned down because the NNDP controlled both the Federal and the West regional Ministries of Information. In a protest memorandum sent to the NBC Board of Governors, the Nigerian Broadcasting Corporation Staff Association condemned 'attempts to ruin the Corporation for political ends – especially during the recent elections in Western Nigeria'. They stated that 'the News Division came under the control of 'a Senior Executive Staff, who approved, suppressed, substituted or doctored news to suit certain ends'. They regretted that, because of repeated breaches of the principles and constitution of the Corporation, the public had soon lost confidence in their news items, expressing their discontent by physical attacks on the Corporation's vans and members of staff. They deplored the practice of ministers, parliamentary secretaries and other politicians of channelling news items through individual members of staff in contravention of the provisions of the ordinance establishing the NBC. They concluded: 'We hope . . . the Board will see to it that, in future, no attempts will be made to ply and bend the Corporation for ends other than that for which it was set up.'[130]

Soon after the election, the NNDP had it announced that it had won 82 seats to UPGA's 11. The returns were transmitted to the Governor of Western Nigeria by the Secretary to the Western Nigeria Electoral Commission. On the strength of these results, the Western Nigeria Governor, Sir Odeleye Fadahunsi, appointed Chief Akintola Premier and asked him to form a government. Earlier, the UPGA had published the detailed results of the election in which the UPGA won 68 seats to NNDP's 26 (including the 16 'unopposed' seats). On the strength of this, the UPGA declared they had formed an interim government in Western Nigeria with Alhaji Adegbenro, acting leader of the Action Group, as the Premier. Alhaji Adegbenro and his nine ministers were promptly arrested and charged with illegal assumption of office.

Thus it dawned on the people of the West that Chief Akintola had got away with his rape of the people's will. In such a situation, there is little left to the people other than a mass uprising. So Western Nigeria erupted, heads rolled and blood flowed. The rioting spread, and in Ibadan, Ijebu-Ode, Igbare-Ode, Mushin, Akure, Ado Ekiti – all over the region – the frustration of the people was expressed in arson, looting and murder. Houses and cars of NNDP supporters were burned. The police were useless, as law and order had completely broken down. The Prime Minister banned the ownership of firearms in Ijebu Province[131] and drafted hundreds of policemen from Northern Nigeria. Most of these could speak neither English nor Yoruba. The only means of communication between them and the Yorubas was violence. Clashes between the police and the masses aggravated the situation.

In mid-November, more than forty days after the West Regional elections, Eyo E. Esua, Chairman of the Federal Electoral Commission (and consequently Chairman of the Western Regional Electoral Commission), wrote a letter to the Western Nigeria Governor on the conduct of the Western Nigeria parliamentary election. He admitted that there was good cause for misgivings about the authenticity of the results. He agreed that several candidates were returned unopposed as a result of improper behaviour of electoral officers. On this he said:

D*

... it was a notorious fact that some electoral officers refused
to accept nomination papers of certain candidates, or failed
to report for duty. Some, in fact, after accepting some nominations of candidates of one political party, thereafter deserted their posts before all other candidates in their constituencies had an opportunity of filing their nomination
papers.[132]

He regretted that, in view of the provision of section 19 (1) (6)
of the Western Region Electoral Regulations, which provides
that

if, after the latest time for the delivery of nomination papers
and the withdrawal of candidates, only one person remains
validly nominated, that person shall be declared elected,

and section 14 (3) of the same Regulations which provides that

the electoral officer's decision that the candidate has been
validly nominated shall be final and shall not be questioned
in any legal proceedings,

the Electoral Commission could lawfully do nothing to check
the irregularities in the election. He expressed surprise at the
leakage of ballot papers since the Commission had handed the
papers to the Commissioner of Police in the conviction that this
would ensure their safety.[133] He observed that the federal
Electoral Act did not apply to the Regional elections and therefore, unlike the Federal Electoral Commission, the Western
Region Electoral Commission had no powers to postpone
elections even if there was likelihood of a breach of the peace.
He made recommendations for changes in electoral laws and
concluded:

I have tried to spotlight in this letter most of the glaring faults
and questionable practices which came to my knowledge
during the last West Regional elections. It is clear that, while
the effective organisation and control of the details of the
election were left directly in the hands of Government of
the day, the Commission was left utterly helpless in spite of
the Commission's desire to remedy the abuses which came to
light. One cannot expect an impotent Commission, therefore,
to perform miracles. Unless we effect the necessary changes
in the electoral laws along the lines suggested, we may as

well say farewell to parliamentary democracy and the rule of law in Nigeria.[134]

The essence of true democracy is that the people should always be free to decide who should govern them and, broadly speaking how they should be governed. Akintola's attempt to deny his people this right is a typical case in which the neutral forces of democracy have been used to pervert democratic principles, because of the absence of the spirit of democracy – which is so essential. Unfortunately, Nigeria imported British democracy, in which the consent of the governed is *sine qua non*, without its spirit.

Esua's belated confessions were of no consequence and did not resolve the crisis. The basic problem remained: that the people were not given the opportunity to choose their rulers. A ruler was being imposed on them against their will.

Only a fresh election (free and fair, of course) could resolve the issue; to form a 'broadbased' government would again be a cowardly compromise which, being uncertain and temporary, could not solve the problem. When Nigeria gained her independence from the British, her people did not bargain for Black Tyranny. The people of Western Nigeria came to be confronted by this menace: they did not want it, and so they reacted against it. They were fed up with the unpopular government of the NNA, headed by Chief Akintola. The attempt to resist the people's will by police or military power only worsened the situation, the more so because, in preparation for the election, the NNDP Government had made a mass recruitment of party thugs into the local authority police. Understandably, the people came to regard the police as a repressive arm of tyranny.

(iii) AFTERMATH OF THE ELECTIONS

The events of the Federal election of 1964 and the Western Regional election of 1965 had thoroughly shaken the faith of Nigerians in the future of democracy in their country. The forces of disintegration had already been set into operation by the fraud of the Federal election; the tyranny of the Western Nigeria election stimulated these forces into a higher tempo.

All this time, the Federal Prime Minister denied that there was anything wrong with the situation in the West, and maintained a studied silence. Commenting on this, the *Nigerian Outlook*, in an editorial captioned 'Speak, Sir', deplored the fact that the Prime Minister was leaving for the OAU Conference at Accra without as much as saying a word about the crisis in Western Nigeria:

> The crisis arising from the Western Nigerian elections is . . . [so] well known throughout the world . . . that the Rhodesian Prime Minister, Mr. Ian Smith, did not hesitate to use it to buttress his argument against giving the Africans in that territory the vote. What kind of a figure does Sir Abubakar expect to cut among the nations attending the Accra Conference, if he goes there without any indications as to what he proposes to do about the tense situation in Western Nigeria? It has been reported that some 30 persons have died in incidents in that Region. Will even this not make the Prime Minister talk? This silence is no longer golden.[135]

The call was, of course, ignored and the 'God-fearing and able' Prime Minister continued to seek for African Unity and world peace, while a part of his country was in chaos. Paradoxically, he went ahead to convene a meeting of Commonwealth Premiers in Lagos to discuss the granting of the franchise to four million Africans in Rhodesia, while a few miles away eight million Western Nigerians were in effect little better off than those four million Rhodesian Africans.

Thus, by the beginning of 1966, it had become obvious that the democratic Constitution of Nigeria was unworkable in the hands of irresponsible politicians. When the Premier of the West could cling to power against the wishes of the people, and when the Federal Premier, because of his commitment to an unholy alliance, could disregard the shedding of innocent blood and refuse to intervene in a clear state of anarchy, the country was doomed unless something was done. On January 15, 1966, something was done in fulfilment of the yearnings of all Nigerians.[136]

4

NORTHERN NIGERIA AND NIGERIAN UNITY

Now, instead of the harmonious voice of unity instilling in the
minds of our people and their children just principles on the
basis of what is right for our nation, there are discordant
sounds of disunity polluting the fountain of human relations
and profaning the tenets of our Constitution by insisting on
who is right and who is wrong. Throughout the vast expanse
of our country, a new crop of evangelists has arisen steeped in
bigotry, sowing seeds of disunity, emphasising our differences,
and pitting brother against brother.

NNAMDI AZIKIWE

Since Northern Nigeria has undeniably played a conspicuous
role in the break-up of the Federation, it is pertinent at this
stage to review certain events in the history of the Federation
in order to ascertain the Northern Nigerian attitude towards
democracy. Northern Nigerian has a predominantly Muslim
population. Traditionally they have a feudal political system,
marked by a stratified social structure. The religion of Islam has
inculcated in children an attitude of subservience, and the region
has thousands of koranic schools. 'Here boys (mainly) were
taught to read and write Arabic. Much of the work consisted
of memorising the Koran. The aim of these schools was to
produce devout Muslims, and train the young to master the
social and religious proprieties of the Muslim community.'[137]
Islam is not only concerned with religious practices, but estab-
lishes a culture with a pervading social pattern. Therefore
Western education, which in the early days of colonalism inevitably meant the forsaking of traditional values for the
Christian doctrine and Western values, was discountenanced by
the Northern Nigerian religious hierarchy. The Southern
Nigerians, on the other hand, received the European Christian
missionaries who consequently established schools in their
part of the country. Thus, while the mission schools were

operating in the South by the mid-nineteenth century, it was not until the turn of the twentieth century that the first school[138] was opened in the North.

It is thus easy to understand the big gap in educational and economic development between the North and the South. This disparity gave the Northerners a feeling of fundamental difference from the Southerners, so that for decades afterwards they found it difficult to regard themselves as one with the rest of Nigeria. The North resented the amalgamation of 1914 and clearly demonstrated it. In his book, *My Life*, the late Alhaji Ahmadu Bello, the former Premier of Northern Nigeria, stated: 'Lord Lugard and his Amalgamation were far from popular amongst us at the time.'[139] Consequently, the Southerners (mostly Easterners) who emigrated to the North and invested their resources there in their genuine belief in one country, were regarded as foreigners[140] by the Northerners. They were quartered in *sabongaris* while the indigenes lived in *birni* ('walled towns') from which the 'strangers' were barred at night. Separate institutions – schools, colleges, courts and police – were established for the Northerners on the one hand and the Southerners on the other.

As stated earlier, Northern Nigeria refused to participate in the Legislative Council at the Centre until 1947 but, supported by the British, it assiduously pursued the system of Indirect Rule as established by Lord Lugard. The significance of this time-lag lies not only in the fact that the South had about twenty-five years' start over the North in the practice of parliamentary democracy, but that it also helped to harden the feeling of difference between the North and the South. That this feeling was not confined to the leaders, but was shared by the average Northerner, is shown by a statement made in 1943 by Mallam Abubakar Imam, editor of *Gaskiya Ta Fikwabo* (a Hausa weekly), at a meeting at WASU House in London. He did not mince words:

> We despise each other. . . . We call each other ignorant. The South is proud of Western knowledge and culture; we are proud of Eastern [culture]. . . . To tell you the plain truth, the common people of the North put more confidence in the white man than . . . their black Southern brothers. . . .[141]

The gravity of the last sentence can be appreciated more fully when it is remembered that, in 1943, Nigerian nationalism was only budding. The preference for expatriates as against Southern Nigerians in the Northern Nigeria Service was expressly demonstrated in the Northernisation policy many years later.

Coleman summarises this as follows:

> . . . The most important single feature of British policy was the effort made to preserve the Muslim North in its pristine Islamic purity by excluding Christian missionaries and limiting Western education, by denying Northern leaders representation in the central Nigerian Legislative Council during the period 1923–47, and by minimising the contact between the Northern peoples and the more sophisticated and nationally minded Southerners temporarily resident in the North. All these aspects of British policy, and others, tended to perpetuate the individuality and separateness of the North.[142]

In December 1949, the Northern People's Congress was formally launched: this marked the awakening of nationalism in the North. That this was not brought about by a shared feeling of opposition against the colonial masters but was 'essentially a defensive reaction to Southern Pan-Nigerian nationalism,[143] can be clearly seen from the declaration of Dikko and Gusau, the leaders of the new Congress. The North, in their view, must and could only be saved by Northerners.[144] Thus, they sought sanctuary in the insularity of regionalism, and their motto was *One North, One People* – a slogan which asserted itself in the Northernisation policy. From the beginning it was obvious that the NPC was intended as an exlusively regional party. It did not contest elections in the South, and took a serious view of what it termed 'incursion into our territory' by other political parties. When, in the 1964 Federal elections, they feared that they might not win all the seats in the North and therefore would not be able to rule the rest of the country, they sought a foot-hold in the South. They found it in Chief Samuel Akintola, late Premier of Western Nigeria, whom they made their puppet in the South while the NPC continued to be the *Northern* People's Congress.

This Northernisation policy is so integral to Northern Nigeria's attitude to democracy in the Federal Republic of Nigeria that it requires an explanation. But first it is pertinent to recall one historical event. During the General Conference held at Ibadan in January 1950, for the revision of the Nigerian Constitution, the Northern delegates demanded that 'only Northern Nigerian male adults of twenty-five years or more, resident in the region for three years, should be qualified for election to the Northern House of Assembly'. In reply, the Eastern delegates entered a minority report, raising an issue of fundamental principle. 'It is in our view invidious,' the Easterners stated, 'that any Nigerian could, under a Nigerian constitution, be deprived of the right of election to the House of Assembly in any Region in which he, for the time being or permanently, has his abode, merely by reason of the accident of birth or ancestry.'[145] This demand was not granted and it was not until the Southern delegates in the interest of unity, had agreed to a Northern demand for 50 per cent representation in the central legislature that the Northern delegates acquiesced.

There have been many attempts to discover the motive for the Northernisation policy. In the following emotional words the late Premier of the North, Sir Ahmadu Bello, revealed and defended the motive. He said:

> I have preached the unity of the North again and again and it is with humility that I accept this clear demonstration of it. . . . The Northerner is regarded in some quarters as a stranger with no right to opportunities in his home. . . . Yet, our policy of trying to see that Northerners are not left behind is savagely attacked and misrepresented. . . . Those non-Northerners who live in the North . . . have enjoyed all rights and privileges, at times even at the expense of Northerners. *If recently Northerners have changed their attitude, others should realise the pent-up feeling.*[146]

The language of this statement reveals a violent passion which seemed somewhat disproportionate, seen in relation to the statement to which it was a rejoinder.[147] The Northern Premier was in fact giving expression to deep-seated resentment which took root more than fifty years before.

Soon after independence, the Northern Nigeria government

embarked on the Northernisation policy. This is a kind of nationalisation, except that the 'nationals' excluded Southern Nigerians. The latter were systematically removed from the Northern civil service, and replaced by Northern Nigerians without the least regard for qualification or experience. Third-class clerks of Northern origin were given accelerated promotion in order to displace Southerners in positions of higher responsibility. After a few months administrative training in the Institute of Administration, school-leavers were sky-rocketed to the position of administrative officers in the Northern government service. Of course, they displaced people, mainly Southerners, who had been in the service for decades and who had lived in the Region for more than half their lives. In the field of education, preference was given exclusively to Northerners in government-sponsored institutions. Children of Southerners who were resident in the North had either to return to the South or to attend mission educational institutions in the North. Even then they had to perform exeptionally well in the entrance examination before they were admitted into the mission schools.

Northern Government secondary and post-secondary scholarship awards were limited strictly to Northerners. All children of Southern parents were excluded, no matter what their academic qualifications or how long their parents had lived and paid taxes in the North. Yet Northern Nigeria is part of the Federation of Nigeria, a country which was called 'Africa's bastion of democracy'. In Eastern, Western or Mid-Western Nigeria the public service was open. Admission to secondary schools was based on the performance of the pupils in the entrance examination. This does not deny that there were irregularities in the public service or in admission of new students to secondary schools. But these irregularities stemmed from the general corruption in the country at the time rather than a bias based on ethnic or regional origin.

The Northernisation policy was also carried to the centre. More than 50 per cent of the Federal Government scholarship awards were given to the North. Inexperienced and un-qualified Northern school-leavers were pushed into the Federal Government service in preference to better qualified and experienced Southerners. This practice prevailed everywhere in the Armed Forces, in Federal institutions of higher learning and in the allocation of amenities.

The greatest anomaly of the Northernisation policy was that foreign nationals were preferred to Southerners, who had early built up the efficient machinery of the Northern public service. The Ibos of the East were deprived of their landed properties; foreign nationals were awarded contracts which qualified Southerners could have taken at lower cost; teachers were recruited from foreign countries at great cost in transportation and allowances, while qualified teachers could have been easily and cheaply employed from the South.

Consequent to the disagreement between the Regional Governments on the figures of the 1963 census, the Northern legislators took the opportunity to make statements which chilled the hearts of all true Nigerians and thoroughly shook their confidence in the prospects of democracy in the Federal Republic. Space prevents the reproduction of all the pertinent statements made in the Northern Nigeria House of Assembly during the Budget session of March 1964; however, the few below are representative.

March 12, 1964: Alhaji Mustafa Ismala Zanna Dujuma, Minister of Establishments and Training:

Mr. Chairman, Sir, since 1959, the Government has laid down a policy. *First Northerners, second expatriates and third non-Northerners.*

March 17, 1964: Mr. Dashi Toklen:

As far as Northernisation policy is concerned, Sir, no chance should be given to Non-Northerners – Ibos' existing certificates of occupancy should be redeemed or should be seized from them and should be issued for two years from now onwards.

Mr. Busar Umari:

. . . The Hon. Premier should from today empower the Minister of Land and Survey *to confiscate all the houses and farms belonging to Ibos. We have finished with them and finished with them finally.*

Alhaji Usman Liman:

. . . North is for Northerners, East for Easterners, West for Westerners and the Federation is for all.

The Minister of Land and Survey, Alhaji Ibrahim Musa Gashash:

. . . having heard their demands, . . . my Ministry will do all it can to see that the demands of the members are met. How to do this, when to do it, all this should not be disclosed now. *In due course, you will all see what will happen.*[148]

A lot did happen, as later events have shown. The fundamental rights of citizens, listed in Chapter III of the Constitution of the Federal Republic of Nigeria, include Section 28 (1):

A citizen of Nigeria of a particular community, tribe, place of origin, religion or political opinion, shall not, by reason only that he is such a person,

(i) be subjected, either expressly by or in the practical application of, any law in force in Nigeria or any executive or administrative action of the Government of the Federation or the Government of a Region, or disabilities or restrictions to which citizens of Nigeria of other communities, tribes, places of origin, religions or political opinions are not made subject; or

(ii) be accorded either expressly by, or in the practical application of, any law in force in Nigeria or any such executive or administrative action any privilege or advantage that is not conferred on citizens of Nigeria of other communities, tribes, places of origin, religions or political opinions.

Section 31 (1): No property, movable or immovable, shall be taken possession of compulsorily, and no right over or interest in any such property shall be acquired compulsorily in any part of Nigeria, except by or under the provisions of the law that

(i) requires the payment of adequate compensation there-fore; and

(ii) gives to any person claiming such compensation a right of access, for the determination of his interest in the property and the amount of compensation, to the High Court having jurisdiction in that part of Nigeria.

As a result of the outrages against the Ibos in the Northern Region, the Ibo State Union prophetically warned:

Now that the Ibos are being victimised merely because they are Ibos; now that Nigeria is considered in many quarters as four or more countries; now that Ibos in Northern Nigeria have no protection under the law nor are their lives and properties safe; *now that the Constitution can be freely violated at the whims and caprice of a section of the community with impunity,* in so far as such violation is aimed at victim-ising the Ibos; the Union demands a revision of the present constitution which has proved unworkable. *The Federation of Nigeria was formed after a protracted round table con-ference of Nigerian leaders. If the leaders are fed up with the Federation, why not call a conference of leaders and dissolve it amicably instead of spilling the blood of the youths of this country for nothing, instead of creating a situation that might lead to spilling of blood before dissolving it . . .?* The Ibo State Union . . . urges political leaders to come together and settle the country's problem in a spirit of give and take.[149]

Unfortunately there were few political leaders in Nigeria with the spirit of give and take. Thus, this prophecy went unheeded and the ship of state drifted helplessly from one storm to another, to the anguish of the common man.

Looking at the Nigerian experience – the excesses and high-handedness of her politicians, the systematic injustice per-petrated by one section against the other – the observations of the Joint Select Committee of the United Kingdom Parliament on the Indian Constitutional Commission report of 1930, perhaps arising from similar experiences, have singular relevance:

Experience has not shown constitutional guarantees of rights to be of any great practical value. Abstract declarations are

NORTHERN NIGERIA AND NIGERIAN UNITY

useless unless there exists the will and means to make them effective. . . . A cynic might indeed find plausible arguments in history during the last ten years of more than one country for asserting that the most effective method of ensuring the destruction of a Fundamental Right is to include a declaration of its existence in a constitutional document.

The constitutional guarantee of rights and freedoms, as a means of restricting the unjust exercise of power by law, is a recent development. Britain, for instance, has no Bill of Rights, and the peoples' rights and freedoms are founded upon the common law, but there is the rule of law, and Britain has a unitary system of government. Entrenched freedoms are considered necessary in Federations, where power is carefully divided between the federating components as a compromise for the safeguard of national unity as well as of sectional identities and interests, and this has been the experience of new nations with written constitutions. From the Nigerian experience, it can now be seen as erroneous to think that, because the procedure for tampering with them is usually long and hard, they would not be easily assaulted by those who govern. Their failure in Nigeria is partly because of a lack of the essential spirit of federalism and democracy on the part of the rulers, and partly because of the fetters which were imposed to limit constitutional guarantees. The Minorities Commission Report[150] of 1958 indeed admitted that a 'government determined to abandon democratic courses will finds ways of violating them . . .', in spite of the provisions.

The Nigerian Constitution in common with other constitutions states that certain guaranteed rights shall be subject to laws 'reasonably justifiable in a democratic society.'[151] Their just application depends on the rulers, and the judges who interpret the law and determine the success and effectiveness of the entrenchment of freedoms in the Constitution.

5

THE JUDICIARY AS A SENTINEL OF FREEDOM AND JUSTICE

> The courts have been appointed sentinels to watch over the fundamental rights secured to the people of Nigeria by the Constitution Order and to guard against any infringement of those rights by the State.
>
> BATE J., in *Cheranci v. Cheranci* (1960), NRNLR, p. 24.

(i) THE POWER OF JUDICIAL REVIEW

The Judiciary in the defunct Federation of Nigeria occupied a unique and important position. It had, by necessary implication,[152] the power of *judicial review* – a right of final say on the Constitution of the country, which was the supreme law, and upon certain acts of the executive. The Nigerian judges, therefore, had the opportunity of defending the Constitution from the ravages of politicians, and of protecting the rights and liberties of citizens by checking both the executive and the legislature in their unwitting play with naked power.

The need to check the excesses of politicans cannot be over-emphasised in a country with a federal system of government, like the then Nigeria, and a written constitution. The role of judges in this respect is essential for the survival of such a federation, and for any enduring democratic society, for it becomes a citadel into which ordinary citizens and minority governments can ultimately retreat, when the rights guaranteed to them in their written constitution are in danger of being jettisoned for political ends. Any judiciary that can discharge this role creditably would be looked up to as a sentinel of freedom and justice.

The Constitution of Nigeria was democratic, with a declaration of rights implying a limitation on the powers of those who governed.[153] It stressed the separation of the three organs of government, the Legislature, the Executive and the Judiciary, each with defined areas of competence, so that no organ could become so powerful as to constitute a threat to one or both of the other organs. It was a constitution designed 'to further the ends of liberty, equality and justice'[154] in the country and in the world at large. It lay with the Judiciary to champion and assure these ends, being the arbiter and interpreter of the supreme constitutional document, and of the laws of the land.

To understand and appreciate how exactly the Judiciary in Nigeria played its part, it is pertinent to examine the basis of its power. How well was the Nigerian Judiciary fitted to play the role of 'protector' aginst the injustices and high-handedness of politicians?

The Constitution of Nigeria guaranteed that its authors should not also be its interpreters. The same was true of the ordinary laws of the land. Otherwise, owing to man's inclination to injustice, the course of justice might be perverted, and the rights guaranteed to the individual in the written constitution would lose all meaningful content. The court, as an outside body set apart and free from both the Legislature and the Executive, could then decide when these rights had been violated or when there had been a perversion of justice. This is the role of the court in all federal states with written constitutions.

Speaking on the powers of judicial review in the landmark case of *Marbury v. Madison*,[155] Chief Justice John Marshall of the United States Supreme Court had this to say:

> The powers of the legislature are defined and limited; and that those limits may not be mistaken, or forgotten, the Constitution is written. To what purpose are powers limited, and to what purpose is the limitation committed to writing, if these limits may, at any time, be passed by those intended to be restricted?

He went on:

> It is emphatically the province and duty of the judicial department to say what the law is. Those who apply the rule to a particular case, must of necessity expound and interpret that rule. If two laws conflict with each other, the courts must decide on the operation of each.

This is the power of judicial review, aptly and succinctly

stated – the power to enquire into the acts of the Legislature and the Executive as a way of ensuring that they do not exceed the limits permitted to them by the written Constitution.

In Nigeria, the Judiciary had never shown itself in doubt as to whether it had the power of judicial review,[156] and rightly considered it a necessary and inevitable concomitant of their general function to interpret the law. In *Cheranci v. Cheranci*[157], Bate asserted that 'the courts have been appointed sentinels to watch over the fundamental rights secured to the people of Nigeria by the Constitution Order and to guard against any infringement of those rights by the state'. The Supreme Court of Nigeria, as the final court of appeal after October 1, 1963, when the Republican Constitution was introduced, had in general terms, and to the exclusion of any other court, original jurisdiction in disputes between the Federation and a Region or between Regions, except that no original jurisdiction was conferred upon the Supreme Court with respect to criminal matters.[158] Any question of interpretation of the Constitution or the Constitution of a Region, arising out of any proceedings in a Nigerian court and involving a substantial question of law, was referable to the Supreme Court.[159] The Supreme Court had exclusive jurisdiction to hear and determine appeals from the High Court of any territory in Nigeria on civil and criminal proceedings on questions as to the interpretation of the Constitution, or as to whether any of the provisions of Chapter III of the Constitution, dealing with entrenched fundamental rights and freedoms, had been violated.[160]

The power to pronounce upon the constitutionality of an act of the Legislature or the Executive is one of great gravity, requiring an enlightened Legislature, an Executive that is not over-zealous and revengeful, and a Judiciary that is upright and courageous, before the exercise of this power can work to the best interests of the nation at large. It has been felt, even in the United States which is a classic federation, that the opinions of a few men sitting on the Bench 'ought not be allowed to override those of the duly elected representatives of the people'. When, for instance, the decision of John Marshall in Marbury's case was handed down, asserting judicial supremacy, Thomas Jefferson, who himself wrote the United States Constitution, argued in a series of letters[161] that each branch of the

American Government is the arbiter of constitutionality in matters normally falling within its own sphere.

In Nigeria, when in 1961 a member of the Action Group, Mr. Doherty, obtained from the Federal Supreme Court an injunction preventing the Federal Government from enquiring into the affairs of the National Bank, many of the country's politicians began to feel that the independence of the Judiciary was becoming a threat to their power. Even the Federal Attorney-General, Dr. Tesilimi O. Elias, who appeared for the Federal Government in the case, argued that the Nigerian Parliament was 'supreme', and that the court had no power to thwart the will of Parliament. The Federal Prime Minister, who was also involved in the case, not only expressed the view that litigation against the Government was becoming frequent but that the courts 'were allowing themselves to be used in a frivolous manner'.[162] In Ghana the Chief Justice, Sir Arku Korsah, was dismissed from the Bench in 1964 for giving a decision not in accordance with the wishes and expectations of the Executive. In Algeria, under Ahmed Ben Bella, the courts were warned to give unreserved support to the Government, or face the consequences of non-compliance.

It requires, therefore, a judge with an exceptionally stubborn fortitude[163] to do justice according to the law, irrespective of what might be the reaction of the Executive or the Legislature in cases where the judgments are unfavourable to them, especially when these organs are bent on subverting the rights guaranteed to the people in the Constitution. The Judiciary is, by comparison, the weakest of the three departments of power. According to Hamilton, in No. 78 of *The Federalist*, as the judiciary has 'neither *force* nor *will*, but merely judgment', it 'must ultimately depend upon the aid of the executive arm even for the efficiency of its judgments'. In his argument against judicial supremacy, Jefferson even went so far as to threaten that he would use 'the powers of the government, against any control which may be attempted by the judges, in subversion of the independence of the executive and Senate within their peculiar departments'.[164]

In spite of these examples of threats and opposition, most federal states have come finally to accept that the power to hold a legislative and executive act invalid is one necessarily vested in the courts to enable them to administer justice according to the law. As Justice George Sutherland stated in the case of *Adkins v. Children's Hospital*,[165] it is:

a necessary concomitant of the power to hear and dispose of a case or controversy properly before the court, to the determination of which must be brought the test and measure of law.

Hamilton, in No. 78 of *The Federalist*, was of the view that in a limited Constitution, such as that of the United States, limitations can only be preserved through the medium of 'courts of justice whose duty it must be to declare all acts contrary to the manifest tenor of the Constitution void'. 'Without this', he went on, 'all the reservations of particular rights or privileges would amount to nothing.' Refuting the argument that this would imply a superiority of the Judiciary to the legislative power, he asserted that:

It is far more rational to suppose that the courts were designed to be an intermediate body between the people and the legislature, in order, among other things, to keep the latter within the limits assigned to their authority. The interpretation of the law is the proper and peculiar province of the courts. A Constitution is, in fact . . . a fundamental law. . . . If there should be an irreconcilable variance between the two (ordinary law and fundamental law) . . . the Constitution ought to be preferred to the statute, the intention of the people to the intention of their agents.

This conclusion presupposes then that the power of the people is superior to both the Judiciary and the Legislature. The will of the people, as expressed in the Constitution, overrides the will of the Legislature as declared in its statutes where there is conflict, and judges are to be guided accordingly.[166]

The main argument against *judicial review* is abuse of the power by judges. Professor B. O. Nwabueze, in his *Machinery of Justice in Nigeria*,[167] accepted that the arguments advanced against judicial supremacy in certain quarters were not to be treated lightly, but he pointed out that judges, owing to their legal training, are particularly qualified to adjudicate in disputes, and that they do approach their duty with great caution.

While striving to uphold the rights and liberties guaranteed to the citizens, they also recognise that the 'power of declaring an Act invalid is not one to be exercised lightly'.[168]

If judges must be free to carry out their high function, the Judiciary must be completely independent of both the legislature and the Executive. An independent court is a fearless court, and only such a court will dare to announce its honest opinions in what it believes to be the defence of the liberties of the people, untrammelled by fear or sense of obligation to the appointing power. Hamilton was quite emphatic in declaring that 'though individual oppression may now and then proceed from the courts of justice, the general liberty of the people can never be endangered from that quarter . . . so long as the Judiciary remains truly distinct from both the Legislature and the Executive'. He went on:

. . . there is no liberty, if the power of judging be not separated from the legislative and executive powers.[169]

Justice Learned Hand of the United States Supreme Court, emphasising the same point, stated in *The Spirit of Liberty* that 'it is a condition upon the success of our system that judges should be independent' and 'their independence should not be impaired because of their constitutional function'.

Where the courts are independent and upright guardians and interpreters of the Constitution and other laws, they go a long way to alleviate the fears of the people generally, and minority peoples and governments[170] in particular.

(ii) THE NIGERIAN JUDICIARY AND THE NIGERIAN SITUATION

Under the Nigerian Constitution of 1963, certain provisions were made in order to assure the independence, and therefore the uprightness and impartiality, of the Judiciary. These were mainly in respect of tenure of office and salaries of judges. After October 1, 1963, when the new Constitution removed appointment of judges from the Judicial Service Commission and vested the necessary powers in the Executive,[171] much responsible opinion in the country felt convinced that a way was provided for the interference of the Executive in judicial functions, for judges might be constrained to show some sense of obligation to the appointing power.

With respect to tenure of office,[172] the provisions assured that judges would not be intimidated by threat of summary dismissal from office. Normally a judge held office till he attained the age prescribed by Parliament.[173] The procedure for removal of judges from office was protracted and would not have been readily resorted to by the Executive. In fact, in the First Republic, there was no instance of a judge being removed from office in this manner. To effect the removal of a judge, both Houses of Parliament would have to present an address to the President praying his removal, and this must be based on inability of the judge in question to discharge the functions of his office, or for misbehaviour – such an address to be signed by the persons who presided at the meeting of each of the Houses of Parliament when the motion was raised. The motion must have been passed by not less than two-thirds of all the members of each House of Parliament sitting and voting.[174]

As further safeguards, salaries of judges were secured or chargeable upon the Consolidated Revenue Fund[175], and such salaries were not to be diminished during the tenure of their office.[176] Judges were not liable for anything said or done by them in the courtroom or in the discharge of their function. By the letters of the Constitution, therefore, the Nigerian judges were safe from political stresses and strains.

After Nigeria gained her political independence in 1960, the country started to experience the 'maladies of infancy' in the acts of her politicians. It became clear that the Executive was bent on interfering with the high function of the Judiciary. The then Prime Minister, Sir Abubakar Tafawa Balewa, openly showed resentment at the verdict given by the court in *Doherty v. Balewa*[177], by stating that the courts were allowing themselves to be used . . . on 'minor' things, thereby making a mockery of themselves.[178] He stated: 'We were dragged to court on the bank inquiry and now we are being dragged to court on the Mid-West.'[179]

When in the same year a verdict was handed down which did not favour the Federal Government, administering Western Nigeria under the Emergency Powers Act, 1961, the Executive refused to take note of it.[180] In this instance, F. R. A. Williams had brought an action seeking a declaration that the Emergency Powers Act, 1961, was unconstitutional, and that the restrictions empowered under SS. 69 and 70 of the Act violated the Fundamental Rights provisions of Chapter III of the Constitution of 1960. He therefore sought an injunction to stop further restrictions. The court, per Bairamian, F. J., refused to uphold the argument of the Federal Attorney-General, Dr. T. O. Elias, that the Governor-General (later the President) could delegate the powers conferred on him by Parliament under the Act to another person – an administrator[181] – and accepted the contentions of Williams, whose freedom of movement under S. 27 of the Constitution was interfered with, that the Executive was wrong in purporting to base its actions on the Act of 1961 and in restricting his freedom of residence and movement.

The attitude of Balewa's minister towards this decision did not conform with the Prime Minister's own statement in *Foreign Affairs*[182] that:

above all, we believe in the rule of law, and in an independent judiciary as an arbiter in dispute. The ready acceptance of both our governments and peoples of the decisions of courts of law even when against them is perhaps our greatest claim to maturity and confidence in our institutions and unity.

As Nigeria's post-independence crises deepened into catastrophe, her politicans showed greater readiness to interfere with the Judiciary and to prostitute the Constitution. In Western Nigeria, the cases of *Adegbenro v. Akintola* and *Aderemi v. Akintola*,[183] stand out. The two cases deal with similar subject-matter, and one of them will suffice to illustrate the point.

The case of *Adegbenro v. Akintola* gave the first sign that the Nigerian Judiciary was succumbing to political pressure – a retrograde step portending disaster for the people. (In an earlier chapter we have referred to the political aspects of this case.) When the Action Group crisis erupted in 1962, Chief Obafemi Awolowo, leader of the Party and of the Opposition in the Federal Parliament, wanted to remove Chief Samuel Ladoke Akintola as Premier of Western Region, as Akintola had fallen out of favour with his Party, under whose ticket he was holding office. Moreover he was no longer prepared to take instructions from his Party chief. On the strength of an affidavit collected outside the Western House of Parliament,[184] in which the majority of members of the House passed a vote of no confidence in Akintola as Premier, Chief Awolowo prayed the then Governor of Western Nigeria, Oba Adesoji Aderemi, to remove Akintola as Premier.[185] This prayer was granted by the Governor, exercising his powers under S. 33 (10) of the Constitution of Western Nigeria; and Chief Dauda Adegbenro was appointed to replace Akintola as Premier. Akintola brought an action to the court alleging illegal removal from office. When the case went up to the Supreme Court of Nigeria, it was held that the clause . . . 'when it appears to him that the Premier no longer commands the support of a majority . . .', under S. 33 (10), did not mean that the Governor's discretion in removing a premier was unlimited. The court asserted that, following the English practice, the vote for the removal of the Premier must be obtained in the House itself before the Governor could validly remove him.

These arguments however, were rejected by the Privy Council, who stated that the Nigerian Constitution was not an effort to reproduce the constitutional practice of England. Viscount Radcliffe said that, by using the words 'it appears to him' in the relevant section, the makers of the Nigerian Constitution had employed their own formula. The Lords held that the judgment as to the support enjoyed by a premier was left to the Governor's own assessment, and there was no limitation to the effect that this judgment must be based on votes obtained in the Western House itself.

Whether this decision was right or wrong is not our concern. What matters is that, by the time it was given, Nigeria was still bound by decision of the Privy Council as the highest court of appeal for the country. If the Nigerian politicans believed in the rule of law, as they had often claimed, this decision would have been respected. Instead, Chief Akintola exerted his influence upon enough parliamentarians to pass legislation, with retrospective effect, nullifying the Privy Council's decision and sanctioning his stay in office. Nigerians marvelled. Akintola's knack for survival came to be generally known as 'Akin-Wonder', a name coined by the Nigerian press.

It was now clear that the fundamental rights guaranteed to citizens in Chapter III of the Nigerian Constitution would be violated by over-powerful executives brazenly and with impunity. The ordinary citizen who had been accustomed to looking to the courts for remedy, now found that the judges themselves were entering into an alliance with their oppressors. Some of these judges even became members of quasi-political organisations masquerading as cultural associations. The Chief Justice of Nigeria, Sir Adetokumbo Ademola, joined the *Egbe Omo Olofin*, an organisation in Western Nigeria which was ostensibly a cultural organisation, but in reality an inner circle or cabal of the NNDP, the political party which Chief Akintola formed after his break with the Action Group. Some of the judges, in fact, became involved in political strife, exposing themselves not only to the influence of those in power, but to the ridicule and comments of laymen. There could not have been, in principle, a greater threat to the rights and freedoms of citizens in a democratic society than this.

The political persuasions of some of the judges became so obvious that, with political cases pending in court, it was possible to predict the likely verdicts. An important case in point was the treasonable felony trial of Chief Obafemi Awolowo and seventeen others in 1962. While for lawyers the decisions provide a wealth of jurisprudence that will have to be studied closely, for laymen who keenly watched that long legal tussle a different consideration applies. Many felt that Chief Awolowo was being persecuted for political reasons. The Balewa Government felt he was a stumbling block that must be removed, and sought to use the court to achieve this end.[186]

As the NNDP was interested in Awolowo's case, it was a foregone conclusion to many Nigerians that Awolowo would find no remedy in the Supreme Court of Nigeria. Chief Justice Ademola confirmed the ten-year jail sentence passed on Chief Awolowo by Justice Sowemimo. Chief Awolowo received much sympathy in connection with his case throughout the country, for a good number of people felt that the case had not been decided on its merits alone. Others felt that the punishment was too heavy.

With the passage of time, the courts in Lagos and the West came to be used as instruments of persecution against the people of Eastern Nigeria. Following the census frauds of 1962–4, the first case in which a Region took the Federation to the court came up. The Eastern Government, convinced that the census counts of 1963 were fraudulent and unconstitutional, decided to take the Federal Government to court.[187] The contentions of the Eastern Nigerian Government were dismissed on the ground of jurisdiction and that the statement of claim disclosed no cause of action. But the East was not convinced. That decision raised doubt as to whether an oppressed people would be well inclined in future to employ legal channels to settle their disputes. It was also seen as an attempt by the court to dodge uncomfortable questions which struck at the root of Nigeria's constitutional democracy. The hope of checking the excesses of politicans through judicial decisions was dashed.

The Lagos University crisis of 1965 provided a series of cases and judicial decisions which buttress the allegations of partiality and pettiness against the Judiciary as constituted in Lagos during the last days of the first Republic. We have seen how tribal and political power was used to effect the removal of Professor Eni Njoku, an eminent son of Eastern Nigeria, as Vice-Chancellor.[188] In one of the cases[189] in which the Students' Union, represented by two of its members, took the Provisional Council of the University to court, seeking an interlocutory injunction to restrain the Council from further closing down the University and alleging that the Council exceeded its powers by the closure of the University, Taylor, the Chief Justice of the Lagos High Courts, awarded costs[190] to both the Provisional Council and the Student's Union. He decided that, although the Provisional Council was wrong in closing down the University, its action was justified in the circumstances since the property of the University was being destroyed by the students. Well, it has to be remembered that what the students wanted was to get the action of the Council declared wrong, and they had not entirely failed in this end. Some people who followed the case, and who knew the situation then in Nigeria, felt that a verdict altogether unfavourable to the Provisional Council would have been unlikely, since certain politicans were interested in the case. But it is not claimed by the authors that the judge was other than fair to his conscience.

There was also the case of T. K. Adams,[191] a law student at the

University of Lagos, who stabbed Dr. Saburi O. Biobaku during the University crisis.[192] What had startled the NNDP was that a Yoruba boy should have committed himelf to such a violent protest against the replacement of an Ibo Vice-Chancellor by a Yoruba man since, in the Lagos University crisis, appeal was made to tribal sentiments. If the NNDP politicians could have found a way of making an Ibo student responsible for the stabbing, or at least of connecting such a student with that incident, they would undoubtedly have done it. But there was no such way. However, while Adams was in prison awaiting his trial, this group of politicians promised to release him if he would state in the court that the Ibo State Union had offered him £20,000 to stab Biobaku. But Adams would neither accept their money nor their condition for his release. This clique of politicians then resolved to see that Adams would be ruined. While the case was still on, Mr. R. A. Akinjide, Federal Minister of Eduction and Secretary of the NNDP, told Adams' girl-friend to go and inform him that he would be jailed for ten years for attempted murder.

However, during the trial a new and unanticipated element arose. Adams was shown, from his past history, to suffer a kind of *personality disorder* from time to time. When in this state he was said to become totally incapable of controlling his actions and appreciating the moral implications of his actions. It was proved that he was in such a state when he stabbed Biobaku. The court was therefore compelled to give the verdict 'Guilty, but insane'. This verdict was upheld in the Supreme Court when the case went on appeal. Adams was committed to the asylum.

'Personality disorder' is not the same thing as madness. Adams had had occasional attacks of 'disorder' in the past, but this could not have warranted his being left in the asylum indefinitely. All through his days in the University of Lagos he maintained an excellent academic record, and was a student who had easily made friends. It lay with the President of the Republic to release him after receiving a report from the psychiatrist in charge of the mental hospital certifying that his condition had again become normal. But the President was powerless if the Executive failed to order a report to be written. No such report was authorised till the military came to power in

E

Nigeria, and Adams had to languish in the asylum, in spite of repeated appeals both by his colleagues and the Nigerian press to get him released. His original crime was that he had identified himself with the side of justice in the University of Lagos crisis. A detractor would say that he had identified himself with the 'Ibo cause'.

Then came a case[193] involving Samuel U. Ifejika, one of the present authors. On June 7, 1965, there were some disturbances on the University of Lagos campus, when the new Vice-Chancellor, Dr. S. O. Biobaku, was assaulted by protesting students.[194] Following this incident, a number of Eastern Nigerian students in the University – Anthony Ojukwu, Samuel Ifejika, Godwin Abajue, E. A. Ekerenduh, Obasi Kalu Obasi, Oji Amogu, Dr. Eni Njoku's driver Augustine Egbue, and a senior lecturer in law at the University, B. O. Nwabueze, were rounded up by the police. A Yoruba student, Oyedele Idowu, was also arrested for assaulting Dr. E. O. Imegwu, a senior lecturer in engineering. In a sense, the arrest of Idowu was unfortunate for the NNDP politicians, and they did everything to see that he was discharged when the case came up for hearing in the Ebute Metta Chief Magistrate's Court on July 14, 1965. It is noteworthy that Idowu's case was taken to the Ebute Metta Magistrate's Court, where his discharge was ultimately secured, while the others had to stand trial at Yaba Magistrate's Court.

The incidents and subsequent trials were marked by various irregularities. Except for Nwabueze and Ifejika, all the others were arrested on June 7, and immediately after the disturbances which marked the opening of the University. Ifejika was arrested on June 8, the day after the incidents, while Nwabueze was first invited to the police station on the 19th to make a statement about the incident on the 7th. On his second visit to the station he was charged with taking part in the disturbances. It was felt that Nwabueze and Ifejika, being the leaders of the academic staff and students respectively, should better be roped in to silence and incapacitate them. All the arrested persons were charged with assaulting Michael Adeyemo, a lecturer in accounts, and causing him grievous bodily harm. Nwabueze and Ifejika were separately charged with assaulting the new Vice-Chancellor, Dr. Biobaku. This latter charge was later withdrawn. Ifejika was separately charged with conduct likely to cause a breach of peace. While Nwabueze was released on his own recognisance, the students and the Vice-Chancellor's driver were committed to prison custody and they remained at the Ikoyi prisons from June 9 to 15, when ultimately they were granted bail by the presiding magistrate, Adeleye Martins. The cases were adjourned till July 16.

When the trials resumed on July 16, there were indications that these defendants were not going to receive a fair trial, and that politics and tribalism were, if possible, going to control the court's ultimate verdict. During a recess in the course of the trials, the counsel for the parties, S. O. Sogbetun (prosecuting State Counsel) and Onyeabo Obi (for the defendants) were invited into the chambers of the Magistrate for discussions connected with the case. While they were there, and purely as a matter of coincidence, the magistrate in question, Ade. Martins, received a telephone call from Dr. E. N. O. Sodeinde, Chairman of the Provisional Council, University of Lagos, and a member of the NNDP, urging him to hurry up with the case because the Government[195] was anxious to see the case go through.

As a result of this incident, when the court resumed sitting, the defence counsel, Mr. Obi, announced to the court that the trial had assumed 'disproportionate dimensions' and as a result he was asking for a transfer of the cases involving his clients to another court, for only thus would the accused have confidence that their cases would be dealt with on their merits. A tremor went through the courtroom, and the magistrate was embarrassed. Inevitably, the case had to be transferred – to court 5, Ebute Metta Chief Magistrate's Court.

However, it was soon discovered there that the defendants had escaped one form of tyranny to be confronted by another more cunning and more intractable. The new magistrate was acting Chief Magistrate Adetayo Awolesi who, as if warned by the experience of Magistrate Martins, was more cordial in his treatment of the accused persons, more restrained and cautious in comments and more careful in his choice of words. His attitude was such that it came as a complete surprise to all the accused when he convicted all of them and declared himself to have believed all the stories told in court by witnesses called by the prosecution. Nwabueze was fined £100, while the rest were fined £25 each. With respect to the charges against Ifejika, only the one in which he was charged with the rest survived the trial at the Ebute Metta Chief Magistrate's Court; the other two charges were withdrawn before the trials at Ebute Metta could take place. An appeal was lodged by the various defendants in all the cases.

Considering the whole trial, Magistrate Awolesi can be described as mild and moderate. He did not commit his accused to prison and the fines he imposed were small. In view of the judicial and political situation in the country then, he could have passed jail sentences on all these people, or imposed very large fines without exciting comment. His political leanings, if any, are unknown. The Broadcasting Station of Western Nigeria radioed the news to the waiting world. The inescapable conclusion is that the Lagos University cases were not decided on their merits. Those involved were convinced that trumped-up charges had been made against them by their opponents. They were also convinced that the facts of those cases had been dishonestly presented.

Many people now began to consider the future of the Nigerian courts. A legal system must ultimately and necessarily be based on confidence. This confidence had certainly been undermined by the political decisions of some Nigerian judges and magistrates during the last days of the first Republic. During the colonial days, and for some time after independence, the Bench in Nigeria remained scrupulously impartial and earned itself a good name. In spite of the protection given to the Judiciary in the Nigerian Constitution, the judges succumbed to political pressure, with the sure result that the high authority of judicial decisions and legal jurisprudence was weakened.

Altogether, only very few Nigerian judges, like Mr. Justice Moses Oyemade, showed determination to resist these pressures. Speaking while presiding over a murder trial involving twelve men from Ogere, Remo Division, Western Nigeria, he said:

I will not allow myself to be intimidated into sending innocent persons to jail. . . . The only thing we have now in this country is the Judiciary. We have seen politicians changing from one policy to another and one party to another, but *the only protection the ordinary people have against all these inconsistencies is a fearless and upright Judiciary*.[196]

Justice Oyemade spoke during the turbulent days in Western Nigeria. His statement provides clear evidence of the executive to use him to achieve their political ends.

A really free, independent and upright judiciary which decides what it thinks to be the law, untrammelled by extra-legal considerations, is a safeguard to be supported at all cost. Such a judiciary could have saved Nigeria.

The Constitution, or any law for that matter, will turn ultimately on the judges who interpret the law. Their particular philosophical attitudes – the way they look upon their responsibility – become of great relevance. It is the duty of judges to uphold the rights and liberties guaranteed to the citizens in the Constitution, and to do justice according to the law. This duty transcends personal interests and political considerations. In a democratic society, the rights and liberties of citizens cannot be abrogated or alienated, the need to do justice at all times is reckoned to be paramount, and the individual is encouraged to work for a society that guards these rights. Only a just society can safeguard and guarantee such rights, and the judiciary can go a long way to help guarantee such a society.

To the question 'What constitutes a good judge?' Arthur T. Vanderbilt gives a good answer;[197]

We need judges learned in the law, not merely the law in books but, something far more difficult to acquire, the law as applied in action in the court room; judges deeply versed in the mysteries of human nature and adept in the discovery of the truth in the discordant testimony of fallible human beings; *judges beholden to no man, independent and honest and – equally important – believed by all men to be independent and honest*; judges, above all, fired with consuming zeal to mete out justice according to law to every man, woman, and child that may come before them *and to preserve individual freedom against any aggression of government*; judges with humility born of wisdom, patient and untiring in the search for truth and keenly conscious of the evils arising in a workaday world from an unnecessary delay.[198]

Without justice, our system is a dead one, and there is neither freedom nor democracy.

When it became clear that the Nigerian judges had proved

themselves broken reeds, oppressed Nigerians started looking for other remedies to safeguard their rights and freedom and protect themselves against political tyranny. The question was not merely that most of the judgments delivered in court during the last days of the civilian regime were not well-received – judges should not in any case be guided by such considerations in giving judgement so long as they are convinced that they are following the law. The question rather was that it did not appear to the ordinary people that judges were following the law. Most of the courts' verdicts were seen by them as designed less to do justice than to disable or punish a political opponent, or to achieve some sectional purpose. The ultimate result of all this was unwillingness on the part of oppressed citizens to seek remedy through the law courts. Jungle or primitive justice took the place of civilised justice. Steadily and surely, anarchy engulfed certain sections of the country, notably Western Nigeria, where political tyranny was the most determined to impose itself upon the people against their will. The hope of building a just society through the Judiciary finally perished, for in the resulting situation, they and all the law enforcement agencies became powerless.

Anarchy is the opposite of legal order and peace. In Western Nigeria and Lagos, the high-handedness and callousness of gangster politicians had driven the people to murder, arson and reckless plunder; those so engaged naturally no longer believed in the obligatory character of the law. They had lost faith in the Constitution, the courts and the judges. They were no longer prepared to accept legal control and from then on, they manifested the freest possible expression of all the latent crude powers of men. Neither the law nor the executive could stop them. But so long as the Nigerian people had decided by their Constitution that their society should be governed by social control and not anarchy, so long as the Constitution had enjoined the sovereignty of the state and not that of the individual, the maintenance of social discipline was indispensable. It was, among other things, to restore this social discipline, to re-establish faith in the Constitution of the land, and to give birth to true "Nigerianism" that the Military entered Nigerian politics on January 15, 1966.

6

THE MILITARY IN NIGERIAN POLITICS: I

> Every true revolution is a programme; and derived from a
> new, general, positive, and organic principle. The first
> thing necessary is to accept that principle. Its development
> must then be confined to men who are believers in it, and
> emancipated from every tie or connection with any principle
> of an opposite nature.
>
> MAZZINI

(i) A REVOLUTION OF THE PEOPLE'S EXPECTATION

Military leaders may be constrained to intervene in the politics
of their country for several reasons. The satisfaction of the
officer's naked personal ambition is one reason. Secondly,
military men may be used as pawns by politicians to achieve
partisan ends. Thirdly, armies may intervene to prevent civil
war, restore law, order and civil liberties, and dethrone corrupt
and inefficient politicians. The January 15, 1966, coup in Nigeria
was a revolution inspired by 'true Nigerianism' and motivated
by a desire to push the country permanently away from the precipice of destruction over which it was then alarmingly hovering.

On the eve of Nigerian Independence in 1960, there were
inspiring speeches about hard work, 'duty to our country',
'sacrifice to our great nation' and other such lofty themes.
Naturally the people, surging with innocent enthusiasm, braced
themselves for the honourable citizenship of the wonderful
and prosperous nation which they were promised. The experience of the first five years of post-Independence Nigeria
shattered these rosy hopes and provided grounds for the most
cynical estimation of the African's competence for leadership.

Within the first months of Independence, as we have seen,
extreme regionalism brought the machinery of democratic
federalism to a grinding halt. Because the political parties had
their bases in (and therefore allegiance to) the Regions, the preponderance in size and population of the Northern Region

upset the principle of federalism in Nigeria. Taking advantage of its built-in 50 per cent representation at the centre, the North sought to perpetuate its position of domination in the country. Superimposed on this was the incompetence and irresponsibility of the politicians. Mediocrities with neither political vision nor personal convictions were put into positions of power. Having nothing to offer the people, they sought to maintain their positions of power and affluence by taking advantage of the emotions of the illiterate populace. They encouraged tribalism and played one ethnic group against the other, and one Region against another.

Under this condition, efficient planning was impossible, and effective policies were frustrated at every turn. To make matters worse, every tissue of the body politic of the country was thoroughly saturated with the bad blood of corruption. In the diplomatic services, the public services and in high and low places all over the country, bribery and kinship were prerequisites for appointments and promotions.

As could be expected, the country made no progress. In spite of her rich and diverse resources, the *per capita* income of the people was still pitifully low. In striking and pathetic contrast to the poverty of the people, ministers and persons in positions of responsibility lived in extravagant splendour – with luxurious cars and palatial houses, and indulging in purposeless overseas tours, during which they lived in the most expensive hotels. Because Nigeria was a neo-colonial country, economic growth was impossible. The leaders followed the advice of their British 'experts' and so-called 'expertise'. Moreover, a sophisticated parliamentary system of government, which requires a high degree of sophistication and discipline for its successful operation, was imposed on inexperienced hands, resulting in more turbulence than progress. In a large land mass torn by tribal and religious animosities, such as Nigeria, the difficulties of operating a federal system were overwhelming. In the words of Mill, 'Government must be made for human beings as they are, or as they are capable of speedily becoming . . .' Speaking in the same vein, Thomas Jefferson stated that representative democracy requires an 'aristocracy of virtue and talent'. Nigeria's first Republic lacked these requirements. Whatever is said in the end, Nigeria of the first Republic placed every human activity in a pecuniary framework. It was not only the politicians or parliamentarians; everybody was involved in this – civil servants, contractors, the corporations, the police. Man was bound to man in Nigeria only by considerations of prudence and advantage.

A pertinent question at this stage is: how much blame can be laid on the masses? Could the country have drifted thus far if the politicians and leaders had set a good example? As *The New Nigerian*[199] pointed out:

> These people aren't, of course, wholly to blame. They have . . . been set a bad example in the past. They have watched others prosper with little or no effort. They have seen the 'dash' become an established part of the scheme of things. They have become part of a machine the overall tempo of which has moved at a snail's pace. They have seen leaders involved in malpractices of all kinds grow rich with no chance of reprimand.
>
> Little wonder then that an air of unreality engulfed many aspects of the public service, with false values abounding and discipline at a low ebb.

Coming to foreign affairs, the country's foreign policy was hydra-headed. Honest foreign investors were scared away by the bad political climate generated by unhealthy regional competition. Adventurous ones exploited the situation for their own ends. The 'ten per cent' bribe to politicians was an open secret. Far from living up to the expectation that it would be 'Africa's bastion of democracy and stability', Nigeria had made herself a laughing-stock in the eyes of the European nations and a disgrace to African states. Naturally, the Nigerian citizens were completely disappointed, and thoroughly ashamed of their citizenship.

Perhaps Nigeria would have managed to live on, but for the fact that the country's maladies not only culminated in grave recurrent national crises but were in turn cast into a bold relief by these crises. We have discussed the Action Group debacle of 1962 and the subsequent Emergency period in Western Nigeria, the Census Crisis of 1962–4, the Constitutional impasse of December/January 1964–5, the Lagos University Crisis of 1965 and the Western Nigeria Election Crisis which was

E*

at its peak by January 1966. In each of these crises, the common
man emerged the worse for it. It was the common man invariably who suffered death or injury, or whose hard-earned money
was wasted. We have seen in our account of these crises how,
for national unity, the people of Nigeria were offered tribal
intrigue; for freedom from white rule, black tyranny; for justice, injustice, nepotism and political intrigue; for national
sacrifice, corruption and greed; and for visionary and selfless
leadership, prosaic leadership and political demagoguery. We
have also seen how the rights and freedoms of citizens were
flouted and how the Republican Constitution was contemp-
tuously desecrated at will. We have seen how the arms of the
law were flagrantly used as instruments of coercion.

Tragically, even the courts, that should have been repositories
of justice and fairness, were not in a position to salvage the
country. Following the abolition of the Judicial Service Commission, the ruling governments filled the Bench with political
sympathisers. Consequently the courts were becoming as corrupt and partisan as the politicians. Most of the High Court
judges and magistrates advised politicians on how to take advantage of flaws in the Constitution to circumvent their responsibilities to the people. Cases in the courts were wantonly
interfered with by ruling governments. As a result, there was
complete loss of confidence in the Judiciary by the people.
So much so that proven cases of electoral irregularities would
not be referred to the courts by losing candidates, because the
futility of such a venture was common knowledge.

When the common people of Nigeria could neither remove
unpopular governments through normal democratic means nor
seek redress in the courts for encroachments on their constitutional rights and liberties, the fate of democracy was completely
and conclusively sealed in Nigeria. In this state of affairs the
people, seeing no prospects for a brighter future, were left
with no alternative but to take the laws in their hands. The fraudulent manoeuvre of the Western Nigeria Election of October
1965 was the last straw. The ensuing chaos in that Region was
an expression of many years of pentup frustration. We have
seen that the North-controlled authorities' response to this
natural demonstration of an indignant people was a show of
force. Hostile Northern soldiers were drafted to this unfortun-

ate Region, and dusk-to-dawn curfews were clamped down on most of its towns. Naturally, the chaos, instead of diminishing assumed anarchical dimensions.

Meanwhile there was resentment in the Army, particularly among the educated middle-rank officers, about the obvious inability of the civilian rulers to hold the country together. This feeling of resentment was further intensified by the use of soldiers in settling political problems.[200] By now the idea was beginning to grow among these officers that it was high time the Army did something to save the country. The matter became a frequent topic of discussion in military circles. For some, however, it was a more serious matter. Among these were Majors Nzeogwu, Ifeajuna, Okafor, Ademoyega and Obienu. To Major Chukwuma Kaduna Nzeogwu, a serious and brilliant young man with a magnetic personality, the fate of the Federation of Nigeria was a matter for serious concern. He was very impatient with the inefficiencies of the current rulers of the country, and was already thinking seriously of a military coup. To this end he and his colleagues had gone about casually sounding the opinions of other soldiers. Major Nzeogwu and his group were thinking of a military take-over in the event of the crisis in the country not being solved, but the turn of events in the country in the last days of 1965 radically changed the time element and precipitated the revolution of January 15, 1966.

Disappointed by the failure of the Army operation to restore order in Western Nigeria, leaders of the Nigerian National Alliance (NNA) were meanwhile making a reappraisal of the situation. Two alternatives were open to them: removal of the rejected puppet régime of Akintola, thereby restoring peace in the West, or the imposition of order in that region by a more drastic measure. The former was a completely disagreeable alternative; a total NNA coup, an idea which was already receiving serious attention, was the only way of silencing all dissident elements. Arrangements for this were hastily completed. There were to be two stages, the first of which would be launched on January 17, 1966. On that day, more Northern troops would be moved into the Western and Mid-Western Regions while, simultaneously, Alhaji Sir Ahmadu Bello, Premier of the Northern Region and leader of the NNA, would conveniently 'seize' power at the centre. The second stage was to follow immediately. An undergraduate of the University of Nigeria, Nsukka, Isaac J. Boro, was supplied with arms and ammunition in order to start an insurrection in the Rivers area of Eastern Nigeria.[201] This was to provide a pretext for the new régime to declare a state of emergency in the East.

To prepare the way, a number of moves were made. The Federal Minister of Defence, Alhaji Inua Wada, a Northerner, issued instructions directing that the General Officer commanding the Nigerian Army, Major-General J. T. U. Aguiyi-Ironsi, an Easterner, should proceed on his accumulated leave. The Inspector-General of Police, Louis Edect, another Easterner, was also to go on leave. His Deputy, Mr. Roberts, a Westerner, was instructed to go on compulsory retirement. He was to be replaced by Alhaji Kam Salem, a Northerner, who in Edect's absence would then be the Police boss. On January 14, Ahmadu Bello, who had returned from a holy pilgrimage to Mecca the previous day, held a top secret meeting in Kaduna with Chief Akintola, President of the NNDP (partner in the NNA), and some senior Army officers. These latter were mainly of Northern origin but included Brigadier Ademolegun, Commander of the First Brigade which had its headquarters in Kaduna, and himself a Westerner. Brigadier Ademolegun had been busy training thousands of soldiers of Northern origin for the particular operations of January 17.

These events did not go unobserved by other military personnel, including Major Nzeogwu and his colleagues, who were now thoroughly apprehensive of the fate of the country. They rightly surmised that, with the Police impotent and the Judiciary corrupt, an introduction of the Army into active partisan politics would rend the already tenuous links that held the country together. It was under these circumstances that they decided to act immediately. In the small hours of the memorable January 15, 1966, they struck.

Everybody expected it, yet paradoxically it was a surprise. The long-suffering and helpless people of Nigeria, taking their cue from military take-overs in neighbouring African states, knew that their salvation lay with the Army. But to them this was mere wishful thinking, for, had they not been told that because of the federal set up in Nigeria a military coup was impossible? Foreign political analysts knew that the situation in Nigeria was ripe for a military takeover, but believed it to be impossible for the same reason of an extensive area and diversified population, and the consequent difficulty in co-ordinated action. The NNA leaders, confident of the success of their plan, were too preoccupied with the details of its after-math to consider other possibilities.[202] The other politicians also knew that, in spite of the apparent impossibility of any change in the *status quo*, all was not very well with them.

Thus, when the heroes of the January 15 Revolution struck, it came as an 'expected surprise' to all and sundry; but, to the disgusted people of Nigeria, it was a *most pleasant* surprise.

(ii) JANUARY 15, 1966

In the early hours of January 14 Nzeogwu, taking advantage of his position as a small-arms instructor in the Military Aca-demy in Kaduna, took a group of soldiers for an extraordinary military exercise around the Ministers' quarters. At day-break, Brigadier Ademolegun received several calls from ministers complaining bitterly of the disturbing noise of mock battle during Major Nzeogwu's exercises. That evening all top Nor-thern military officers were in Lagos, ostensibly to attend Briga-dier Zakari Maimalari's regimental reception. In Lagos too were Majors Ifeajuna, Obienu, Okafor and Ademoyega. Ifea-juna was in charge of Signals, which had headquarters in Lagos. Okafor headed the Federal Guard. Obienu and Ademoyega were both from the Abeokuta Garrison.

In the early hours of January 15, Major Nzeogwu took his men to Sir Ahmadu's well-fortified castle on the first phase of the Northern operations. Fortunately for the revolution-ariès, because his meeting with Akintola had ended at a late hour, Sir Ahmadu was sleeping in his lodge, a thing he had rarely done since the crisis. Not unexpectedly, the Sardauna's guards opened fire on them. The exchange which followed lasted long enough to make Nzeogwu fear that time was run-ning out; and the success of the coup was in jeopardy. With him were Sergeants Maman Manga and Duro (both Norther-ners), each armed with an 84-millimeter Carl Gustaf, and Ser-geant Yakubu Adebiyi (a Mid-Westerner), who loaded the guns for them. Battering the Sardauna's castle walls with these, they gained entrance into the castle and engaged the defending guards in a close battle. Nzeogwu tossed grenades as he changed from one room to the other searching for the formidable Sardauna. Eventually the Sardauna, who could not be arrested within the short time available, was killed amidst his many wives and concubines who, in a bid to protect him, had heaped themselves on him.

Before 5.30 a.m. all phases of the Northern operations were completed. The Ministers who were earmarked for arrest were arrested on schedule. The radio station was surrounded; so were all government buildings, the power stations and other important installations. Brigadier Ademolegun was shot; so was his wife. Kano airport was also seized by soldiers, and closed to all flights (in innocent obedience to an instruction signalled from Lagos by Ifeajuna). The first indication for civilians and top army officers that anything was amiss was the smoke from the dead Premier's smouldering lodge. Those who had heard the sounds of battle in the lodge assumed that, as on the previous evening, the soldiers were practising again. It is said that Col. Shodeinde, woken up by the noise, phoned an enquiry to Brigadier Varman, Commandant of the Nigerian Defence Academy, who dismissed his fears by informing him that it was a mere practice.

In Lagos and Ibadan, operations had started almost simultaneously with the Kaduna operations. A group of soldiers led by Major Ademoyega, a Yoruba himself, had swooped from Abeokuta on the Premier's lodge at Ibadan. Chief Akintola, who, only a few hours earlier, had returned from his meeting with the Northern Premier, put up a grim fight with his bodyguard, a group of well-trained and well-armed men who, since the crisis, had accompanied the Premier wherever he went. After about two hours exchange of fire the revolutionaries smashed the resistance, killing Chief Akintola in the process. Chief Fani-Kayode, his deputy, was arrested. The Radio Station was seized by soldiers obeying instructions signalled by Ifeajuna. By this time it was nearly daylight, and Ademoyega and his men made straight for Abeokuta where, to their chagrin, they were arrested by men loyal to Ironsi.

The operations in Lagos were not as successful as those in Kaduna and Ibadan. Major Obienu was the officer-in-charge of the reconnaissance squadron, and had the all-important assignment of moving his armoured vehicles down to Lagos from Abeokuta and seizing Ikeja – including both the Airport and the barracks of the 2nd Battalion. After the operation in Lagos, instead of going back to Abeokuta he lingered in Ikeja barracks. It is strongly believed that it was through him, perhaps inadvertently, that the coup leaked to Ironsi. When ultimately he tried to go back to Ikeja it was late and he was arrested by troops loyal to the GOC.

By this time, Captain Oji, who was given the assignment of arresting Ironsi, led a group of soldiers to his house and pulled a revolver at him. On a stern and thundering reprimand from the Commander, however, he dropped his gun. Ironsi's first instinct was to protect the Prime Minister. On arriving at his residence he found he was too late. So he dashed to Ikeja via Ikorodu Road. At a military road-block near the Ikeja estates, he was blatantly refused passage by the guarding revolutionary soldiers, who said they did not care who he was. He had to turn round and take the Mushin Road, a distance of about twenty miles. At the military road-block there he had more luck. A thundering order – 'Get out of my way' – from the towering Commander broke the resistance of the revolutionary soldiers and he drove through. At the Ikeja barracks, he contacted the officer commanding the 2nd Battalion, Lt.-Col. Njoku, who sounded an alarm and rallied his men around the General. From there he sent contingents to surround the Radio Station, the Airport and important public buildings including the ministers' quarters.

Meanwhile, Majors Ifeajuna and Okafor had arrested the Prime Minister, Sir Abubakar Tafawa Balewa, who followed quietly, and the Finance Minister, Chief Festus Okotie Eboh, who whimpered pleas of mercy and promised the soldiers thousands of pounds. For this he received a beating. Before this, Lt.-Col. Unegbe, the Quartermaster-General, was shot because he refused to give the revolutionaries the key to the armoury. So were Brigadier Maimalarin and Lt.-Col. Pam, who resisted arrest and were killed in the ensuing encounter. Thence the Majors made for the Broadcasting House. Finding, to their surprise, that the place was already surrounded by men loyal to Ironsi, they ordered their own men to fire at the guards. This was the first indication that things were not working according to plan. This time their men refused to obey orders. Afraid of their men now, the two Majors deserted them and made for the East, taking the captives with them. In a panic, they killed these two men and left them somewhere along the Lagos–Abeokuta Road. By the time they got to the East, a distance of about four hundred miles, it was daylight and the helpless Majors went into hiding.

Ifeajuna, who headed the Signals division, had signalled instructions to Enugu ordering them to 'arrest Premier, Ministers' and to seize the Broadcasting House and other installations. These instructions were carried out by the unsuspecting battalion in Enugu. When later, having, with the help of the 2nd Battalion, entrenched himself in the Police Headquarters, Ironsi called on the battalions all over the country to support him, they pledged their loyalty immediately. The revolutionaries heard these disheartening developments from their hiding place and, abandoning their intention of carrying out the planned arrests in the East, fled back to Lagos.

In Benin, capital of the Mid-West Region, the same instructions as were sent to Enugu had been received and obeyed. The reader may have observed from the foregoing accounts that Benin and Enugu were not the immediate concern of revolutionaries. The reason is not difficult to find. First it must be realised that the five majors who planned the coup were in subordinate positions. Secrecy was therefore paramount. To this end, it was necessary to limit the comprehensive plans to themselves only. Again, as seen from their locations – Nzeogwu, Kaduna, (North); Okafor and Ifeajuna, Lagos; Obienu and Ademoyega, Abeokuta (West) – they had nobody stationed in either the East or the Mid-West. In the East there were no middle-rank officers of their calibre whom they could trust to carry out the plans. In the Mid-West however, the Region having existed for only about three years, there was no effective force, and therefore the revolutionaries surmised that, with the other regions in their control, the dislodgment of the politicians in that Region would be an easy matter. Obviously they trusted in the popularity of their cause to carry them through as soon as the top Army officers and powerful politicians were arrested. Furthermore, they conjectured that with Lagos – the seat of

the Federal Government and the North, the abode of the bulk of
the Nigerian Army and military installations – under their control, the rest of the country would easily capitulate under heavy
threats.

The morning of Saturday, January 15, 1966, was charged
with uncertainty and bewilderment for most Nigerians. There
were conflicting rumours about what had happened the previous night. These rumours could not be confirmed because the
telephones were dead. The presence of stern-looking soldiers,
who were guarding strategic buildings all over the country,
and the menacing patrol of army jeeps and armoured cars were
more alarming than helpful. So was Radio Nigeria, which played
High Life music all the time. In the regions the situation was
not clearer. In the East, crowds who had gone to see off the
visiting President of Cyprus, Archbishop Makarios, at the
Enugu airport, watched in alarm as, the moment the august
visitor took off for Lagos in a helicopter, Premier Okpara was
taken away in an army van.

Hopes rose high when a report from Cotonou announced that
the Army had seized power in Nigeria. The report quoted an
unidentified spokesman of the new régime as saying that the
Army had taken over 'to bring an end to gangsterism and disorder, corruption and despotism'. It further said that the statement had ended with the words: "My compatriots, you will
no longer be ashamed to be Nigerians."

At 10 a.m. the Federal Parliament, which was in session,
met for only a few minutes. Only 33 out of the total of 312
Members turned up, and these having, to their terror, found the
parliament building swarming with armed soldiers, were only
too pleased when R. B. K. Okafor (promoted a Minister the
previous day)[203] moved for adjournment in view of the absence
of a quorum.

At 1.50 p.m. the NBC read a statement from the Cabinet
Office. It announced:

> In the early hours of this morning, January 15, 1966, a dis-
> sident section of the Army kidnapped the Prime Minister
> and the Minister of Finance and took them to an unknown
> destination. The General Officer Commanding and the vast
> majority of the Nigerian Army remain completely loyal to

the Federal Government, and are already taking all appropriate measures to bring the situation under control. All essential public services continue to function normally. The Federal Government is satisfied that the situation will soon return to normal and that the ill-advised mutiny will be brought to an end, and that law and order in the few disturbed areas of the country will soon be restored. All public buildings and establishments in the Federal Territory are being guarded by loyal troops.

In the evening, Major Nzeogwu, who was now in control of the Northern Region, made a broadcast over Radio Kaduna. He said:

In the name of the Supreme Council of the Revolution of the Nigerian Armed Forces, I declare martial law over the Northern Provinces of Nigeria. The Constitution is suspended and the legal Government and elected Assembly are hereby dissolved. All political, cultural, tribal and trade union activities, together with all demonstrations, and all unauthorised gatherings, excluding religious worship, are banned until further notice.

This was followed by ten proclamations, which warned, among other things, that 'looting, arson, homosexuality, rape, embezzlement, bribery, corruption or obstruction of the revolution, sabotage, subversion, false alarm, and assistance to foreign invaders, are all offences punishable by the death sentence'.

Meanwhile, there was a meeting at the Police Headquarters in Lagos. Present were Alhadji Zanna Bukar Dipcharima (NPC, Cabinet Minister), Alhadji Nuhu Bamali (NPC, Foreign Minister), General Ironsi, senior police officials, Dr. T. O. Elias (Attorney-General), and Sir Francis Cumming Bruce (British High Commissioner). Also present were Dr. Nwafor Orizu, Acting President of the Federation,[204] and Dr. K. O. Mbadiwe, (NCNC, Minister for Aviation.) The meeting did not arrive at any decisions as the Ministers were angling to be appointed Acting Prime Minister. Dr. Orizu, on his part, said he would not make any such appointment until he had contacted Dr. Azikiwe.

In the Northern Region, Major Nzeogwu set up administra-

tive machinery in Kaduna. The Permanent Secretaries were to
head their Ministries. The Government was to be headed by
Alhadji Ali Akilu. Everything in that Region was working with
frightening efficiency. The trains were on schedule, civil servants came to work on time, telephone girls were no longer
rude and put callers through promptly, queues disappeared
in the post offices and banks, and electric and water supplies
were continuous. Almost single-handedly, Major Nzeogwu
ruled the North efficiently for a full week. The remaining senior
Army officers in the North had no alternative but to support
him. By now he was threatening to march on the South. Major
Hassan Usman Katsina,[205] who was in charge of the Reconnaissance Squadron in the North and had become Nzeogwu's
right-hand man, moved his armoured divisions down to Jebba
in readiness for the assault on Lagos.

Down in the South, the situation was still confused. On
Sunday, January 16, however, there was another cabinet meeting in Lagos. Ironsi also met Commodore Wey of the Navy
and Alhaji Kam Salem, now acting Inspector-General of Police.
At 11.50 p.m. Dr. Nwafor Orizu, in a broadcast, told the nation
that, consequent on the advice of the Council of Ministers,
they had, in view of the situation in the country, decided
to hand over the government of the country to the Armed
Forces, and that he had invited the General Officer Commanding the Nigerian Army, Major-General J. T. U. Aguiyi-Ironsi,
to take control. This announcement was immediately followed
by a broadcast from General Ironsi, announcing that he had
been formally invested with power as Head of the Federal
Military Government and Supreme Commander of the Armed
Forces. He announced decrees suspending the office of the President, the Prime Minister, the Executive Council, the Legisla-
tures, the regional Governors and Premiers, and the Constitution. He further announced that there would be Regional Military Governments headed by Military Governors. He added
that the Chief Justice and all other judges, the Nigerian Police
Force, the Special Constabulary and the Civil Service would
continue to function as before. All native authority and local
government police would now be under the control of the Inspector-General of Police.

He said his Government would honour all agreements entered into by the previous Government, and would continue to maintain the existing external relations. He warned that he was determined to maintain law and order in the country, and would declare Martial Law in any disturbed area.

On Monday, January 17, Major Nzeogwu announced that, having reached a five-point agreement with General Ironsi, he had 'surrendered' to the General. (Ironsi confirmed this at his first press conference.) The points agreed upon were:

(i) a guarantee of safety for himself, his officers and all men who took part in the January 15 revolution,
(ii) a guarantee for them of freedom from legal proceedings then or at any later time;
(iii) compensation should be paid to the families of all officers and men who lost their lives during the coup;
(iv) the release of all officers and men who were arrested in the West;
(v) a promise that 'the people whom we fought to remove will not be returned to office'.

However he refused Ironsi's invitation to Lagos until Lt.-Col. Nwawo, his life-long friend, was flown in from the United Kingdom to assure him of his safety.

The foregoing describes the course of that fateful January revolution. It failed in the sense that events did not turn out in the way the revolutionaries had planned. It succeeded in the sense that the Nigerian gangster politicians were routed. At least it gave the country a chance – a chance to start again under new, purposeful leadership, and a chance to resuscitate itself from the putrefied society it had become, into a hate-free and propsperous nation. For this, millions of Nigerians expressed their unreserved gratitude to the heroes who had the courage to do what was thought impossible.

In a personal interview at the Independence Layout, Enugu, on May 21, 1967, Major Nzeogwu gave the following as reasons for the coup:

(i) The unrest in the West had assumed anarchical dimensions, and had great possibilities of spreading to other parts of the country.
(ii) The projected take-over of the country by the NNA,

with the assistance of highly placed Northerners in the Army, portended a bloody disintegration of the country.

(iii) It was necessary to purge the country of its social evils – bribery, tribalism, bureaucracy, nepotism, feudalism and other social injustices.

(iv) There had arisen a class of 'presumptuous chosen leaders' who forgot that their powers were derived from the people, and were running the country for their own benefit.

(v) Simpering under foreign eulogies on its democracy and stability, the civilian rulers had let the domestic affairs of the country come under the remote control of imperialists. In external affairs, the leaders sought to play up to the tune of foreign flatteries resulting in lack of coherence in the country's policy statements.

(vi) Because of the Nigerian leaders' lack of any plans and the consequent drift of the country, the Nigerian populace had developed a sometimes too emotional, but often too soft and apathetic, approach to vital issues. It was necesary to whip them up and reorientate them so they would appreciate things objectively, and to bring them to realise that national issues are also personal issues.

(vii) The country needed a more realistic unification, a centralisation of vital agencies, and the building of a nation where 'every citizen belongs everywhere'.

(viii) The civilian leaders had proved completely incapable of managing the affairs of the country.

Perhaps unfortunately, the nationalist major did not have his chance. Mazzini, in the statement quoted at the beginning of this chapter, has rightly averred that no revolution is complete unless those who believe in it are allowed to direct its programme. We shall come to this point later. Meanwhile, let us direct our attention to a few questions which have been often asked and to which wrong answers have been given as many times as the questions have been asked.

Like all events in history, the revolution of January 15 has been subjected to all shades of interpretation; it stands clearly however, as one of the most often misconstrued of historical events. The standard-bearers of this misinterpretation were notably the BBC commentators and the leaders of Muslim countries. In spite of the fact that all Nigerians received the military takeover with an obvious joy expressed by nation-wide jubilations, the BBC called it an 'Ibo-Coup'. The leader of a neighbouring Muslim African state condemned the 'dastardly assassination' of the Sardauna, and closed his country's borders with Nigeria. In Khartoum, Sudan, the Muslim Brotherhood organised a demonstration protesting against the 'massacre' of Sir Ahmadu Bello and Sir Abubakar, whom Sudan's Muslim press represented as 'martyrs of Islam killed by imperialism and Zionism'. In English, Hausa and Arabic, Radio Cairo made powerful denunciations of 'Kafferi onslaught on the very citadel of Islam in Nigeria'.

Seven senior army officers were killed by the revolutionaries in the process of executing the coup. These were:

Brigadier Z. Maimalari (Northerner)
Brigadier S. Ademulegun (Westerner)
Colonel Kur Mohammed (Northerner)
Colonel S. A. Shodeinde (Westerner)
Lt.-Col. A. Largema (Northerner)
Lt.-Col. J. Y. Pam (Northerner)
Lt.-Col. A. C. Unegbe. (Easterner.)

The questions have been asked (i) Why only one Ibo officer (Lt.-Col. Unegbe) was killed during the coup? (ii) Why they killed the Sardauna, Chief Okotie-Eboh, Chief Akintola and Sir Abubakar, leaving Dr. Okpara of the East and Chief Dennis Osadebey, Mid-West Premier? Why were such controversial figures in the Federal Cabinet as Dr. K. O. Mbadiwe not also killed? Was it not because the Ibos carried out the coup in order to rule the country?

A study of the reasons for the coup as given by Nzeogwu himself will provide answers to these questions. The immediate cause of the revolution was the projected take-over of the Government of the Federation by the NNA with the aid of Northern senior Army officers. The fundamental cause was the fact that the civilian rulers had proved incapable of holding the country together. The plan of the revolutionaries was to arrest all senior Army officers, all the civilian rulers and all persons in positions of responsibility including members of the Judiciary and senior police officers. These would have been publicly tried (after exhaustive and expansive enquiries to ascertain how they individually or collectively contributed to the decay of the Federation), and the culprits would be punished in accordance with the gravity of their offences. Because these arrests could not be done at once, they had to be done in stages. First, the Prime Minister, the Premiers, the GOC and the Brigadiers had to be arrested or the coup would fail. Sir Ahmadu Bello and Chief Akintola resisted arrest, and so lost their lives. so did Brigadiers Ademulegun and Maimalarin who were, moreover, actively involved in the NNA coup. The coup failed in the East, so Majors Okafor and Ifeajuna did not carry out their duties as planned. Even then was Dr. Okpara not the most national-istic, the most progressive, the most dynamic, and the most popular of the four premiers in the country? The Mid-West, for reason already given, was not in the immediate plan and so their Premier was not arrested. Lt.-Col. Unegbe had to be killed because, by refusing to give out the key to the armoury, he posed the first serious threat to the success of the coup. The other Lt.-Colonels were deeply involved in the NNA coup and had to be arrested immediately because they were in a position to frustrate the coup. They lost their lives because they resisted arrest. The GOC was not arrested because Captain Oji lost his nerve in the dominating presence of the Commander. The Prime Minister and the Finance Minister were both killed by their panicking captors when the latter realised they had failed to capture Lagos. Moreover, was it not the same Okotie-Eboh who demanded 10 per cent of the value of any contract as a bribe before awarding such a contract? Was it not the same Okotie-Eboh whom foreign correspondents described as 'Afri-can dash-master'? Had not this same man tried to bribe the soldiers who came to arrest him with bundles of pound notes? Did such a man deserve to live?

In the light of all these factors, can the coup of January 15, 1966, rightly be described as an 'Ibo coup'? Majors Ifeajuna, Obienu and Okafor were Eastern Ibos, Major Nzeogwu was a West-Niger Ibo, and Major Ademoyega was a Yoruba. In spite of the tribal origins of these planners, could the coup be regarded as Ibo-instigated? To answer this question fully it is pertinent to take a retrospective look at the history of Nigeria. This should reveal that nationalist-spirited Nigerians have been Southern Nigerians and particularly Easterners. Moreover, it would have been foolish to include any Northerner in the comprehensive plan when it was already known that they were planning a Northern coup. This is more so when it is remembered that the majors were in subordinate positions, and they therefore considered secrecy an essential part of the plan.

Even though the coup was planned by Southerners (four-fifths of whom were Ibos) it was executed by people from all sections of the country. It is pertinent to quote a *Daily Times* publication on this issue:

Explaining the background to the coup, Major Nzeogwu said that five men were concerned with planning the operation. 'On Saturday morning the officers and men thought they were going out only on a night exercise. It was not until they were out in the bush they were told the full details of the plan. They had bullets, they had been issued with weapons but I was unarmed. If they had disagreed they could have shot me,' he said. 'Most of those concerned with the revolt in the North were Northerners,' he added. 'It was a truly Nigerian gathering, and only in the army do you get true Nigerianism. All those who took part in the coup had received no rewards. They did it for the good of their country. This is why we have gone out of our way to avoid bloodshed. We are anxious for peace.'[206]

It is remarkable, however, that through the haze of cries of 'Ibo coup', there were foreign commentators who could see that the majors acted in the interest of all sections of the country. *The Economist*, commenting on the Nigerian military takeover, stated:

... even those to whom military coups are abhorrent on principle must concede that only the army could put an end to a situation that had become intolerable and could not be remedied by less drastic means,[207]

Colin Legum, *The Observer's* Commonwealth correspondent, put it this way:

This month's mutiny sharply broke the cycle of escalating suspicion, hostility and violence. But it also introduced a new and much more hopeful note into Nigerian politics.

For although the mutiny's ringleaders were all Ibo, support for the military regime is not confined to any one tribe. The popular reaction in all their regions shows widespread dissatisfaction with all the old parties. The political class had become discredited. Young Nigerians, it appears, had come to look with strong disfavour on the way in which the old politicians sought to exploit tribal and regional suspicions to maintain their power.

The mutiny, therefore, marks a real break with the past in Nigeria. The crucial question is whether these new ideas, which now command the centre of Nigeria's politics, can be translated into a different kind of Constitution that can protect legitimate regional interests while at the same time providing the country with a central Government with sufficient authority and power to hold the country together. This is the challenge facing General Ironsi and his Young Turks.[208]

It was in the search for a solution to this crucial problem that Major-General Johnson Thomas Umunnakwe Aguiyi-Ironsi got lost – partly because of his ignorance of the geography of politics, partly because of his unpreparedness for the journey into which chance had pushed him, and partly because of the wickedness of human nature and the tragedy of misplaced trusts.

(iii) IRONSI'S REGIME

The announcement of the hand-over of the Government of Nigeria to the Armed Forces was greeted with nationwide jubiliation. Messages of support poured into the State House. All the political parties, trade unions and students' organisations expressed their unreserved support for and loyalty to the new regime.

In a statement signed by its acting General Secretary, Chief Koluwole Balogun, the NCNC declared that the Army, being the bulwark and sanction of any civil government, had come in to safeguard the parliamentary democracy, the rule of law and respect for human dignity – principles for which the masses had fought with sweat, blood and tears in the struggle for independence. The AG, in a statement signed by acting leader Alhadji Adegbenro, described the take-over as a 'continuation of the people's struggle to preserve parliamentary democracy and the unity of the Federation'. The NPC, in a statement signed by Alhaji Hashim Adaji, saw the take-over as the only solution to the many crises into which the country had been plunged. Other statements of support came from the National Union of Nigerian Students, the Nigerian Youth Congress, the Joint Action Committee of the Trade Unions, the United Labour Congress, the Nigerian Workers' Council, the NNDP, the Zikist Movement, the Benson Youth Brigade, cultural and Church organisations, and natural rulers, including the Obas of Lagos and Benin. There were students demonstrations in the Nigerian universities in support of the new military Government. Cheering crowds poured into the streets, as the happy demonstrators marched past their homes and places of work. Some of the placards read: 'Down with tyranny, away with feudalism', 'Tyranny is Dead', 'New Nigeria is born', 'Nigeria is now really independent', 'Welcome, Ironsi; but release our heroes'. The Nigerian press, without exception, and in no equivocal terms, declared their support for the take-over. After a visit to Nigeria, J. D. F. Jones, the diplomatic correspondent of *The Financial Times*, said of the popularity of the Army take-over:

> The enthusiasm is infectious, and marks a happy contrast with the years of growing disillusion and suspicion that lay behind Nigeria's much-lauded 'Democratic Experiment.'[209]

Meanwhile, General Ironsi, now fully saddled in office, appointed Military Governors to head the four Regional Military Governments. He also set up, as organs of the Federal Military Government, a Supreme Military Council and a Federal Executive Council. The Governors were: North, Major Hassan Usman Katsina, son of the Emir of Katsina; East, Lt.-Col. Chukwuemeka Odumegwu Ojukwu, Oxford-trained son of Nigeria's business tycoon, Sir Odumegwu Ojukwu; West, Lt.-Col. Adekunle Fajuyi; Mid-West, Lt.-Col. David Ejoor. The Supreme Military Council comprised General Ironsi, Commodore Wey (the Navy chief), Lt.-Col. Kurubo

(Head of the Air Force), Brigadier B. A. Ogundipe (Chief of Staff, Supreme Headquarters), Lt.-Col. Yakubu Gowon (Chief of Staff, Army Headquarters) and the four Military Governors. The Federal Executive Council comprised all members of the Supreme Military Council, the Inspector-General of Police and his Deputy. As Supreme Commander of the Armed Forces and Head of the Federal Military Government, Ironsi was to preside over both Councils. On the inclusion of the Regional Military Governors in the Federal Executive Council (which took up the duty of the Council of Ministers), General Ironsi said he considered it necessary because it underlined 'the fact that there is now only one Government in Nigeria'.

With transparent enthusiasm and sincerity, the military men embarked on the much needed national reconstruction which would transform the old suspicion-plagued Nigeria into a strong, united new Nigeria. In this they received enthusiastic co-operation from the people. The riots in Western Nigeria and in the Middle-Belt territory ceased. Millions of people in these areas who, as an expression of their complete loss of confidence in the governments of the Federation, had for long refused to pay their taxes, willingly resumed payment. All over the country there was obvious dedication to the ideals of the new regime. Nor did the new leaders fail to live up to the people's expectations. General Ironsi appointed members to national study groups to study the problems of national unity, constitutional review and the development of the national economy. He revoked the appointments of the Chairmen and Boards of Federal Statutory Corporations and replaced them with new appointees, mostly from the Federal Ministeries.

In the regions, the Military Governors were no less busy. In Enugu, Lt.-Col. Ojukwu declared that the Nigerian citizens must 'realise that we are determined to turn our own back for ever on the unproductive drift of yester-year' which he described as 'ten wasted years of planlessness, drift, incompetence, inefficiency, gross abuse of public office, corruption, avarice and gross disregard of the interests of the common man'. He abolished all provincial Assemblies and the post of Agent-General for Eastern Nigeria in the United Kingdom, suspended the activities of the regional and provincial scholarship boards and the salaries of board members of Government corporations not engaged in administrative and executive duties, and directed that all powers and functions of the former Governor, Premier and Ministers of each region would be exercised by the Military Governor. Appointment, promotion and discipline of senior staff in the public service of the region would be made by him with the advice of the Public Service Commission. The former Regional Governor, Premier, Ministers, Provincial Commissioners and parliamentary secretaries should vacate their 'official residences and surrender any Government property, including cars, in their possession'. He warned the debtors of Government to liquidate such debts. He further warned against corruption, dereliction of duty and careless talk, and thanked the people 'for your widespread expressions of goodwill and support'.

In the North, Major Hassan Katsina announced that he would operate on the administrative structure established by Major Nzeogwu. He declared:

> Everyone must realise that we are one nation, irrespective of tribe, from which each of us originated. Our experiences in the past have shown that the political parties have not worked for the common good but for sectional interests. I do not need their greetings or congratulations, as this is not the time for jubilation or flattery, but for hard work and selfless service. This is the way to reach our goal of satisfying the aspiration of the common man.[210]

In the West, Fajuyi revoked the appointments of all managing committees administering the Local Government Councils throughout his region. He also revoked the appointments of all members of joint boards responsible for customary courts, education, water schemes and forestry, and replaced these committees and joint boards with sole administrators. He further restored the salaries of Obas, which had been suspended or reduced to a penny by Akintola's régime, and ordered that no customary courts in the region should handle criminal cases.

In the Mid-West, Ejoor abolished the Public Service Commission, the Mid-West Agent-General's office in London and management committees, and suspended tax assessment committees. He established a recruitment committee and stopped chairmen, executive directors, and members of all boards and corporations from carrying out party functions. The number of ministries in the region was reduced from 20 to 11.

Throughout the Federation, concerted efforts were being made on all fronts to re-establish the country and revivify its body politic into a new lease of nationhood. Bans that had been placed on certain daily newspapers in some regions were lifted. Enquiries were instituted in numerous institutions, and suspects of fraud arrested and committed to assizes with unprecedented dispatch. Chief Pius Nwoga, the former Eastern Minister of Town Planning, and his permanent secretary, Uche Okoye, were charged to court with corruption and conspiracy to defraud the Eastern Nigerian Government. Chief Odoffin Bello, former Commissioner of Police for the Western Region, was sentenced to three years' imprisonment on charges of corruption and abuse of office. He was charged with receiving £2,500 from Oba C. D. Akran, Finance Minister in Akintola's Government, with a view to protecting offending NNDP supporters from detention or punishment. Emmanuel Olawaiye, Assistant Commissioner of Police in the West, was charged with abuse of office and stealing £162, property of the state. Solomon Olujobi, Superintendent-General of the Western Nigeria Local Government Police, was charged with receiving £500 from Chief Adeyi, NNDP Minister of Works and Transport, and another £500 from Oba C. D. Akran, in order to show favour to NNDP supporters. Also arrested were seventeen ministers and functionaries of the former NNDP-controlled Government. They were charged with stealing the sum of £62,045 18s 2d, property of the Western Region Marketing Board.

This wave of national purgation, set into operation by the soldiers, gave the people of Nigeria assurance of a brighter future for the country. Commenting on this, a correspondent of *The Economist*[211] said that Nigeria would now emerge 'stronger, cleaner, and a more promising recipient of aid and investment'. He continued:

A clean sweep has been made not only of politicians but of political appointees in corporations . . . and a start has been made in dismantling the patronage system on which regional politics rested.

In a front-page comment, *The Daily Times* had this to say:

Let's hand it to the Army. They're doing a fine job . . . they have taken long strides in a short time – and done it with such a minimum of fuss. . . . Nigeria knows more calm today than it has in three years . . . The Army has spent the first 30 days pulling down what was left of the house that crumbled under the sheer weight of curruption, illegality and mismanagement. It has put the teeth of its tractors to the debris of ill-founded boards; it has put its shovel to corporations slit and made rickety; it has brought in the heavy-duty mowers and moved mass concrete into areas where the murk of filth had been prepared as bedrocks.

In a few weeks, the task of preparing the site for a new nation would have been complete. AND THEN THE GREAT QUESTION IS – What next?[212]

Indeed the big question was: 'What next?' This was the crucial point where General Ironsi's problems began. One incongruous feature that was evident during this national cleansing period was the fact that no cleansing was done in Northern Nigeria. Whereas ex-politicians were arrested and detained in Lagos and the three regions in the South, their counterparts in the North were not only in free circulation but were returned to positions of responsibility. This was the bane of Ironsi's régime, and the root of events which forced Walter Schwarz of *The Guardian* to observe ruefully that 'even a well-meaning military régime cannot obliterate the tribal tensions which make Nigerian politics.'[213]

Because the main feature which had frustrated the first attempt at democratic government in Nigeria was the extreme regionalism which was a result of the nature of the Federal Constitution, it was natural therefore that any effort to create unity in the country should be directed towards eradicating this disuniting factor. That this was General Ironsi's policy is shown by this statement:

I am convinced that the bulk of our people want a *United Nigeria* and that they want in future one government for Nigeria and not a multitude of governments. They want one government whose units of legislative and administrative devolution would, on the one hand, be nearer to the people than the old Region was, and on the other, be of such a size most likely to satisfy local needs, but of such limited powers as not to constitute a danger to the *Unity of Nigeria*.

This is the aim of the Supreme Military Council, this is the frame of reference within which all our measures of national reconstruction – political, economic and administrative – must be formulated, this is the common guideline for all the study groups that have been appointed or may be appointed in future to advise and assist me in the achievement of our great national objective of creating one Nigeria.[214]

It was in the pursuit of this policy that he promulgated the fateful Decree No. 34 which banned political organisations, ended the Federation and unified the Civil Services. As admitted by foreign commentators, the decree proposed no new changes but formalised conditions which were already existing under the military régime. A *West Africa* correspondent said:

> Careful examination of these sections of the speech show that the constitutional and administrative changes proposed are intended to apply only to the three-year period for which, the General said, military rule was thought necessary. And since military rule has in fact put an end to the federal form of government the speech was not proposing any remarkable change.[215]

The West African correspondent of *The Economist* aptly explained the involvements of the decree thus:

> In fact, the decree did little more than formalise an existing state of affairs. Nigeria has had what amounts to a military form of government ever since the military take-over in January, the regional military governors take their orders from General Ironsi in a way the regional premiers never did from the Federal Prime Minister. Under the decree the former regions are called 'groups of provinces,' but they have the same boundaries and are under the same military governors as before. Although nominally unified, the five former civil services remain separate, each under its own civil service commission. Only the higher appointments

(those worth more than £2,000 a year) will be made on a
national instead of a regional basis.[216]

Unfortunately, in Nigeria, as in most African, Asian and Latin-
American countries, where the standard of literacy is very low,
laws and decrees are never fully understood by a vast majority
of the populace, and what they know of new laws is invariaby
what they are told by the people whom they look upon as leaders
who should know. The North has the lowest percentage of
literacy in Nigeria, and one of the lowest in Africa. This fact
was taken advantage of by the many sections in that region
who saw in the prospect of a clean and united Nigeria a serious
threat to their selfish ends.

We have already mentioned the former politicians who,
though discredited in the period immediately following January
15, had exploited their new positions to ingratiate themselves
into the hearts of the gullible masses of Northern Nigeria.

Then there were the expatriates (mainly British) resident in
Northern Nigeria, who can rightly be called the largest contri-
butors to the break-up of the Federation of Nigeria. Great
beneficiaries of the Northernisation policy, they saw in the military take-over an end to their long years of paternalism in that
region, the reward of which had been positions in the higher
echelon of the Northern Nigerian civil service and corporations.
They saw in Decree No. 34 a document which gave constitutional permanence to their displacement from their privileged
positions as 'expert' advisers to the Northern Nigeria Government, and substitution by qualified Nigerians from the South.

Then there were the Northern Nigerian civil servants, most
of whom owed their high positions to the Northernisation
policy. Next came the University students who had already
become accustomed to the prospect of top executive posts as
soon as they left their degree examination halls, with the atten-
dant huge purse which is further swelled by a chain of 'allowances'. These also were beneficiaries of regionalism, and saw
in its abolition the end of a life-long dream.

Finally there were the party functionaries – the local officials
and strong-arm men who earned their living from the party
purse; the contractors who won contracts not because of the
high quality of their previous work nor because of their low

tenders, but on account of their material and moral support for the ruling party; and these were the political appointees who were constantly haunted by the prospect of suffering the fate of their counterparts in the other regions.

These people, who fed on the decay of the nation, were naturally disgruntled when the dirt was swept away by the soldiers, and would have given anything to return to the 'good old days'. It was natural that the idea of an uprising should appeal to them; and it was therefore in them that the expatriates found a most willing tool for their designs. Being accustomed to reaching the masses through their emotions, they effectively expounded the concept of domination which was necessary to arouse the indignation of the impressionable populace.

When Decree No. 34 was announced on May 24, expatriates, particularly those in the Ahmadu Bello University, Zaria, urged the Northerners to 'protest' against the military Government. They reminded them of the death of Sir Ahmadu Bello, Sir Abubakar and the Northern officers, and the leadership of the military regime by Ironsi (an Ibo) as evidences of the plan of the Ibos to dominate the country. Decreee No. 34, they informed their audience, gave a legal sanction to this plan. A strong campaign against the Government was mounted, and student groups travelled to the main centres of the region 'explaining' to the people the 'dangers' which the decree portended for the North, among which was the absurdity that very soon there would be more Easterners in the North than Northerners. This sort of preposterous propaganda achieved the desired effect on the Northern populace, it did not even occur to them that the population of the East is less than half that of the North. The students succeeded in convincing them of the necessity for an uprising. On May 29, after a series of all-night meetings in which they were addressed by expatriate staff of the University, the students thronged into Zaria and Kaduna to demonstrate in favour of a demand for the secession of Northern Nigeria from the Federation.

This was the cue for which the illiterate masses, who were by now emotionally fully charged, had been waiting. In Kano, Zaria, Katsina, Jos, Bukuru, Gusau and Sokoto, waves of murder and arson erupted simultaneously. Hundred of Easterners

F

resident in the North were killed, and their property looted or destroyed. Many others escaped to the South. In Sokoto and Gusau, Roman Catholic churches were attacked. Commenting on these events, Lloyd Garrison of *The New York Times* said:

> ... there was nothing spontaneous about the demonstrations that fuelled these hostile passions. They were staged at the same time in three widely separated Northern cities.[217]

West Africa analysed the root of the riots thus:

> The riots in Northern Nigeria which followed this [Ironsi's] speech, are generally thought to have been the responsibility of politicians disappointed in their expectation that they would soon be returned to the fruits of office, a well as of people who feared that the General's announcement meant that the control over Nigeria, which the preponderance of population gives to the Northern provinces, was now being arbitrarily ended. While even a military régime would be wise to allow peaceful demonstrations as a safety valve, what those responsible hoped to achieve by these violent means is not clear. ... At any rate *it is clear that the demonstrations were essentially tribalistic, anti-Ibo, in nature, and should not be elevated into serious expressions of political thinking about the constitution.*[218]

Indeed, the riots, like all expressions of savagery, were not directed towards any clear objective and the planners themselves who had hoped to achieve their private ends by the 'protests', never envisaged that the unreasoning masses would degenerate to such depths of savagery. This is borne out by the evidence Dr. Eva Sansome, a senior lecturer at the Ahmadu Bello University, Zaria, who with her husband, an expatriate professor in the same university, was deeply involved in the uprising; she confessed to an Eastern lecturer that they did not envisage that a 'mere strong protest' against 'the unification of the civil service' would involve so much destruction of life and property.[219]

General Ironsi's reaction to the riots and massacres was to launch an enlightenment programme to explain to the Northerners that, contrary to their understanding of his government's intention, the decree was a temporary measure designed only for the administrative convenience of the military régime. Hassan Katsina, the Military Governor of the North (by now promoted to the rank of Lt.-Col.), himself explained that 'we in the Army have got a unified command and it is the methpo we are used to'. General Ironsi followed this publicity drive by asking Lt.-Col. Katsina to have a meeting with the Emirs in order to discover their grievances. He further summoned at Ibadan a consultative meeting with the traditional rulers all over the country. Then he embarked on a meet-the-people tour of the four regions. It was during his tour of the Western Region (having visited both the North and the Mid-West) that a group of Northern Nigerian soldiers kidnapped and murdered him and his host, Lt.-Col. Adekunle Fajuyi, the Military Governor of Western Nigeria. The details of the events of that morning of July 29, 1966, will be discussed in the next chapter. Meanwhile, let us attempt an analysis of the methods by which this unfortunate man sought to carry out a task which he neither asked for nor envisaged.

First, how did the prevalent sentiment of tribe affect his administration, and what efforts did he make to disentangle himself? Can any Nigerian ever rule this country with the mutual respect and trust of all peoples of Nigeria? And finally, can *National Unity* ever be achieved while the seeds of tribalism continue to germinate in the Nigerian soil?

Though, by its nature and implication, a military rule is dictatorial, General Ironsi did not for a moment succumb to the temptation of dictatorship, but all the time lived up to his determination to serve, rather than lord it over, his people. In his eagerness not to hurt tribal feelings, and to dismiss the notion that the military régime was Ibo-orientated, he went out of his way to placate the Northerners in a way that suggested that he was sorry for a wrong which had been done to them. Whereas the ex-politicians in the South were subjected to the most intensive inquiries, their counterparts in the North were not even detained for security reasons. He distrusted, or gave the impression of distrusting, army officers and men of Eastern origin, and surrounded himself with Northern soldiers and wards. He effected promotions of Northern officers without reference to the seniority list. For example, Lt.-Col. Yakubu

(a Northerner) was appointed Army Chief of Staff in spite
of the fact that he was neither the most senior nor the best
qualified officer to hold the post.

When confidential reports were sent to him he treated them
most unconfidentially. On two occasions, when delegations
of Southerners resident in the North came down to report on
anti-government plots in that region, he called Northern
officers around him and asked the informers to make the reports in their presence. Even when these reports were supported
with data and photographs, and further substantiated by his
own cross-checking, he was hesitant in bringing the culprits
to book. This had the natural consequence of making his
informers keep mute when they saw or heard things that were
prejudicial to peace in the country.

This impression of regret which he gave the Northerners was
further borne out by his continued detention of the prosecutors
of the January 15 coup in spite of the fact that every Nigerian
(including Ironsi himself and the Northerners) was pleased
with the overthrow of the corrupt civilian régime, and in spite
of his personal pledge of safety to Major Nzeogwu. While it is
admitted that his hesitation to comply with the Northern demand for the public execution of the revolutionaries[220] was
influenced by this pledge, it must be stated that he lacked sufficient courage to release them in accordance with his pledge
and conviction. On matters concerning the North, General
Ironsi's decrees were either conveniently forgotten or watered
down to something less than ordinary laws; eventually they
were left to be forgotten.

That General Ironsi acted with good intentions is indisput-
able, but that he also displayed ignorance of state craft is only
too obvious. He failed to realise that in the realm of politics,
and even in the most liberal democracy, mere goodwill without
some measure of force cannot achieve anything. For though
one may be acting oneself with good faith one cannot guarantee good faith on the part of the other party. After the May
riots he merely issued a statement saying that the Military
Government was aware that the disturbances were incited by
'some Nigerians in collusion with certain foreign elements', and
'sincerely hoped' that 'these foreign elements are not being
backed by their respective governments'. A more realistic

approach would have been to repatriate all the foreigners who were involved in the disturbances, and detain all their Nigerian accomplices. This is where a compromise should be struck between realism and ethics in order to achieve a purpose, otherwise it would be mere sentimentalism.

Politics is a twilight zone where ethical and coercive factors must inevitably interpenetrate, and it is for these essential factors to work out their own tentative and uneasy compromises. Ironsi failed to realise this, and so failed to release enough force to back the central purpose of his administration – that of giving Nigeria *unity*. In this he is not to blame. He did not seek to play the role which chance thrust upon him. Nor was there anything in his earlier career which had prepared him for such a role.

Mazzini's immortal words have again been vindicated. Here is the tragedy of a well-intended revolution grossly frustrated by a man who was neither part of the revolution nor shared the ideas of those who planned it. Nzeogwu and his colleagues had a vision and a conviction. Perhaps they should have been given the chance to make this vision a reality. Had the revolution been completed, Nigeria, the misdirected giant of Africa, would perhaps by now be strong, prosperous and united, a true leader on the African continent.

General Ironsi was the unfortunate pawn in the hands of fate, a man to whom providence assigned a task which he was not well equipped to accomplish. A prototype of the bureaucratic warlord, he took too much for granted and paid too dearly for it.

7

THE MILITARY IN NIGERIAN POLITICS
II: THE JULY 29 MUTINY

Man may be a little lower than the angels, but he has not yet
shaken off the brute. His passions, his thinking, his body
carry their origins with them; and he fails, if he vaingloriously
denies them. His path is strewn with carnage, the murderer
lurks always not far beneath, to break out from time to time,
peace resolutions to the contrary notwithstanding.

JUDGE LEARNED HAND

(i) THE NORTH AND SECESSION

Major-General Ironsi's placatory policy in Northern Nigeria,
particularly his apologetic reaction to the ill-advised May riots
and massacres, had the summary (though paradoxical) effect
of deepening the Northern people's ill-conceived fear of domination. Therefore, in spite of the robust nature of the General's
goodwill and his unusually wide national perspective, they
came to believe very strongly that his regime was not in their
interest. Thus the age-old idea of secession began once more
to appeal to them very strongly.

Secession has for many years attracted the people of Northern
Nigeria. We have seen, in Chapter 4, their approach to the
question of Nigerian unity. As far as they were concerned, a
united Nigeria was one in which the North ruled; and whenever
their position of dominance was jeopardised, the clarion call
was always 'secession'.

For instance, it will be recalled that, in January 1950, at a
General Conference held at Ibadan, Western Nigeria, to discuss
final proposals for revising the Richards Constitution of 1946,
the North, in keeping with its policy of 'domination or secession', announced to the Conference that, unless the Northern
Region was alloted 50 per cent of the seats in the Central
Legislature, it would ask for separation from the rest of Nigeria,
as has been the case before 1914. When ultimately it was

allocated forty-five seats, while each of the other regions (East and West) had thirty-three, the Northern delegation refused to vote. In the interest of Nigerian unity, a Select Committee of the Legislature let the North have its way; and once again the South acquiesced in the political domination of Nigeria by the North, so that Nigeria might remain one political entity.

The late Sir Ahmadu Bello, President of the Northern People's Congress (NPC), in his book *My Life*, admitted that there was persistent agitation for secession in Northern Nigeria. He said:

> ... There were agitations in favour of secession; we should set up our own; we should cease to have anything to do with the Southern people; we should take our own way . . . . I must say it looked very tempting. We were certainly 'viable', to use the current phrase; we could run our own show; the Centre would have to hand over to us our share of Nigeria's accumulated sterling assets.[221]

The Northern Nigerian undergraduates whose demonstration sparked off the May massacres carried placards, some of which read: 'Let there be secession.'

It is pertinent to reproduce here the closing section of an anonymous letter written from Yola, Northern Nigeria, and dated June 10, 1966, which read as follows:

> We are not in fact accepting Federal and there should be no Unitary Government for us. *We in the North should either rule Nigeria or there should be no Nigeria.*[222]

It was in this spirit that the mammoth pogrom of July 29 and the following days was planned and executed. At first, however, the military officers of Northern origin were not inclined to the idea of a coup. So the former Northern political leaders recruited and trained about 500 men from neighbouring African states who, either because they have predominantly Muslim populations or because of other interests, are sympathetic to the Northern cause. In this, the Northern politicians were actively helped by the NNDP men, their erstwhile colleagues in the corrupt civilian regime. Proficient in the act of subversion and inducement, they directed their own efforts towards in-

ducing the Northern military personnel to join their side. The
discovery of the sum of £126,000 at the house of Oba C. D.
Akran, former NNDP Finance Minister, on January 20, 1966,
is significant in this regard.[223] Subsequently, the Northern
officers were not only inclined to the coup, but played very
leading roles in its planning and execution.

(ii) JULY 29, 1966

The aim of the July 29 massacre was two-fold:

(i) to split the country and effect the secession of the North
from the rest of Nigeria;

(ii) in the alternative, to re-establish the hegemony and
domination of the North in the Federation.

In accordance with these aims, the Federal Military Government, as led by General Ironsi, had to be overthrown. The
General himself must be eliminated. Lt.-Col. Yakubu Gowon
was selected as the man who would replace Ironsi. He had been
General Ironsi's Army Chief of Staff (Defence Headquarters)
and a member of the Supreme Military Council. He had returned to Nigeria from Britain less than forty-eight hours
before the Revolution of January 15, and the fact that he was
appointed the Army Chief of Staff a few weeks after January
15, 1966, and subsequently a member of the Supreme Military
Council, shows the amount of confidence General Ironsi
reposed in him – confidence he betrayed. His position gave
him the opportunity to study the inner workings of the National
Military Government, preparatory to his revolt. It was natural
therefore that he should become the 'Chief controller and Co-
ordinator of Operations' of the '*Araba*' (meaning 'Secession
Day' in Hausa), the code name given to the July 29 mutiny.[224]

If, after the operations, there were obstacles to the Northern
design of ruling the Federation, then Lt.-Col. Yakubu Gowon
would declare himself the 'Supreme Commander' of the new
Republic of the North. In this event, the Nigerian flag would
be replaced in all Northern territories by the new Northern
Nigeria flag made up of red, yellow, indigo, green and khaki
stripes.[225] If, on the other hand, there were no obstacles, and
the North could, by this revolt, assure for itself, once more,
dominance over the rest of the country, then Gowon would

instead declare himself 'Supreme Commander of the Armed Forces and Head of the National Military Government' of Nigeria.[226]

On July 28, 1966, General Ironsi addressed the country's natural rulers at Ibadan. In the evening he retired to the Government House, Ibadan, with his host, Lt.-Col. Adekunle Fajuyi, the West Military Governor. With him were Lt.-Col. H. M. Njoku, officer commanding the 2nd Brigade, Lt. Nwankwo, the Supreme Commander's Air Force aide-de-camp, and Lt. Bello, his Military aide-de-Camp. Late that evening the 'Araba' was launched into operation in many parts of the Federation,[227] Southern Nigerians in General Ironsi's bodyguard were removed, and a group of twenty-four Northern soldiers was sent to reinforce the remaining Northerners. Before midnight the Ibadan Government House was already surrounded.

Meanwhile operations had started at Abeokuta in Western Nigeria. A group of Northern soldiers broke into the officers' mess and shot Major Obienu, Lt. Orok (both Easterners), and Lt. Okonweze (Mid-Westerner). An alarm was sounded, and Southerners who responded to it were arrested and locked up in the guardroom and the armoury, which had by now been emptied of its contents and converted into a guardroom. Then the Northern troops, now fully equipped with arms and ammunition taken from the armoury, went hunting, both in the barracks and in the adjourning civilian houses, for Southern troops who had failed to answer the alarm. Some of those caught were locked up, others were shot at sight, depending on the whims of their Northern captors. Later the Westerners were sifted out from the other Southerners and released. At sunrise, the non-commissioned officers (NCO's) amongst the detainees were brought out and shot, their bodies being bundled into a vehicle which was made available for the purpose.

Back in Ibadan, news of the disorders had reached the Government House. The Supreme Commander's Military ADC, Lt. Bello (a Northerner!) had disappeared. So had Lt.-Col. Fajuyi's ADC. Following a brief conference between the Supreme Commander, his host and Lt.-Col. Njoku, it was decided that Njoku should hurry down to Lagos in plain clothes, take over control and quell the uprising. On his way a group of Northern

F*

soldiers fired at him, wounding him in the thigh. He returned
fire and made straight for the University Teaching Hospital,
Ibadan. He had scarcely been admitted there for treatment
when his assailants tracked him to the hospital. Fortunately,
with the help of some hospital staff, he managed to escape to
the Eastern Region.

The sound of the exchange of fire warned Ironsi and his host
that they were in trouble. So they sent Lt. Nwankwo downstairs to find out what was happening. When he got downstairs,
the Lieutenant was arrested and detained by the guards. When he
did not return for some time, Lt.-Col. Fajuyi went downstairs
and was himself arrested and detained. At about 9 a.m. on July
29, Major Danjuma, who was in command of the guards, took
some of his men upstairs, and after quizzing the Supreme
Commander, saluted him and ordered his arrest. The three
captives were stripped naked, tied up and, amidst floggings and
beatings, bundled into separate police vans. Led by Lt. Walbe,
Lt. Paiko, Warrant Officer I. Baka and Company Sergeant-
Major Useri Fegge, the special team selected for the purpose
took the captives to a small stream about ten miles along the
Ibadan-Iwo road, where the torture was continued. At this
stage Lt. Nwankwo escaped. Enraged by this, Lt. Walbe and
his men sprayed Major-General Ironsi and Lt.-Col. Fajuyi
with machine-gun bullets.

At the Letmank Barracks, Ibadan, the process was the same
as at Abeokuta. The armoury and magazines were seized by
Northern troops, the alarm was blown, the Southern soldiers
arrested, and the non-commissioned officers of Eastern origin
among them shot and bundled away in a waiting van. Then
there followed a room-to-room hunt of Eastern soldiers, but
this time the killings and arrests were accompanied by the
raping of wives and looting of the property of the Easterners.

There were, however, a few differences. At 10 a.m. (July 29),
Lt.-Col. J. Akahan, Commanding Officer of the 4th Battalion
at Ibadan, called an officers' meeting. He did not attend. The
officers of Eastern origin who attended were arrested and locked
up in the guardroom. At night they were transferred to the
tailors' shop, into which were then thrown hand-grenades. The
few surviving officers were shot as they tried to escape. Their
corpses were bundled into a van and conveyed to a mass grave

already prepared at the outskirts of the town. The next day Lt.-Col. Akahan disarmed the Northern soldiers and caused it to be announced that the fleeing officers should return, as their safety was now assured. Some Eastern officers who were in hiding in the city returned, but, at night, Northern soldiers attacked them with guns and knives, killing all they caught. Those who escaped fled to the East.

The same pattern was followed in the remaining Southern military stations – Apapa, Ikeja, Lagos island and Yaba. In the absence of General Ironsi, Lt.-Col. Gowon was in overall command, and thus had a free hand to direct the operations. He later moved to Ikeja, where he established his headquarters. It is pertinent to note that, for over twenty-nine days after July 29, the Northern Nigeria secessionist flag of red, yellow, indigo, green, and khaki stripes was flown in the Ikeja barracks.

In the North, the pattern was not much different except that operations did not start until the night of July 29. Here, however, ghastly bestialities were committed in broad daylight, and here too the atrocities were committed by both civilian and military authorities alike. In Kaduna, the Eastern officers were rounded up, sentenced to death and taken in batches to a waiting firing squad in the outskirts of the town. In Kano, an alarm summoned the soldiers for parade at the basket-ball pitch. Then, as in other places, the Easterners who were present were arrested and locked up. Some were removed to unknown destinations. Others were tortured and eventually murdered. Some managed to escape and, after sleeping in the bush for days, finally found their way to the East. There were many who did not make it, however. The unfortunate ones ran into search parties of Northern soldiers, who invariably shot them at sight.

One thing that is peculiar to the July operations is the revolting bestiality that marks every aspect of it. Some victims were not even given the 'mercy' of a quick death from a bullet, but were slaughtered with knives. Others were made to swim in ponds of faeces for several hours before being finally shot. It is difficult to understand the depth of hatred that must have driven the Northern soldiers to these sadistic acts, the more so when it is realised, that, a few hours before the holocaust, the Eastern soldiers shared the same sleeping accommodation and dined at same table with their executioners. It cannot be argued that these killings were a sudden outburst of pent-up grievances. All available evidence points to a detailed and exhaustive programme – a premeditated and cold-blooded extermination of Easterners in the army. This is borne out by the uniformity of the procedure for carrying out the massacres in the different military stations, with slight modifications depending only on the degree of bestiality of the commanding officer and the whims of the executioners. The scrupulous separation of Western Nigerians from the Easterners before the latter were executed goes a long way to support premeditation. The genocide of the later months of 1966[228] is still more conclusive as evidence.

Another point which must be mentioned here is that the killing of the Eastern soldiers was indiscriminate. No attempt was made to ascertain whether any Eastern soldier was Ibo, Ibibio, Efik, Ijaw or Ogoja. As soon as the Yorubas were sifted from the detained Southerners, the rest, including Mid-Westerners were marched off to the firing squad, which is usually preceded by some torturing. Of the total of 43 officers killed, 33 were Easterners, 7 from the Mid-West, and 3 from the West. The number of other ranks killed is estimated at 200, but, due to the fact that records of newly trained soldiers are not available, only 170 can be accounted for. Of these 153 were Easterners, 21 Mid-Westerners, and 3 Westerners.

In the East, the operation *Araba* was a complete failure in spite of the fact that, of the 950 soldiers in the 1st Battalion at Enugu, 700 were Northeners. By a stroke of sheer luck, Captain Ogbonna had escaped the killings at Abeokuta. Not realising the extent of the plans, he phoned the Quarter-Masters-General of a number of military stations to report what he believed to be an isolated mutiny. Fortunately the Quarter-Master-General at Enugu (a Northerner) did not receive the call having gone out to get the Northern soldiers ready in full war dress. As soon as the report reached Lt.-Col. Ogunewe, the Officer Commanding the 1st Battalion, he contacted Lt.-Col. Odumegwu Ojukwu, the Eastern Military Governor, who took immediate precautionary actions. He ordered the immediate disarming of all soldiers, sealed off the armoury, called in the Mobile Police Force, and moved into the Police Headquarters from where he

contacted Brigadier Ogundipe, Chief of Staff, Supreme Headquarters, and the next senior officer in the absence of General
Ironsi, whom he urged to assume command and leadership.
In the course of his discussions with Ogundipe, he learnt that
the rebels were in firm control of Lagos and would only agree
to a ceasefire on two conditions, viz.:

   (i) that the Republic of Nigeria be split into its component
       parts,
  (ii) that all Southerners resident in the North be repatriated
       to the South, and all Northerners resident in the South
       be repatriated to the North.[229]

This is understandable for the rebels were not certain about the
co-operation they could get from the South, especially as they
had failed in the East.

(iii) DIPLOMATIC MANOEUVRES

Bewildered by the success of his revolt at the Centre, but aware
that he had failed in the East, and rather fearful of the reaction
of the people of Eastern Nigeria, Lt.-Col. Gowon decided to
declare Northern Nigeria a separate state immediately. To this
end he prepared and tape-recorded a speech. This speech did
not, however, go on the air, for, as the result of advice and
pressure from British and American diplomats, sections of his
statement containing the declaration were deleted only a few
minutes before his broadcast. He had been advised that the
North, in the event of secession, would be the poorer, and the
greatest sufferer. It would become land-locked, having no
access to the Southern ports and harbours. Moreover, there
were some military officers of Northern Nigerian origin who
were attracted by the idea of ruling the whole country.

These pressure groups not withstanding, Lt.-Col. Gowon's
revised statement still betrayed the same desire for Northern
secession. On Monday, August 1, 1966, he made a broadcast to
the nation over the network of the Nigeria Broadcasting Corporation (NBC). After reviewing the events in the country he categorically declared that the basis of unity did not exist for the
people of Nigeria. This broadcast which started at 11.15 a.m.,
came after three days of unmitigated tension and anxiety,
during which the nation had waited to hear, from the rebels or

from any other authoritative source, what had happened to the Supreme Commander and the Federal Military Government. Turning to what he considered 'the most difficult part but most important part of [his] statement', he said:

> As a result of the recent events and other previous similar ones, I have come to strongly believe that one cannot honestly and sincerely continue in this wise . . . Suffice it to say that putting all considerations to test – political, economic as well as social – the base for unity is not there. . . . I therefore feel that we should review the issue of our national standing and see if we can help stop the country from drifting away into utter destruction.[230]

However, reassured by foreign agents and Southern colla-borators, Lt.-Col. Gowon dropped the question of secession and assumed the office of Head of the National Military Government and Supreme Commander of the Nigerian Armed Forces. Now entrenched at the Centre, he still had the problem of persuading his fellow Northerners, who still very much wanted secession, to forgo the idea, at least for the time being. After all, if the North was ruling Nigeria, what more could the North desire or get out of her political association with the rest of Nigeria? In the words of Gowon himself, 'since the end of July, God, in His Power has entrusted the responsibility of this great country of ours, Nigeria, into the hands of *another Northerner*. . . .'[231] Emphasising the same point, he said:

> Here I would like to repeat what I have said earlier. The responsibility for the well-being of Nigeria is today in our hands. . . .[232]

Because 'another Northerner' had came to power in the Centre, there was jubilation and merriment throughout North-ern Nigeria, following Gowon's broadcast of August 1, 1966. Muslim schools were reported closed in celebration of Ironsi's overthrow and displacement by 'another Northerner'. Certainly, for the North, the events of July 29 were proper and right. For the rest of the country, however, they were a cause for anxiety and tension, uncertainty and confusion. Thus *The Daily Times*, in an editorial during those turbulent days of heightened tension, had to warn:

When in a country that is governed by the armed forces, members of those forces are involved in the kind of revolt which we have all witnessed in the past four days, all responsible people, however restrained they may be in their emotion, know that the follow-up is usually anarchy . . . facing the blunt truth, we are moving towards the brink of anarchy, for the military men of our country have been killing themselves that it cannot truthfully be said that there is an effective Nigerian Government. . . .[233]

That same editorial concluded by stating that the fifty-four million people who inhabited the former Federation of Nigeria had 'very grave cause for anxiety'.[234] People were being killed like rats in those days of maximum danger. Gowon's soldiers could no longer subject themselves to discipline and command, and these soldiers freely helped themselves to any atrocities that appealed to their sadistic nature. The law enforcement agencies were quite powerless in the situation.

At Aburi, Commodore J. E. A. Wey, Head of the Nigerian Navy and a member of Ironsi's Supreme Military Council, claimed that he had been properly placed in all that went on in Lagos on July 29, 1966. He stated that there was complete indiscipline among the rank and file in the Army in Lagos, and soldiers could not take orders from officers as they had done in the past. Therefore, it was inconceivable, if not impossible, that Brigadier Ogundipe or any other officer next below him could have assumed command, for the rebels would not obey nor accept control. Thus, when the Eastern leader, Col. Ojukwu, appealed to Ogundipe to take control, the latter could not accept, even though he considered the idea fair and proper, because the rebellious faction was not likely to accept him.

The truth is that negotiations for a cease fire started soon after the rebels gained control at the Centre. On the night of July 30, at about 2 a.m., some NNDP and Northern leaders held a series of meetings to discuss the rebellion. In the course of the planning of the *Araba*, long before July 29, they had agreed among themselves that if the rebellion succeeded, Lt.-Col. Gowon should assume leadership. In the cease fire negotiations of July 30, therefore, in which the East was not represented, the plan to put Gowon in office was again sanctioned. Brigadier Ogundipe, the next in command, was dropped out. Gowon was preferred because, according to the Northern view after July 29, he 'had done everything'. The Northern leaders insisted upon a Northerner being at the head.

On the part of Gowon himself, he readily and happily held himself out for leadership. As a man who came from the Middle-Belt, then still smarting under the oppression and injustices of the old civilian regime in Northern Nigeria, Gowon would be most eager to create the Middle-Belt into a separate state. This state would be pulled out of the Northern state to go its independent way. But if he was assured that ruling the whole of Nigeria would not present much trouble, he and his people would be happy that at last they had the opportunity of lording it over their former oppressors and rulers – the Fulani Emirs. His people might then drop the idea of secession – the idea of seceding not only from Nigeria but also from a new Republic of the North. It was with this kind of idea that he was encouraged to develop the idea of ruling Nigeria as one political entity. Lt.-Col. Gowon, then, was not 'a soldier reluctantly in government', as he had been portrayed by both Commodore Wey and by the Nigerian Government publication on the crisis.[235] At best, it could be said that the Commodore was deceived by the events of July 30.

As far as the Northern leaders were concerned, they were sure that Gowon's hold upon power at the Centre was only temporary. The balance of power was so worked out that, though Gowon nominally held executive authority, the real power of the Central Government lay again with the Northern Emirs, as had been the case in the civilian government.

Commodore Wey's logic was that, if the rebels would obey no one other than their leader, why should leadership and command not be conceded to such a leader? But the question that could properly be asked here is this: should a nation hand over the command of its Army and its Government to anyone simply because he is the leader of a rebel gang that has seized power? The next in command in the Army hierarchy (after Ironsi) should automatically have succeeded, pending a more permanent settlement in the future. And if Gowon was anxious to preserve the peace and unity of the country, he should at once have invited leaders from all parts of the country to decide on the future destiny of the nation.

Gowon had embarked upon his rebellion not so much because he had any real grievance against Ironsi's régime. He was rather being used as an instrument to assure Northern domination and hegemony. But he saw in the process a chance of saving his people of the Middle-Belt area. This is further supported by the fact that the July 29 revolt had no ideology. In his first broadcast to the nation, Gowon pledged 'to continue the policy laid down by the Supreme Commander on January 16, 1966, published on January 26, 1966'.[236] If he had nothing new to offer to the nation immediately, it is difficult to read any other motive into his rebellion than the desire for personal power, and the commitment to be the instrument through which the Northern domination and hegemony could be perpetuated.

But in all this, Lt.-Col. Yakubo Gowon was not acting on his own initiative. We see at once the diplomatic manoeuvres of some Western countries, actively geared to satisfy their imperialistic interests in Nigeria – interacting with the avowed and true desires of the Northern people. Lt.-Col. Gowon was the instrument through which these interests and desires – all in an uneasy juxtaposition – were to be fostered and satisfied. Later developments clearly show that these interests and desires, being in direct conflict, could not work out their uneasy and tentative compromises without further bloodshed in Nigeria.

Unlike the January 15 coup, the rebellion of July 29 was known to some Western diplomats well before it took place. We have already discussed how foreign nationals in the Northern civil service and the staff of Ahmadu Bello University became personally involved in its planning and execution. Many of these persons were Britons. In the light of the British role in colonial Nigeria, and in the Biafra-Nigeria war, it is difficult to believe that these Britons did not receive the active collaboration and support of their embassies. Generally, foreign interest in the July revolt was to restore the Northern hegemony and dominance at the Centre. Some Western powers had always considered that the North would be easier to manage than any other region in the Federation of Nigeria. So long as Northerners remained in power at the Centre, they could easily be manipulated to serve as agents for neo-colonialism. The Northerners, on their part, in their pathological distrust of the people of the South, were always prepared to listen to their foreign advisers.

One problem which these foreign advisers had to combat was the strong and persistent sentiment for secession in the North – a sentiment which had been exploited in full to bring about the revolt of July 29. For obvious reasons (the same reasons for which Britain has given Nigeria active military support against Biafra[237]) secession was considered not in the best economic interest of some foreign powers. Therefore, after the overthrow of Ironsi, such powers worked hard to see that the rebels did not effect the disintegration of Nigeria – and here an economic sophism was used. Lt.-Col. Gowon was persuaded to drop the idea of secession. But the Northern masses could not for long be persuaded by this argument, as would be shown later.

Gowon's usurpation of the post of Supreme Commander of the Armed Forces and Head of the National Military Government – the title borne by General Ironsi – carried with it a number of implications: first legal. A legal government existed in Nigeria since, on January 15, Nzeogwu teamed up with Ironsi, and his activities in the North became part of the functions of the Ironsi régime. If he had refused to accept Ironsi's authority, they would have had to fight it out to establish their legal positions. The January 15 coup had therefore established a legal order in Nigeria under General Ironsi, and this, being the purpose of a government, was the determining factor of its legality.[238] Ironsi was thus heading a second republic with a new Constitution as established by the series of decrees which he promulgated. The question is: could Gowon validly and legally have declared himself Supreme Commander and Head of the National Military Government? If General Ironsi who held these dual functions was dead or missing, is it not naturally and legally to be expected that the next senior officer in the chain of command should assume leadership? The Army, as constituted at the time of Gowon's asumption of office, had at least half-a-dozen officers whose seniority in the Army Command was not in dispute, and who were members of the Supreme Military Council.[239]

Now Lt.-Col. Gowon claimed that there was no change in government but only a change in leadership; leadership had been handed to him by the mandate and sanction of the Supreme Military Council. This could not be true considering that, at the material time, the Supreme Military Council never met. The Eastern Military Governor, Lt.-Col. Ojukwu, for instance, was never in Lagos, where Gowon was supposed to have been given the mandate, nor were the other Military Governors known to have met in Lagos for that purpose. They were all at their stations when Gowon assumed his functions. The argument that these Governors, who with a few other officers constituted the Supreme Military Council gave Gowon his mandate *in abstentia*, is supported by neither precedent nor by the Constitution of the Second Republic. There was no procedure before that time – not even before Aburi[240] – whereby an absentee member of the Council could validly state his own views by comments or by concurrence, without being physically present at its meetings. Previous meetings of the Council clearly vindicate this point. Nor could it be argued that Gowon got a majority of members of the Supreme Military Council to sanction his assumption of office. Not only had the Supreme Military Council never adopted this principle for arriving at its previous decisions, but it was physically impossible for Gowon to obtain such a majority in Lagos, unless the regional Governors assemble there. In the light of the above, Gowon had not been validly appointed.

If, on the other hand, the July event was a coup, and Gowon was thereby the head of a third republic, then since his coup had failed in the East, while he had forcibly established legal order in the North, West, Mid-West and Lagos, his exercise of authority should clearly be restricted to these areas in which he was in effective physical control. A *de facto* situation had been created. For the sake of order and continuity, while the *de jure* authority has lost control – be that loss temporary or permanent – the right of exercise of authority is conceded to the *de facto* authority within the area of its effective physical occupation. This does not mean that the government has been recognised *de jure*. Granted that Gowon's rebellion succeeded in other parts of the former Federation of Nigeria, excepting the East, on what basis could Gowon have made any claim also upon Eastern Nigeria? – and on what basis could he have declared himself Head for the whole country?

Quite apart from logic and the legal aspects, the rebellion of July 29, 1966, can not, by any stretch of liberal judgment, be described as a popular revolt – a revolt supported by the entire or almost the entire mass of Nigerians, including those of all the regions. The revolt of January 15, 1966, had had that character and been sanctioned by the people themselves. It also had a national and ethical purpose. The revolt of July was an extension of the pogrom which started on May 30, 1966, and had had, as one of its aims, the annihilation of Easterners, Eastern officers and men in the Nigerian Army and Eastern civilians. The ultimate aim was the restoration of the dominance and hegemony of the North.

What is being most important is that the revolt of July 29 totally destroyed the discipline of the Nigerian Army. For the Supreme Military Council, or any of its members for that matter, to have sanctioned the leadership of Lt.-Col. Yakubu Gowon meant, to all intents and purposes, writing permanent indiscipline into the future history of the Nigerian Army.

At Aburi, Lt.-Col. Ojukwu stated the case against Gowon in very eloquent terms. Before Aburi Lt.-Col. Gowon, in his telephone talks with Col. Ojukwu, had twice brought up the question of Supreme Command. On those two occasions Ojukwu made his objections quite clear. He 'would not recognise' Gowon but, in the interest of peace, he 'would co-operate' with him.[241] His logic was that headship of the Army should not be conceded to a person purely on the grounds that such a person was at the head of a group of rebel soldiers who had their fingers poised on the trigger. If this was done it would result in a tragic precedent, for any other person tomorrow could take over command precisely on the same ground, and it would not matter to such a person whether he was acceptable to the people or not. Lt.-Col. Ojukwu would furthermore not recognise Gowon as Supreme Commander because the former Supreme Commander was declared missing and nothing had been said about his whereabouts. To underline the validity of this claim, Gowon had appointed Col. Robert Adebayo, an officer senior to himself, as Acting Governor in Western

Nigeria, presumably acting for Lt.-Col. Adekunle Fajuyi, who was also declared missing.

If Gowon was not holding Lagos by sheer force of conquest (for in that case it would not be proper for him to lay claim to the East, which he was *not* holding), and was anxious for order, discipline and hierarchy in the Military Command, what he should have done was to allow the next most senior army officer to General Ironsi to convene a meeting of the Supreme Military Council, which was then the country's highest executive body, to discuss how to get on with the business of government in the absence of the Supreme Commander. If the situation was such that the Council could not meet – this it certainly was – then it could be arranged for personal representatives of members to meet in Lagos with a view, not to taking any major decision, but to recommending how to normalise the situation in the country. The question of leadership could be settled later, while somebody was put in an acting position. Lt.-Col. Gowon adopted none of these procedures. He proclaimed himself Head of Government and Supreme Commander outright, while at the same time maintaining that he had not staged a coup.

In this contradiction lay the problem to which were directed the initial efforts towards a peaceful settlement of what became known as 'Nigerian Crisis 1966'. But the bane of the subsequent break-up of the Nigerian Federation lay not so much in this contradiction as in Lt.-Col. Gowon's addiction for contradictions, and his lack of realism and clear convictions which have made him an easy instrument for other interests.

Meanwhile, the East was hoping that events would force realism on Gowon. For example, it was constantly felt that the contempt with which the average Fulani Emir regarded the Middle-Belters would make the Fulani Emirs unwilling to tolerate the Gowon leadership for long. A conflict was always being expected, and the East in particular hoped very much to be able to exploit this situation in order to effect the freedom of the Middle-Belters. Its propaganda in those initial days was directed to achieving this objective. But foreign diplomats were always at work to smooth over any major difficulties confronting the Northern oligarchs. It was this intervention from foreign diplomats which postponed, if not frustrated, the desire of the

Middle-Belters to free themselves from the Fulani oligarchy. The same intervention was to frustrate subsequent attempts to find a lasting and peaceful solution to the Nigerian Crisis, as later events have shown.

8

EFFORTS TOWARDS SETTLEMENT: I

It is of great importance in a republic not only to guard the
society against the oppression of its rulers, but to guard one
part of the society against the injustices of another part.

The Federalist, No. 51

(i) A CONCERN FOR PEACE

The tragic events of July 29, 1966, jolted the beliefs of many
Nigerians in the future of their country as one nation, and
brought the country to the brink of anarchy. For more than
three days the rebels continued their mass slaughter – and
officers and men of Eastern Nigerian origin were their victims.
They would not agree to a cease-fire unless the Republic of
Nigeria was split into its component parts, and Southerners
resident in the North were repatriated to the South, and
all Northerners resident in the South repatriated to the North.
The whereabouts of the Supreme Commander, Major General
Ironsi, was not disclosed to the people. For many days, there
was no effective Nigerian Government. While the Northern
populace considered the situation proper for merriment and
rejoicing, these events had aroused very strong feelings among
the people of the South, especially the people of the former
Eastern Nigeria, for whom they were a calamity. The situation
was such that unless something was done quickly, the country
might be drawn into a civil war. It was certainly Nigeria's
darkest hour.

In the face of this heightened tension, the Military Governor
of the East, Col. Ojukwu, threw in his weight on the side of
peace and legal order. He was principally concerned with how
to stop the killings and save the Nigerian Federation. Against
the advice and persuasion of officials and friends who were
anxious for his safety, he went to the Eastern broadcasting
studio to appeal for calm, and for the maintenance of law and
order in Eastern Nigeria. After reviewing briefly the wanton

and deliberate massacre effected by Gowon and his men on July 29, he appealed to the people of Eastern Nigeria 'not to give expression to their feelings in any violent form, but to co-operate with the law enforcement authorities in the assurance that [their] rights of self-determination will be guaranteed'.[242] He disclosed the effort he had made so far to get the rebels to stop their mass murder and suggested that, after the killings had been stopped by those who started them, 'the next step would be to open discussions at the appropriate level to allow other sections of the Nigerian people to express their views'[243] as to the future association of Nigeria.[244]

From the foregoing, it was clear that Col. Ojukwu was prepared to 'co-operate', but he would not 'recognise'. He also had justifiable doubts as to whether the people of Nigeria could ever live together as members of the same nation. But, whatever might be the future of the country, things had to be negotiated. A peaceful settlement had to be preferred to intimidation and the use of force for political purposes. And the Eastern leader carried with him the mass of his people who, in spite of their strong feelings against the anarchists from the North, demonstrated their maturity and loyalty to the Governor by heeding his appeal for calm once more.[245] The Easterners restrained themselves from revenge, retaliation or any precipitate action.

One of the results of the July massacre was that the oneness of the Nigerian Army could no longer be maintained. Officers and men in the Army no longer trusted each other. Soldiers had killed their fellow-soldiers with whom, in the past, they had shared the same barracks and eaten together in comradeship. Officers had killed or planned the killing of their brother-officers with whom they had drunk in the same mess. The only path of reason, therefore, lay in a general disengagement of troops. Troops would then return to their particular regions of origin. This point was made quite clear to Gowon by the Eastern Governor, and both of them agreed to the repatriation of all soldiers to their home regions. This decision was later endorsed at the meeting of representatives of Military Governors held in Lagos on August 9, 1966.

The meeting of August 9, 1966, came about as a result of Ojukwu's concern for order and peace. It has to be remembered that, in his first broadcast after the July 29 mutiny, he had condemned the unilateral decisions being taken by the rebels concerning the future of the country, and had suggested that the most appropriate procedure would be 'to open discussions at the appropriate level to allow other sections of the Nigerian people to express their views, as their Northern compatriots have recently done, as to what form of association they desire for themselves. . . .' Gowon was ultimately persuaded to take this approach. He therefore convened a meeting of representatives of the military Governors for August 9, 1966.

The day before the representatives started their meeting in Lagos – on Monday, August 8, 1966 – Lt.-Col. Gowon made a broadcast to the nation. He announced that the Military Governors of the North, East, West and Mid-West had agreed with him that there was an urgent need for discussions at the appropriate level 'to pave the way for the people to express their views as to the form of association they desire for themselves'.[246] He also indicated his intention to modify or nullify, sooner or later, the provisions of any previous decrees which assumed extreme centralisation.[247] Referring to the general lawlessness and insecurity in the country, he promised that he would do everything to stop further bloodshed, so that people could once more enjoy a complete sense of security and freedom in the Republic. It was therefore with high hopes and great expectations that the meeting of personal representatives of the Military Governors began in the Committee Room of the Senate building in Lagos.

The Governors themselves could not attend that meeting personally for obvious reasons. Great tension and general insecurity then prevailed in the country. The Governors therefore had to send representatives. Not that these representatives had a magic formula for safeguarding their own lives, but they would attract less attention than the regional Governors themselves. The Eastern Governor's position was, from all available evidence, especially insecure. Since the coup had been directed against Southerners and since it had been a failure in the East, clearly nowhere in Nigeria was safe for Easterners, as the soldiers of the North were continuing to kill them. It was therefore obvious that the Governor of the East, above all, was a wanted person and had he travelled to Lagos at that time he might well have been eliminated by the Northern soldiers there. That the East still sent its own representatives in this general situation, shows what sacrifices it was prepared to make for the sake of Nigerian unity. The men sent were all of high calibre and standing.

The aim of the meeting of August 9 was to find immediate means of stopping the country's drift towards anarchy and of reducing tension. All the regional representatives to that meeting appeared eager for a lasting solution. Three days before the meeting, on August 6, 1966, and barely one week after Gowon's take-over at the Centre, a conference of Northern emirs and chiefs had been summoned by the Military Governor of the North, Lt.-Col. Hassan Katsina, to advise him on the future of Nigeria. That Conference had sat for three days, ending on August 8 From its recommendations it is clear that proper consideration was given at the meeting, not only to the immediate problems facing the country, but also to the important issue of the future form of association for the country. It recommended, *inter alia*, that Northern delegates to future constitutional talks to be called shortly should ask for a confederation or a loose league of states. This would ensure that in future 'sectional interests [would] not [be] allowed to lead to disastrous results'.[248] From all records available it was also evident that the North was more concerned in those days about the form of association it could negotiate than with restoration of law and order in the country. The same conference of August 6 also recommended that Alhaji Kashim Ibrahim (Adviser to the Northern Military Governor) and the Northern Attorney-General, Alhaji Buba Ardo, should represent the North in any future talks on Nigeria's future. They would be accompanied by the Etsu of Nupe, the Ochi Idoma and the Emir of Yawuri, with two officials, Alhaji Usman Sarki and Ajene Ukpabi, as advisers.

The representatives in Lagos for the other regions were:

For Lagos: Chief Ishola Bajulaiye, the Eletu Odibo; Chief Jas Ogundimu, the Oloto; and Major Mobolaji Johnson, the Military Administrator of Lagos.

For the East: Professor Eni Njoku, Vice-Chancellor, University of Nigeria (later of Biafra), Nsukka; Mr. Christopher Mojekwu (former Attorney-General, Eastern Nigeria,); and Mr. N. U. Akpan, Chief Secretary to the Government of Eastern Nigeria.

For the West: Professor Akin Mobogunje of the University of Ibadan and Dr. Festus A. Ajayi, Solicitor-General, Western Nigeria.

For the Mid-West: Chief T. A. Salubi; Dr. Christopher Okojie and Mr. D. P. Lawani.

Officials from the Central Government in Lagos included Mr. B. O. Kazeem, Solicitor-General of the Republic of Nigeria. The conference of August 9 was opened by Lt.-Col. Gowon. In his address to the representatives he stressed the need for frank and free discussion and, to assure that the deliberations were held in an atmosphere of confidence, the press was barred from the meeting. The leader of the Northern representatives, Alhaji Kashim Ibrahim, was appointed chairman. After two days of meeting, the conference adjourned for a week, but recommended as follows:

(i) Immediate steps should be taken by the Supreme Commander to post military personnel to barracks within their respective regions of origin.

(ii) Having regard to its peculiar position, the question of maintainance of peace and security in Lagos should be left to the Supreme Commander in consultation with the Military Governors.

(iii) A meeting of this Committee or an enlarged body should take place in a week's time to recommend in broad outlines the form of political association which the country should adopt in the future.

(iv) Immediate steps should be taken to nullify or modify any provisions of any decree which assume extreme centralisation.

(v) The Supreme Commander should make conditions suitable for a meeting of the Supreme Military Council urgently as a further means of lowering tension.

Apart from the first recommendation, which was only partly implemented, Lt.-Col. Gowon never implemented any of the other agreements.[249] It was essential that, for internal peace and order to exist once more, trigger-happy soldiers who constituted the rebel gang should be sent into the barracks. Moreover, since the type of confidence essential for comradeship no longer existed in the Nigerian Army, it seemed logical and most proper that soldiers should, for the time being at least, be confined to their regions of origin. The Government of Eastern Nigeria repatriated all the Northern soldiers who were in the East back to the North, as agreed. The Lagos Government failed to reciprocate, but retained some 30 per cent of officers and men of Eastern Nigerian origin in the Nigerian Army as hostages. The soldiers repatriated from the East were even allowed to go with their weapons, and given every decent treatment as a further demonstration by the Government of Eastern Nigeria of its faith in agreements reached and in civilised standards. The Lagos Government on its part dispatched the Eastern soldiers in the North to Eastern Nigeria with no weapons for their self-protection. In fact, they were mocked and molested before they were allowed to embark upon their journey.

All through the period before the final break with Nigeria – before Biafra's declaration of Independence – Gowon was repeatedly reminded to implement the agreements of August 9, even by Yoruba leaders.[250] But he would not keep faith and remained adamant to these demands. Gowon saw rather in the presence of Northern troops in Lagos and Western Nigeria the surest way to maintain his dictatorial hold on these territories. In fact, far from removing the troops, he from time to time dispatched many hundreds more from the North to these places, as if to reinforce the soldiers already there. He was eager to perpetuate the Northern presence, and saw in the massing of Northern troops in Lagos and the West a way both of assuring his own personal security and imposing Northern rule on the people of these areas. Gowon fully realised that the moment the Northern soldiers were removed from the West and Lagos, the people, especially the Westerners, would immediately seize the opportunity to free themselves from the Northern rule.

On the part of Eastern Nigeria, the repatriation of the Northern soldiers (even though the Nigerians would not reciprocate the gesture) would remain the finest diplomatic victory scored since the crisis of July 29, 1966. This repatriation took place, not immediately after July 29, but some weeks later, in

September 1966. Gowon's foreign advisers and collaborato.. could not stop the move before it was too late. Certainly, on the part of Gowon, it was the gravest error; by force of logic – the logic of the situation – it was most proper. With Northern troops at Enugu, perhaps the East could have been intimidated into accepting dictation from the Lagos Government, as was the case in the West and in Lagos, for the Northern soldiers far outnumbered the Eastern soldiers there at the time. The ratio stood at three-to-one in favour of the North. These Northern soldiers obviously collaborated with Gowon and his gang and were certainly hostile to the Eastern Government and people. Perhaps, without their repatriation, Eastern Nigeria could not have succeeded in taking the path of honour by proclaiming, on May 30, 1967, the independent, sovereign Republic of Biafra. To the extent, therefore, that Gowon was prepared to honour the agreements of the August 9, 1966, it was certainly an advantage to Eastern Nigeria, and a lever which facilitated their march to self-determination and progress.

But the above is not to be understood to mean that the Government and people of Eastern Nigeria were all the time looking for a suitable opportunity to take their own separate way. The Eastern Nigerian declaration of Independence was the result of many years of political injustice and oppression, of calculated acts of bad faith and ill-will, and of a well-planned programme of extermination. The removal of the Northern troops could be said, therefore, to have facilitated the just cause of an injured people when all hopes of a negotiated settlement of the crisis had been lost, and when their detractors were still spoiling for further assaults upon their life, honour, liberty and happiness. Perhaps, if Gowon had kept faith, if he had shown remorse for the wrongs done, if he had shown any readiness to abate the atavism and savagery of his troops, the East would not have seceded.

(ii) THE AD HOC CONSTITUTIONAL CONFERENCE:

(a) *Lagos as a Venue?*

Another opportunity to settle the Nigerian crisis by peaceful negotiation presented itself during the Ad Hoc Conference on the Nigerian Constitution which opened in Lagos on September 12, 1966. According to the recommendations of August 9, this Conference was to have been called about August 17, about three weeks earlier. Because of the non-implementation of those recommendations, there was still tension and insecurity throughout the country. Soldiers, rather than being confined to the barracks, were still left at large and thus able to harass and intimidate the civilian population. Easterners in Lagos, the North and the West, both civilians and soldiers alike, were still being massacred in large numbers, with the result that, in an editorial of August 30, 1966, *The Daily Times* of Nigeria called attention to these indiscriminate killings, stating that 'right now, our streets are littered with unburied bodies in their thousands'.[251]

In the same month the Military Governor of the Mid-West, Lt.-Col. David Ejoor, had to complain to Lt.-Col. Gowon about the action of some armed soldiers who swooped on the Benin prison on Tuesday, August 16, 1966, forcibly removing some soldiers believed to have participated in the January 15, 1966, coup, but who were then in protective custody. The armed soldiers were believed to have come from Ibadan, Western Nigeria. This violent challenge to legal order in the Mid-West came about in spite of David Ejoor's pledge of loyalty to the Gowon régime on Wednesday, August 3, 1966.

Lt.-Col. Hassan Katsina, the Military Governor of the North, also bore testimony to the general disorder and lawlessness in the country at that period. Being anxious about the indiscipline among his troops, he had to warn soldiers in Kaduna about continued acts of violence, intimidation and lawlessness. He spoke about the need for discipline and regimentation. Katsina was addressing the Kaduna Army units during an inspection tour of Northern Nigeria. He repeated the same warning at the week-end preceding September 12, 1966 – the day the Ad Hoc Conference was scheduled to begin in Lagos. He spoke about some 'misguided' people 'thinking that only by acts of lawlessness could they achieve their objectives'.[252]

In this kind of situation many people naturally felt themselves insecure, not least the delegates to the Conference. From time to time, in both August and September 1966, administrative directives had to be issued by the Lagos Government to fleeing civil servants and corporation staff who could not return to their posts because of the general situation in the country. For instance, in about mid-August, a circular letter signed on behalf of H. A. Ejueyitchie, the acting Secretary to the Gowon Government, by S. A. Akenzua, was sent to all permanent secretaries and heads of non-ministerial departments, as well as chairmen of statutory corporations and state-owned companies, warning all public servants to return to their posts immediately, or face 'dismissal from the Service without formality'. Yet the Gowon régime could do nothing to assure their safety if they returned. In late September 1966, another ultimatum was issued to fleeing workers, this time to return to their posts by October 15, 1966, or face automatic dismissal.[253] This ultimatum was issued by Lt.-Col. Gowon himself.

The press reacted immediately to this unreasonable call. *The Tribune*, in a front-page editorial on Tuesday, September 27, 1966, pointed out that for the Government to adopt the measure of dismissing workers would be 'very regrettable indeed', since it had failed to give protection to its fleeing workers – a protection they were entitled to, 'whatever their backgrounds and identitities. . . .' It reminded Gowon that 'no sane man, especially one that makes a living from his honest sweat, will wake up one morning and then decide to abandon his work knowing full well the consequences of such an action . . . ' *The West African Pilot*, writing in the same vein and on the same date, in an editorial titled 'Nigeria's Nightmare', stated that the talks going on in Lagos 'should act as a palliative'. Instead, 'in the midst of the talks there has been mounting tension'. *The Daily Times*, writing on September 28, 1966, pointed out that as 'the accepted leaders of the people resume their important talks on the future of the country in Lagos today, millions of the people they represent and speak for are living in a state of tension. They have genuine fears that their lives are in danger.' It went on:

> There are many mad and lunatic-fringe men roaming about today, acting on their own, without any authority or instruction from either the army authorities or any civil organisation.[254]

Even the Northern Nigerian Government-sponsored daily, *The New Nigerian*, under the headline: 'At stake – the Future of the North', appealed to its violent, trigger-happy countrymen to end their violence, since the North would suffer for it.[255] Essential services could not be maintained because of the exodus of fleeing workers from the North. It is hard to see how Gowon expected the fleeing workers to come back in this kind of situation. It would be all well and good if they decided to go back, 'but sending them back', according to *The Nigerian Outlook* (an Eastern Nigerian Government newspaper), 'is like asking them to go to their graves without as much as a protest'.[256] All these comments go to show the general state of tension and insecurity before and throughout the duration of the Ad Hoc Constitutional Conference. If Gowon had confined soldiers to the barracks, as was agreed in the meeting of August 9, this kind of situation would not, perhaps, have arisen, and tension could have been greatly reduced.

According to the recommendation of August 9, which spoke about leaving the question of maintenance of peace and security in Lagos to 'the Supreme Commander in consultation with the Military Governors' – a recommendation that was spearheaded by the Eastern representatives at that meeting, it was envisaged that security in Lagos should be handled by the police, since then soldiers would be in their barracks. The recommendation that a meeting should be convened a week after August 9 arose from an anxiety to effect a speedy settlement of the Nigerian crisis before further troubles could develop. But Lagos would not act quickly, and the killings continued. The delay became so irritating to responsible opinion within and outside the country that *The Daily Times*, in an editorial on August 30, 1966, called on the Lagos Government to delay no longer in convening a meeting to discuss the future of Nigeria. It pointed out that tribal war was still going on and that the killings had continued.[257] It called on the National Military Government to 'act swiftly' and get the people's representatives together to talk things over in Lagos, for 'speed is vital in these days of tension'.[258]

It was this general state of affairs, including the Lagos attitude to the situation, which compelled the Eastern Consultative Assembly, when it met at Enugu between August 30 and September 2, 1966, to express doubts about the wisdom of sending any delegation from Eastern Nigeria to Lagos. They in fact passed a resolution, which read as follows, that:

It was agreed that while Eastern Nigeria is willing and anxious to attend the Constitutional Conference and present her case, an atmosphere conducive to safety and the absence of molestation is a *sine qua non*. This atmosphere does not exist at present anywhere in Nigeria and the Assembly therefore suggests that some neutral ground be insisted upon, for example, the OAU Headquarters at Addis Ababa.[259]

The fear was in fact amply borne out by events in Lagos and other places. Apart from the fact that Easterners continued to be targets for mass killings, there were two bomb explosions in Lagos on the day preceding the September 12 meeting, i.e. on Sunday, September 11, 1966, in the early morning, one at the Federal Palace Hotel (where the delegates must have been expected to lodge during the duration of the Conference), the other at No. 6, Okotie-Eboh Street, Ikoyi, Lagos.

Nevertheless, out of his belief in the oneness of Nigeria and his faith in the durability and sanctity of a negotiated settlement, the Military Governor of the East, Lt.-Col. C. Odumegwu Ojukwu, summoned on September 9, 1966, thirteen delegates who would represent Eastern Nigeria at the Lagos Conference. These delegates had great misgivings about their personal safety and did not disguise their feelings. But the Governor did everything humanly possible to guarantee it. He received personal assurances from Lt.-Col. Gowon that the delegates would be safe in Lagos. He even insisted on and obtained, apart from the telephone assurances, a coded message from Lt.-Col. Gowon, accepting personal responsibility for the safety and free conduct of the Eastern delegates, and this was followed by a guarantee in writing, under Gowon's personal signature, giving his word of faith and honour, as a soldier, that nothing would happen to the delegates. After the bomb blasts which took place in Lagos, the Eastern Governor renewed his plea for assurances about the safety of the Eastern delegation. Gowon readily gave them. As a further precautionary measure for assuring their safety, the names of the Eastern delegation were not disclosed or made public until the delegates had arrived in Lagos.

To reassure the people of former Eastern Nigeria who had spoken out against sending delegates to Lagos, and who had

G

urged that the meeting be held elsewhere since the Northern troops were still in Lagos, the Eastern Governor made a broadcast to the nation in the early morning of September 12, 1966, just before the Eastern delegation left Enugu, assuring Easterners that he had done everything he could to assure their safety, pointing out the urgent need for 'finding solutions to the unfortunate problems which now beset a country we have all come to love so much – problems which have in recent months, and more so in recent weeks, assumed disastrous and bloody proportions'.[260]

The Eastern party left for Lagos in a special flight on September 12. The party arrived in Lagos late[261] and were met in conditions of heavy security, mounted by the Nigerian police. The delegates were first taken to the National Hall and later to the *Eastern Flats*, where they stayed throughout the duration of the Conference. This house, a two-storey building overlooking the Lagos lagoon, was barricaded and also guarded by the Nigerian police during their stay there. Other delegations arrived earlier than September 12.

The full lists of all the regional and Lagos delegations were:

For the North: Alhaji Kashim Ibrahim, Adviser to the Northern Governor (leader), Alhaji Buba Ardo (Solicitor-General, Northern Nigeria), Alhaji Usman Sarki. With them were Ochi Udoma, the Etsu of Nupe and J. S. Tarka.

For the East: Professor Eni Njoku (leader), C. C. Mojekwu, E. B. Ndem (lecturer in anthropology, University of Nigeria), Chief Allagoa, the Amanyanagbo of Nembe. M. T. Mbu joined the team two days later, having travelled from London. There were seven alternative delegates: Chief Douglas Jaja, the Amanyanagbo of Opobo, A. E. Bassey, Professor Anthony N. A. Modebe, Dr. Kalu Ezera, Miss Mary Ededem, John Odey and I. Kogbara.

For the West: Chief Obafemi Awolowo (leader),[262] Professor Hezekiah Oluwasanmi (Vice-Chancellor, University of Ife), Chief Olu Akinfosile (a former Federal minister under Abubakar régime). They were accompanied by three advisers: Oba Samuel Akinsanya, Odemo of Ishara, Prince Alade Lamuye, and Dr. Festus A. Ajayi (Solicitor-General, Western Nigeria).

For the Mid-West: Chief Anthony Enahoro (leader), Chief J. I. G. Onyia and Dr. Mudiaga Odje. Advisers were S. O. Ighodaro, Rufus Ogbobino and Dr. T. M. Yesufu.
For Lagos: Lateef Jakande (leader) and Dr. Tesilimi O. Elias (former Federal Attorney-General). Their advisers were Femi Okunnu and the Eletu Odibo, Chief Ishola Bajulaiye.

The nation had waited for the starting of the Conference with high hopes and justifiable anxiety. The various regions had had ample time during the long intervening period between August 9 and September 12 to prepare themselves adequately for a full discussion on the Nigerian problems, to hold full consultations with their own people and to get the necessary briefings on what line to take at the Conference. An official announcement that the Ad Hoc Conference on the future of Nigeria would begin at the National Hall, Lagos, on Monday, September 12, 1966, was made in Lagos on Wednesday, September 7, 1966, almost a week before the actual meetings. The main purpose of the Conference was disclosed. Nobody, therefore, could claim to have been taken by surprise. The announcement stated, *inter alia*, that 'the main task of the Conference will be . . . to make recommendations as to the type of constitution which will satisfy the aspirations of the various ethnic and linguistic groups'[263] in Nigeria.

On the part of the Eastern delegation, there was a firm resolve to put a halt to the recent disastrous trend of events in Nigeria by finding a lasting and realistic solution to the problems besetting the country. In the words of the Eastern Governor, in an address to the people of Eastern Nigeria on the morning of September 12, 1966:

At this Conference our delegates will put forward plans to ensure equality and fair play for all citizens of this country; to minimise friction in appointments and in the distribution of national amenities; to eliminate the possibility of any region controlling the central authorities to the detriment of other regions and for ever remove the possibility of any one region holding the others to ransom; to ensure maximum protection for the citizen outside his region of origin; to ensure the orderly development of each region at its own pace; and to generate mutual confidence and responsibility between the various regions of this country.[264]

These were the problems of Nigeria in perspective. Everything which had led to friction in the past, all the causes of the recent bloody events, would have to be courageously and frankly discussed. Their mandate, according to the opinions and views expressed by the generality of the people of Eastern Nigeria and as resolved by the Consultative Assembly, were summarised in the following six broad principles:

(i) To acknowledge that the country is on the brink of anarchy and everything must be done to ensure the security of life and property.

(ii) The fact of very deep-rooted differences in religion, culture, attitude, outlook and rate of development existing in the country should be recognised and accepted.

(iii) The necessity of allowing each region to develop in its own way and at its own pace should also be recognised and accepted.

(iv) Since the control of the Centre has been the ever-living main source of friction and tension between the different regions, thereby threatening national solidarity and integrity, the distribution of functions between the regions and the Centre should be reviewed and so arranged that only such subjects and functions as will engender the minimum of suspicion and friction among different groups are allowed in the hands of the Federal Government.

(v) The composition of the organs of the Federal Government should be so arranged as to give no one region an advantage over another.

(vi) The subject of representation and the method of selecting such representatives should be carefully gone into. We would like to see the practice of a Federal General Election abandoned.[265]

(ii) (b) *Proposals of the Various Delegations: Form of Association*

The most realistic and sincere approach to the Nigerian problem demanded the adoption of these principles. These principles were based on the belief of the people of Eastern Nigeria that the rest of Nigeria was eager for lasting and practicable solutions to the problems of Nigeria. Gowon's address to the opening session of the Conference also indicated hopes along this line, and appeared to have been guided by the same principles. In an address to the delegates on the afternoon of September 12, 1966, opening the Conference, he told them that they might later be called upon to consider such matters as:

   (i) the distribution of powers as between the Regional Governments and the Central Government;
  (ii) the territorial divisions of the country; and
 (iii) the system for selecting representatives to the legislature.[266]

This would depend on the form of government the delegates chose for the country. Gowon limited the scope of the Conference by ruling out either break-up of the country or a unitary form of Government, but he allowed the delegates to choose one among the following three systems of government for the country.

   (i) a Federation with a strong Centre or a Federation with a weak Centre;
  (ii) a Confederation;[267] or
 (iii) an entirely new arrangement which would be peculiar to Nigeria and not yet found in any political dictionary.

After Gowon had addressed the Conference and left, Sir Kashim Ibrahim, leader of the Northern delegation, was elected chairman of the Ad Hoc Conference. A Steering Committee made up of the leaders of the various regional delegations prepared an agenda. It contained two items which were expressed as follows:

   (i) consideration in broad outlines of the form of association suitable for Nigeria in the future; and
  (ii) interim arrangements.

It then appeared that the work of the Conference would proceed without difficulties and that delegates were in a frame of mind to co-operate and seek honest solutions to Nigeria's problems.

On Tuesday, September 13, 1966, the second day of the Conference, the meeting began at 10 a.m. The Northern delegation circulated its memorandum with a brief introduction of the points it contained. It made it quite clear that a new form of association was what Nigeria needed, not federalism, since the passion generated within the last six years between the peoples of Nigeria had greatly weakened 'the base of our association'. Noting that Nigerian leaders had in the past 'pretended for too long that there are no differences between the peoples of this country', it emphasised that the peoples of Nigeria 'are different peoples brought together by recent accidents of history'. It therefore recommended that each of the existing four regions of Nigeria 'should be constituted into an autonomous state', as each Region in the past had managed to preserve some measure of order and a sense of unity within its confines. It advocated that the component states should have a kind of Common Services Organisation, similar to the East African Common Services Organisation, in which the component states would be able to co-operate on economic matters without political unity. Subjects or groups of subjects which were of common interest should be delegated to a Common Services Commission. According to the delegation:

> The leaders of such a country must be ever prepared to grope for new ways of association, while to preserve the aspirations of the individual groups will, at the same time, preserve some forms of association which will bring about co-operation in fields which are of mutual interest to all the groups without bringing the component groups into direct physical or economic conflict.[268]

According to it, the Federal system which carried us to independence proved a disaster.[269] On the other hand, a unitary system was tried for the administrative convenience of the colonial masters.[270]

Explaining the working of this new type of association, it stated that 'any member state of the Union should reserve the right to *secede* completely and unilaterally from the Union. . . .'[271] It recommended that each state should have its own Army, Air Force, Police, Civil Service and Judiciary; but there should be a Navy composed of personnel from all the

States in proportion to the population of each state.[272] The Common Services should include, among others, money matters, communications, telecommunications and postal services, citizenship, immigration and emigration, weights and measures, customs and excise, foreign affairs and foreign trade.[273]

It will be seen from the foregoing that Northern Nigeria was eager to sever all its links with the rest of the country. The introduction accompanying its recommendation implied to all intents and purposes, that the North no longer wanted to 'pretend' or 'assume' anything. The Nigerian leaders had pretended very much in the past that the base for unity was there.

After the North had introduced its paper, the Western and Mid-Western delegations proposed that the Conference should adjourn, to meet again on Thursday, September 15, 1966. The Conference had sat that day for less than an hour. Their reason for asking for adjournment was to allow the other delegations time to produce their own memoranda. But it should be constantly borne in mind that the various regions had had sufficient notice of the meeting of September 12. All responsible views agree that that meeting had been long overdue. It was expected, therefore that, when the Conference finally started, delegates would have been ready and prepared to act with a sense of urgency, for delay meant further troubles for the country. It was on this ground, therefore, that the Eastern delegation objected to the adjournment and insisted that, before the Conference adjourned, all the other regional delegations should at least make a general statement showing the approach they intended to adopt on the Thursday. Such statements could later be supported with more detailed memoranda.

The Eastern delegation was in a hurry to get down to business, because it was convinced that, unless decisions could be reached quickly, the country might experience further bloodshed. It therefore, proceeded to outline briefly its general position[274] on the vexed question of Association. It stated that, in spite of all that had happened in the country in recent months, the component parts of Nigeria could still associate politically. But this association must be based on the lessons of the past. Areas which had caused conflict, rivalry and bitterness in the past between the various governments should be carefully looked into with a view to removing or minimising such possibilities. Much would depend on the way power was shared between the central and regional governments. It suggested that more powers should go to the Regions in order to make the Centre less attractive, as the struggle for power in the Centre would remain a potential cause of conflict.

After the Eastern delegation had briefly explained its position, it expected the other delegations to do the same. But they still maintained that the Conference should adjourn. Since nothing was forthcoming from them, the Conference adjourned after sitting for about one hour and thirty minutes, to resume again on Thursday, September 15.

On the resumption of the Conference on Thursday, the remaining delegations – the East, the West, the Mid-West and Lagos, in that order – presented their memoranda. It became apparent that, apart from the Mid-Western delegation, all the other delegations wanted a loose form of association of states in which the Centre would be weak.[275] Apart from the Mid-West again and Lagos, all the other regional delegations sanctioned the right of the associated units in the Federation to secede unilaterally. On the question of Armed Forces and Police, the East, West and Lagos wanted Central Army, Police, Air Force and Navy. The North recommended that each state should have its own Army, Air Force and Police, while the Navy should be centralised.[276] And apart from the Mid-West, which reserved its position on the whole matter, the other delegations wanted some form of central defence arrangement to be organised, in the Eastern viewpoint, as occasion might demand, for defence against external aggression. On financial arrangements, the North, East, West and Lagos agreed that revenue should be allocated on the principle of derivation. The Mid-West reserved its position.

(ii) (c) *Proposals of the Various Delegations: Creation of states*

On the question of the creation of more states, only the Mid-West wanted immediate action on the matter by the setting up of an expert commission to study and report on the creation of states. In fact, the matter came up on Friday, September 16,

1966, when it was made a subject of debate by the Mid-Western delegation. The stand of the West and Lagos was that, in the event of Nigeria remaining a Federation, there should be an immediate creation of more states including the creation of Lagos State. In the alternative of establishing a Commonwealth of States, creation of states was still envisaged. The Eastern position was that, as much as each state should have the right of self-determination, the question of creation of more states should be subject to referendum and, since this would lead to all sorts of delays, and therefore also delay the determination of the future of Nigeria, the matter should be left for the mean time until more urgent issues were settled.

The question of the creation of more states came about as a result of a conspiracy between the Northern and Mid-Western delegations to break the Eastern solidarity and postpone the urgent issues of the time. If the matter had not been handled very carefully, it would have frustrated the work of the Conference. In fact, the September Conference shows not only how progress was hampered by the way fundamental and secondary issues jostled one another, but also the haggling, lobbying and filibustering that attended the work of delegates.

Right from the start of the Conference, some political adventurers and men with vested interests from minority areas of the country saw the opportunity to carve out new areas of influence for themselves, instead of directing their minds to the more urgent matters of the time. They lobbied the delegates for support, and even presented memoranda to the Conference. There were several groups of lobbyists for separate states. Three such groups were asking for the re-grouping of the Yorubas of the Ilorin and Kabba Divisions of Northern Nigeria with Western Nigeria. They also wanted Calabar and the Rivers areas of Eastern Nigeria to be made into a separate state. One of the groups was demanding a Middle-Belt State and the creation of three other states in the North: North-Western State; Northern State; and Bornu State. This same group called also for the creation of two states in the East: Eastern and Southern States. They also wanted the West to be split into two – Western State; and Lagos and Colony State.

There was nothing wrong in calling for the creation of more states in the country, but this could not be one of the ways of

G*

easing the tensions of that time. First things should be considered first. Secondly, most of the people who lobbied the delegates for the creation of more states never got the mandate of their people, but acted purely on their own and from selfish motives. Nor could it be said that they agreed among themselves. In fact, on a number of occasions, they quarrelled among themselves on the question of what areas should come within a particular state, or what people should be grouped within a particular area. It is hardly reasonable to expect a nation, in tension and despair, to wait while these differences were ironed out. But these lobbyists were able to secure the ready assistance of the Mid-West, egged on by the North, and the Mid-Western delegation could not be persuaded to restrain its enthusiasm and accept the logic of the situation, until the Ika Ibos of the Mid-West also called for their own separate state.

The explosive nature of the state issue necessitated a public statement from both the Northern and Eastern delegations during the week-end. On Friday night, both Alhaji Ibrahim and Dr. Eni Njoku, leaders of the Northern and Eastern delegations respectively, issued their first public statement on the matter. The two statements were incorporated in a communiqué issued at the end of a meeting of the heads of delegations to the Conference. Sir Kashim Ibrahim, stating the Northern stand, was quoted as saying that the Northern view on the question of creation of states had been subject to misrepresentation and distortions in the Nigerian press. The North denied that it was opposed to creation of states. The statement went on:

> By way of amplification, I should like to point out most emphatically that the Northern delegation stands in favour of creation of more states anywhere in Nigeria, *if the majority of the people directly concerned express such a wish*.[277]

Dr. Eni Njoku, expressing the Eastern viewpoint, stated:

> The Eastern delegation does not believe that the splitting up of the country into more states at this stage is what we need in order to normalise conditions of life in this country and provide a sense of security for its inhabitants.[278]

The East pointed out that as the country was in the grip of fear, suspicion and mistrust, only an immediate constitutional arrangement made on the basis of the existing regions could save the country:

> To split the country into more states now will involve a long-drawn out process of inquiries, commissions and plebiscites, taking up many months or even years, which we cannot afford under the present crisis.[279]

It therefore suggested that creation of new states should be the 'internal responsibility of the Region' and that 'the initiative for the creation must come from the Region in which the state is to be created'.

This position must be considered the most realistic. A state does not come into existence by a *fait accompli*. As the Northern statement admits, the issue must be sanctioned by the 'majority of the people concerned'. This necessarily involves holding a plebiscite or a referendum. Consulting the people themselves is most important. An article in *Nigerian Opinion*, discussing the 'Real Issues at the Lagos Conference', emphasised the same point by stating that:

> *First*, new regions should be created *only when* the wishes of the people have been fully assertained.[280]

To do otherwise, using the language of Mr. Matthew Mbu,[281] commenting on the Lagos programme for creation of states, would be comparable to the Queen of Hearts in *Alice in Wonderland* who said: 'Verdict first, evidence afterwards.'[282]

There were also such questions as delimitation of boundaries, surveying the areas, and other related issues such as settlement of titles to land. To have attempted to create states under the condition of the time would have been like going rat-hunting while the homes were burning. All that was of concern to the Lagos Government was how to break the Eastern solidarity.

The Eastern Military Government had all along showed itself aware of the delicate issue of minorities and was eager to build a society free of minority fears and in which there would be justice for all. Some people are inclined to the view that in all political societies there must be a political minority. But that could be no argument for hoping that the solution would lie in the creation of new states. Here, the conclusions and recommendations[283] of the Henry Willink Minority Commis-

, appointed by the Colonial Office in 1958, to enquire into the fears of minorities and the means of allaying them, become relevant. The Minority Commission stated that it did not feel persuaded to agree that the creation of more states would solve minority problems in the then Nigeria, even though some of those who appeared before it had argued in favour of this exercise.[284] It stated that 'on its own merits – a separate state would not provide a remedy for the fears expressed. . . .'[285] It also expressed the view that in considering the problem, it was 'impressed by the fact that it is seldom possible to draw a clear boundary which does not create a fresh minority. . . .'[286]

Because of issues of secondary importance, like that of creating states, that were introduced during the first week of the Ad Hoc Conference by some delegates, not much progress was made. In fact, after five days of meeting, all that was achieved was the presentation of memoranda by the various delegations. There had not even been discussion of these documents. Chief Awolowo, in the course of the Conference, stated that 'some people want a more prolonged approach to the work of the Conference', and accordingly, 'it has now transpired that we have not made much progress after five days of meeting. . . .'[287] The North in particular appeared to be in no hurry to get down to business, and had started to reflect upon its memorandum introduced earlier. In spite of the strong statement of Chief Awolowo, the Western delegation lent itself to the delaying manoeuvre of the North by supporting immediate discussion of the state question. The Eastern delegation maintained all through that speed was essential, and repeatedly expressed concern about the general situation in the country.

(ii) (d) *Conflict on the Constitution*

On the afternoon of Tuesday, September 20, 1966, the Ad Hoc Conference reassembled, to be faced with a volte-face by the North. The main question was what kind of political association Nigeria should have. There could not have been much difficulty in finding this out, as in the previous week delegations had submitted their memoranda stating their views on this subject. It was naturally expected that discussions would start on these memoranda. It was with surprise, therefore, that the Eastern delegation received an announcement by the

Northern delegation, when the Conference resumed, that it was going to introduce another memorandum. The North now asked for a Federation with a strong Centre, for immediate agreement on the thorny question of creation of more states, and for the removal of secession from any future Constitution. The other delegations behaved as if they had expected, and in fact encouraged, this reversion of stand by immediately associating themselves with the views of the Northern delegation. The Eastern delegation, however, stated that it would maintain its former stand until the Northern delegation could explain in greater detail what it meant by 'effective central government'. If it turned out that the North meant a different thing from a loose form of association, the East would not agree to it, as such a stand was unwise under the circumstances of the time. The Northern delegation agreed to supply more details on their new stand in another memorandum. The Conference, therefore, had to adjourn in order to allow it to do this and to submit its new proposals for study.

The Northern *volte-face* was influenced by a number of factors. First, during the previous week, diplomatic and sectional pressures had been piling up against the Northern stand. With Gowon at the centre, the Middle Belt appeared to be in a powerful position to control not only the North as a whole, but also the Central Government. Since, in such a position, it would not be controlled by the Fulani oligarchy in the North, under whom it had suffered oppression in the past, there was no point in again seeking for an independent Middle-Belt State. It considered, therefore, using its new position of influence at the Centre to effect the creation of a Middle-Belt within a Nigerian Federation with a strong Centre in which it would retain control. This was the best advice it could get from foreign advisers in Nigeria, who wanted to keep Nigeria together at all cost because of their vested interests. Secession would by implication be ruled out. This new stand spearheaded by the Middle-Belt inevitably caused some upheaval within the Northern delegation, as there was a powerful body of opinion in the North which was still insisting on a loose form of association in which the associating states would have the right of secession. As a result of the new development, some members of the Northern delegation flew to Kaduna for consultation during the week-end preceding the resumption of the Conference on Tuesday, September 20. The matter was of such a serious nature that the Military Governor of the North, Lt.-Col. Hassan Usman Katsina, flew to Lagos on Monday, September 19, to consult with Lt.-Col. Gowon. Gowon and his men were in the stronger position, and the decisions finally reached had to be in support of creation of more states and of a strong Central Government with no right of secession to the component states.

The second factor influencing the change of policy consisted in the people and institutions with vested interests who had started speaking out against a loose form of association. Here we have to note particularly the role of *The Daily Times* of Nigeria, one of the country's national dailies of which Cecil King,[288] a Briton, was Chairman.

As far back as August 25, 1966, in a front-page editorial captioned 'Whither Nigeria?', *The Daily Times* expressed its opposition to Confederation in very strong terms. This editorial was prompted by the conclusions reached by the Conference of Northern Leaders of Thought, which ended its meeting in Kaduna, Northern Nigeria, on August 8, 1966. They mandated their delegation to the future constitutional talks to ask for a Confederation or a loose league of states – exactly what *The Daily Times* did not want. On September 14, 1966, when the first plenary session of the Nigerian leaders' summit on the future of the country was just producing its agenda, *The Daily Times*, as if to forestall or prejudice the work of the Conference, and in spite of its self-righteous disavowal of any such intention, published an editorial entitled 'We Say No to Confederalism', in which it stated that it wanted *only Federalism for Nigeria*.[289] On Saturday, September 17, 1966, it addressed another editorial to the '14 Wise Men' holding constitutional discussions in Lagos to the same effect. *The Daily Times*, as an institution and as a business concern, was only too anxious to see that its financial interest was not jeopardised in the possible break-up of the Nigerian Federation. It saw in Confederalism the surest road to the disintegration of Nigeria. It considered that only a united Nigeria would assure it the largest sale with the minimum of difficulties.

But what exactly the North meant by an 'effective Central Government' did not become clear until the Conference resumed on the afternoon of Wednesday, September 21, 1966, when they circulated their new memorandum. The apparent agreement between the new Northern stand and the attitudes of other delegations other than the East was found to be unreal. There was in fact, no unanimity, nor much common ground for discussion. In the first instance, an attempt was made by the other delegations, except the East, to define their stand in terms of known political terms. They said they wanted a federal form of Government. The Eastern delegation, however, maintained that a mere political label would not do. What mattered was the exact content of delegations' memoranda in respect of items allocated to the central and regional governments. It suggested, therefore, that the Exclusive Legislative List should be examined in the light of the memoranda submitted by the various delegations with a view to knowing what items should remain with the Centre.

Following this suggestion, the Conference went through the subjects in the Exclusive Legislative List of the 1963 Republican Constitution. Delegations were asked to indicate that they did not wish a particular subject to remain in the List by saying 'No'. At the end of this exercise it was found that all the other delegations, in fact, indicated about the same number of 'Noes' as the Eastern delegation, and it was clear that any central government left with only the items left to it in the Federal List by the Conference could not be described as a strong or, to use the language of the Northern delegation, an 'effective' Central Government. In fact, only about nine subjects were left on the Exclusive Legislative List, and they were mostly subjects of secondary importance. They included such subjects as trade marks, weights and measures, patents, copyright and accounts of the Federal Government. A sub-committee consisting of two members from each delegation was set up to study the views of the delegations on the various subjects, with a view to reporting, when the Conference reassembled, the areas of agreement and difference. Another week was nearly over, and the Conference adjourned till the Wednesday of the following week, in order to await the report of the sub-committee.

In the meantime, the terms of reference of the sub-committee were extended to include all matters in the Concurrent Legislative List, the structure of the Central Government and the question of creation of states. A number of financial matters such as bills of exchange and promissory notes, borrowing of moneys both within and outside Nigeria, capital issues, currency, coinage, legal tender and exchange control, were refered to the financial experts for consideration and advice, with a view to enabling each Region to borrow abroad, to issue its own promissory notes, and to play an effective part in determining the monetary policy of the whole country.[290] These experts, drawn from all the Regions, and including representatives of the Federal Government and Central Bank officials, were to report to the sub-committee well before the resumption of the Ad Hoc Conference on Wednesday, September 28. When the Conference resumed on that date, the sub-committee was ready with a comprehensive report showing areas of agreement and disagreement. The report was adopted.

At this stage, the only logical thing to do was to adjourn the Conference so that the various delegations could go back to consult with their governments. The Conference was on the point of doing this when Lt.-Col. Gowon sent a message expressing disapproval of the idea and demanding that the leaders of the various delegations should see him on the next day, Thursday, September 29. When they did see him, he insisted that the Conference should continue until October 1, because, according to him, there were rumours that the East would secede on that date. He was adamant to the assurances of leaders of the delegations that the adjournment that had been proposed the previous day was necessitated by the fact that the Conference could make no further progress until the various delegations had consulted with their governments. The other leaders of the delegations stated further that they were prepared to continue the Conference until October 3, 1966, in view of the fears of secession expressed by Lt.-Col. Gowon. The leader of the Eastern delegation protested on the ground that the Eastern delegation was scheduled to report to the Eastern Consultative Assembly on Friday, September 30. Moreover, the Conference had lasted for a long time, leading to the extended stay of the Eastern delegation in Lagos. In spite of these reasons, it was decided that the Conference should go on until Monday, October 3.

But on that same September 29, 1966, when Lt.-Col. Gowon was holding a meeting with the delegation leaders, a fresh wave of violence started in Northern Nigeria and Lagos, claiming thousands of Eastern lives and lasting several days. This was the third phase of the pogrom[291] and the only conclusions that could be reached was that the Northern soldiers had realised that secession could no longer be conceded to the North by the Ad Hoc Conference, and that they embarked upon the mass killing of Easterners in Northern Nigeria in order to remind the Conference that the idea of one Nigeria was unrealisable. They wanted to intimidate the delegates into reconsidering their present stand. It was in this kind of tension and terror that the Ad Hoc Conference wrote up an interim report at Gowon's insistence. Gowon wanted to announce progress to the nation. This report was submitted to him on September 30, 1966[292] – before the Conference adjourned on October 3. The other delegations wanted to publicise a similar report in the press, but the Eastern delegation objected to this on the ground that it had not yet reported to its principals, being mere delegates, not plenipotentiaries. Its decisions needed ratification. Secondly, to publish the report meant that those at home would be told the decisions reached before their delegates could come home and report to them. Again, this protest was not heeded and the interim report was published in the Nigerian press in part, but as a Federal Government statement.

(ii) (e) *The Interim Report*

The interim report reveals major areas of agreement and disagreement between the Regions. It also reveals interesting alignments. Fourteen items were unanimously accepted to remain in the Exclusive Legislative List:

   (i) Accounts of the Government of the Federation and officers, courts and authorities thereof, including audit of those accounts (Item 1, Exclusive Legislative List);
  (ii) Archives, other than the public records of the Governments of the Regions since the twenty-third day of January, 1952 (Item 2, Exclusive Legislative List);
 (iii) Copyright (Item 8, Exclusive Legislative List);

   (iv) Deportation of aliens (Item 12, Exclusive Legislative List);

   (v) Extradition (Item 16, Exclusive Legislative List);

   (vi) Legal proceedings between the Government of the Federation and any other person or authority or between the Governments of Regions (Item 21, Exclusive Legislative List);

  (vii) Patents, trade marks, designs and merchandise marks (Item 30, Exclusive Legislative List);

 (viii) Pensions, gratuities and other like benefits payable out of the Consolidated Revenue Fund or any other public fund of the Federation (Item 31, Exclusive Legislative List);

  (ix) Powers, privileges and immunities of each House of Parliament and its members (Item 33, Exclusive Legislative List);

   (x) Public Relations of the Federation (Item 35, Exclusive Legislative List);

  (xi) Tribunals of inquiry with respect to all or any of the matters in the Exclusive Legislative List (Item 39, Exclusive Legislative List);

  (xii) Water from such sources as may be declared by Parliament to be sources affecting more than one territory (Item 41, Exclusive Legislative List);

 (xiii) Weights and Measures (Item 42, Exclusive Legislative List);

 (xiv) Matters incidental or supplemental to the above (Item 45, Legislative List).

It is clear from the above list that the areas of agreements were not many, and that the subjects actually left with the Central Authority were not controversial and were not of major importance, nor were they such as could make for 'an effective Central Government' or a Federal Government with a 'strong Centre'. Yet the Federal Government press conference aimed at making the Nigerian people believe that the Ad Hoc Constitutional Conference recommended 'an effective Central Government' for Nigeria by stating with gusto that fourteen items were agreed. These items were not listed. In fact, the powers of the Central Government were greatly reduced, while the Regions gained substantially more powers.

Nine further items were left in the Exclusive List, with provisos
which had the effect of permitting the regions to operate in
these areas or altogether safeguarding Regional interests. The
items in question are:

(i) Aviation (Item 3, Exclusive Legislative List);
(ii) Immigration, including visas (Items 18 and 29, Exclusive Legislative List);
(iii) Nuclear energy (Item 28, Exclusive Legislative List);
(iv) Emigration (Items 18 and 29, Exclusive Legislative List);
(v) Posts, telegraphs and telephones, including Post Office
savings banks (Item 32, Exclusive Legislative List);
(vi) Railways, including ancillary transport and other services (Item 37, Exclusive Legislative List);
(vii) Federal highways (Item 40, Exclusive Legislative List);
(viii) External Affairs (Item 15, Exclusive Legislative List);
(ix) Meteorology (Item 24, Exclusive Legislative List).

Even though it was agreed that external affairs and meteorology should remain in the Exclusive Legislative List, there was
no unanimous agreement reached with regard to the Federal
position in these matters. In external affairs, the West and Mid-
West and Lagos proposed that it should remain on the Exclusive List. The East proposed it should remain in the Exclusive
List, subject to the following four conditions:

(i) Appointments to foreign missions and appointments
within their establishments should be on a quota system
based on equality of representation among the Regions,
as had been suggested by the East, and the Mid-West
Delegations in the case of item 36: 'Public Service of the
Federation'.
(ii) All diplomatic and consular posts in the United Nations
Organisation, the Organisation of African Unity, and in
foreign and Commonwealth countries, should be held
in rotation for fixed periods, as stated below, by suitable
indigenes of the member Regions of Nigeria:

Head of Mission   2 years
Head of Chancery ⎫
Counsellor   ⎬ 3 years
Heads of Division ⎭
Other Staff   4 years

(iii) The following Missions – namely London, Washington, United Nations, New York, Bonn, Paris, Brussels, Rome and Moscow – should not be headed at the same time by more than two indigenes of any one Region, and any Region that had within the preceding twelve months had one of its indigenes as Head of Mission to one of these countries should not immediately be allowed to have another representative from such a Region to head such a Mission.

(iv) The Regions should have power to enter into treaties and agreements with foreign powers in the interest of trade and commercial development of the Region; any Region that so desired might appoint a commercial attaché or counsellor to a Nigerian mission abroad.

The North accepted the second and third provisos; the Mid-West reserved its position on proviso 1 and the first sentence of proviso 4. On meteorology, there was a proviso that the Government of a Region should have power to establish and maintain its own meteorological service. The North reserved its position in respect of this proviso.

The reports dealt in some detail with the all-important question of the Armed Forces and the Police in any future Constitution. Interestingly, there was a lot of agreement here. All the delegations agreed that the Army, the Navy, the Air-Force and the Police should be regionalised, though with some form of central control. There would be a Defence Council, charged with operational control of the regional units during certain emergencies, such as external aggression. This Defence Council would consist of the Head of State, the Heads of Regional Governments, the Chief of Staff, Regional Commanders, and the Minister of Defence. For the Police, the position was similar, but with minor variations. The powers of the Regional Commanders would cover training, ordnance depots, army stores and operational control. The Regional Commander would be responsible for securing public safety and public order within the Region and could be given directions by a Security Committee in that Region, of which both the Governor of the Region and the Commissioner of Police, among others, would be members. It was also clearly stated that regional armies would be established which would be composed entirely of personnel indigenous to each Region. It is difficult to understand on what basis anyone could still have described a Central Government with no Army of its own, strictly speaking, as a 'strong Central Government'. With the regionalisation of the Army, the weakness of the Central Authority became apparent and the growth of regional power more obvious. It did not matter what label this form of government might finally be given.

There are other items on the Exclusive List like mines and minerals – including oilfields, oil boring, geological surveys and natural gas, which require brief mention because of the Northern attitude. As for these items, only the North insisted that they should be left in the Exclusive Legislative List. It should also be recalled that, in its first memorandum to the Ad Hoc Conference, the North accepted that revenue derived from these resources and other resources of the Federation should be allocated on the principle of derivation. In its second memorandum, reversing its original stand, it would appear that the North wanted only revenue from oil and minerals to be federally controlled, and other revenues to be on the basis of derivation. It is this kind of selfishness and greed which made the work of the Ad Hoc Conference difficult, and finally led to Gowon's dismissal of the Ad Hoc Conference itself, for unless what the North wanted was conceded to it, decisions reached were as good as no decisions at all. The Conference could reach no agreement on the question of revenue allocation, and the matter was deferred until future meetings.

The greatest divergences appear in respect of the structure of Government at the Centre, and often the North and the East were at opposite poles on this issue. This deals with the three arms of the Central Government – the Legislature, the Executive and the Judiciary. Details of the answers given to the above questions were contained in the memoranda submitted by the various delegations.

On the thorny question of the creation of new states, two questions were asked. One was whether more states should be created in the country, to which the North, West, Mid-West and Lagos answered 'Yes'. There was also a question whether a plebiscite should be held to determine the wishes of the people in each proposed state. The position of the East had been made quite clear during the constitutional talks.[293] When it appeared that the first statement of the East on the question was being misinterpreted as meaning that the East was opposed to the creation of more states, the Eastern delegation was constrained to make a second statement on the issue in which it stated that the East was 'not opposed to creation of states.' It further stated:

> Indeed, we are pleased to hear that the North has now agreed to the creation of states because the size of the North was one of the weaknesses of the First Republic. It is therefore a great gain for Nigeria that the North has now agreed to the creation of more states.[294]

(iii) A 'NATIONAL' CONSTITUENT ASSEMBLY?

The Ad Hoc Conference finally adjourned on Monday, October 3, 1966, for three weeks, in order to enable delegates to report back and have consultations in the Regions and Lagos on the progress so far made. The various delegations would also attempt, during this interval, to get briefings on the other aspects of the new Constitution which, so far, had not been considered.

The All Nigeria Constitutional Conference had been designed to work out a framework for Nigeria's future. In a sense, it could be regarded as a drafting body: there was no draft constitution by experts presented to it for ratification; but it was free to seek a new basis of association – to draft a new Constitution for Nigeria, based on the realities of Nigeria's past and present experiences. Even though its three weeks of meeting had been chequered, it was still generally hoped that out of its discussions and decisions would emerge a reconstructed and regenerated Nigeria. But the intentions in Lagos were not yet clear. Nor could one determine in the light of the talks so far the real desires of the inscrutable North.

For the new wave of murderous activities which the North unleashed, even while the Conference was going on in Lagos, and on the eve of Nigeria's sixth independence anniversary, Lt.-Col. Ojukwu, the Eastern Governor, had to warn, in a Republic Day Broadcast over the network of the Eastern Nigeria Broadcasting Service, that 'no settlement will be acceptable to the East without stoppage of these atrocious inhuman acts. . . .'[295] But he also expressed hope that in spite of all, and given goodwill, objectivity and a sense of realism, it would still be possible to salvage Nigeria from the present shambles. In spite of extreme provocation, untold humiliations and personal losses, the Government of Eastern Nigeria was still keenly interested in the search for a solution to the Nigerian crisis.

The next stage of discussions was due on October 24, 1966, but it did not take place. The Eastern delegation could not come to Lagos for the Conference because of the continued massacre of Eastern Nigerians in Lagos, Western Nigeria and the North. Efforts were made to find an alternative venue to Lagos because of the insistence of the East that Lagos was unsafe, and that Lagos could only be accepted as a venue if the Northern troops were removed from there and the West. These efforts were insincere in that no attempt was made to deal with the root-cause of the situation in Lagos. At a stage, the Mid-West was suggested as a venue, but the East again refused to go there, on the grounds that that Region was easily accessible to the Northern troops from Western Nigeria.

Gowon's idea was that an immediate return of Northern troops from Lagos and the West to the North would leave the Federal capital and the West with virtually no troops at all, as there were not enough Westerners in the Nigerian Army. But most of the troubles in these areas – the West and Lagos – were the work of Northern troops. If they left there would be less trouble and violence; the police alone would be enough to keep peace and order in these areas. There could never have been a reliable guarantee that the Northern troops would not misbehave if the delegates assembled again for a resumed Conference. For the East, either Lagos and the West would have to be cleared of Northern troops to make it possible for the Conference to resume in Lagos, or, as an alternative, the Conference could be held outside Nigeria – in Addis Ababa, Liberia or Switzerland.[296]

On November 17, Lt.-Col. Gowon postponed the talks 'indefinitely', having come to a decision that the Ad Hoc Conference offered no hope of a way out of Nigeria's constitutional impasse. In a broadcast on November 30 he announced that he would set up a representative Constituent Assembly to work out a constitution for a stable federation. The Constituent Assembly would be preceded by a constitutional committee of experts to work out a draft constitution which would be presented to the Assembly for ratification. Yet, Lt.-Col. Gowon disavowed any intention to impose a constitution on the country. Not only was this action unilateral and sudden, but he took pains to state what structure of Government at the Centre he wanted for Nigeria. Confederation was ruled out for, according to him, it would be unworkable and would deepen the present conflict in Nigeria. He said that Nigeria should be divided into no fewer than eight states, and no more than fourteen states. Lt.-Col. Gowon for the first time indicated that he would not hesitate to use force to impose his ideas on the Nigerian people in the name of preserving the Nigerian Federation. He said:

I have always preferred peaceful solutions to our problems ... but if circumstances compel me to preserve the integrity of Nigeria by force, I shall do my duty to my country.

Boastfully he continued:

It is easy enough for me to mobilise enough forces to deal with any dissident or disloyal group.

Still on his draft constitution for Nigeria, Lt.-Col. Gowon announced that detailed machinery for selecting delegates to the Assembly, which would consist of at least one person from each of the existing administrative divisions,[297] as well as representatives of special interests such as trade unions, professional associations, chambers of commerce, industry, and women's organisations. Civilians 'who are known to believe strongly in the continued existence of Nigeria as a federation' would be appointed into the Federal Executive Council to help the Federal Military Government carry through its programmes.

Gowon's unilateral dismissal of the Ad Hoc Conference and the broadcast of November 30, 1966, require a number of comments. *First*, the Ad Hoc Constitutional Conference was almost reaching decisions on a number of issues when Gowon dismissed it. From this dismissal can be deduced that the Conference was not arriving at the kind of decisions favoured by Lt.-Col. Gowon. In fact, the Ad Hoc Conference was moving towards

Confederation or a loose form of association. In the broadcast
of November 30, Gowon immediately seized the opportunity
to state his disapproval of having a confederal system of
government. Even though on September 12, when he opened
the Ad Hoc Conference in Lagos, Gowon left the delegations
free to consider a confederacy, he was, from this point on, no
longer prepared to have confederalism discussed in any constitutional talks. In the future, he was going to take no chances
at all. He therefore decided not only to present a draft constitution embodying his wishes to a future constitutional body,
but to set up a Constituent Assembly, whose members would
owe their appointment to him. In this way it would be possible
to pack the Assembly with men agreeable to his views, and who
would have a sense of obligation to the appointing power.
Gowon's wishes were to have a strong Central Government,
to carve out a state for his people – the Middle-Belt State – and
to increase his personal power, if possible through the constitutional machinery. Paradoxically, it was Ironsi's attempt to do
the first which had led the Northerners to kill him. The second
objective was borne out in the twelve states created by Lt.-Col.
Gowon without consulting the peoples and Governments of
Nigeria and the third was already on the way to being achieved,
as Gowon gradually but firmly installed himself as a dictator.

Secondly, even if the Constituent Assembly were not obliged
to accept Gowon's own views, the mere fact that a draft
constitution would be presented to it would leave it with little
discretion. The members, being personally selected by Gowon,
would certainly try to act in his favour by ratifying the draft
constitution, or try to wear the garb of objectivity by modifying
only the non-fundamental issues in the draft presented to them.
It must be remembered that even the Ad Hoc Conference had
not been able to agree on a number of issues, because of very
deep divergencies between the views of regional delegations on
these issues. Could the draft by the experts have attempted or
been able to reconcile these divergencies?

Thirdly, the Constituent Assembly was not only going to be
composed of people personally picked by Gowon himself, but
was going to be made up of at least 100 persons, unlike the Ad
Hoc Conference, which was a small body of fourteen men, carefully chosen from all the regions and Lagos by their govern-

ments. It was also going to include representatives of non-political bodies like the trade unions, women's organisations, and so on, as already mentioned. This large aggregation of people was perhaps expected to debate the delicate constitutional problems of the time and arrive at a generally acceptable compromise. The venue for their meeting was expected to be Lagos. At the time their meeting was being planned, the East was already protesting about having Lagos as the venue because of their fear of molestation by Northern troops. If the small Eastern delegation would not come to Lagos because of the situation there, was it reasonable to expect that a larger delegation would agree to go to Lagos? And if Gowon would not remove his troops from the West and Lagos, was he sincere in his eagerness to have the East represented in a future talk on Nigeria's future, or to hold the Conference at all? Perhaps he was looking for a pretext to justify his gradual but sure assumption of the role of a dictator in Nigeria's politics and government. It is perhaps only in this role that he could have the supreme capacity to impose his wishes on the peoples of Nigeria. The East, from this stage, became seriously concerned about their fate and began to question critically Gowon's sincerity on the question of Nigerian unity. Gowon's actions meant dictatorship, and the East was not prepared to play with dictators.

The question of having Lagos as the venue was no longer one that the East would be prepared to dally with, as the price would certainly be paid in blood. The only other thing to be done in order to save Nigeria was to seek a neutral and friendly ground where the problems of Nigeria could be discussed in an atmosphere of freedom, devoid of fear, intimidation and blackmail. Such an opportunity came a few months later in the Aburi summit meeting of Nigeria's military leaders, and after it was seen by Lagos that the solution to the crisis did not lie in the setting up of a Constituent Assembly.

9

EFFORTS TOWARDS SETTLEMENT II: THE ABURI ACCORD

> To negotiate with forces that are hostile on matters of prin-
> ciple means to sacrifice principle itself. Principle is in-
> divisible. It is either wholly kept or wholly sacrificed. The
> slightest concession on matters of principle infers the
> abandonment of principle.
>
> WILHELM LIEBKNECHT

(i) MEETING OF THE SUPREME MILITARY COUNCIL

(a) *Search for a venue*

With Gowon's dismissal of the Ad Hoc Constitutional Conference and assumption of dictatorial powers, the hope of
settling Nigeria's crisis by non-violent and constitutional
method became very slim. The situation was worsening every
day, with nobody able to arrest the trend towards greater disaster. The drift to anarchy had started once more. Even well-
meaning Nigerians began to despair of the peace prospects for
the country. In Eastern Nigeria in particular, there developed a
strong sentiment for separate existence as the only way of
assuring the survival and honourable existence of Eastern
Nigerians in the face of Gowon's dictatorship and the general
hardship, humiliation and brutality brought upon them by
their fellow countrymen. This sentiment was reaching a level
of revolutionary explosiveness where even the popular Government of the Region was finding it difficult to restrain the people
in their increasing resolve to lead a separate life and to avenge
the wrongs done to them.

The massacre of thousands of Easterners resident in the
North, Lagos and the West had increased not only bitterness
but many other problems as well. Between May and December
1966, in a massacre that took three main phases, at least 30,000

Easterners lost their lives, and more than 50,000 others were wounded, maimed or disfigured. The general sense of insecurity among Easterners led to an enormous population shift in which about two million Easterners left other parts of the Nigerian Federation to return to their homeland in the East. This brought about a refugee problem. There was hardly a family in Eastern Nigeria that was not bereaved of parents, children, relations or at least confronted with the problem of refugees. Thus in the East, about the end of 1966, there was a great deal of bitterness in men's hearts and a diminishing hope about the continued existence of the Nigerian Federation.

However, just before Christmas, Nigerians witnessed a dramatic and surprising move to save Nigeria; but it was also a desperate move. The four civilian advisers to the four regional Governors – Alhaji Kashim Ibrahim (North), Dr. Francis Ibiam (East), Chief Odeleye Fadahunsi (West), and Chief Jeretin Mariere (Mid-West) – met in Lagos to consult on the situation with Lt.-Col. Gowon. After a five-hour meeting with him, they issued a communiqué stating that they had agreed that a meeting of the Supreme Military Council was urgent and necessary if the impasse was going to be resolved. This meeting had failed to take place since July 29, when Gowon came to power, because the venue of the meeting had been such that, for reasons of security, all the regional Governors could not attend. The regional advisers, therefore, proposed that such a meeting should be held in Benin, not in Lagos, Benin being considered the safest place for such a parley.

The regional advisers also made recommendations on other aspects of the crisis. They recommended that troops should be repatriated to their regions of origin, as had been agreed at the meeting of representatives of Military Governors held on August 9, 1966; that the security of Lagos should be left to Lt.-Col. Gowon; and that the proposed Benin meeting should discuss the reorganisation of the Army. Also attending the Lagos meeting were Commodore J. E. A. Wey, Head of the Navy; Major Mobolaji Johnson, Military Administrator of Lagos; Mr. Omo-Bare, Deputy Inspector-General of Police; and a number of other officials.

The meeting of these civilian advisers and officials ultimately yielded nothing to the country by way of resolving the crisis.

According to its communiqué, the meeting was said to have been very frank – held 'in a most pleasant atmosphere'. Yet at the end of its deliberations, and in spite of its recommendations, the country remained without a new formula for peace.

The Christmas and New Year of 1966–7 passed in a cold and unpleasant atmosphere of hatred, distrust and bitterness. The Christmas message or broadcast to the nation by the Eastern Governor dwelled in many places on this tragedy and the gloom that had struck the nation. According to him, 'unhappiness and gloom' had descended 'upon practically every home in Eastern Nigeria'. 'In the national context', he went on, 'age-long confidence and ties have been broken, confidence has been undermined and in some cases destroyed and fear is invading every mind and human motion.'[298] It was the Governor's belief that Nigeria had reached this stage because men had preached without practising the message and significance of Christmas.

All along, however, the Government of Eastern Nigeria had adhered consistently to the principle that it was essential to settle the Nigerian crisis by peaceful negotiations. It was convinced that, with every day that passed, events were taking a more dangerous turn, and very quickly they could reach a point of complete and irreparable disaster. It constantly expressed the need to convoke a meeting of the Supreme Military Council, as the highest executive authority in the country, to tackle the urgent problems confronting the country. It maintained all through that unless Northern soldiers were removed from the West and Lagos and repatriated to their region of origin, such a meeting could not be held in Nigeria. The East would not attend a meeting in any area or in the vicinity of any area occupied by Northern troops. The Eastern Government put forward a number of alternative venues for the meeting, notably Addis Ababa, Liberia or Switzerland. Lagos, feeling that this suggestion detracted from Nigeria's sovereignty, would not listen, and in fact maintained that the meeting must be held in Nigeria, even without the removal of Northern soldiers. A point of complete stalemate was therefore reached.

Thus it was a matter of great surprise to the nation to be informed, with the dawn of the new year, that their military leaders had eventually agreed to meet outside Nigeria. The meeting was kept top secret. The Nigerian military leaders

were, in fact, already at Peduase Lodge, Aburi, Ghana, where
the meeting was held, on January 4, 1967, before the generality
of Nigerian people knew what was happening. To Easterners
in particular, most of whom heard the news for the first time
from the BBC, and who had all along opposed any move by
their Governor to meet other Nigerian military leaders outside
the East except on neutral ground, the news was received with
disbelief and astonishment. Some other Easterners, who had
become convinced that nothing constructive and rewarding
would come out of such a meeting, could neither understand
the wisdom of the Governor in attending nor appreciate why he
should on this occasion act contrary to the expressed fear and
anxiety of his people. Ojukwu's safety was their paramount
consideration.

The Governor was, however, determined, even at the risk of
his own life, to make another great move to save his country
and prevent bloodshed and anarchy. In his own explanation[299]
of why he went to Aburi, the Eastern Governor had this to say:

I did so, firstly, because after the events of July 29, 1966,
there was no single authority in Nigeria which could command the allegiance and obedience of the entire peoples of
Nigeria, or give protection to their lives and property. It
became imperative, therefore, to re-create the Supreme
Military Council in such a manner as to re-establish its
authority and ensure its impartiality in matters affecting
Nigeria as a whole, thus removing the possibility of the central authority being solely controlled either by a Northerner,
an Easterner, a Westerner or a Mid-Westerner. Secondly, in
order to preserve the integrity of the country, a solution must
be found to the question of national leadership and chain of
command within the Armed Forces. The Aburi meeting was
intended to provide and did provide a working basis for
solving the problem. Thirdly, it was necessary to arrest the
drift in the country and to control the situation, so as to
enable constitutional arrangements to be made in an atmosphere devoid of fear, tension and suspicion. I did not go to
Aburi as an Easterner, I went there as a Nigerian seeking a
satisfactory solution to a Nigerian problem. I did not go to
Aburi to seek powers for myself, nor did I go there for a

picnic. I went there to work in order to save this country from disintegration.

Nigerians in general received the news with mixed feelings, in some cases with supressed enthusiasm. The nation waited for the outcome of the talks.

(i) (b) *The Aburi Meeting*

From the actual discussions at Aburi, one gets the impression that the military leaders felt a sense of remorse for the way they had acted in the past, dissipating their energies on things that did not really matter, engaging in the same pettiness and hypocrisy of which the former civilian leaders had been accused, and totally forsaking military honour and principles to become easy prey to the selfish manipulations of the very politicians from whom power had been wrested in the quest for a better life for all. They came, therefore, with an attitude of objectivity, sincerity and realism, to engage in an exercise which almost amounted to drawing up a new constitution for the country. The basis of their exercise lies in the supreme position and authority of the Supreme Military Council as the country's highest executive authority. It was indeed a unique opportunity to save Nigeria.

The Aburi meeting lasted two days – January 4 and 5: but they were two days in which vital and far-reaching decisions were taken, and many issues that had caused concern in the past were cleared up. They included the following: reorganisation, administration and control of the Army; preparation of statistics of existing Army strength; return of Army personnel of Northern Nigerian origin to the North; recruitment and training of soldiers of Western Nigerian origin; announcement of the death of Major-General J. T. U. Aguiyi-Ironsi and Lt.-Col. Adekunle Fajuyi; re-definition of the powers of the Federal and Regional Governments; repeal of Decrees tending towards over-centralisation; functions of the Supreme Military Council; appointments to diplomatic and similar posts; the Federal Civil Service, Armed Forces and Police; rehabilitation of displaced persons and recovery of their properties.[300]

During the deliberations there were serious, tense moments as well as moments of laughter and cheers, and altogether the atmosphere could not have been more cordial and friendly. In attendance were Lt.-Col. Yakubu Gowon; Col. Robert A. Adebayo, Military Governor of Western Nigeria; Lt.-Col. C. Odumegwu-Ojukwu, Military Governor of Eastern Nigeria; Lt.-Col. David Ejoor, Military Governor of Mid-Western Nigeria; Lt.-Col. Hassan Usman Katsina, Military Governor of Northern Nigeria; Commodore J. E. A. Wey, Head of the Nigerian Navy; Major Mobolaji Johnson, Military Administrator of Lagos; Alhaji Kam Salem, Inspector-General of Police; and T. Omo-Bare, Deputy Inspector-General of Police. It was an impressive gathering of Nigeria's military leaders.[301]

Opening the meeting, Lt.-Gen. Joseph A. Ankrah, Chairman of Ghana's National Liberation Council and Head of the Government of Ghana, who played host to the Nigerian dignitaries, appealed to them to be sincere in searching for a solution to the Nigerian crisis. He reminded them that 'through the annals of history we have not seen failures with military statesmen'[302] and, according to him, 'when military personnel do take over the reins of Government they have proved their worth . . . Soldiers are always statesmen'.[304]

The meeting that followed this address was regarded as a 'round-table' discussion in which, according to Ankrah, there was no 'head' or 'tail'.[305] The military leaders had agreed on an agenda before the Aburi summit. The meeting would try to:

(i)   resolve the question of leadership within the Army, restore the chain of command which had become badly disrupted, and examine the crisis of confidence amongst the officers and soldiers which had rendered it impossible for them to intermingle;

(ii) evolve ways and means of carrying on the responsibility of administering the country until a new Constitution had been determined; and

(iii) tackle realistically, the problems of displaced persons.[306]

These were embodied in the agenda of the Aburi meeting.[307]

On the first day of the meeting, and before any discussions on the agenda could be gone into, the Military Governor of the East, Lt.-Col. Ojukwu, with a sense of the dramatic, put forward a resolution calling on the military leaders to 'renounce the use of force as a means of settling the present crisis in

Nigeria . . .', and to reaffirm their faith 'in discussions and negotiations as the only peaceful way of resolving the Nigerian crisis'. The military leaders were to hold themselves 'in honour bound by this declaration'. This resolution was adopted by the military leaders and was later embodied in the communiqué[308] issued by the Council at the end of its first day of meeting. Nigerians heaved a sigh of relief that, after all, the crisis in their country might be settled by peaceful negotiations.

Ojukwu proposed this resolution out of a genuine desire to lessen the tension in the country and effect a speedy return to peace and mutual confidence. Before Aburi, Lagos had accused the East of planning secession and of trafficking in arms. The East, in return, had accused Lagos of preparing for war against her, and of an arms build-up. At Aburi, Col. Ojukwu repeated this accusation, producing one of the most dramatic moments of the discussions. He mentioned the 'Apollo arms deal' with Italy in which a number of individuals, with documents from Lagos, were involved. Gowon admitted that there was such a transaction, but stated that there was no 'back-handed business', as the purchase, according to him, was intended 'for the whole army'. He qualified his statement, however, by saying that everybody would have shared in the purchase 'if the situation [had been] absolutely normal'. The point was that the situation was far from being normal.

Ojukwu was strongly of the view that Gowon's arms deals were not intended to benefit the units of the Nigerian Army in Eastern Nigeria. It was his hope that this question of purchasing arms should be settled first, otherwise, if the military leaders failed to reach immediate agreement on the matter, the Aburi meetings might be used by some people as a cover for an arms build-up in the country. As would be seen in the discussions, the other military Governors also got interested in the whole question of sharing and keeping every region fully aware of the current arms position. The Governors were also interested in strengthening their respective regions.

(i) (c) *The Aburi Decisions*

Having regard to the great fear and suspicion which led to accusations and counter-accusations of an arms build-up in

H

different parts of the country, the military leaders were greatly relieved by the joint declaration renouncing the use of force as a means of settling the crisis and affirming their faith in peaceful settlements through discussions and negotiations. Thereupon they went straight to the agenda, discussing the items frankly, expressing and accommodating free and personal opinions, tackling the problems and taking unanimous decisions magnanimously. Thus, by the end of the two-day meeting, they had reached agreements on all the items in the agenda.

The following are decisions unanimously reached:

(i) A Military Committee comprising representatives of the Regions should meet to take statistics of arms and ammunition in the country. Unallocated stores of arms and ammunition held in the country should be shared equitably between the various commands in the Federation.

(ii) The Army should be reorganised in order to restore discipline and confidence. Specifically,

   a. the Army should be governed by the Supreme Military Council which would be chaired by a Commander-in-Chief of the Armed Forces and Head of the Federal Military Government;

   b. Area Commands under Area Commanders and corresponding to existing Regions should be created;

   c. during the period of the Military Government, Military Governors should have control over Area Commands, for internal security;

   d. a military headquarters, comprising equal representation from the regions and headed by a Chief of Staff, should be established;

   e. a Lagos Garrison, including Ikeja Barracks, should be created.

(iii) In accordance with the decision of August 9, 1966, Army personnel of Northern Nigerian origin should return to the North from the West. In order to meet the security needs of the West, a crash programme of recruitment and training was necessary but the details should be examined after the Military Committee had finished their work.

(iv) The Supreme Military Council should deal with all matters of policy including promotion to top executive posts in the Armed Forces and the Police.

(v) The Legislative and Executive authority of the Federal Military Government should be vested in the Supreme Military Council, to which any decision affecting the whole country should be referred for determination, provided that, where a meeting was not possible, such a matter must be referred to the Military Governors for their comments and concurrence.

(vi) Appointments to the Diplomatic and Consular posts as well as to superscale posts in the Federal Public Service and equivalent posts in the Federal Corporations must be approved by the Supreme Military Council.

(vii) With a view to promoting mutual confidence, all decrees or provisions of decrees passed since January 15, 1966, which detracted from the previous powers and positions of the Regional Governments should be repealed. Law Officers of the Federation should meet in Benin on January 14, 1967, and list all the Decrees or provisions of Decrees concerned, so that they may be repealed not later than January 21, 1967, if possible.

(viii) A meeting of Permanent Secretaries of the Ministries of Finance of all the governments in the Federation should be convened within two weeks to consider ways and means of resolving the serious problems posed by displaced persons all over the country.

(ix) Displaced civil servants and corporation staff (including daily-paid employees) should continue to be paid their full salaries until March 31, 1967, provided they have not secured alternative employment. The Military Governors of the East, West and Mid-West should send representatives (Police Commissioners) to meet and discuss the problems of recovery of property left behind by displaced persons.

(x) The Ad Hoc Constitutional Committee should resume sitting as soon as practicable, and the question of accepting the unanimous recommendations of September 1966 should be considered at a later meeting of the Supreme Military Council.

(xi) For at least the next six months there should be purely a Military Government having nothing to do with politicians.

(xii) The deceased military leaders should be accorded full Military Honours due to them.

(xiii) All Government information media should be restrained from making inflammatory statements and causing embarrassment to various Governments in the Federation.

(xiv) Lt.-Col. Ojukwu should keep his order, that non-Easterners should leave the Eastern Region, under constant review with a view to its being lifted as soon as practicable.

(xv) The next meeting of the Supreme Military Council should be within Nigeria at a venue to be mutually agreed.

The Aburi meeting was marked by a sincerity and realism which had been conspicuously absent in the history of Nigerian politics. The tape-recorded version of the meeting revealed a readiness to recognise and accept the stark realities of a country which had already been torn asunder by hate and rancour. It revealed in the live voices of the members of the Supreme Military Council a frank desire to make the best of an already bad situation. It revealed a complete absence of hypocrisy, a realisation of the facts of the day, and an acceptance of the tragic circumstances of a tottering nation. It expressed a hope in the possibilities of salvaging the country from destruction by a practical approach – an approach which recognised as a precondition for solving the nation's problems the restoration of trust and confidence among the disaffected people of Nigeria. These are what became known as the *Spirit of Aburi*. It is a spirit of peace and brotherhood, a social strategy aimed at staying the hands of mischief and anarchy, a preference for peaceful discussions and negotiations to war-cries of subjugation and domination. The spirit of Aburi lacked pretensions. Suspicion, fear and distrust for years harassed independent

Nigeria, and this distressed 'colossus of Africa' had become known as 'big-for-nothing Nigeria'; this 'bastion of democracy' had experienced repeated events which gave the white races of the world strong reasons seriously to doubt the ability of the black African to rule himself. The spirit of Aburi was a sincere attempt to eradicate once and for all this destructive virus.

The Aburi decisions provided Nigeria with a positive and practical framework for survival. There is no doubt that, if the military leaders had kept the terms of these agreements, Nigeria would have taken a step, nay a big leap, towards her sure survival. But, alas, the Aburi agreements were not given a trial.

It has been stated that the Nigerian military leaders were already in Peduase Lodge, Aburi, Ghana, before the astonished Nigerian populace had any hint of the meeting. In Eastern Nigeria, however, the news was not very well received. Why should their Military Governor risk leaving their Region in spite of their express objections? In trying to answer this question, they were gripped with one fear: that Lt.-Col. Ojukwu might have gone the way of others before him. Had he compromised his convictions and his people's wishes at last 'in the interest of national unity'? It was to allay these fears that, at about 2.15 p.m. on January 6, he addressed a crowded press conference at Enugu in which he tried to explain the Aburi agreement to the people of Eastern Nigeria. He stated that he had

> hurried to make this statement to you because of the misgivings which I understand are prevalent in this Region as a result of this meeting.[309]

According to the Aburi decisions, all decrees or provisions of decrees passed since January 15, 1966, which detracted from the previous powers and positions of the Regional Governments were to be repealed not later than January 21, 1967. When January 21 arrived, however, these decrees were not repealed. Instead, on January 26, Lt.-Col. Gowon called a press conference in Lagos in which he repudiated Aburi and contradicted Lt.-Col. Ojukwu's version.[310] From these contradictions, it now became obvious that the mysterious spirit of

Aburi, which had promised a restoration of peace and normalcy, was not real.

It will be helpful at this point to attempt to compare and contrast the salient points in the addresses of the two military leaders in order to appreciate their areas of divergence.

(i) *Reorganisation of the Army*

LT.-COL. OJUKWU	LT.-COL. GOWON
(a) Army to be governed by the Supreme Military Council.	One Army under a unified command, but the Army and Air Force Councils and the Navy board to continue to function 'as at present'.
(b) Council to be chaired by a Commander-in-Chief.	(Not mentioned, but [c] below implies continuation of the post of Supreme Commander.)
(c) Military Headquarters of equal regional representation headed by a Chief of Staff.	Military Headquarters (composition not mentioned) 'directly under me as the Supreme Commander'.
(d) Area Commands under Area Commanders and corresponding to existing regions.	Area Commands under Area Commanders who will take instructions from Military Headquarters (See [c] above).
(e) No mention, but preponderance of indigenes of an area in the corresponding Area Command is implied by the very factors that necessitate the establishment of area commands.	Preponderance of indigenes of an area in the corresponding Area Command, but 'we definitely decided against Regional armies'.
(f) There will be a Lagos Garrison including Ikeja.	(No mention.)
(g) For duration of Military Government, Military Governors to have control of Area Commands for matters of internal security.	Military Governors can use Area Commands for internal security but with express permission of Head of Federal Military Government.

(ii) *Powers and Functions of Supreme Military Council*

(a) All matters of policy, including appointments and promotions of persons in executive posts in	Matters of policy in Armed Forces and Police vested in the SMC, but Army, Air Force, Police Councils,

the Armed Forces and the Police, to be dealt with by the Supreme Military Council.

and Navy Board to continue 'as at present'.

(b) Decisions affecting the whole country to be determined by the Supreme Military Council. Comments and concurrence of Military Governors required where a meeting is not possible.

(No express mention.)

(c) Supreme Military Council, Federal Executive Council, Regional Executive Council to remain.

(No express mention, but same is implied.)

(d) Appointments to:
    (1) Diplomatic and Consular Posts,
    (2) Senior Posts in the Armed Forces and Police,
    (3) Superscale Federal Civil Service and Federal Corporation Posts to be approved by Supreme Military Council.

Top posts, such as Permanent Secretaries and Ambassadors, to be approved by Supreme Military Council. Federal Public Service Commission and Police Service Commission to remain.

(iii) *Displaced Persons*

Salaries of displaced persons to be paid in full until March 31, 1967.

Salaries of displaced persons to be paid up to March 31, 1967, but each case to be considered on its merit. Financial difficulties of corporations to be appreciated.

(iv) *Type of Association*

Politically, Regions to move slightly apart for safety of the nation. Decrees or parts of them which detracted from the previous powers of the Regions to be abrogated.

If allowed to fall apart, the country will disintegrate. 'We have agreed to return to the status quo ante January 17, 1966'. Decrees or parts of Decrees which tended towards over-centralisation to be repealed.

It is clear from the above that the basic difference between the two interpretations of the Aburi Agreements is the question of the kind of political association between the component parts of the country; while Ojukwu interprets the Agreements to mean a confederation, Gowon insisted on an 'effective Central authority'.

If it is realised that up till this time the public were still ignorant of the real Aburi decisions, their utter confusion and disappointment at this point can be appreciated. So the question now arose: What was really agreed upon at Aburi? One thing was only too obvious: the belatedness of Lt.-Col. Gowon's statement on Aburi was irresistibly suggestive that probably he had succumbed to pressures, apparently adverse to the Aburi Accord.

This probability became a certainty when it was learnt that on January 20, 1967 (a day before the implementation of the Aburi Agreement was to commence), a meeting of Federal Permanent Secretaries made certain recommendations[311] to the Federal Government which, to all intents and purposes, constituted a complete repudiation of the Aburi Agreements. The similarity in phraseology and reasoning between the text of these recommendations and Gowon's speech is significant.

One distressing fact was manifested by this revelation. Lt.-Col. Gowon gave his interpretation of Aburi, not because he was convinced that this was what the decisions really meant. Rather, it was *in spite of* the knowledge that it was *not* what the decisions meant. Therefore, it was a deliberate attempt to renounce decisions unanimously reached. This is further supported by the fact that there was no implementation even of what might be considered as minor decisions. The Finance Committee had not met; the Military Committee did meet, but disagreed and broke up. Salaries of displaced persons remained unpaid. Giving the reason for the 'not-so-fast progress in the implementation' of the Aburi Agreement, a Federal Government statement explained that 'the speed with which these matters are handled must of necessity be dictated by administrative and other circumstances of the country, some of which were unforeseen at the time the decisions were taken'. This escalated the tension and suspicion which the implementation of the Aburi Agreement was supposed to allay.

Subsequent to Gowon's press conference on January 26, 1967, the Federal Military Government circulated to the Regions a draft decree which by-passed all the major decisions taken at Aburi.

(i) It retained the title of 'Supreme Commander' as against the Aburi decision to alter it to Commander-in-Chief.

(ii) It retained the title 'President' instead of 'Chairman of the Supreme Military Council', as agreed at Aburi.

(iii) It enlarged the membership of the Supreme Military Council, to include 'Head of the Nigerian Army', Chief of Staff of the Armed Forces and 'Chief of staff of the Nigerian Army'. Aburi only agreed on a Chief of Staff at the Military Headquarters.

(iv) It vested executive and legislative power either in the Federal Military Government or in the Federal Executive Council. This was contrary to the Aburi decision that the legislative and executive powers of the Federal Military Government should be vested in the Supreme Military Council.

(v) It ignored the Aburi agreement that appointments and promotions to top executive posts in the Armed Forces, Police, Federal Public Service and Corporations must be approved by the Supreme Military Council.

(vi) It restored sections 70, 71 and 86 of the first Republican Constitution without restoring the safeguards provided in that Constitution. Thus, contrary to the Aburi agreement, it gives Gowon the power to declare a state of emergency anywhere in the country.

Consequently, this draft was rejected by the Military Governors. A second draft decree was prepared and circulated by the Lagos Government. This also fell short of the Aburi decisions.

(i) Whereas the Aburi agreement required the concurrence of the Military Governors on *all* matters affecting the whole country, this draft limited the requirement of concurrence to a few specific cases.

(ii) Whereas the Aburi agreement conferred the power of appointment of and removal of Judges of the Lagos High Court and of Justices of the Supreme Court of Nigeria, on the Supreme Military Council, this draft vested it in the Head of the Federal Military Government, thus depriving the Council of its legitimate right as the sovereign authority.

(iii) The Aburi agreement was that only those provisions

H*

of decrees which detracted from the powers of the
Regions

    iv. This draft restored the suspended provisions of
the First Republican Constitution which did not affect
the powers of the Regions.

This second draft decree was, of course, not acceptable to the
East.

Contrary to the Aburi decisions, troops of Northern origin
were still in the West. Thus rumours of an intensive arms build-
up in Northern Nigeria heightened the Eastern Nigerians' fears
of the intentions of Lagos.

It was under these conditions of fear and uncertainty that
Lt.-Col. Ojukwu, the Eastern Military Governor, decided to
give direction and motive to the aimless drift of the country.
In a radio broadcast on February 25, 1967, he declared:

> Today all the high hopes and confidence borne out of Aburi
> seem to be waning. There is evidence that those in authority
> in Lagos are determined to repudiate or evade the agreements
> reached unanimously. Unnecessary confusion has been
> infused into the whole issue both from within and from with-
> out, and the country is once again drifting dangerously.

Explaining the reasons for his statements, he said:

> Having regard to . . . the great uneasiness which appears
> to be pervading the Region, as a result of actions on the part
> of the Government in Lagos . . . I have no alternative but to
> make this statement, for two reasons: first, to assure the
> people of this Region that I am bound in honour to the
> Aburi agreements, and secondly to call for continued calm
> and intensified vigilance.

He regretted that the Lagos Government had published the
document *Nigeria 1966*, in spite of his mutual agreement with
Gowon that the publication be withheld because it detracted
from the Aburi spirit. He disclosed that this 'was the first act
from Lagos after Aburi which shook my confidence in what we
tried to do at Aburi'. He said that Lt.-Col. Gowon's press conference on the Aburi agreements 'virtually amounted to a
denunciation of the agreements'. He listed several breaches of

the Aburi agreements by the Lagos Government. Commenting on the reasons which had been put forward to support these breaches, he declared: 'If anybody went to that meeting unprepared, then one can only infer that he was not seriously concerned with the said problems which had beset the country, let alone how to solve them.' He declared:

> The survival of this country, its normalcy and peace, hinge on the implementation of the Aburi agreements. . . . Once the agreements are implemented, Nigerians will be assured of a faster and more peaceful march to the goal of normalcy.

Then came the ultimatum:

> . . . if the Aburi agreements are not fully implemented by March 31, 1967, I shall have no alternative but to feel free to take whatever measures are necessary to give effect in this Region to those agreements.

He warned that the East cannot be intimidated into accepting any form of dictation, but will crush any agressors. Concluding, he declared:

> Fellow countrymen and women, *on Aburi we stand.*
> There will be no compromise.[312]

As a sequel to this broadcast, Lt.-Col. Gowon gave an address to Heads of African Diplomatic Missions in Nigeria. He told them that that meeting was important because he expected them 'to send dispatches to your Governments which will reflect as much as possible an objective analysis of the situation in Nigeria'. The address contained his own version of the Aburi agreements. He concluded it with:

> All I am trying to do is to hold this country together. I am still trying my best to do so by peaceful means. We however live in a situation where we may be forced to take preventive measures to avoid a disaster. You can all use your good offices to help.

It became certain, to the chagrin of most Nigerians, that the Aburi Accord had failed.

But what exactly could be said about the obligatory character of the Aburi Accord? Principally, the Aburi meeting of the

Supreme Military Council was intended to establish a basis of confidence which is a precondition for return to normalcy. Strictly speaking, one would agree with Lt.-Col. Gowon that the members of the Supreme Military Council did not go to Aburi to write a new Constitution for the country. Aburi was not intended to do this, nor to give Nigeria a third Republic; it was intended only as an amendment to the Constitution of the second Republic, under whose powers the Supreme Military Council was acting in the first place. Lt.-Col. Gowon never doubted or behaved as if he doubted that he was acting under Ironsi's Constitution. The very fact of the Aburi summit itself showed clearly that the July 29 revolt never established a third Republic for Nigeria. If Gowon was prepared to act under Ironsi's Supreme Military Council, he should also be prepared to subject himself to the existing Constitution until it was amended by the Council itself.

At Aburi, a unanimous decision was reached that, instead of a Supreme Commander, the country should now have a Commander-in-Chief, who would be selected by the Supreme Military Council itself. This was a logical step to be taken since the former Supreme Commander was no longer there. This was the condition under which the East would recognise Lt.-Col. Gowon's leadership. But this depended on the implementation of the Aburi agreements. Thus, there was a reciprocity of pre-conditions. The Supreme Military Council took a decision which amended the Constitution, replacing the post of Supreme Commander with that of a Chairman who would be called Commander-in-Chief. This new post was to be filled by a selection of the Supreme Military Council, particularly as the former Supreme Commander was no more. Much as the effectiveness of these decisions depended on putting them in the form of a decree (as was the practice during Ironsi's administration), the recognition of Gowon's Government (though not necessarily his leadership) by the East depended on the implementation of these decisions; thus Gowon was morally bound to implement Aburi.

Furthermore, the Aburi agreements were decisions of the Supreme Military Council, which no one member of the Council had power or authority to repudiate or modify. Any alteration of such decisions must necessarily be made by the Council

as a body. If Gowon had subjected himself to Aburi de
the East would have recognised his Government;
modification of the agreements amounted to an assum
dictatorial powers.

Thus breach of faith and downright selfishness had killed the
Aburi spirit. Why did the Aburi meeting fail? It did not fail
because it was unable to activate the patriotism of the Nigerian
military leaders and the Nigerian people. The tape-recording
of the meeting and the acclamation with which the meeting was
received showed that all were genuinely concerned with the
survival of the country. The Aburi meeting failed because of
pressure-groups who, pursuing private motives, manoeuvred
events by threatening here, and persuading there. Lt.-Col.
Ojukwu and Lt.-Col. Gowon, the two leaders who finally
emerged at the two opposing ends, were champions of diverging
interests.

Lt.-Col. Ojukwu, the Military Governor of Eastern Nigeria,
found himself, by Providence, accepting the challenge of
championing the cause of the persecuted people of Eastern
Nigeria. These people, frustrated by the futility of many years
of one concession after another 'in the interest of national
unity', embittered by the crass ingratitude of a people whose
homes they had helped to develop, and brutally shocked out
of their strong belief in Nigerian unity by six months of a
savage pogrom, returned home from other parts of the country,
determined to give a trial to a form of association, which
amounted virtually to separatism.[313] To them, the Aburi agreements were the only practical solution to the continued existence of Nigeria. Everywhere in the Region the cry was: 'Confederation or secession.'

Lt.-Col. Gowon, a non-Hausa-Fulani from the oppressed
Middle-Belt Area of the Hausa-Fulani-dominated Northern
Nigeria, had led a Northern revolt which overthrew Ironsi in
July 1966. His position was complicated. He had to compromise
with three pressure groups: the Hausa-Fulani aristocracy, who
wanted secession or domination of the rest of Nigeria; his
(Gowon's) backing gunners of Middle-Belt origin who wanted
freedom from their Muslim oppressors; and imperialistic
Britain which, seeing greater economic gains in a Nigeria
dominated by compliant Northerners, advised against seces-

sion or confederation. The dilemma in which these groups
threw Lt.-Col. Gowon was reflected by his vacillations and
contradictions. But his problems were not yet ended. Superimposed on this pressure from three directions was the frustrat-
ing manoeuvre of misguided Federal Civil Servants. Each time
the story of the last days of the Federation of Nigeria is told,
the betrayal of the Nigerian people by these selfishly-motivated
'top civil servants' will be remembered as the greatest disservice
to the nation of all. The cloud of disaster continued to hang
over the nation like the mythical Sword of Damocles.

10

THE DECLARATION OF INDEPENDENCE

... Prudence, indeed, will dictate that Governments long established should not be changed for light and transient causes; and accordingly all experience hath shewn, that mankind are disposed to suffer, while evils are sufferable, than to right themselves by abolishing the forms to which they are accustomed. But when a long train of abuses and usurpations, pursuing invariably the same object, envinces a design to reduce them under absolute Despotism, it is their right, it is their duty, to throw off such Government, and to provide new Guards for their future security ...

The Declaration of American Independence, July 4, 1776

(i) THE SURVIVAL EDICTS AND THE PUSH

(a) *The Stand of the East*

One thing that was remarkable in the Nigerian Crisis of 1966–7 was the consistency of the stand of the Eastern Nigeria Government. When, in 1960, Britain launched the Nigerian ship of state into independence, Nigerians as well as the Western World hoped that here was one nation which would surely develop into a show-piece of democracy in Africa. The Federation of Nigeria was looked upon as the most promising African country. However, by November 1965, the promise was proving a mirage. By November 1966 it was obvious that the Nigerian experiment was a total failure. The disillusioned people of Eastern Nigeria who, since the inception of Nigeria, had championed the cause of a united country, were forced out of their reverie and made to realise that it was impossible for this great political experiment to work under existing conditions. Thus they came to the inevitable conclusion that the political and economic structure of the country must be reviewed with a sincerity and realism that would recognise the political realities that existed in Nigeria. Among other facts it must be recognised that the pogrom of May, July, September and October 1966 proved conclusively the failure to merge the diverse peoples of Nigeria into a unified nation, the failure of the Federation to guarantee all citizens the rights of life and property, the complete rupture of the bond of comradeship which existed in the Nigerian Army, and the necessity for the removal of the areas of friction if the Federation was to survive. Having regard to these facts, a form of association had to be found in which conditions that led to the events of 1966 would never arise. A unity that is not based on mutual respect and goodwill is abstruse and a sham. Therefore, the East put forward proposals which would ensure that every Region developed according to its own pace, uninterrupted and without interference. This meant a looser form of association which would reduce to a minimum those things which had given rise to friction, make it impossible for one Region to dominate another, and create conditions which would, in the near future, generate confidence and respect among the disaffected peoples of the Federation.

In the Aburi meeting of the Supreme Military Council, under the influence of the mysterious 'Aburi spirit', realism prevailed and the participants rightly took decisions which ran parallel with the Eastern Nigerian proposals. Therefore, the East insisted on the implementation of the Aburi agreements because this was the only realistic and practical solution to the Nigerian crisis, an inevitable solution at which anyone who sincerely believed in the continuation of the Federation would arrive.

The stand of the East on the Aburi agreement was not only due to the political and constitutional reorganisation of Nigeria which it provided, but also due to the economic and fiscal consequences which should flow directly from this reorganisation. Under the fiscal arrangements of the first Federal Republic of Nigeria, financial resources were transferred from the wealthier to the relatively poorer regions. The basis for such transfers was the promise that every citizen of the Federation could move freely anywhere in the Federation, establishing business or seeking employment without fear of prejudice or discrimination. Thus every citizen could benefit from the distribution of the resources of the Federation. However, following the pogrom of 1966 and the consequent irreversible shift of population to the East, there was a population explosion in that Region, to which more than two million surviving Easterners had returned home. Some were maimed, but all were destitute. Because no Eastern Nigerian could establish himself in the North, the foundations on which the fiscal transfers were based became irrelevant.

The following facts will illustrate the assistance of the East to other parts of the Federation *for the year 1965:*

	Federal Total	Eastern Nigeria contribution	Percentage
Exports	£263 million	£99 million	38%
Tax revenue	£140.7 million	£48.4 million	35%
Population	55.7 million	12.4 million	22%

Of Tax revenue the East was given £19.6 million, i.e. 14%.

Thus with 22 per cent of the Nigerian population, Eastern Nigeria contributed 38 per cent of Federal exports and 35 per cent of the Federal tax revenues, while she received back 14 per cent of the tax revenues. Additionally, in the same year the Federal Statutory Corporations realised a surplus of £5·4 million in their operations in Eastern Nigeria.

With the tragic events of 1966, which resulted in population re-distribution, the East experienced a sudden growth of 16 per cent in her population, which imposed on her grave economic and social problems. She therefore maintained that, since each Region alone was saddled with the responsibility of looking after the welfare of its peoples, the economic and fiscal consequences which must follow the political reorganisations must be such that each Region should control its own resources in order to be able to meet these responsibilities. Explaining the Eastern stand, Lt.-Col. Ojukwu stated:

I have a duty to the 14 million people of this region who are very anxious for an opportunity to rebuild, rather than lick their wounds.[314]

This statement concisely but eloquently portrays the attitude of the people of the East. They did not seek to stay slightly further apart because 30,000 of their kith and kin had been

massacred, but because of the consequences of these massacres.
They did not seek revenge, nor did they solicit pity. All they
wanted was an opportunity to accept the challenge of reconstruction, and to tackle the problems forced on them by the
aftermath of the pogrom. This attitude was devoid of any
emotion, but faced the hard facts of the existing circumstances.
It could not have been more realistic.

(i) (b) *Repudiation of the Aburi Agreements*

Unfortunately, the chances of the Easterners having this
much-need opportunity became more remote with each passing
day. According to *The Economist*,[315] soldiers who find that
they have power in their hands but who have no political
philosophies or ideas in their heads are in a sorry state and
constitute a danger to peace and progress. This is true indeed,
for they are vulnerable to one of two things: (i) the inebriety
of power; (ii) the wiles of self-motivated 'expert advisers'.
The Nigerian example gives a classic illustration of this fact.
Urged by the 'expert advice' of the top Federal civil servants,
cajoled by the persuasive 'benignity' of the British diplomats,
coerced by pressures from Northern Nigeria, Lt.-Col. Gowon
made statements and took actions which, apart from being
inconsistent, frustrated hopes of a peaceful settlement of the
crisis.

Contrary to the Aburi agreements, recruitment into the
Nigerian Army continued in all other parts of the country
except the East. The Federal Government continued to import
arms and ammunition, most of which were sent to the North,
ostensibly for safe storage. This naturally excited the suspicion
of the East. As has been stated in the last chapter, the meeting
of the finance officials had not taken place, and the meeting of
military officers, which had made an encouraging start, was
unilaterally postponed by Lagos. Appointments to the diplomatic service were made without reference to the Supreme
Military Council and, to worsen matters further, Easterners
serving in foreign embassies were put into situations where they
were forced to resign. Employees of the Federal Statutory
Corporations operating in the East, such as the Railway and
the Coal Corporations, were refused their salaries. Therefore,
already saddled with the marathon task of rehabilitating her

two million refugees, the East had to absorb displaced diplomats, as well as remit advances for the salaries of employees
of Federal Corporations. Contrary to the agreements reached
at Aburi, salaries of Federal civil servants were not paid up to
March 31, 1967.

If the above lapses of the Federal Government discredited
it before the East, its reasons for these lapses and the inconsistency of these reasons subjected it to ridicule before the world.
First was the contention that the Military Governor of the
East had misinterpreted the Aburi decisions. When, however,
following a persistent demand by the press, the Eastern Government published both the minutes and the tape-recordings of the
Aburi meeting, the Federal Government dropped the question
of interpretation and decided to adopt the Aburi decisions with
amendments, which reflected the 'objections' of a group of
Federal Permanent Secretaries. Giving reasons for this action,
it explained that some of the Aburi conferees (i) went to the
meeting unprepared, and (ii) did not understand the agreements
reached at the meeting; therefore it was considered necessary
to refer the decisions to 'civil service experts' for final advice.
These reasons sound ridiculous, considering that the agenda of
the meeting was prepared and agreed upon long before the
meeting. It looks strange that the comments of the 'civil
service experts' on decisions of the Supreme Military Council
should be accepted in their entirety without further reference to
the Supreme Military Council.

As a sole reason for failing to honour the agreement to pay
Federal employees who had been forced to flee their places of
work, the Lagos Government said that, because some railway
wagons were lying in the East, it was unable to raise the money
required for the payment. But these wagons were in the East
when the agreements were reached at Aburi.

On March 17, the Federal Government promulgated a
Constitution (Suppression and Modification) Decree 1967.
Among other things, it limited the area in which the concurrence
of all Military Governors was required, it enlarged the Supreme
Military Council, and it arrogated to the Supreme Military
Council the power to declare a state of emergency in any Region
'with the concurrence of the Head of the Federal Military
Government and of, at least, three of the Military Governors'.

These are, of course, a departure from the Aburi agreements; whether or not the meeting of the Supreme Military Council which sanctioned this decree was properly constituted does not alter this fact. Lt.-Col. Ojukwu did not attend the Supreme Military Council's meeting in Benin because of the presence of Northern soldiers (in the West), the removal of whom had been agreed upon in Aburi. Yet the decree did not receive his concurrence before being promulgated. Commenting on this issue, an editorial of *Nigerian Outlook* quoted Col. Adebayo, the Western Military Governor, as saying that, although a meeting of the Supreme Military Council would be regarded as properly constituted if any Military Governor was absent, 'but as agreed at Aburi, any Military Governor not present will be given the opportunity to express his comments on, and concurrence with, the decision taken in his absence, *before* they are implemented.' He was quoted as having further argued that, although 'decisions by majority would have been the best thing in ordinary circumstances, in the present situation in the country one has to admit that such a rule could lead to open disagreement and conflicts, and to the revival of tension which everything must be done to reduce'.

Therefore this decree failed to recognise that the Nigerian situation had passed the stage in which decisions on matters affecting the whole country could be justifiably taken by the majority vote of representatives of the various governments of the Federation. Such majority decisions can only be justified in federations where *all* citizens, irrespective of region of origin, can freely and safely live, seek employment and establish business in all parts of the country. The atmosphere of fear and suspicion created by the brutal killings of 1966 had, if only temporarily, made this type of government impossible in Nigeria.

The Constitution (Suppression and Modification) Decree 1967 was rejected by Eastern Nigeria, not only because it unilaterally modified Aburi agreements, but also because it contained those provisions of decree 34, for which thousands of lives of Eastern Nigerians were lost. Thus, in spite of the steady approach of March 31, 1967 – the day of the expiry of the Eastern ultimatum – there was no sign of change in the Lagos attitude.

(i) (c) *The Survival Edicts*

The month of March 1967 can very rightly be called 'the solidarity month' in Eastern Nigeria, for it is a month singularly marked by mass demonstrations of support for the stand of the Eastern Nigerian Government in the crisis. Starting from Enugu, these demonstrations spread like wildfire, and within a few days, the whole Region was engulfed by mammoth rallies. From the villages, indignant Eastern Nigerians poured into the cities. They came from all walks of life – students from universities and other institutions of higher learning, students from secondary schools, primary school pupils, nurses, trade unionists, doctors, lawyers, engineers, market women, farmers, fishermen, hunters – they all came out in their thousands. One rally followed another. From street to street they marched carrying placards and chanting anti-Gowon hymns. Some of the placards read 'On Aburi we stand', 'Gowon honour agreements', 'Ojukwu we are behind you, go ahead', 'Ojukwu, no more compromise', 'Ojukwu give us arms', 'Confederation or secession', 'Aburi or nothing', 'Aburi or Unilateral Declaration of Independence', 'Ojukwu ever, Gowon never', 'Ojukwu our Hero', 'Solidarity for ever', 'We federate no more', 'Down with vandals', 'Remember the pogrom'. Hundreds of thousands of such placards bore different inscriptions but they proclaimed the same thing – a people driven to the wall and united in the singular determination to give no more ground – because there was no more ground to give.

From the hills of Ogoja, from the mangroves of Brass, from the forests of Arochukwu, from the farmlands of Abakiliki, from the creeks of Bonny, from Awka, Aba, Uyo, Onitsha, Port Harcourt, Bende and all parts of the Region, delegations of chiefs and elders, student unions, trade unions and cultural organisations, paid visits to the State House to submit memoranda to Lt.-Col. Ojukwu affirming their loyalty to and support for him and his Government.

Meanwhile, Lagos was busy importing arms, planning naval exercises in the Eastern waters and test flights over Eastern Nigeria. This was probably meant to intimidate the people of the East. As if to support this, the threatening voice of Lt.-Col. Katsina, Military Governor of Northern Nigeria, rang through the already charged atmosphere. He declared that he needed only two hours to crush the East if given permission by Lagos. To this provoking statement, and Lt.-Col. Gowon's threat to use force against the East, Lt.-Col. Ojukwu simply stated that the East had no intention to secede unless it was pushed out. He defined 'push' as meaning physical attack or economic blockade. These threats only succeeded in strengthening the Eastern determination to resist any attempts at domination to the end. The mass demonstration increased in tempo, assuming a magnitude comparable to the Chinese Cultural Revolutions. Commenting on this, an editorial of the *Nigerian Outlook*[816] stated:

. . . Eastern Nigeria has witnessed an unprecedented unity of purpose . . . Lt.-Col. Ojukwu has done no more than giving tongue to the wishes of the people.

Things have happened in Eastern Nigeria and things are still happening. All the incidents coming as they do from the will of the people have one central purpose – to safeguard the integrity of Eastern Nigeria as an indivisible unit free from the humbug of indolent neighbours, who have no faith in hard work and merit as necessary ingredients for happy living.

We would like to direct outsiders' attention to numerous solidarity demonstrations that are taking place in all corners of Eastern Nigeria at this hour of the nation's trial. We would like Hassan and his compeers to brood over the recent mass rallies of workers of Eastern Nigeria who have gone to so great an extent as to volunteer a fraction of their monthly salaries in defence of Eastern Nigeria.

As if to give the final whip to a willing horse in a race, Peter Enahoro (alias Peter Pan,) a renowned Nigerian journalist and, until a few weeks earlier, editor of *The Daily Times*, wrote:

Inexorably, it seems, Nigeria limps painfully towards dismemberment. Unless Eastern Nigeria, under the stubborn leadership of young Lt.-Col. Emeka Odumegwu Ojukwu surrenders to pressures from Lagos, Lt.-Col. Yakubu Gowon, by the grace of mass murders the self-proclaimed Head of State, will 'take police action' against the 'recalcitrant' Eastern Region.

Lt.-Col. Odumegwu Ojukwu must not yield, Eastern Nigeria must not capitulate.

For once in the history of Nigeria, let us witness a strong leadership and let us see a section of the national community that is sufficiently strong in its beliefs to resist the temptations of compromise.

Nigeria totters on the brink of disintegration. Some people counsel that yet another compromise will restore our balance. I do not believe that a mere resumption of equilibrium is what Nigeria needs today. What she needs is total withdrawal from the precipice.[317]

Prophetically he warned:

I enjoin Lt.-Col. Odumegwu Ojukwu to brook no compromise. Let Nigeria begin its nation-building on a proper foundation at last. Confederation will not break up the country. *On the contrary, it is enforced federation that will lead to more strife and bitterness.* And out of that chaos only disintegration can follow.

Let Nigerians gradually learn the value of unity. Until they come to appreciate the need for unity, that goal will remain an elusive prize.

There is a vacuum in the absence of a leader around whom the entire nation can rally both on political and military fronts. Which is why many Nigerians now feel that a very loose Federation – for want of another word called *Confederation* – is the immediate solution to the present crisis. . . . Nigerians will gradually learn the need for unity. But in an era when the Ibo man can no longer live in the North and the Hausa man can no longer live in the East, it is the height of folly to speak of a tight Federation. . . . A tight Federation requires trust. Give Nigerians time to rebuild that trust.

Let's settle now for a loose Federation. A temporary confederation.[318]

When on March 31 it became evident that Lagos had not the least intention of implementing fully the Aburi agreements but preferred a stalemate because the East suffered by it, the Government of Eastern Nigeria opted for survival by issuing five 'Survival Edicts'.

On March 31, 1967, the Military Government of Eastern Nigera issued an edict entitled 'the Revenue Collection Edict 1967', ordering that all monies collected on behalf of the Federal Government in Eastern Nigeria should be paid to the Government Treasury in the Eastern Region. The edict also stipulated that all monies payable to the Government of Eastern Nigeria under the edict should be paid through the Treasury in the manner provided in this or any other edict or as the appropriate authority might from time to time prescribe. It also prohibited any payment or transfer of money to the Government of Eastern Nigeria in any matter other than through the Treasury. The law came into effect on April 1, 1967. Offenders were to face a special tribunal. Minimum sentence of £500 for a federal corporation or a federal institution, and three years imprisonment for an individual, would be passed on conviction. Giving a five-point reason for this edict, the Government of Eastern Nigeria explained that it was to enable it to meet the financial responsibilities imposed upon it by both the refugee problem and the non-implementation of Aburi. It further explained that the edict was meant to prevent Lagos from accumulating more debts to Eastern Nigeria. Lagos was indebted to the Region to the tune of about £11 million. The edict was expected to secure to the Region £20 million as against £19·5 million due to it by allocation.

The Revenue Edict was followed immediately on April 17 by the Legal Education Edict and the Statutory Bodies Edict. The former established the Eastern Nigeria Law School, to ensure legal education for the Eastern Nigerian students who could not go to the Lagos Law School to continue their courses because of the situation in the country. The latter established a Statutory Bodies Council and transferred ten central government-owned agencies to it. The bodies affected were: Electrical Corporation of Nigeria, the Nigerian Airways (WAAC Ltd.), the Nigerian Broadcasting Corporation, the Nigerian Coal Corporation, the Nigerian National Shipping Lines Ltd., the Nigerian Ports Authority, the Nigerian Produce Marketing Company Ltd., the Nigerian Railway Corporation, the Department of Posts and Telegraphs and the Citizenship and Leadership Training Centre. The edict was meant to enable corporation services to be continued, sustained and expanded, so that

Eastern Nigeria might be able to pay her refugees who were employed in these corporations. The Aburi meeting agreed that the Federal Government should pay these salaries till March 31; Lagos did not honour this agreement.

On April 18 the Court of Appeal Edict followed. It established an appeal court in Eastern Nigeria. This was necessary because Eastern Nigerians could not go to Lagos for their appeal cases for reasons of personal security and judicial prejudice.

Finally, the Marketing Board Edict was published on April 19. This gave the Eastern Nigeria Marketing Board more powers. Under this arrangement, Eastern Nigeria could market its produce direct to overseas countries and could thus retain its profits.

These edicts were received with acclamation by the people of Eastern Nigeria. Acclaiming the Statutory Corporation Edict, the *Outlook* described it as a Survival Edict 'because the keynote underlining the promulgation of the Edict stems from a passionate attempt to halt Lagos' plans to strangulate the economy of this Region by abdicating its responsibility for running and maintaining the corporations concerned'.[319] Messages of congratulations which came to the Military Governor from different parts of the country included ones from the Eastern Electricity Workers' Union and the Nigerian Coal Miners' Union.

(d) *Counter Measures*

The Eastern Nigerian Government's Survival Edicts were not kindly received by Lagos. As a counter-measure, Lt.-Col. Gowon proceeded to impose a diplomatic, economic and military blockade against the East.

Notes were sent to foreign governments emphasising that the situation in Nigeria was 'an internal affair' of the country. The Eastern Nigerian border with Cameroun was sealed off, and the Cameroun consulate in Enugu was closed. All passports which had earlier been issued to officers of Eastern Nigerian origin, who had transferred to the Eastern Nigeria Public Service, were cancelled. *The Push had started*.

On April 1 the Lagos Government declared that Eastern Nigeria's Revenue Edict was 'illegal and unconstitutional',[320] and advised 'all those indebted to it to continue to meet their obligation in the usual way'.

On April 4 Nigerian Airways suspended flights to Eastern Nigeria.

On April 5 Lagos froze all foreign transactions in Eastern Nigeria.

On April 19 the Nigeria Produce Marketing Company, Lagos, directed firms to deal directly with it and declared that it would be illegal to deal with any other authority, or for any-one to ship produce without its permission. Ships which were bound for the Eastern Ports were diverted to Lagos for evacuation and collection of customs dues.

A meeting of some members of the Supreme Military Council (without Ojukwu) announced 'stern measures' against Eastern Nigeria for 'defiance of Federal Authority'. They also drew up what was described as a 'political and administrative programme on action for preserving the federation of Nigeria'. Gowon, in an address to diplomats in Lagos, threatened to create States in the East by decree (and backed by forces, if necessary) in order to 'protect the minorities' in the East, if Lt.-Col. Ojukwu implemented his threat of secession.

This threat typifies the attitude of Lt.-Col. Gowon in the Nigerian crisis. His actions were intended to be punitive rather than to resolve the crisis. On April 29 he declared that Savings Bank deposits made in the East, after March 31, as well as savings stamps, certificates and premium bonds sold in the East, would not be recognised by the Federal Government. *The Push was now fully on* – and the nation was drifting very dangerously.

(ii) FINAL ATTEMPTS TO SAVE NIGERIA

From the account preceding this section it would appear as if there were no voices of reason anywhere in the Western and Mid-Western Regions of Nigeria. Such voices were to be heard from time to time, particularly as the crisis approached the point of no return. However, for individual reasons, these voices were weak and ineffectual.

As far back as March 27, 1967, a 'peace parley' comprising Col. Adeyinka Adebayo, Lt.-Col. David Ejoor, Commodore Wey and Timothy Omo-Bare, the Deputy Inspector-General of

THE DECLARATION OF INDEPENDENCE

Police, flew to Onitsha, Eastern Nigeria, to make 'a f
appeal' to Lt.-Col. Ojukwu not to carry out his thre
unilaterally implementing the Aburi agreements at the er
March. One significant point about this parley is that all the
four were members of the Supreme Military Council and were
signatories to the Aburi agreements. If they were sincere in
seeking a peaceful solution to the crisis, the best and most
effective way of 'stopping Ojukwu from carrying out his threat'
would have been to direct their 'frantic appeal' to Lt.-Col.
Gowon to implement the Aburi decisions unamended. However,
the delegation held a detailed and frank discussion in which
Lt.-Col. Ojukwu made clear to them (perhaps unnecessarily,
because they had always known it) the position of the East.
Under the irresistible logic of the Eastern stand, the delegation
undertook to get Lt.-Col. Gowon to do two things: (i) to make
sure that the debt owed to the East was paid by March 31;
(ii) either to repeal those sections of the Constitution (Suppression and Modification) Decree 1967 (i.e. Lagos Decree No. 8.),
which were obnoxious to the East, or to suspend the entire
decree. They also agreed to get the North to express their
remorse for the atrocities of 1966 against the Easterners by a
public apology. Sadly enough, nothing came out of this and
none of these things was done.

With the swift exchange of economic blows which marked the
greater part of April, there were significant changes in the
attitude of Western and Mid-Western Nigerians to the crisis.
In the West where, earlier on, the Nigerian crisis was regarded as
a two-cornered tussle between the East and the North, there
arose a gradual but noticeable realisation of the true issues
involved. The presence of Northern troops in their Region was
deeply resented by the Westerners, but they could not give
voice to this resentment for fear of assaults by the Northern
soldiers. The resentment did, however, receive expression in a
series of secret meetings, the decisions of which were never
announced.

In mid-April, Lt.-Col. Gowon announced that the Ad Hoc
Constitutional Committee[321] would resume its conference to
draft a Constitution for Nigeria. This was supposed to be the
first step towards the return of the country to civilian rule. Of
course, this amounted to a deliberate refusal to tackle the basic

problem that faced the country. The position of the East had
been made clear. As agreed in Aburi, the best chance for the
survival of the country lay in the Regions moving slightly
apart. The implementation of the Aburi decisions would
demonstrate an acceptance of this fundamental principle. It
was therefore a pre-requisite for any constitutional conference,
since the latter would have to work out the details of the fundamental principle. The East would therefore not attend any
constitutional talks unless the Aburi decisions were implemented.

Other Regions of Southern Nigeria agreed with this view,
but were afraid to speak up. However, on May 24, 1967, a
step was taken towards Southern Nigerian solidarity. Chief
Obafemi Awolowo, who had been acclaimed 'leader of the
Yorubas', on his release from prison[322] the previous year,
resigned as leader of the Western Nigerian delegation to the
Ad Hoc Constitutional Conference. In a letter to Col. Robert
Adeyinka Adebayo, Military Governor of Western Nigeria,
Chief Awolowo said that one of his reasons for resigning was
the 'documented tension between the Hausa tribe of Northern
Nigeria and those Yorubas resident in that Region'. He accused
some Federal Government circles of trying to help Eastern
Nigeria out of the Federation, so that they would form a new
Federation on their own terms from among the remaining
units. He said the Federal Government had failed to respect the
consensus among the majority of people in the West and Lagos
that the Northern troops in these two territories constituted an
'army of occupation', and that their non-removal had reduced
the territories to the status of a 'protectorate'. He declared:

... If you want to save the Federation from complete disintegration and the constituent units from mutual destruction,
we must embark now on a four or five years' venture on
Confederalism.[323]

On May 1 a meeting of the Western Nigerian Leaders of
Thought declared their stand on the Nigerian crisis in a six-
point resolution. One of the resolutions stated that, in view
of the existing circumstances in the country, Western Nigeria
would no longer participate in the work of the Ad Hoc Committee on Nigeria's constitutional proposals, nor would they

comment on the programme of the Supreme Military Council. Another resolution demanded that every effort should 'be made to keep the East in the Federation on a basis which recognises the mutual interests of all the Regions, even if this means a constitutional arrangement that is looser than hitherto'. Another resolution declared that in the event of any component units seceding or being forced out of the Federation, Western Nigeria should automatically become independent and sovereign.

Addressing the Conference earlier, Chief Awolowo stated that in the face of the West, Mid-West and Lagos' declared opposition to the use of force in solving the Nigerian crisis, any military attack on the East could only be a war favoured by the North alone. He went on:

... If the true position of such a war is to preserve the unity and integrity of the Federation, then these ends can be achieved by the very simple devices of *implementing the recommendation of the committee which met on August 9, 1966, as re-affirmed by a decision of the military leaders at Aburi,*[324] on January 5, 1967, as well as by accepting such of the demands of the East, West, Mid-West and Lagos as are manifestly reasonable, and essential for assuring harmonious relationships and peaceful coexistence between them and their brothers and sisters in the North.

Disagreeing with the proposition that an attack on the East could be likened to Lincoln's war against the Southern States in America, he stated that, first, the American Civil War was aimed at the abolition of slavery; secondly, it was a war between an English-speaking people, who stuck to the principle of good conscience and humanity, and fellow English-speaking nationals. He added:

A war against the East, in which Northern soldiers are predominant, will only unite the Easterners or the Ibos against their attackers, strengthen them in their belief that they are not wanted by the majority of their fellow Nigerians, and finally push them out of the Federation. . . . It is my considered view that whilst some of the demands of the East are excessive within the context of a Nigerian Union, most of such demands are not only well-founded, but are designed for smooth and healthy association amongst the various national units of Nigeria. . . . If we are to live in harmony one with another as Nigerians, it is imperative that these demands and others which are not here related, should be met without further delay by those who have hitherto resisted them.[325]

Chief Awolowo's resignation was followed in a quick succession by the resignations of both Mr. Lateef Jakande and Sir Kashim Ibrahim, the leaders of the Lagos and Northern delegations respectively. Sir Kashim gave no reasons for his resignation. Mr. Jakande said he saw no useful purpose in the Conference since the East would not be present in the meeting. On May 3 the Mid-Western Region joined the chorus of Southern solidarity. After a seven-hour meeting, the Region's Constituent Assembly opted for a confederation. On the same day, an official announcement from Lagos stated that the Ad Hoc Committee meeting had been adjourned indefinitely. In the light of the preceding developments this did not come as a surprise. However, it was expected that, since most of the Southern delegations[326] expressly favoured a loose federation, the Lagos Government would reconsider its stand in the interest of the nation. Lt.-Col. Gowon's answer to these expectations were:

. . . The day we say confederation, it would be goodbye to Nigeria, since confederation meant a willing grouping together of independent sovereign states.[327]

This was, of course, in line with the decision of a meeting of the Northern Nigerian emirs, natural rulers and leaders of thought, that a federation with a strong centre was the only form of political association suitable for Nigeria. Commenting on this resolution, the Students' Union of the University of Ife, Western Nigeria, said it was 'a further justification of the accusation levelled against the North that it wants to dominate the Federation'. The students added that, in a letter to Lt.-Col. Gowon, they had told him that the only solution to the present impasse in the country was a confederal system of government, as this would allow the wounds of the recent past to heal.[328]

An additional call for confederation came from Professor Fafunwa of the University of Ife. Following a meeting of professors, lecturers and senior administrative staff of the University of Ife called by Professor Fafunwa himself, he sent a telegram to the military leaders, saying:

> Loose federation can still mean one currency, one Army, one Foreign Ministry and one Federal Parliament. I commend this arrangement to the Supreme Military Council and people of Nigeria.[329]

In spite of these calls and the obvious popularity of the idea of a confederal system of government, Lt.-Col. Gowon stuck to his guns. Even Lt.-Col. Ojukwu's call for the mediation by some African heads of state was rejected. The Lagos reason for this was that it was an insult to the integrity of the country as it meant that Nigeria could not solve her own problems. This of course amounts to shying away from the truth because the fact is that Nigerians had proved incapable of solving their own problems. To what extent Gowon's reason was motivated by national pride is clearly shown by the fact that, whilst he consistently rebuffed efforts of African heads of state to mediate in the crisis, he was only too eager to call in British troops 'to neutralise the Mid-Western Region'.

Early in May a group of Nigerians formed a new peace-body called the Nigerian Conciliation Committee (NCC). The members were: Chief Obafemi Awolowo, Dr. S. A. Aluko, Alhaji Kashim Ibrahim, Dr. R. A. B. Dikko, Chief J. Mariere, Mr. S. Ighadoro, Dr. S. I. Audu, Chief I. O. Bajulaiye, G. B. A. Coker, Alhaji Z. B. Dipcharima, Alhaji Abdul Waid Elias, Dr. L. A. Fabunmi, Dr. Babatunde Williams, Professor T. M. Yesufu, G. K. Amachree and Dr. Okoi Arikpo.[330] On May 6 a four-man delegation, led by Chief Obafemi Awolowo and comprising Chief Jeretin Mariere, Dr. S. A. Aluko, and Chief J. I. G. Onyia arrived in Enugu to plead with the East to send delegates, – Dr. Francis Ibiam, Adviser to the East Military Governor, and Sir Louis Mbanefo,[331] Chief Justice of Eastern Nigeria, were named – to attend a meeting of the Committee. The East found it difficult to understand the basis on which the Committee was formed. To begin with, Mr. Amachree and Dr. Arikpo – two self-exiled Eastern Nigerians in whom the

East had no confidence – were members. Moreover, it looked strange that whilst other members of the Committee were invited personally, the Eastern Nigerian Government should be required to appoint delegates. The East rejected the Awolowo delegation's invitation because it could not be expected to participate in mediating in any crisis directly involving the Region (one might as well ask Ojukwu to mediate in the Nigerian crisis), and the Chief Justice could not be involved in politics, the Judiciary being sacrosant. However, the East offered proposals, one of which was that for such a committee to be in a position to achieve effective results it should be made up of people mandated by their Governments, with the Regions equally represented and having equal status.

The Committee refused these proposals and went ahead to meet. This was followed by a communiqué, issued by Dr. Fabunmi, the secretary of the Committee, giving five recommendations to the military leaders. These were as follows:

(i) That the economic sanctions taken against the Eastern Regional Government after the publication of its recent Edict (the Revenue Collection Edict No. 14 of 1967), affecting collection of Federal Government revenue, be lifted immediately;

(ii) That the East Regional Government should revoke all measures whereby it took over Federal institutions and departments in that Region;

(iii) In view of the urgency of this matter, the two Governments should give effect to this recommendation within one week;

(iv) That immediate steps should be taken by the Supreme Commander to post military personnel to barracks within their respective Regions of origin;

(v) Having regard to its peculiar position, the question of maintenance of peace and security in Lagos should be left to the Supreme Commander in consultation with the Military Governors.[332]

The Committee gave May 26 as the dead-line for effecting these recommendations.

On May 20 Lt.-Col. Gowon announced that he had accepted all the recommendations of the Conciliation Committee. He further announced that financial transactions between the East and the rest of the country would resume on the 23rd, and expressed the hope that Lt.-Col. Ojukwu would reciprocate by repealing the revenue edicts. This, of course, Lt.-Col. Ojukwu would not do for obvious reasons: experience had taught him and the people of Eastern Nigeria to hesitate before taking Lt.-Col. Gowon's words at their face value. A lifting of the blockade, followed by an immediate payment of the debt owed to the East, would have demonstrated Lt.-Col. Gowon's sincerity.

The trouble with peace missions in the Nigerian crisis before the war was their refusal or inability to tackle with realism and objectivity the basic problems that faced the country. The recommendations implicitly recognised Lt.-Col. Gowon as the Supreme Commander of Nigeria. Secondly, they amounted to a return to pre-March 31 conditions, without making provisions for the next step. Admittedly the recommendations were not meant to provide a solution to the crisis. In fact, the withdrawal of Northern troops from the West would pave the way for negotiations. But further negotiations were made unnecessary by the refusal of Gowon to abide by decisions reached in previous meetings. In the light of past records of dishonoured agreements and unfulfilled promises on the part of Lagos, such a reconciliation committee would have recommended a positive step in the right direction. It is not enough to retrace a step wrongly taken. What stops this step from being taken again unless efforts are made to prevent it? Members of the peace mission knew full well that the Eastern Nigerian revenue edicts had been provoked by the non-implementation of the Aburi agreements. They should have at least recommended that, as agreed at Aburi, the salaries of Federal workers in the East be paid up to March 31. It was not even necessary to lift the Federal blockade against the East before promulgating the decree which had been overdue since January 21, 1967. This was the crux of the matter, the primary cause. The survival edicts and the economic blockade were simply effects which would disappear if the primary cause was removed.

What we are indicating is that a reconciliation is useless unless it is a full reconciliation. There is no half-measure. A return to the position before March 31 was no solution. The

I

Federal Government decree of March 17, which amended the Aburi agreements, was still in force. Any supposedly reconciliatory move which did not go back to the position at the end of the Aburi meeting on January 5, 1967, was insincere and was therefore bound to fail. This is because, in the history of the Nigerian crisis, the Aburi meeting stands clearly as the only concerted attempt to find a realistic solution to the problems facing the country.

Thus, because of either the insincerity or the incompetence of the peacemakers, even the final attempts to save the tottering Nigerian nation failed. The Federal Republic of Nigeria had gone too far on its way to becoming a prominent example among the 'federations that failed'.

(iii) POINT OF NO RETURN

The final attempts to save Nigeria succeeded only in one thing. They convincingly showed that Gowon's glib and platitudinous talk of 'my duty to my country' and 'my desire to do what is best for our dear country' lacked the sincerity they conveyed. His determination to create states by decree without seeking the views of the people, the North's arrogant intransigence and threats to overrun the 'stubborn East', and the ever-mounting Federal arms build-up (most of which were stored in the North) – all these and more were conclusive evidence that the Federation of Nigeria had no chance of survival. Its days were certainly numbered.

In Eastern Nigeria the mass demonstrations which had started in March were now raging on in full spate. This time, however, there was a new dimension to their demands. The demonstrations were no more just a 'Solidarity March', but a 'Liberation March'.[333] They demanded immediate secession of Eastern Nigeria from the rest of the Federation.

On May 13, 1967, in a mammoth rally at the Enugu Stadium, more than 80,000 demonstrators called for the declaration of an independent state of Biafra; then on May 23, 1967, at least 100,000 demonstrators marched through the streets of Port Harcourt making a similar call. Some of their placards read: 'The Federation of Nigeria is dead', 'East will never be enslaved', 'Unilateral Declaration of Independence of the

Republic of Biafra', 'Ojukwu declare us a sovereign state as the basis for unity is dead'.

On the same day about 40,000 demonstrators converged on Oji River from the five counties of the province. Some of the placards read 'Bye-bye to Nigeria' 'Declare a sovereign state of Biafra now!' In Nsukka thousands of demonstrators, including undergraduates and lecturers, buried a mock coffin of 'Nigeria' amidst shouts of 'Biafra We Hail Thee, Nigeria We Nail Thee'. In Calabar more than 60,000 people stormed the sports stadium where, after passing a resolution demanding secession, they inaugurated a branch of the Eastern Nigeria Movement for National Liberation. In Aba over 200,000 citizens from all walks of life formed a forest of green leaves and placards and charged through the streets chanting 'liberation songs'. They launched what they called 'Operation Amputation' and buried two mock coffins of Lt.-Col. Gowon and Lt.-Col. Hassan Usman Katsina. Some of the placards read: 'Aba Youths are ready to fight', 'RIP Nigeria', 'Long live Biafra', 'The die is cast', 'Forward with Biafra', 'Gowon has gone too far and the Push is complete'. Indeed the Push was complete, for in Uyo, Okigwi, Yenagoa, Umuahia, Abakiliki, and in all the major and minor cities of Eastern Nigeria, the demand for secession was in the same tone – urgent, insistent and impatient.

Meanwhile, the Military Governor of Eastern Nigeria, Lt.-Col. Ojukwu, had called a meeting of the enlarged Eastern Nigerian Consultative Assembly for May 26, to discuss the current Nigerian crisis with a view to taking decisions on the next step which the East should take. This meeting was looked upon by all Nigerians – though for different reasons – as crucial. As May 26 approached, the liberation marches in Eastern Nigeria increased in tempo. An *Outlook* editorial[334] summed up the situation thus:

Today's meeting of the Eastern Consultative Assembly is crucial. It takes place in conditions of revolutionary rising expectations of the people of Eastern Nigeria, made manifestly clear in the resolutions, the events and happenings of the past few weeks. It takes place at a time when the Nigerian crisis approaches inexorably its culminating point.

A lot of developments have taken place in the general

political situation in the country since the Assembly's last meeting last year. In the intervening period the crisis has passed from one stage to another, experiencing its low and high tides, but still pursuing its intractable course to a nameless destination that seems more and more to be unavoidable.

Within this period hopes rose with Aburi and were terribly frustrated soon afterwards by the non-implementation of Aburi; steps were taken or not taken by Lagos in order to strangulate the East economically; steps were also taken by the East to prevent itself from being strangulated; more Regions joined the East in calling for a realistic and objective approach to the problems facing the country.

In the same period also, the North has remained impassive, almost immutable in its intransigence, certainly indifferent to the increasingly concerted efforts of the South for a quick, honourable and lasting solution to the crisis.

It is against this background of frustrated hopes and bad faith that the Assembly will consider the present and the future. One thing is certain. The indefiniteness of the crisis is now unbearable and the people expect the Region to take a definite step forward. This Region cannot effectively tackle its many gigantic and pressing problems under uncertainty or in a state of perpetual tension. They demand action, they want a positive step taken, they want a decision. If the East is to survive it must first disentangle itself from the internecine embrace that ever was the lot of a progressive people to get into. The moment of decision has come. It is our fervent hope that the Assembly will have the courage and patriotism to make the right decision in the interest of the peace and prosperity of the people they represent.

As members of the Consultative Assembly arrived at the Legislature at Enugu for the meeting, they were applauded by thousands of placard-carrying demonstrators who urged them to 'hearken to the desires of the people'. Students of the University of Nigeria distributed documents arguing the cause of secession. One of the documents exhorted:

. . . We are now making history. Be a part of this history. Immortalise your name by exercising your discretion judiciously in the present crucial political decision. 'Secession' reflects the cross-current of Eastern Nigerian public opinion. Confederation is not a better substitute because it is at best a veiled federalism and an unnecessary prolongation of our agony... We can save ourselves and posterity the continuing uncertainty of a dubious unity by making hay now that we can see the sun still shining. . . . God speed you all.

Addressing the meeting, Lt.-Col. Ojukwu declared:

Your meeting today is very crucial. The East is at the cross-roads. . . . I find it necessary to put all the facts before you indicating the issues, the difficulties and the dangers, so you can examine them fully and advise me on the path we are to follow from now on. As usual, I call upon you to be free, frank and objective.

He proceeded to give an account of the remote and immediate causes of the crisis, and of the events that marked its every stage. Then he concluded:

No Easterner would want to pass through the events of the past ten months again. Only a loose association, call it confederation or what you may, can ensure this. But Gowon and the North have categorically rejected confederation. The position of the East, indeed the West and Mid-West on the one hand, and that of the North on the other, are at once irreconcilable. It is for you as representatives of the 14 million people of Eastern Nigeria to choose from (a) accepting the terms of the North and Gowon and thereby submit to domination by the North, or (b) continuing the present stalemate and drift, or (c) ensuring the survival of our people by asserting our autonomy. If we have no alternative to the third choice, we shall leave the door open for association with any of the Regions of the country that accepts the principle of association of autonomous units. . . . I consider it my duty to warn that if we are compelled to take that decision we must be prepared for a period of real sacrifice, hardship and inconvenience. To start with, we may be without friends for a period. We may have to face the hostilities of the North acting in desperation. For a time there may be financial and economic difficulties. There will be the problems of external communications, of immigration, including passports.

After deliberating on the matter for two days, members of the enlarged Consultative Assembly declared that in consideration of the facts . . . .

    (i) that the Eastern Nigerians had always been in the forefront of the struggle for a united and prosperous Nigeria;

    (ii) that they cherish certain inalienable rights which include the rights of life, liberty and property;

    (iii) that they demonstrated these beliefs by settling in and contributing immensely to the development of other parts of the Federation of Nigeria;

    (iv) that following the genocide of 1966, perpetrated against the Easterners by the Northerners, the consequent conversion of two million Easterners into refugees, and the remorseless and arrogant attitude of the Northerners, they painfully realised that the Federation of Nigeria had failed;

    (v) that all efforts to find a practical and just solution to the crisis were frustrated at every turn by acts of bad faith on the part of Gowon;

    (vi) that the Federation of Nigeria had forfeited any claim to their allegiance by these acts and by economic, political and diplomatic sanctions imposed against them by the Gowon régime;

they had mandated 'His Excellency, Lt.-Col. Chukwuemeka Odumegwu Ojukwu, Military Governor of Eastern Nigeria, to declare at the earliest practicable date Eastern Nigeria a free, sovereign and independent state by the name and title of the *Republic of Biafra*'.

A few hours later, Lt.-Col. Gowon repealed the Constitution (Suspension and Modification) Decree, 1967, which attempted to implement the Aburi agreements. He thus resuscitated the provisions of decree No. 1 as modified by decree No. 9, which returned the country to a federal system of government. Now acting unilaterally, he followed this up by declaring a state of emergency in Nigeria, and carved the tottering country into twelve states, three of which were in the East, six in the North, a Western State, a Lagos State and a Mid-Western State.

Meanwhile, following the mandate given him by the people of Eastern Nigeria, Lt.-Col. Ojukwu proceeded to appoint administrators to the twenty provinces of Eastern Nigeria which were created in January.

At this stage it was obvious that Nigeria had reached the end of its journey of existence. In a doleful editorial[335] captioned 'The Plunge', *The Daily Sketch* remarked:

Events have moved fast in Nigeria within the last few months. Whatever is going to be the outcome of these events is anybody's guess. One thing is certain, Nigeria has taken a big plunge. Future is bleak and nebulous. . . . It looks very much today as if all hope is lost.

Perhaps it is too late to continue to appeal for calm. Perhaps it is too late to entreat the rulers and their advisers to think of the masses of Nigeria in whatever they are doing. We do not think, however, that it is too late for praying. . . . Our prayer therefore, is: may God guide us aright.

It was certainly too late for appeals and entreaties. The nation had taken 'the big plunge' and Eastern Nigeria had been pushed beyond the point of no return. 'Prudence, indeed, will dictate that Governments long established should not be changed for light and transient causes.' These are the immortal words of the American Declaration of Independence. Eastern Nigerians were forced to declare their sovereignty by grave and enduring causes. They suffered injustices and abuses while they were sufferable. But when a catalogue of bad faith and duplicity (on Gowon's part) and arrogant intransigence (on the North's part) had evinced an unmistakable design to place them under an absolute and perpetual domination, it was their right, nay, their duty to provide for themselves such a new government as they should think fit to assure their own safety and security.

Thus at the dawn of that momentous Tuesday, May 30, 1967, the firm, slow and articulate voice of Lt.-Col. Chukwue-meka Odumegwu Ojukwu brought the good tidings to the 14 million anxious Eastern Nigerians. In a radio broadcast,[336] he declared: 'Fellow countrymen and women, You, the people of Eastern Nigeria:

* *Conscious* of the Supreme authority of Almighty God over all mankind, of your duty to yourselves and posterity;
* *Aware* that you can no longer be protected in your lives and in your property by any government based outside Eastern Nigeria;
* *Believing* that you are born free and have certain inalienable rights which can best be preserved by yourselves;
* *Unwilling* to be unfree partners in any association of a political or economic nature;
* *Rejecting* the authority of any person or persons other than the Military Government of Eastern Nigeria to any imposition of whatever kind or nature upon you;
* *Determined* to dissolve all political and other ties between you and the former Federal Republic of Nigeria;
* *Prepared* to enter into such association, treaty or alliance with any sovereign state within the former Federal Republic of Nigeria and elsewhere on such terms and conditions as best to subserve your common good;
* *Affirming* your trust and confidence in *me*;
* *Having* mandated *me* to proclaim on your behalf, and in your name, that Eastern Nigeria be a sovereign independent Republic,

now, therefore, I, Lieutenant-Colonel Chukwuemeka Odumegwu Ojukwu, Military Governor of Eastern Nigeria, by virtue of the authority, and pursuant to the principles, recited above, do hereby solemnly proclaim that the territory and region known as and called Eastern Nigeria, together with her continental shelf and territorial waters, shall henceforth be an independent sovereign state of the name and title of *The Republic of Biafra*'.

This proclamation was greeted with wild and unrestrained jubilation all over the country by joyous crowds who thronged the streets shouting '*Hail Biafra*'.[337] Schools and shops were closed. Offices were deserted. Men, women and children, old and young – everybody joined in the jubilation. Students of the University of Nigeria (later University of Biafra) jumped out of their halls in their pyjamas and nightgowns for sheer

joy and congratulated one another. Thus Nigeria, a federa~~~
created and destroyed by Britain, has unhappily taken a well-
deserved seat among the federations that collapsed. Out of its
decadence has emerged a young, virile, and amazingly promising
African nation – the Republic of Biafra.

11

A RETROSPECT

(i) BRITAIN AND THE FEDERAL CONCEPT

Looking back at the whole history and political experience of Nigeria and the Biafra-Nigeria conflict, a number of conclusions and comments would appear pertinent at this stage. First we direct attention at Nigeria's federalism. From the history of Nigeria, it was obvious that Nigeria was not one country, but several 'countries' – brought together by a forced political amalgamation. This amalgamation was effected and maintained in spite of deep-rooted differences and suspicions between the various tribal groups, arising from the factors of culture, language and geography, and the impact of foreign influence. The various Constitutions, from the colonial days to independence, expressed the country's disunity and sought to impose political and economic 'unity in diversity'. From 1914, when the Colony and Protectorate of Southern Nigeria was joined to the Northern Protectorates, to 1960, when Nigeria achieved political independence, no fewer than five attempts were made to fashion a charter that would help Nigerians to live together as citizens of one and the same nation. The failure of the attempts illustrates the difficulty of working out a satisfactory solution to the problems of governments in a society with such deep-rooted differences. Thus, in spite of the enthusiasm with which Nigeria accepted her independence from Britain, sophisticated observers were able to come to a conclusion that Nigeria remained more of a 'geographical expression' than a nation. True nationhood and unity were yet to be achieved.

Nigerian disunity could be attributed in part to the colonial Constitutions. The Richards Constitution of 1946 set out as its aim the promotion of Nigerian 'unity in diversity'. The motive might have been acceptable, but the truth of the Nigerian experiment in regionalism, which that Constitution ushered in, was that ethnic and tribal loyalties immediately found expression in geographical terms and therefore got intensified. Inevitably, the Richards Constitution became a dividing line in Nigeria's constitutional development: before it, the tendency was towards unification and centralisation; after it, the keynote in Nigeria's politics became separatism and greater decentralisation. Ironically, it was that Constitution that for the first time brought the North and the South under one Central Legislative Council. However, the establishment of a Regional Assembly in each Region served as a focus for sectional loyalties and as a forum for championing sectional claims. Indeed the Richards Constitution compromised Nigerian unity.

The Lyttelton Constitution[338] of 1954 gave Nigeria a federal structure. But it did not aim at creating true federalism for Nigeria. It retained the anomalies inherited from the Richards Constitution and allowed, not only the size of the North, but also a 50 per cent representation of the North in the House of Representatives. Federalism is a system of government in which there is a division of powers between a central government and a number of regional or state governments, each government, whether central or regional, supreme in its own allocated area of authority and at the same time co-ordinating with the other governments. Sir Ivor Jennings was of the view that 'nobody would have a federal constitution if he could possibly avoid it'.[339] Perhaps, in the Nigerian circumstances also, federalism is the last form of government that should have been contemplated, and the matter was made worse by the peculiar absurdities of the country's Federal Constitution. Two characteristics pointed out by Dicey as necessary – earlier and looser connection and the existence of a federal sentiment – were clearly lacking in the case of Nigeria. The various peoples of Nigeria had existed independently and separately before colonial rule. After the British came to impose their rule and a common government, they resisted it. The North, in particular, did not think that there could ever be a meeting-point between them and the South, and wanted to go its own separate way. Nor did the peoples of Nigeria, when a federal constitution was thrust upon them, show capability in playing the complicated game of circumventing sectional frictions while working out the rigidities, technicalities, excessive legalism and conservatism that are inherent in a federal constitution. In spite of the para-

phernalia of federalism and parliamentary democracy, Nigeria
was neither a nation nor a democracy by the time of the military take-over of January 15, 1966. The North arrogated to itself the right to pursue an independent foreign policy, and considered itself to have a greater tie with the Arab world than with
the rest of Nigeria. A very good illustration of Nigeria's hydra-
headed foreign policy was the difficulty the Federal Government once ran into while seeking loans from Israel. When Ahmadu Bello, the Northern Premier, then on an Arab tour, heard of
the Federal Government's move to get a loan from Israel, he
declared that, as far as he was concerned, Israel did not exist.
Of course, since the NPC, of which he was also the President,
was in control of the Federal Government, the matter was
naturally dropped. The NCNC Government of Eastern Nigeria,
on the other hand, never hesitated at any time to work in association with Israel, which the North and Lagos had rejected.
There were many Israelis in the East in various capital projects. But since the East could not secure loans outside Nigeria
without Federal Government approval, she paid herself for
every project.

Most of Nigeria's ills have been blamed on the British, if
only as a comforting resort. But this approach is not irrational
in many cases, where it is possible to understand the motives
behind the British Government's actions. A pertinent question
in this discussion is: what was the motive behind Britain's
creation of Nigeria as a federation? To answer this question,
it is necessary to refer to similar attempts by Britain in the
different parts of her now defunct empire. As a trade-dependent
nation, Britain did not overlook the concept of economies of
scale in her economic activities in foreign lands. She aimed,
in all cases, at the maximum exploitation of the economic resources of colonial territories. In the case of larger territories,
this meant expanded markets. She thus developed a positive frenzy for the federal concept as the most effective political
contrivance for achieving this economic purpose. Thus, in
different parts of the world – in Malaysia, the West Indies,
South Arabia, Central Africa, East Africa and Nigeria, federations were imposed. The ultimate disintegration of these
federations supplies plentiful evidence that they were impositions
effected, not with a view to assuring harmony in the lives of

the peoples involved, but to assuring maximum exploitation by the imperial and colonial power.

In the former Nigerian Federation, an ephemeral unity was given to the country for the same hope of economic gain. British administrators paid greater attention to the economic than to the political unity of the country. The theoretical data for economic planning was defined as making the physical and industrial resources of the various regions complementary to one another. Common governmental services and transport facilities (roads, rail, harbours, air transport) were planned and maintained. A common currency was instituted for the country, while the total fiscal policy was geared to becoming a counterweight in the direction of unity. A National Economic Council was organized and retained from 1955, with regional and federal representatives, as a forum for considering economic problems and encouraging the co-operation of all the regional governments in economic matters. A Joint Planning Committee was established in 1958, including other organs like a Loans Advisory Council, to deal with economic planning and the distribution of loans. The mineral wealth of Eastern Nigeria was to be exploited to the total advantage of the whole country, especially the poorer regions looking for capital for industrialisation and other capital projects. The need for planning from the Centre was constantly emphasized, the reason being to secure the most efficient use of economic resources, raw materials, technical skills and outside investment. Nigerians were constantly reminded of their interdependence. No Region or Government in the Federation, it was said, could exist without the others.

In spite of exertions in this direction on the part of our colonial masters, they acted as if they were unaware that Nigeria's single most basic problem was *sub-nationalism* – a term which has variously been referred to as tribalism, provincialism, regionalism, sectionalism or even communalism, each of which made for group loyalty and group solidarity along ethnic, linguisitic and cultural lines. The fact of the Nigerian experience would tend to lead one to the conclusion that this refusal to recognise the problem of sub-nationalism was both deliberate and advantageous. Lord Lugard tolerated Northern conservatism and parochialism in his anxiety to adopt the system of *indirect rule*. Other instances from the creation of Nigeria abound, leading clearly to the conclusion that the British administrative and political policies tolerated, or even encouraged, tribal and regional separateness. The North was encouraged to look different and to develop along its own lines, and the natural consequence of this policy was that the North did not feel itself to have anything in common with the South. Its dealings with the South after independence smacked of racism.

In the desire to serve regional, rather than national interests, intense and unhealthy rivalry developed between the various regions in all fields of economic development – in the siting of the Federal capital projects, in campaigning for foreign loans and in investment. The North used its position as a majority group and controller of the Federal Government to obstruct economic ventures and slow down development in other regions. The Federal Government itself inevitably became a tribal Government; being manipulated by the North, it became partial in the siting of Federal industries and projects, as happened in the case of the Iron and Steel complex, which was done on a political, rather than economic basis.[340] As Eastern Nigeria, under the able leadership of Dr. M. I. Okpara, offered the most sustained and stubborn resistance to Northern domination and hegemony, the Northern Nigeria-controlled Federal Government discriminated against her in the siting of Federal capital projects. Before the break-up of the Nigerian Federation, the siting of Federal institutions in the various regions of the country was as follows:[341]

(i) *Northern Region*

    a. Federal Department of Veterinary Research, Vom;
    b. Agricultural Research Institute, Samaru;
    c. Institute for Trypanosomiasis Research, Vom and Kaduna;
    d. Military Headquarters, Zaria;
    e. National Munitions Factory, Zaria;
    f. Nigerian Military Academy, Zaria;
    g. Air Force Headquarters, Kaduna;
    h. International Airport, Kano;
    i. £78 million Kainji Dam Project;

j. Jebba Paper Mills;
k. Bacita Sugar Industry, Ilorin.

(ii) *Western Region*
   a. University of Ibadan and several associated institutes;
   b. University College Hospital, Ibadan;
   c. Headquarters of the Federal Department of Agricultural Research;
   d. Headquarters of the Federal Department of Forestry Research;
   e. Cocoa Research Institute of Nigeria, Ibadan;
   f. Federal Industrial Research Institute, Oshodi;
   g. Nigerian Institute for Stored Products Research, Ibadan;
   h. Headquarters of the National Archives, Ibadan;
   i. Police Training College, Ikeja;
   j. International Airport, Ikeja;
   k. The proposed £15 million Rockefeller/Ford Foundation's Institute for Tropical Agricultural Research, Ibadan;
   l. The Nigerian Institute for Social and Economic Research (NISER), Ibadan.

Eastern Region
   a. The Oil Refinery (joint venture with Shell-BP and the Eastern Government);
   b. The Nkalagu Cement Factory (joint venture with the Eastern Government).

Mid-Western Region
   a. Nigerian Institute for Oil Palm Research, Benin.

These facts speak for themselves.

There was also, as a result of Nigeria's tribalism, an unhealthy rivalry between the various regions of Nigeria on economic matters. Former Nigerian politicians acted purely to satisfy regional, rather than national interests. Whenever they went on economic tours or 'missions' abroad, they organised loans on a regional basis and each regional mission succeeded or failed, depending on the astuteness of the mission members and the standing and political influence of the region in the foreign country involved. The rivalries and jealousies existing between the regions made it virtually impossible for an industry ultimately established with such borrowed capital to find a ready market in a region other than that in which it was sited. Rival industries were established and even administrative directives about industries to be patronised were issued to government departments.[342] People patronised products from their own particular regions, and governments directed propaganda campaigns against industries situated in other regions. The industries and capital projects in the country, rather than becoming complementary to each other, were planned along independent lines. In fact, with a little adjustment, each region could have existed entirely on its own.

(ii) CONFEDERALISM AS AN ALTERNATIVE

What then could have been the answer to Nigeria's explosive internal situation? Since Britain did hardly anything positive to give Nigeria true unity, perhaps a confederal system of government could have been adopted. This was the only logical step that could have been taken if the component parts of the Federation were to avoid direct and headlong collision. The kind of situation that existed in Nigeria called for contraction of political and territorial unity and for a looser form of political association, aimed at minimising friction. The component or associating states, by establishing a kind of Common Services Organisation, would achieve economic co-operation without the political unity which had proved to be disastrous. Confederation is by definition an association of a number of states for the purpose of co-operation (usually economic) and joint defence, but the central authority does not have a direct power over the citizens of the associated states. There are examples like the Germanic Confederation (1815–66), the Confederation of the Netherlands (1580–1795) and the Confederation of American states (1861–5). East Africa, which had a purely economic confederation, provides an excellent illustration of the solution that could have been applied in Nigeria. It also illustrates the fact that you cannot impose a federal arrangement, or indeed any form of government, upon an unwilling people and hope that such a political arrangement would stand the test of time.

East Africa was the last major centre of colonial rule in Africa. There, Britain tried to impose a federal set-up upon the people. Since the attempt was stoutly resisted, the effort came to nothing. But Britain had used a clever device by setting up (under the East Africa High Commission Order-in-Council, 1947, London) an East African High Commission, which came into being on January 1, 1948, replacing the East African Governors' Conference which had been in being since as long before as 1926. The new arrangement, even though falling short of a political union, and dealing principally with economic co-operation, also made for the establishment of an East African Central Legislative Assembly. The ultimate result was that it joined Kenya, Uganda and Tanganyika together in a form of functional federation. Within the arrangement, there were to be inter-territorial services in the fields of communications, transport, higher education and research.

Because the High Commission was understood for what it was – an economic fetter for the advantage of the British colonial power, which could be used in the future as a pretext for a white-dominated political federation – it was not popular among African nationalists. Tanganyika and Uganda, in particular, were highly critical and distrustful of it, and their fears were amply borne out by the imposition of a federation on the Africans of Northern Rhodesia and Nyasaland. The people of Kenya regarded the High Commission as a bureaucratic structure dominated by British officials.

When, therefore, Tanganyika became independent, she seized the opportunity immediately to call on the British Government to give assurance that her further participation in the Commission would be made compatible with her new sovereign status. At a Constitutional Conference in Dar-es-Saalam in March 1961, this point was clearly emphasised. In June 1961, therefore, it was agreed to establish a new organisation to be known as the East African Common Services Organisation, in which Tanganyika, Uganda and Kenya would participate as equal partners in a mutually beneficial economic association, responsibility for it being vested in the East African Common Services Authority. The areas of co-operation included, *inter alia*, Railways and Harbours Administration, Post and Tele-communications, Civil Aviation, Customs and Excise, Income Tax, Accounts and Audits, Meteorological Services, Research and Statistics. The new organisation clearly demonstrated how sovereign states can achieve economic co-operation and unity without political unity or association. A political unity in East Africa could have been disastrous as it has been in Nigeria, since there too tribalism is a very powerful centrifugal force.

The Nigerian context did not permit of a political union. Centrifugal overwhelmed centripetal forces, and deepened group antagonism and group loyalty. Friction developed from time to time between the various groups, and finally reached a bloody climax in the pogrom of 1966, which claimed 30,000 lives from Eastern Nigeria (Biafra) alone. Something similar to a tribal war started between Biafra and Nigeria when Gowon declared his war of genocide on July 6, 1967 – deepening tribal animosity and bitterness, and depopulating great areas in the two countries.

Perhaps, in spite of Nigeria's tribalism, with the right kind of leadership, the situation might have been saved. Right leadership here means a leader with the right kind of political vision and understanding – charismatic and evangelising and ready to accept the challenges posed by the country's peculiar situation with a statesmanlike approach in all things. There would be conflict certainly, for this is a political and human society – but it would not have got out of hand. But this is only a tentative view, not a categorical assertion – for, in Nigeria's actual experience, no leader ever came forward who was totally acceptable to the various peoples of the whole country. General Ironsi's case illustrates the fact that, even where there is a leader with sufficient goodwill and a fair portion of statemanship, the bitterness and tribalism of Nigeria can still generate force that will obstruct the building of true nationhood.

Because there was no acceptable leader, and because the bitterness between the various ethnic and tribal groups continued, confederation could have been the most realistic set-up for Nigeria. Here the powers at the centre would no longer be attractive. Any leader at the centre would have been easily accepted because the people would have recognised that such a

leader did not hold any effective power, at least enough to interfere with the independent development and progress of the associating states. Indeed, leadership at the centre would have been
rotational.

When the Ad Hoc Conference on the future of Nigeria met in
September 12, 1966, the North for once showed realism by
acknowledging that the only realistic approach to the Nigerian
crisis was political disengagement between the various regions.
In the first plenary session of the Conference, which was chaired
by one of her sons, Alhaji Kashim Ibrahim, the Northern delegation recommended that, in place of federation, Nigeria
should have a Common Service Organisation, after the examples of East Africa and Central Africa.[343] This new kind of
association would make co-operation possible in the fields of
mutual interest to all groups without bringing these groups into
direct physical conflict. The areas of co-operation, according to
the Northern paper to the Conference, should include Currency,
Central Banking, Telecommunications, Postal Services, Transport, Weights and Measures, Immigration and Emigration, Citizenship, External Publicity and Information, Customs and Excise and Foreign Trade. There was to be a Central Defence
Commission, while movement from one state to another should
be free.

The other Regions showed the same measure of realism by
supporting a loose form of association, in which the Centre
would be much weaker than the Regions. Except for the Mid-
West, all the other Regions, including the North, supported
the right of every Region to secede unilaterally from the
Federation. However, as soon as it became evident that the
Conference would recommend a confederal form of government for Nigeria, Lt.-Col. Gowon dismissed the Ad Hoc
Committee. It will be recalled that the Aburi Accord also recommended a loose form of association. If such a plan had
been adopted, Nigeria would thus have been saved – saved from
disintegration and a useless war.

The main point was that Lt.-Col. Gowon had been made to
believe that confederalism would ultimately bring about the
country's disintegration. But there are instances in political
history to prove him wrong. The United States of America,
today a very powerful nation, proud of her political heritage and

destiny, confederated before federating. Switzerland has continued to be a confederation in name but has acquired tendencies towards greater unity, so much so that some political analysts consider it today a federation for all practical purposes. On December 1, 1967, there was a meeting of East African leaders in Arusha, Tanzania. Kenyatta, Nyerere and Obote (the leaders of Kenya, Tanzania and Uganda respectively) met to wind up the East African Common Services Organisation, an economic confederation which had been given effect on December 9, 1961, and to form a new East African Economic Community. The absence of political union did not mean that there could be no economic co-operation, and the fact that there is only economic co-operation today does not mean that there could be no political union tomorrow. There is nothing stopping the East African countries from associating politically in future, if they so desire. The point of emphasis is that this must come about as a result of the genuine desire of the people themselves.

Before the break-up of Nigeria, Biafra continued to stress that the only reasonable path for the present time was confederalism. Nigeria vacillated, and ultimately took the downward path to self-destruction. After Biafra became independent, she still left the door open to Nigeria to accept economic co-operation in place of political union. Up till today, in spite of Nigeria's stubborn stand on the side of political union, Biafra has continued to extend the hand of fellowship to her. The Biafran Declaration of Independence embodied a clause which read that Biafra should 'keep the door open for association with, and would welcome any sovereign unit(s) in the former Federation of Nigeria, desirous of association with us for the purpose of running common ties. . . .' The same point was repeated by the Government of Biafra after the capture of the Republic of Benin, and was demonstrated in practical terms when Biafra resumed economic ties and co-operation with the people of that Republic. The same point was made while the OAU Peace Committee was in Lagos.

In spite of the Biafra–Nigeria war and the bitterness that has been generated, the authors believe that Nigeria still has the opportunity to look dispassionately and realistically at the future in the hope that the illusions of today might be disabused by the realities of practical experience. It is possible that Biafra could still co-operate with Nigeria economically. Once bitter enemies and antagonists might tomorrow become the best of friends. And let the lessons of Arusha be constantly borne in mind.

12

POSTSCRIPT:
MY PEOPLE SUFFER

by ARTHUR NWANKWO

(Dedicated to Mr. H. Obu and Dr. Okechuku Ikejiani)

I have seen things in Biafra this week which no man should have to see. Sights to scorch the mind and sicken the conscience. I have seen children roasted alive, young girls torn in two by shrapnel, pregnant women eviscerated, and old men blown to fragments. I have seen these things and I have seen their cause: high-flying Russian Ilyushin jets operated by Federal Nigeria, dropping their bombs on civilian centres throughout Biafra.

WILLIAM NORRIS
The Sunday Times (London), April 28, 1968

I became fully politically conscious in my first year in College in the United States. I saw the affluence of the American society. Consciously or unconsciously, that affluence influenced by belief in large political units as the salvation for African peoples. I looked on the Federation of Nigeria to which I belonged as the greatest hope for Africa. Naturally I believed to the hilt in the unity of that country and dreamed of a powerful, united, vast and populous Nigeria. All through our major national crisis I wrote to brothers, relatives and friends, enjoining, pleading, cajoling for a united country. I lost no opportunity, even in the most informal note, to plead the cause of national unity – at all costs. In spite of the continued drift of the Federation, I continued to hope, even in face of news of growing internal disharmony, tribal, social and political.

Then January 15, 1966, and the coup – the unsuccessful coup. When I heard the news first, I went out with a couple of other Africans and had an expensive and wild evening. Later, I heard the details, and about Major-General Ironsi, and wasn't so happy. Had he any political background? He could shoot, but could he rule? But after a month or so, I began to change my mind. After all, the General seemed to be doing well. His sincerity was transparent, and his National Reconstruction sounded promising – at least from the distance.

Then, on July 29, 1966, two hundred officers of Eastern Nigerian origin were mowed down. The pogrom followed – 30,000 Eastern Nigerians systematically massacred in successive outburts of hateful passion. From far away in the United States it looked unreal: as distant as the colonial history we studied in the high school. Came January 1967, and the Aburi meeting of the Nigerian Supreme Military Council in Ghana. The agreement in Ghana gave me joy, because it meant a chance for peace and meaningful unity. My joy was short-lived. For very soon it became obvious that Gowon would not honour the Aburi Agreement. There followed the federal blockade, then an impasse and then secession. Biafra was born. On July 5, 1967, the eerie silence of Nsukka Province was shattered by those fateful bullets that started the war. Gowon had launched his police action. The poor villagers were forced out of their homes. Till today – one and a half years later – they are still homeless (i.e. those surviving, for thousands have since died), and still fly from pillar to post – for dear life's sake.

At that time I had just obtained my Master's Degree, at Duquesne, Pittsburgh, USA, and I began to think of going home. I was inside blockaded Biafra five days after leaving New York, and found what I'd never seen anywhere – a mountain of smouldering injured feeling, the grim and quiet determination that characterises a man who has been shocked out of a long dearly-held illusion, and is determined to have no more of it. You could feel it gnawing at you from the entire atmosphere, further intensified by the hardship caused by the blockade. It is true that Biafra's case for a right to separate existence has been very eloquently put forward in pamphlets, over the radio and by personal contacts. But beyond doubt is the fact that you cannot fully comprehend the gravity of the situation unless you visit Biafra.

To me, Biafra was quite different from the Eastern Nigeria I left five years before. There had been a great transformation. Before I left the country the spirit of Nigerian nationalism dominated the everyday life of the then Eastern Nigerians. The Ibos were the proudest Nigerians, within and without. The

National Council of Nigerian Citizens, the only nationalist political party in the old Nigerian Federation, derived the bulk of its support from Eastern Nigeria. Eastern Nigerians took pride in speaking Hausa or Yoruba amongst themselves. They often damned traditional customs to intermarry with the people of the other regions of the Federation. They lived and worked in other parts of the country – perhaps they did all this because they are go-getters by nature. Perhaps, too, they were adventurous. And perhaps because their Region was too small to contain and sustain them. These are reasons which have been advanced to explain away their nationalism. But after all is said and done, it must be admitted that the then Eastern Nigerians took Nigerian nationalism in their stride. No matter what one would choose to read into their motive, the inescapable fact is that all through the history of Nigeria, they were in the vanguard of the struggle for Nigerian Unity. Dr. Azikiwe, then the leader of the NCNC, vehemently opposed regionalisation, which later turned out to be the bane of the Federation.

Now, this loyalty – like the unappreciated love it was – has been turned from it's ungrateful object to a new smaller but more meaningful and appreciative object. A new kind of nationalism has emerged: Biafran nationalism. Why the change? This is a question most foreigners have never stopped to ask themselves. Why should a people who have for over fifty years consistently stood for a large united political entity now fight to uphold a secession? And who are the people branded as Ojukwu's lieutenants? Of *Dr. Nnamdi Azikiwe*, the charismatic father of African nationalism, even the most narrow-minded human bolt in the monstrous war machine that is today choking the young Biafran Republic will admit that, on several occasions, in order to keep Nigeria one, he entered into compromises which earned him the disfavour and even the jeers of his erstwhile adorers. Today, even Zik has run out of compromises.

Dr. Akanu Ibiam, Vice-President of the World Council of Churches, with an integrity untarnished in any way. A man of God with a personal life whose unblemished character is recognised at home and abroad. Everyone who has associated with Dr. Ibiam will agree that he is not a man who can be used as an instrument for personal ambition, particularly where the defence of that 'ambition' entails loss of scores of thousands of human lives.

I don't want to mention Dr. Michael Okpara (in spite of his nationalist outlook) because someone might bring up the irrelevant argument that he was a regional premier of the Federation and thus contributed to the regionalism that destroyed the country. For a similar reason, too, I won't include Matthew Mbu, S. Dikibo, Dr. K. O. Mbadiwe, and a host of others. I am interested in internationally respected dignitaries, like Bishop Arinze, Bishop Uzodike, Mr. N. U. Akpan, General Effiong, and others who are not politicians, and whose age, position and training make it incongruous for them to support a secession which, in their opinion, is rash and unnecessary. The stubborn question is: What is it that has rallied these people behind the crusading banner of secession? The hackneyed explanation that Biafra is the child of a frustrated attempt to dominate Nigeria cannot stand a close examination. For when a man leaves all his life-time fortune and friends for a new and uncertain future, the reason cannot be transient. There must have been strong reasons which compel him to prefer the uncertainties of the future to the certainties of the present. Nor can it be rightly said that Biafrans were cajoled to come home by men who wanted power, for the average Biafran is an independent thinker. The ease and speed with which erstwhile political crowd-pullers fall out of grace for any unpopular action or statement in the former Eastern Nigeria underlies this fact. Even now, just one wrong step from Lt.-Col. Ojukwu and the very peasants in Biafra who drop their picks to shake adoring fists will spit into his face in obvious and profound contempt.

Thus one fact stands clear: the Biafran secession was a popular and spontaneous desire. It was not just an alternative; it was a last resort. No race, community or group of people, put in a similar position to the Biafrans, will act otherwise. We only have to look into the pages of history to see that people have done graver things for more transient reasons.

If the massacres of 1966 had been limited to a coup in which General Ironsi and a number of leaders (even if they were all Ibos) were killed, the matter would have remained political, its scope limited to a smaller circle comprising, by and large, only the politically conscious. But the massacres were not directed only against the leaders and prominent men. They were directed against Biafrans – just Biafrans – men, women and children. This is the element which brought the matter home to the people: the fact that whether you played politics or not, you were qualified for death so long as you were a Biafran. This made the crisis a social problem in which every Biafran felt committed.

So much effort has been expended trying to cut the number massacred from 30,000 to 10,000, as if 10,000 is the permissible limit for the toll of a pogrom. Ten thousand is a large number of people to lose, and this is putting it mildly. After all, the blacks in both Rhodesia and South Africa have not lost half as much, yet the whole world is raising hell against the white regimes in those two countries.

In a statement entitled 'Why we recognised Biafra', the Government of Tanzania said: 'Once a large unit stops believing that the state is theirs, and that the Government is their instrument, then the unity is no longer viable'. Definitely the loss of 10,000 (not to say 30,000) relatives, fathers, mothers and children, is sufficient reason to make any group or community consider themselves unwanted. But even this did not push Biafrans to secession. Long after the 1966 massacres and the consequent exodus of over 1·8 million Biafrans from other parts of the Nigerian Federation, the concept of an independent Republic of Biafra was still a far cry from the desires of the people of the then Eastern Nigeria. The pogrom was not so much the factor which influenced the secession as the fear of a repeat performance of the killings. And nothing fortified this fear more than the fact that the perpetrators of these killings gloated over, rather than showed remorse for, their barbarous deeds. Nor did the Gowon régime give any sincere impression of disapproving the killings, much more punishing the sadistic culprits. Thus, when the Aburi Agreements were dishonoured by the Lagos régime, it did not need a mass communication medium to convince the people that their security could not be entrusted to anybody outside the Eastern Region. The transference of loyalty from Nigeria to Biafra was complete. This is not to say that, hitherto, there had never been calls for secession. Indeed, after the massacres there were bitter groups who strongly believed that secession should be declared immediately. There were even cases of men who armed themselves with machetes and made for Northern Nigeria to avenge their relatives. (Of course, they were held back by friends and surviving relatives.) Not surprisingly this group of zealots were mainly from the refugees from Northern Nigeria who were still incensed by the terror they had seen there in those months of the massacres. Up till late February 1967 the group had been a negligible and ineffective minority. By May, however, they had had their last laughs. For then, they could smack their lips with satisfaction and say to their more conservative friends, 'I told you so'.

All I have been trying to say is that the Biafran secession was unanimous and spontaneous. It wasn't the plot of a clique; nor one man's ambition. If anything is true, it is that Col. Ojukwu was pushed into declaring the secession on May 30 by forces within Biafra and by the acts from Lagos which further activated those forces.

Living in Biafra today is like a nightmare, for one counts oneself fortunate for every hour one has lived through. Food prices have risen a hundred-fold. Garri, which is the staple food, used to be less than a penny a cup. Now it's more than a shilling (twelve pennies) a cup! Yet it is the basic and commonest foodstuff which even the poorest must afford or starve. Such things as meat and fish are now exorbitant luxuries. Salt costs £105 to £120 a bag! And so on. To appreciate the situation, it must be realised that the buying power of money (particularly of local foodstuffs) is particularly high in underdeveloped countries. For example, whereas the average Biafran (before the war) could dine comfortably in a local hotel with a shilling, an average American would need at least a dollar fifty to do the same. Of course, it should be realised that the *per capita* income was much higher in the United States.

One can then imagine a situation where an average Biafran can't have a satisfactory meal on five shillings! And to crown the misery the earning power is less by more than a half now. The peasant farmers have been driven out of their lands, their crops destroyed and set ablaze by the Nigerian Army. The heavily burdened government is the only employer and its employees are (inevitably) paid *allowances* and not salaries. With an increased number of dependants, heavily reduced wages, and prices multiplied tenfold, the average Biafran is forced to concentrate on the progressively more difficult job of keeping from starvation. This is the story for the average Biafran who earns an income (no matter how small) or who has a relative who does so. There are millions of others who are below this fortunate average. These are the desperate refugees, no less than six million in number, unemployed, destitute, driven from their homes and deprived of their lands – their only means of livelihood – which have been blazed into desolation by the invading Nigerian Army. It is from this miserable group that two to three thousand die every day of hunger and disease. And as you go along the streets of Biafra, you would see them everywhere, under trees, in empty school buildings – just any-where there is any kind of shelter. You would see them, all dried up and without flesh, their creasy and scaly skins dragging on their protruded bones, their eyes hollow and pale and their bearings gaunt. But to them, in their own personal way, the fight is on, the fight for survival. As you pass, they present withered bony palms for alms. They have the courage to swal-low traditional pride and beg! An unthinkable thing before the war. They are about the streets in families, the woman, grim-faced, carrying a crying, hungry child; the rest stumbling blindly after her; all of them miserable, living skeletons, picking their weary way through the more fortunate but no more happy crowd, in search of just sufficient food to postpone the inevitable parting of ways between body and soul. At first the alms came, freely and generously. But soon they became only a trickling, as the shortage of circulating money became more acute. Civil servants go for months without their slashed allowances. And almost always the bank vaults are dry. In any case, most of the fortunate ones walk about with little or no money in their pockets (and of course nothing in the house). And none is sure of the next meal. Under this condition, the refugees receive little and they die of hunger and of exposure to the elements of nature. The extended family, that resilient traditional umbrella in whose comfortable and protecting shade the Biafran always finds a welcome place in times of need, is useless today. The umbrella itself has been torn to pieces by the invading Nigerian forces. Makeshift refugee camps are set up in every available space (which is rare).

After my first visit to a camp I couldn't sleep for two days. Before then the full impact of the suffering of my people had never really struck me. It was terrible enough to live from hand to mouth, not sure of the next meal; to think of such things as electric lights, gas stoves, fans, air conditioners, milk, ice cream, cake, beer, tinned food, soft drinks and anything that savoured of twentieth-century civilisation (except, of course, guns, bombs and modern instruments of destruction) is to think of luxuries of far remote times.

My first visit to the refugee camp was not planned. I ran across an old school-mate whom I hadn't seen for years. He was an administrative officer-in-charge of one of the camps. He invited me for a weekend and I went. The camp was in what used to be an elementary school compound. (Education is also a thing of the past world in embattled Biafra.) My friend graduated from a Nigerian university and shared a room with a co-worker – also a graduate of the same university. The first thing my host did was to take me round the camp. It was a nightmarish affair. The refugees clustered in groups (family groups, probably) and gazed listlessly at us as we passed. Of course they were human skeletons. There were hundreds of children, with swollen tummies and legs, large skully heads, withered chests, pleated and sallow skins, yellowish hairs, flattened buttocks and sunken pale eyes.

As we approached the last building, my host stopped and smiled sadly.

He said: 'Would you like to go there also?' He pointed at the small white house.

'Why, of course,' I said. Then on second thoughts I asked: 'Who are these?'

His sad smile broadened and then was gone. He looked straight at me and said: 'They are people who are about to die.'

His sad smile returned again and he asked: 'You want to see them?'

I nodded, and we walked towards the small white house. As

we approached, a strong revolting stench sprang at us. I remembered that stench from my early school days – years before. A man accused of burglary had been stoned to death by an angry mob. His corpse lay in a street gutter for three days before sanitary officers took it away. For those three days, that vicinity was deserted because of the sickening smell of the decaying flesh.

Now, as the same stench rushed at us, I recognised it immediately. It was the smell of death. It grew in intensity faster than we approached, and pushed at us. My nostrils protested violently. I would have turned back but I was ashamed to turn my back on my people, condemned to death for no fault of theirs.

I looked at my host, his face was calm and grave. That sad smile still hung on it. He couldn't speak. He made signs indicating that I should hold my handkerchief to my nose. I obeyed.

We walked into the house of death. We saw then those who were about to die. They sat all about the floor and gaped unseeingly before them. Dead but alive. They didn't turn their heads or flick their eyelids to show they noticed our presence. They simply sat still, oblivious of the multitude of flies which flirted around them, and oblivious of the ghastly smell that hung heavily in the air.

We went from room to room, my host leading, and I following blindly behind him. In one of the rooms there were three dead bodies, in another, four. Here the stench was so thick you could almost touch it. My host inspected each corpse. I watched his face most of the time. The sad smile was gone but the gravity remained. I noticed that he held nothing to his nose. Then I looked around again and saw them. Not the corpses, but the living dead. And I was ashamed to hold by handkerchief to my nose. I quickly and angrily removed it.

This attracted my host's attention and he looked curiously at me. I glared back at him and his stubborn sad smile returned to his face. We turned and retraced our steps. My host's steps were hurried now.

Outside, and beyond the domain of the sickening stench of death, I asked the questions that had been welling up in my mind.

'Just why should these people be left to die?'

My host didn't speak for a while. Then he said, 'Because nothing can be done about them.'

'What do you mean?' I asked.

'Just that they are beyond help. They can't take food because it means nothing to them. They've been hungry so long, they have lost interest in food. Give them food and they just stare at you. They've lost interest in the world. All they await is death.'

His voice was tremulous, but he still hurried. I asked him why the hurry.

Without turning he said: 'I have to have the dead removed and buried.' Then he turned to me. 'That's all we can do,' he said, and hurried off.

I intended staying in the camp for three days. But so upset was I that I picked up my little travelling kit and left the camp that same evening. My host was sorry that I had to leave, but he understood. There was no fuel, so there was no public transport. Luckily I got a ride on a military truck. Its destination was an army camp twenty-five miles from Aba. I passed a most uncomfortable night there. The next day I got another ride, this time on a bicycle. It took me to within ten miles of Aba and I trekked the remaining distance. I arrived at Aba twenty-four hours after leaving the refugee camp.

At first I regretted that visit, because for the next seventy-two hours I had terrible nightmares. I was haunted by those glassy, vacant eyes of the inmates of the house of death. I was ashamed to have a meal while those condemned inmates waited for the comfort of death. And even as I ate, it came and they followed it, willingly from a world which had been unfair to them. These days I don't regret the visit any more. Rather I have been reinforced in the depth of my appreciation of the sufferings of my people.

But the living skeletons in the refugee camps were not alone on their journey. Countless others followed them. Victims, not of starvation, but of violent deaths, deliberately inflicted by the Nigerian land and air forces. Only yesterday I was plodding wearily home in the baking heat of the equatorial sun when there was an air-raid. There were the usual reactions you get when Aba is bombed. Men, women and children thronged into the streets trying to locate the bomber or bombers. Frightened ones ran helter-skelter – achieving nothing practically.

'It's not bombs this time' yelled a soldier. 'It is rockets. You won't see them coming – for heaven's sake go into the house!' No one heard him. I dived into the nearest building. I found myself taking cover in the ground floor of a storeyed building. There were women and children cuddling together, their lips moving in sibilant prayers. I could hear 'Jesus Christ' and 'God' repeated over and over again. A little lad of about nine looked at me with starry eyes from behind the protective embrace of his supplicating mother. He shared the embrace with his brothers and sisters who also muttered prayers for divine protection.

Then there were footsteps from the staircase above. A man with a very angry countenance hurried down. He had a double-barrelled rifle in both hands. As he came down he stuffed two bullets into it. He didn't look at me. He just gave a hard stare at the woman with the starry-eyed boy, and went into the pandemonium of the street, shutting the door behind him. The woman gazed back apprehensively at the retreating figure of her husband.

Meanwhile the menacing drone of the Nigerian bomber had become very loud, muffling the angry bark of anti-aircraft fire. The prayers of the women and children grew with it. Suddenly the lad with the starry eyes disengaged himself from his mother's embrace and ran into the street. Terror-stricken, his mother yelled his name and rushed after him. Instinctively, I pulled her back. Just then there was a deafening explosion above the din. I went down on the concrete floor. The women and children did the same as particles whistled above us into walls and furniture. The building shook so violently I thought the explosion was in our midst. There were agonising cries from the street outside. I regained my feet immediately and bounced out into the street.

The sight that met my eyes gave me a feeling of nausea. Sprawled along the street was a rippling sea of violently writhing bodies. Chilling moans charged the hot noon. At my feet, on the steps, the mangled body of the ten-year-old boy with the starry eyes lay in a pool of his own blood.

Instantly I stooped and felt his pulse. His body was still warm but the boy was certainly dead. Just then his mother rushed out, saw her dead son and fell on him, wailing piteously. The father came too; carrying a dangling left arm in his right hand. His gun wasn't on him. Red warm blood spouted out of his left shoulder and covered his left arm and one side. But his attention was not there. He stared agonisingly at the remains of what was once his son.

Meanwhile the hubbub had grown to something more than a din. The soldier had been busy keeping off the wailing crowd, and he now yelled at me to help. I left the dead boy with his parents and leapt into the midst of the writhing, blood-smeared bodies. The first I came to was a young woman of about twenty-five. Her right leg was smashed into a bloody pulp.

She said to me. 'Please, please help me. Don't let me die.' Not knowing exactly what to do, I held her shoulders. Then the next moment she threw her head backwards and died. *She died in my hands.* A tremor travelled through my whole frame and I quivered violently. For a moment I felt dazed and sick. Then a voice barked, 'You! What are you doing there?' It was the soldier. 'If she is dead, leave her and come this way.'

By now the clanging of racing ambulances had added to the chaos. With the help of Red Cross workers, who were now on the scene, we quickly loaded the dead and dying into ambulances, volunteered private cars and hand-pushed trucks. Some of the wounded died in transit to the hospital. All together that particular raid claimed one hundred and twenty-five lives. There were at least five hundred wounded.

I got home sick and tired. I just sat down and stared at the bloodstains on my clothes. I felt my head swell as I saw in my mind's eye the girl with the smashed leg. It was her anguished eyes as she pleaded 'Don't let me die'. I saw another: the body of a middle-aged woman. I had come upon her and, finding no blood on her, had thought she had merely swooned. I was mistaken, for she was stone dead. A closer look disclosed that the death bullet had entered her head at a point above the right ear.

An icy feeling crept up my spine and I shook my head to dismiss the picture. Just then, a commotion outside attracted my attention and I went out into the street. A long frenzied

K

column of men, women and children were marching up the street. They shook their fists, chanting:

> We are Biafrans
> Fighting for survival,
> By the name of Jesus
> We shall conquer.
>
> They may bomb us,
> Killing all our children,
> But by the name of Jesus
> We shall conquer.

This was the effect of each air-raid. It intensifies the belief of the people that their survival lies in resisting to the bitter end. It doesn't cow them into submission as it is meant to do. The main victims of Nigerian bombing missions in Biafra are civilians. Out of a total of 4,000 victims (this figure is still soaring), only about twenty were soldiers. The same proportions are true of the general death toll in the war. The total of lives so far lost is soaring rapidly towards three-quarters of a million, out of whom about eighty to ninety thousand were soldiers. The rest were civilian victims of starvation, disease, air-raids and the cold-blooded massacres that are carried out by the wild Nigerian soldiers on entering any town. The pattern is the same everywhere. Males of any age are lined up in hundreds and shot. The girls and women are despoiled to death. Farms are plundered and crops set ablaze. The children and the surviving women are left to starve to death. The result is that almost all civilians flee before advancing Nigerian soldiers. Some are forced by hunger to return to their embattled villages to scout for crumbs.

The case of the Federal Army lieutenant, Macauley Lamurde, who was executed before a hastily gathered audience of foreign journalists for 'breaking his Code of Conduct' by killing an Ibo youth called Matthias, again before foreign witnesses, is well known, and 'greatly embarrassed' the Nigerian Government (see *Newsweek*, September 9, 1968). The 'great embarrassment' is, of course, not that one Nigerian officer killed an Ibo boy. It was because the killing was done before foreign observers. This explains the unusual anxiety of the Lagos Government that the execution of the perpetrator should also be done before witnesses – foreign witnesses. Just to demonstrate that discipline can be maintained in the Nigerian Army.

A point that slips out of consideration is that Lt. Lamurde was an officer in whose charge were scores of 'other ranks' whose wildness equals the barbarism of the hordes who sacked Rome. Secondly, Matthias's story is the only one reported, because it is the only one so far witnessed by foreigners. If it took place in spite of those foreign observers, at a time when the Nigerian Government had invited an international observer force to observe its conduct of the war, one can imagine what has been going on.

This brings us to the team of observers invited by Nigeria from Britain, Poland, Sweden, Canada, the OAU and the United Nations, to disprove the allegation of genocide on the Biafran people. The total number of observers was no more than ten, their task: to observe the conduct of war on at least fifty fronts encompassing a land area of at least five thousand square miles. To perform this duty the observers should necessarily have accompanied all the Nigerian companies of soldiers on all their attacks. That is, they had to be present on all fronts, at all times. This, of course, included Biafran counter-attacks. For ten men to do all this presumes that they possess qualities which are something near omnipotence. This cannot be said of General Alexander, the British representative, nor of any of his team-mates. So far, the International Observer Team has proved the eyewash that it is.

Its first and second reports absolve the Nigerian soldiers of the charge of genocide on Biafrans. These were consequent to two visits of a few days each to the Northern and Southern sectors of the war. That is, the reports were based on experience gathered after spending a few days in some areas already over-run by the Nigerian soldiers. This is not only naïve but also ridiculous! How do the members of the team know what happened when the drugged soldiers invaded the area in the first instance? One of the reports says that the Nigerian soldiers were seen feeding the Biafran civilians in the areas they have captured. It continues: 'The fact that there were Ibos in these areas speaks for itself.' Strange reasoning . . . The fact that there are Ibos alive does not mean no Ibos were killed! This is the point. Genocide is genocide, and is bad enough whether complete or partial. Not all Ibos have to be dead before genocide can be established.

The observers witnessed distribution of food to refugees. Would General Alexander or any of his team-mates sincerely say that he really expected to see otherwise on such an invitation? Of course, the visits were expected, duly announced and well prepared for. Therefore, you would expect nothing but the best behaviour from the Nigerians. It is comparable to inspection days at school.

On October 4, 1968, two British missionaries (the Rev. and Mrs. Albert Savory) and two International Red Cross workers were shot by the Nigerian soldiers when they entered Okigwi. In a protest letter to the Nigerian Government, the International Committee of the Red Cross quoted an eye-witness account. The relief workers, it said were deliberately shot by the Nigerian soldiers in a clearly marked Red Cross hospital. The Nigerian officer who was present during the murders was either unable or unwilling to stop the shootings.

Before this there had been garbled reports about the soldiers being drunk, and their officer making fruitless attempts to hold them in check. If these reports were meant to show that the event was an accident, they merely begged the question. But this is not my concern here. The important thing is that it happened to white people, recognised as Red Cross workers. In a half-hearted attempt to exculpate the killers, a BBC Correspondent inferred that the whole concept of the Red Cross as a humanitarian and neutral organisation is strange to Africans in general. I do not want here to dwell on this insult to the African personality. The point I want to make is that, if the Nigerian soldiers found it difficult to consider relief workers as neutral 'because they fed their starving enemies', what was the fate of the 'enemies' themselves when they caught up with them? The answer follows simply: unquestioning and instantaneous execution. The observers were supposed to be in this sector of the war observing its conduct when this incident took place.

Yet they went back and reported that they found the Nigerian soldiers disciplined and well-behaved.

After the deaths of the four white people followed a wave of indignant cries from different parts of the world. The Red Cross sent a 'strong protest note'. World news media, except the British Broadcasting Corporation, condemned it. But conveniently forgotten was the fact that *three hundred* Biafrans were shot with these men in Okigwi. Nobody wants to see a connection between the Biafran charge of genocide and the cold-blooded shooting of the four white people. After all they would say, the other is Africans killing their brothers. It is an African problem. The whole idea of African brotherhood, as it is being practised today, and as it is being paid lip service by those who pretend to African leadership, is an absolute sham – as much a sham as the concept of an observer force.

My people suffer. This is an undeniable truth. That they have been made victims of genocide is a stubborn fact – international intrigue notwithstanding. And I mean genocide in its internationally understood meaning – that is, systematic extermination of a race or community by mass murder, or by imposing conditions that make survival impossible. For genocide is genocide – whether by bullet or starvation – so long as it is wilfully inflicted on its victims.

The Nigerians continue to do to death thousands of Biafrans in the thick jungles, in the little abandoned and forgotten 'houses of death' and at street corners – by bullets, by starvation and disease, and by mental breakdown. The last needs further elucidation.

The psychological effect of this war on the total Biafran population has been most profound, though this is hardly recognised. The knowledge that one stands a very good chance of being dead the next minute is a rather exacting strain. One moment you are chatting with a neighbour, a friend or a brother. The next moment a bomber swoops into the town, there is an explosion and he is dead. It could have been you. And there is no knowing that it won't be your turn next. When a bomber arrives, my younger brother usually says 'Say your last prayer which may not be your last'. He does it jovially; but how profound it is!

There is no philosophy in death. It must come sooner or later.

But conditions in Biafra make it come sooner than later. For there have been many who have broken down under the crushing strain of fearing death. A close survey of the death toll in Biafra shows that, apart from those who die of bombs, rockets, bullets and malnutrition, most of the others (i.e. those who, we say, died peacefully) are the aged and the weak or ailing-hearted. The old men and women give up rather than face the prospect of losing their sons, of starving to death, and of evacuating a place which has been home to them and their ancestors for centuries.

Today there is a general feeling of insecurity in Biafra. This adds to the mental strain. It is not out of place to find soldiers (stragglers, no doubt) making a most excruciating nuisance of themselves. On one occasion, while I was walking down a street, I jingled a few coins in my palm. A soldier stopped me and asked me what I had in my palm. I told him it was money. 'Give it to me!' he ordered.

I asked him why. He said it was because I was hoarding coins. I told him I couldn't be hoarding *five shillings* (the value of the coins). The man wouldn't listen and threatened to use force. By now I was pretty angry. I made him understand that he was trying daylight robbery and that I wasn't ready to part with my money even if it meant a physical showdown. When the bully recognised the futility of his venture he quietly left me alone with a face-saving warning against 'hoarding money'.

On another occasion I had a rougher deal. I was coming home from work. The time was about 6.35 p.m. (Wartime Biafran Civil Service operates a 56-hour working week). Three young fellows stopped me and said that I was arrested for breaking the dusk-to-dawn curfew.

'But it's not 7 p.m. yet,' I protested.

'Curfew starts 6.30 now,' one of them told me curtly.

'When did the change start?' I asked. 'It was not announced.'

'Look, man, explain that to the Ward Leader,' I was told and pushed on along the street.

By the time we got to the Ward Leader's house it was after seven and there were many other prisoners arrested both before and after 7 p.m. The Ward Leader, a middle-aged private citizen who had never tasted authority in his life, would listen to no one. I passed the night (which proved a very long one) on

my two feet in a cell so congested that there was just enough
space for standing. We were released the next morning only to
hear that there had been no change in the curfew time.

Thus, added to the strain of the knowledge of the closeness
of death, is the fact of the uncertainties of living, the fear of life
itself. This combination makes a terrible experience.

Now we come to the pertinent questions: Why do Biafrans
suffer? Are these hardships inevitable? Could the misery have
been less? If so, what are the factors responsible?

The Biafran struggle, like all struggles, has generated a current
of forces which have a scope far larger than and beyond the
confines of a simple, straightforward conflict between Nigeria
and Biafra. Because the world has become more compact as a
result of improved communication, and because man is long-
nosed and incapable of keeping out of other people's affairs, a
ripple in the social order of one part of the world sets off a
current in the social or political order of another part thousands
of miles away. No community in the world is completely
isolated and self-contained; a problem here has its consequences
somewhere else.

The misery of the Biafran population is many times more
than it would have been had the present Nigeria-Biafra war
been a clear-cut armed conflict between a sixteenth-century
African people called Nigerians and another sixteenth-century
African people called Biafrans.

Biafrans suffer today as a result of two factors: the interested
parties beyond and behind the Gowon Government, and the
moral and spiritual decadence within the Biafran society.

The Biafran secession was a stage in the conflict between the
contradictions which existed in the social, cultural and political
patterns of the old Nigerian Federation. Britain's role in em-
bedding and intensifying these contradictions is obvious from
the history of the Federation (see Chapter 1). For the first few
weeks after the outbreak of the Nigeria-Biafra war, Britain
claimed neutrality in the conflict. Eventually, however, following mounting evidence against it, the British Government
could no more sustain its denials of backing the Nigerian

Government. She owned up and gave reasons. These were: (i) 'Britain has been the traditional supplier of arms to Nigeria and cannot let her down in her time of need.' That was said by a British Cabinet member. (ii) 'We have to continue our arms supply to Nigeria if we must maintain our influence over here.' That was another Cabinet member. And finally: (iii) 'We want to found one Federal Nigeria.' This came from none other than the British Commonwealth Secretary, Lord Shepherd, himself. Now let us take these points one by one:

Firstly, it is an utter fallacy to state that Britain had been the traditional supplier of arms to Nigeria. Nigeria stopped buying British rifles and machine-guns in 1964. Up till then Nigeria had purchased from Britain just twelve Ferret cars and two Saladins. Nigerian arms purchase was as follows: artillery guns and rifles from Italy, machine-guns from Germany, and mortars from Israel. Moreover, examples abound of instances when Britain stopped supplying arms to its traditional buyers on account of internal trouble in their territories. The Buganda debacle in Uganda is a case in point.

On the second reason for backing Nigeria, the question might first be asked: What need does the British Government have of influencing the Lagos Government? According to a British Government spokesman, this influence is necessary so that Britain can be in a position to bring about a peaceful settlement of the bloody conflict. A number of events have exposed this for the absurdity that it is. In the first place, the war is dragging towards the close of its second year, yet nothing has been seen of British influence in effecting a peaceful solution. It is not doubted that Mr. Wilson's Government has an influence over the Lagos Government. In fact, 'influence' is too mild a word to use in describing the relationship between the two governments; 'control' would be a more fitting word. But the obvious point is that the British Government desires a negotiated settlement of the crisis. Britain sowed and tended the seeds of discord in the Nigerian Federation, fanned the flames of hate and belligerence, frustrated peace moves before the secession and, after the secession, her diplomats urged the unwilling Nigerians into waging a war on Biafra, for there is no doubt that the different Nigerian regional governments were as fed up with the Federation as the Biafrans were. Left to themselves, Biafrans and Nigerians would have had enough of this war to come to the conference table with reasonable terms for peace. This makes nonsense both of the argument of 'influence' and of British professions of desiring a peaceful settlement. For, up till the time of writing, the Nigeria-Biafra war could have ended the moment the British Government really wanted.

This brings us to reason number three. 'We want to establish one Federal Nigeria.' This statement gives the impression that the phrase 'One Federal Nigeria' is self-explanatory, and is synonymous with all that is desirable in life. 'One Federal Nigeria' existed from 1914 until 1967: what did it achieve? What did it mean to its citizens? One crisis after another.

After all is said and done, no matter with which party or parties one's sympathy lies in Nigeria's post-independence crisis, it must be accepted that the Biafrans had the most gruesome experience out of the accumulation of those crises, but other members of that Federation also had experiences which they would rather not go through again. So when the British Government talks of founding One Federal Nigeria, it is pursuing a cause which is more to its own aggrandisement than in the interests of those for whom it is supposed to be founded. And is it not absurd that Britain should decide what is right for a people who were supposed to be politically independent eight years ago?

The nations of the world are today in what Thomas Hobbes called a state of nature. On the international level there is no superior authority to control the passions of every nation, because no nation recognises any final authority above itself. Moral sanctions have no place in international politics. The ultimate deciding factor is might. The Soviet invasion of Czechoslovakia in August 1968 and South Africa's seizure of the South West African trust territory are contemporary testimonies to the rightness of might in international politics. The determinant of where a nation applies its might is its interests, and the ultimate basis of these interests is economic.

This is the nature of the international society in which young and tender African nations find themselves – a world in which the big nations have the economic, diplomatic and military means to control the behaviour of the weak nations. This power

K*

holds Africa and Africans in a bondage that ridicules the concept of African independence.

It is in this light that we must see the attitude of African
countries in the Nigeria–Biafra war. The OAU met in Kinshasa
in September 1967 and appointed a Committee to look into
the conflict. After several postponements, excuses and counter-
excuses, four of the six Heads of African States who comprised
the Committee finally assembled in Lagos to tackle their much-
feared assignment. The meeting lasted a few hours, and consisted of an address by the Head of the Nigerian Government
and a few casual remarks by the Committee members. The
result was a communiqué calling on Biafra to renounce secession.

This was an obvious bungling. Without going into details,
it will suffice to say that the contempt which it aroused from
world opinion sent the Committee into another attempt. This
resulted in the Niamey (Niger Republic) and Addis Ababa
(Ethiopia) peace talks, which were abortive. Then followed the
OAU Assembly in Algiers in September, where a resolution was
passed calling on the Biafrans 'to cooperate with Nigeria in
maintaining the integrity of Nigeria'. Its utter meaninglessness
in the context of the Nigeria–Biafra conflict is obvious and
does not require further comment.

One thing, however, is clear. The Organisation for African
Unity is a misnomer. It is not a society of independent African
nations whose interests are towards African emancipation,
unity and advancement. Eighty per cent of its members are
mouthpieces for masters in London, Washington, Moscow,
Paris and even Cairo and Pretoria. The OAU is a boiling pot
of mixed loyalties. Unfortunately very few African countries
have laid any psychological foundations, or instilled sufficient
national consciousness for real nationhood. The Black is awake
but is paralysed. His central nervous system is infected, his
brain benumbed. Africa's problem is its leadership. Out of the
host of supposedly independent African nations, only a handful
can claim any form of independence.

Because of the ignorance of most African leaders of the
answer to the question 'Whither Africa?', they have fallen
victim to blackmail and to cheap and hackneyed arguments.
One such meaningless expression which has been sold to the

gullible Africans is 'the need for Unity'. The argument is put
forward that Africa must not be allowed to disintegrate – that,
if the Biafran secession succeeds, Africa will balkanise into the
numerous tribal groups which make it up. Thus unity must be
maintained at all costs, and the 'territorial integrity' of the
existing African countries must be maintained.

Unity is not achieved by magic. It depends on the will of the
people. That the Nigerian Federation did not break up earlier
was, more than anything else, due to the will of the then Eastern
Nigerians to continue to live together, with the peoples of the
other regions and to give the Federation yet another chance.
The pogrom of 1966 destroyed this will.

In Nigeria, with the death of the will to live together and the
loss of confidence in the Federal State, the basis of unity was
destroyed. Whatever unity that exists in Nigeria today is based
on the common hatred for the Biafrans. Unity should be based
on love and understanding, which is voluntary. According to
the Ivorian President Houphouet-Boigny, 'When therefore will
my black brothers understand the necessity of breaking with
this fatality which has wanted and still wants, alas, that Blacks
be killed with impunity or kill themselves with impunity? If we
cannot yet, as a result of the present weaknesses of our material
means, prevent people from killing us, at least we have the possibility of stopping not only killing ourselves, but also, refuse
to let others help us to massacre ourselves. But our race continues to bleed from this double haemorrhage. . . .

'Among ourselves we must tell the truth even if it hurts, even
if it goes contrary to what we believe to be our own interests.
But we have all inherited from our former masters not nations,
but states where the links between the different ethnic groups
put together by the colonisers are very fragile. Our first objective is to build a nation, to realise national unity which is a precondition for all harmonious development. But it is a difficult
task, a long range operation, which necessitates on the part of
all, and the leaders in particular, constant efforts of patience,
tolerance, comprehension, generosity and love of a transcendent
nature rising above personal consideration, above tribe, and

above quarrels between generations – by the obstinate search for peace through dialogue. . . .

'Unity will be the fruit of the common will to live together and should not be imposed by one group upon another with force. . . .

'If we are all in agreement in the OAU in recognising the imperious necessity of unity, unity as the ideal framework for full development of the African man, we cannot admit, for ourselves, that it should be his grave. We say yes to unity in peace through peace, unity in love and through brotherhood. We say no to unity in war and through war, or unity in hatred. Unity is for the living and not for the dead. . . .

'If our brothers fighting cannot live together in a federation, let them accept peace as neighbours, peace between neighbours being, finally, a bridge of love, of fraternity, linking the two of them.'

This comes from one of the few African statesmen who can interpret political concepts in terms of the aspirations of living people. President Nyerere leads the United Republic of Tanzania – a most successful experiment in willing unity. His recognition of Biafra goes a long way to show the emptiness of the balkanisation theory. Rather than lead to the disintegration of Africa, the Biafran issue will strengthen African unity because it will serve as a standing warning to African governments and peoples against the tragic consequences of intolerance and abuse of political power. The word 'imperialism' is a *sine qua non* in the vocabulary of African statesmen. From the way most of them use it, it becomes an urgent necessity to redefine the term. For if even known African mouthpieces of foreign capitals accuse other African leaders of being imperialist stooges, then the term imperialism has assumed a new meaning.

Apart from Britain, Russia and the United States of America have contributed immensely to this fratricidal war of West Africa. Russia, with the promise of a bridgehead in Africa, has maintained a steady flow of Ilyushin bombers and other military hardware. The American Central Intelligence Agency has frustrated every genuine initiative, both from within Africa, and from Europe, aimed at bringing the war to an end.

The factors external to Africa which intensify the misery of the Biafran peoples were penetratingly summed up in an article entitled 'Biafra: Let Them Eat Oil' by Robert Fitch and Mary Oppenheimer, published in *Ramparts* Magazine (San Francisco, USA) on September 7, 1968.

Nearer home another by no means small contributor to Biafran misery is the incompetence, confusion and uncertainty of African leadership. The Nigeria-Biafra conflict has been described as an essentially African problem. As a result some well-disposed European nations and organisations have been scared away from contributing to its solution lest they should be termed imperialists. But alas! Africa has shown a dismal incapacity to settle her own problems without dictates from foreign interests.

So far we have looked at the *external* factors threatening Biafra's survival. Now we will look inside Biafra itself, where a number of ills are aggravating the country's sufferings. These ills I would prefer to call contradictions.

First, between military personnel, and between different wings of the armed forces, there are tensions which, to say the least, are not in the best interest of the Biafran nation. Many a battle has been lost because Colonel X has disagreed with Colonel Y or because of the rivalry between Division U and Division V.

Secondly, amongst most military men there is the mistaken belief that the war is being fought by the soldiers alone. Thus the much-used derogatory term 'idle civilian'. The civilians resent this, for they alone appreciate the deprivations they suffer to support the fighting men. They also know that the arms the soldiers fight with, the food they eat, the money they are paid, the diplomatic battle, the propaganda battle and the moral support which the soldiers enjoy, are all results of efforts from the civilians. This leads to bad blood between the two groups. The binding force and the cushion which has harmlessly absorbed these jolting shocks of dissension has been the reality of the presence of the invaders. Everyone is only too aware of the dangers of allowing the enemy to win. Nonetheless there is an urgent need for improved public relations between the two groups. The need becomes more urgent now that civilians are binding themselves into guerrilla organisations for the defence of their homes. It is not uncommon these days to find villagers attacking conventional soldiers retreating from the enemy in their homes.

Thirdly, the civil service is meant to stabilise the country at all times. Governments come and go but the civil service remains. In war-time Biafra, this is not the case; civil servants as well as politicians are actively engaged in war efforts. They are a powerful presence in the Directorates – institutions established to meet the emergency needs of the warring young nation. In these Directorates are not only the politicians but also thousands of young and impatient university lecturers, graduates and undergraduates and former employees of oil companies and other large business concerns who have ceased operations because of the war, who are in too much of a hurry to co-operate with the officious civil servants, who, they say, are ineffective, inefficient people, bogged down by the 'civil service mentality'. The civil servants, on their side, resent the threats of these 'upstarts' and cling desperately to their traditional way of doing things. The consequence is much bad-blood, pettiness and intrigue.

The fourth contradiction is the disparity in living standards between the composite peoples of Biafra. On the one hand are the big government officials. On the other are the common men. The former have cushioned themselves from the shocks of the war and insulated themselves and theirs from its stark realities. The latter have borne the brunt of the war. The former still indulge in peace-time niceties even as thousands of the latter starve to death. While some children pine away in the houses of death, others still have monthly gifts of expensive toys to play with while their well-fed parents indulgently watch them in air-conditioned rooms, sipping beer and smoking cigarettes. While there isn't petrol to send food and arms to the soldiers in the front, some people have enough to drive their girl-friends on pleasure trips.

Relief materials which are meant for the starving people are diverted into private homes and finally find their way into the market on sale at exorbitant prices to the very people to whom they were sent. Yet when a town is threatened, the men in cars are the first to flee even when evacuation is not necessary. Sadly enough they make no arrangements or leave any instructions as to how important official documents should be evacuated. The unfortunate ignorant commoner stays in the city until enemy shells start falling; if he survives the first shells, he leaves the city on foot, carrying whatever of his belongings he can.

Yet the common man fights the war. His children, his brothers fight the war, die in the fronts. The high officials hide their children behind civilian 'essential duties'. When I say high government officials or civil servants, I mean some. Certainly the very top policy-makers have been exemplary. Nonetheless, their genuine efforts are frustrated by those whose ultimate duty it is to execute their directives.

It is a cause for hope that, at the time of writing, these ills are being gradually overcome. Frauds are being fished out and ruthlessly dealt with. Relief materials now reach the victims. A school of orientation has been established, and public relations have been improved.

Nonetheless, Biafra still has a long way to go. Our misery has been greatly aggravated by our own debasements. Until these contradictions are resolved we shall continue to suffer more than we should.

In this postscript, I have tried to establish a number of facts. First, the Biafran secession is a product of neither the calculated schemes of one, two or more self-seeking megalomaniacs, nor the passing whim of an emotionally misguided populace. It is the end-product of a number of consistent provocations which gradually but surely broke down the ardently held illusions of a virile republican people. The provocations comprised bitter experiences in the individual and collective lives of the Biafran people. This is why the transference of loyalty, from extreme Nigerianism to die-hard Biafranism, was so total. And this is why, on the question of Biafra's sovereignty, there is a unanimity of opinion amongst all communities and classes in Biafra.

Next I recounted the tragic suffering of the Biafrans – the

agony that is their lot today – and followed this up by a cate-
gorisation of its causes. It is important to add something here.
No account of the Biafra society, during this war period, will
be complete without a mention of the 'dissenters'; to pretend
that they do not exist is mere self-deceit. It is from this group
that we have the tools of the Lagos Government. They can be
classified into two major classes. The first consists of ardent
dissenters. These are people who, for reasons of past individual
experiences, personal convictions, biases of the heart or of the
head, or for other reasons, are strongly opposed to the Biafran
secession. Here there can be further classifications. There are
those who have been so embedded in the rotten politics of the
old Federation that they have come to identify the Biafran
Government with its predecessor in the pre-1966 years. Thus,
if they were opposed to the ruling National Council of Nigerian
Citizens in the then Eastern Nigeria, their reservations were
transferred to the Biafran Government. On this group, the
change in the personalities in power and the traumatic events
of 1966–68 are completely lost. There are also the ambitious
opportunists who see in the Nigeria of a multi-state structure
great chances of big executive posts. The men of these two
groups are from the non-Ibo-speaking areas of Biafra.

In the second class belongs the apathetic type. These are not
sufficiently attached to any cause to want to suffer for it, and
this class is naturally more numerous than the first class. They
were among the first refugees to Biafra from various parts of
Nigeria when the massacre began. True to type, when the suffering mounted in Biafra, they obligingly crossed again, where
they are spared for political reasons. Among this class are Ibos
as well as non-Ibos. One thing is certain: as soon as the sufferings cease in Biafra, most of the people in this group will
quickly return to Biafra.

These two groups are rather the exceptions without which
every rule looks unnatural. Combined, they score less than a
generous 5 per cent of the entire Biafran population, which
leaves a conservative estimate of 95 per cent Biafrans who are
today faced with total extermination.

King Croesus of Lydia once said: 'No one is so senseless as
to choose of his own free will war rather than peace, since in
peace the sons bury their fathers, but in war the fathers bury

Leaders of Biafra. From left: Mr. Jaja Nwachukwu, Sir Louis Mbanefo,
Dr. Nnamdi Azikiwe, Lieut.-Col. Ojukwu, Dr. Michael Okpara.

Biafra: the Civilians' War
Above, in front of the 'House of Death' (page 273 ff.).
Opposite page: above, after a Nigerian air raid on Eke Market Motor
Park at Nomeh, near Awgu; below, the remains of Biafran civilians
killed by Nigerian incendiary bombs.

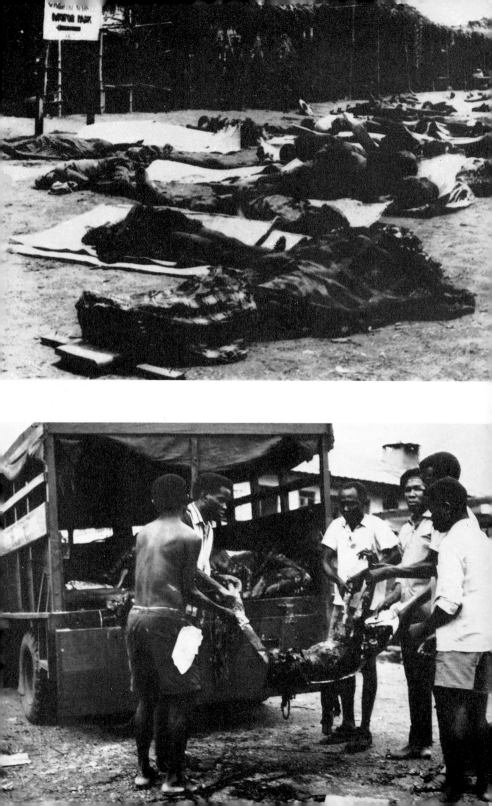

Above, a solidarity rally at Aba in support of the Biafran Government; below, Biafran soldiers moving towards the front.

their sons.' In Biafra today parents have not only buried their grown-up sons but have also watched their infant children die agonising deaths from starvation, exposure and disease. Yet there is law and order in Biafra. There was violence in Chicago because a Negro was refused a drink in a pub. There are strikes and revolts all over the world for such discomforts as delayed pay, insufficient salary and raised costs. Yet in Biafra today, costs of the basic necessities of life have multiplied a thousand-fold, incomes are halved and living is almost intolerable. Yet the people do not grumble. Rather they are ready to sacrifice and suffer a little more so that the country may survive. If there are any discontents, they are directed against Britain, against the OAU, against hoarders, against fraudulent officials but never against the Government. For so committed is everybody to the urgent question of survival that any attack on the Government is synonymous with self-mortification. For the first time in Africa, there is a burning nationalism which is genuine and selfless. It is appalling what a high quality of men have died in Biafra. Yet all young men rush into the Army, in spite of the obvious inferiority of Biafran armour in comparison with Nigeria's sophisticated weapons.

The picture is not peculiar to the home front alone. Young Biafran students and professionals rush home from the comparative safety of foreign lands. Why all these apparent suicidal acts? This is a question which few foreigners have really asked themselves. One has to agree with Mokwugwo Okoye (*The Beard of Prometheus*, p. 157) that 'men are activated by the environmental, instinctive and hereditary factors more than the ideological: it is the needs, their beliefs which are the mere by-products of their environment and experience.' This is by way of an answer to the question above. Biafran attitudes and beliefs today are a product of bitter experiences, and experience is so good a teacher that it is almost impossible to unlearn a lesson it has taught. And according to Dr. Kenneth Kaunda (in *Zambia Shall Be Free*): 'When people understand a cause, become prepared to suffer for that cause and see glory and honour in such suffering, it is indeed just impossible to suppress them or the cause they stand for.'

This is why this war must be stopped. It is futile. Its prolongation is an unnecessary increase in the misery that is the lot of

Biafrans today – a suffering that intensifies rather than mitigates the will of the people.

No one doubts that a larger political unit carries with it greater international status, yet we must admit that when such a larger unit lacks a sense of unity amongst its peoples, the end of the union is defeated, for then the unit turns into a boiling pot of strife and dissension. In such a case it would be better to arrive at a relationship which, while enjoying the benefits of wide international co-operation, would avoid too close a contact which might give rise to tensions and, therefore, strife.

Biafra is a child of tragedy born out of a willing option of a people who have been sobered by a common bitter experience to seek a common destiny in their quest for self-determination. She has shown the capability and the mental and emotional personality of independent nationhood. Blockaded into exploiting its resources, Biafra has produced her own weapons – bombs, rockets, rifles etc. – refined her crude oil, processed her salt, and built gunboats under the most adverse conditions.

Biafra will add to the positive forces in African leadership; this is why Biafra must be saved from destruction. But above all the suffering must stop. A people cannot be destroyed in the name of unity. My mind revolts at this barbaric war where there is no code of conduct and where civilians die much more than the soldiers. At the time of writing, the death rate in Biafra is ten thousand daily! To the Biafrans, the only alternative is mass slaughter. The only solution to this human dilemna is Biafran sovereignty. In the long run it will be to the interest of Nigeria and indeed of Africa. For when Biafra finally takes her place within the human community, it will be to the pride and benefit of Africa; the symbol of African revolution where the contradictions in a society have been resolved by the purgative effect of bitter war.

I see Biafra as a proud nation, proud of her culture, and of her technology. For out of this suffering will emerge a world power with something new to improve the lot of the human species. Biafra must live. The sufferings of its peoples must end now.

Umuahia, Biafra,
October 1968

REFERENCES

INTRODUCTION

1. See *Introducing Biafra* (Government Publication), Span Ltd., Port-Harcourt, Vol. 1, p. 10.
2. O'Brien, Conor Cruise, 'A Condemned People', *The New York Review*, December 21, 1967.
3. Nduka, Otonti, *Western Education and the Nigerian Cultural Background*, Oxford, 1964, p. 91.
4. O'Brien, op. cit.
5. See House of Lords debate, February 13, 1968.
6. *Introducing Biafra*, op. cit., p. 11.

CHAPTER 1

1. See Kirk-Greene, A. H. M., 'Who Coined the Name "Nigeria"?' *West Africa*, December 22, 1956, p. 1035; Coleman, James S., *Nigeria: Background To Nationalism*, University of California Press, Berkeley and Los Angeles, 1958, p. 44.
2. Orizu, Nwafor, A. A., *Without Bitterness*, Creative Age Press, New York, 1944, p. 111.
3. Ibid., p. 112.
4. Wheare, Joan, *The Nigerian Legislative Council*, Faber and Faber, London, 1949.
5. Ibid.
6. Ibid.
7. See Cowan, L. Gray, *The Dilemmas of African Independence*, Walker and Company, New York, 1964, p. 5.
8. See Anene, J. C., *The Boundary Question*, delivered at a Seminar on the problems of Pan-Africanism, May 29, 1964.
9. Ibid.
10. See Kirk-Greene, A. H. M., *Peoples of Nigeria*, pp. 5–8; Azikiwe, Nnamdi, 'Tribalism: A Pragmatic Instrument for National Unity', *President Azikiwe: Selected Speeches*, (1960–64), Daily Times Publication, p. 24, column 3.
11. *Azikiwe: Selected Speeches*, op. cit., p. 24, column 3.
12. Statesmen in Britain, as well as powerful and influential merchants, before the abolition of the slave trade, tended to consider this trade, not from a moral point of view, but as a great commercial activity very vital to Britain's prosperity and strength. Thus Britain became the most notorious slave-trading nation. See Fage, J. D., *Introduction To The History of West Africa*, 3rd Ed., Cambridge University Press, 1965, p. 99. Not until equally powerful contrary economic arguments were offered did such statesmen and merchants agree to give up the trade. Adam Smith, who wrote in 1776 *The Wealth of Nations*, argued that in the long run, it would pay Britain better to keep the African labour in Africa to produce raw materials required by British factories rather than transporting them to the New World, with the risk and waste of travel. Britain was at that time

entering the era of Industrial Revolution and mass production. Africans left in Africa would also provide a market for manufactured goods. The expensive and unparalleled effort of the British Government to abolish the West African slave trade shows that the humanitarian impulse and the sentiment of justice could hardly be divorced completely of all selfishness. But to that extent the African, indeed the world, benefited. The lead which Britain took to stop the trade, in the words of Lecky, must be 'regarded as among the three or four perfectly virtuous pages in the history of nations'. However, because of the misgivings which some British merchants continued to have about the slave trade, even after its abolition, Sir Thomas Fowell Buxton had in 1839 to publish *The African Slave Trade and its Remedy*, in which he argued that the slave trade could profitably and effectively be replaced by legitimate trade, industry and agriculture, and investors in slaves would not after all lose their money. This came under the slogan 'The Bible and The Plough': the Bible should accompany the plough and the traders' goods.

13. Barker, W. A., *et al.*, *A General History of England* (1832–1960), Black Ltd., London, 1960, pp. 68–83; 190–5. The Parliamentary Select Committee set up in 1865 to look into Britain's foreign commitments, and chaired by Sir Charles Adderley, following the feeling of the age, recommended unequivocally that 'all further extension of territories or new treaties offering protection would be inexpedient. . . .' The change of this policy later portrays, among others, a confusion of the time between *laissez-faire* and collectivism, in spite of the fact that the British Parliament accepted Sir Charles' recommendations. For a good description of the perplexity and confusion of the period, see Young, G. M., *Portrait Of An Age*.

14. Palmerston was Foreign Secretary of Great Britain from 1830 to 1851, except during the Tory ministry of Peel from 1841 to 1846.

15. Ibid, p. 68.

16. Beecroft was particularly qualified for his assignment. He came to Fernando Po about 1827, when it was occupied by Britain for operations against the slave trade. When Spain took over the island in 1843 it appointed Beecroft Governor. Between 1835 and 1840 Beecroft had had the opportunity of exploring the Niger and the West Coast hinterland and therefore knew the place better than most other Europeans. He had also served in the British Navy.

17. However in 1872 the Consul for the Bights of Benin and Biafra was entrusted with the necessary powers by the British Government. This could be regarded as the first official step on the part of the British Government to take a hand once more in the acquisition of territory in West Africa. This step was to be made complete and total following the competition of European powers in Africa which culminated in the Berlin Conference of 1884–5.

18. Akitoye was first crowned King by the Oba of Benin in 1841, but he was not popular. He was expelled by Kosoko, the favourite of the Lagos Chiefs, in 1845, and he sought political asylum in Abeokuta. It is actually much in doubt who was more interested in the slave trade – Kosoko or Akitoye. Certainly Kosoko was a big slave-trading king and probably resisted the British attempt to stop this lucrative source of income. But it is doubted whether Akitoye could not have done the same were he in office at the material time. While in exile, Akitoye formed friendly associations with big-time slave dealers of Abeokuta and Badagry and sought help also from a notorious but very wealthy slave dealer there – one Domingo Jose. All these are against the evidence that Akitoye was opposed to the slave trade. At best, it could be said that he only saw in co-operating with the British the only way of regaining his throne through the use of the British naval power. Beecroft, on the other hand, knew very well that a man

in Akitoye's position and predicament would be easy to handle and that the sanction of his interference would ultimately produce a puppet king in the Lagos throne who would be more readily prepared to do his bidding.

19. The big question is whether Dosunmu had a right to transfer Lagos to the British Crown without the authorisation or the local chiefs and the people themselves. Traditionally, the African idea of kingship or chieftaincy was that a king ruled, not for himself but for the people and held his power in trust for them. Their sanction would be necessary for any far-reaching decision of this nature. This sanction was lacking in this case.

20. Akpofure, Rex and Michael Crowder, *Nigeria*, Faber and Faber, London, 1966, p. 134.

21. Furnival, J. S., *Colonial Policy and Practice*, Cambridge University Press, 1948, p. 4.

22. The Royal Niger Company was paid about half a million pounds for the loss of its privileged position and for properties acquired from it.

23. The First battalion of the West African Frontier Force (WAFF) was assembled at Lokoja on April 16, 1898.

24. Crowder, Michael, *The Story of Nigeria*, Faber and Faber, London, 1962, p. 213.

25. See McPhee, Allan, *The Economic Revolution in British West Africa*, London, 1926, pp. 108 ff.

26. Coleman, op. cit., p. 42.

27. See *President Azikiwe: Selected Speeches*, op. cit., p. 23, columns 3–4.

28. For an evaluation of the British attempt to give Nigeria political and economic unity through Federalism, see Chapter 11: 'Retrospect'.

29. O'Brien, Conor Cruise, 'A Condemned People', *The New York Review*, December 21, 1967.

30. For a distinction between a colony and a protectorate see Phillips, Hood, *Constitutional and Administrative Law* (3rd ed.), Sweet and Maxwell, London, 1962, pp. 706, 780, 753–60.

31. The Aba Women's riot of 1929 in Eastern Nigeria was a demonstration of opposition against Indirect Rule in the South, and the *Warrant Chiefs* that were created with it.

32. See Roome, William J. W. 'Strategic Lines of Christian Missions in Africa', *International Review of Missions*, V, July 1916, p. 354.

33. O'Brien, op. cit.

34. See Coleman, op. cit., p. 133.

35. For a fairly good account of troubles arising from the Southern demand for self-government in 1957, see Davies, H. O., *Nigeria: The Prospects for Democracy*, Weidenfeld and Nicolson, London, 1961, pp. 92–4.

36. See Coleman, pp. 275–6.

37. The Western politicians saw in Dr. Azikiwe's uncompromising and innovatory political ideas, coupled with his journalistic activities, a formidable threat to their aspirations for leadership. They thus sought to restrict his activities and influence to his home region.

38. Legum, Colin, 'Can Nigeria Escape Her Past?', *The Observer*, January 30, 1966.

39. *Legislative Council Debates*, March 20 to April 2, 1947, Government Printer, Lagos, 1947, p. 208.

40. Ibid.

41. Ibid., p. 212,

42. Awolowo, Obafemi, *Path to Nigerian Freedom*, London, 1947, pp. 47–8.

43. Note particularly the Western Nigerian Election of 1951.

44. At the time of Independence in 1960, Nigeria had an area of 373,250 square miles and in population was the fourth in the Commonwealth and thirteenth in the world. The population census result of November 2, 1963, stated her population to be 55 millions. It was the economic argument turning largely on the alleged advantages of the economics of scale that prompted Britain to create the Nigerian Federation. See Chapter 11: 'Retrospect'.

CHAPTER 2

45. Ottah, Nelson, 'The Rise and Fall of Chief Awolowo', *Drum*, November 1963, column 2., p. 25. See also Ikejiani, Okechukwu (ed.), 'Education and Tribalism', *Education in Nigeria*, Frederick A. Praeger, New York, p. 116.

46. Legislative Council Debates, 1947, op. cit., p. 212.

47. Azikiwe, Nnamdi, *Respect for Human Dignity* (Inaugural Address at his Installation in 1960), Government Printer, Enugu, 1960, p. 2.

48. Ibid., pp. 11 and 12.

49. Ibid., p. 15.

50. Ibid., pp. 14–15.

51. See Wallerstein, Immanuel, *Africa: The Politics of Independence*, Vintage Press, New York, 1961, pp. 98–9.

52. See notably, 'Our Nation Swoons in Despair'; 'An Appeal to the People of Nigeria'; 'Caring Enough . . .', all broadcasts to the nation by Nnamdi Azikiwe on March 23, May 6, and October 1, 1964, respectively.

53. Note statement by R. B. K. Okafor, MP (formerly a member of the Zikist National Vanguard and later NCNC Federal Minister) after Azikiwe re-appointed Balewa Prime Minister in spite of the rigging of the Federal Elections of 1964. Mr. Okafor stated that 'Zikism' had outlived its usefulness and was no longer a living ideology.

54. Ottah, op. cit., p. 25 (*Drum*).

55. See post.

56. Majekudunmi was accused of issuing his restriction orders in a way that favoured the UPP.

57. Although the Colonial Government, through its District Officers, made every effort to check evasions, it came to be alleged that the census of 1952–3, could not be accurate because many Nigerians avoided being counted out of the belief that the census was required in order to increase taxation.

58. See *Mr. Prime Minister* (a selection of Speeches by Alhaji Abubakar Tafawa Balewa), Nigerian National Press, Lagos, 1964, p. 183.

59. Ibid., p. 183.

60. Ibid., p. 184.

61. Ibid, p. 184.

62. Ibid, p. 184.

63. Ibid, p. 184.

64. Ibid. p. 185.

65. *Census Controversy: One North or One Nigeria?* Government Printer, Enugu, 1964, p. 3.

66. Ibid., p. 3.

67. Ibid., p. 4.

68. Ibid., p. 5.

69. *Mr. Prime Minister*, op. cit., p. 186.

70. At the end of the seven-month old emergency in January 1963,

S. L. Akintola, the suspended Premier of the Region, retained his premiership. This was possible because of the coalition his party, the UPP, struck with the NCNC. When the census row developed, the NCNC naturally expected the UPP to reject the census figures. But Akintola had other plans. About March 10, 1964, while the census controversy raged, he changed the name of his party to Nigerian National Democratic Party (NNDP) and soon after declared he was forming an all-party Government in Western Nigeria. But that was his plan for kicking out the NCNC, which had calculated on a long-term political gain in which Akintola woud ultimately be ousted.

71. *Sardauna Accepts Census Figures: Answers Critics One By One*, Gaskiya Corporation, Zaria, 1964, p. 2.

72. See Supreme Court Judgment, per Brett, J. S. C. 29/6/64 in the Attorney-General, Eastern Nigeria *vs.* the Attorney-General of the Federation. See also Chapter 4 of the present work.

73. Census is the 4th item on the Concurrent Legislative List. In the event of a conflict between the Federal and Regional law on the matter, the Federal law, under S. 69 (4) of the Nigerian Constitution, would have primacy. This could have the effect that the Federal Parliament could pass laws on the census without consulting the Regions, and such laws would override Regional laws where there was conflict. It would then appear that the Prime Minister, under the Constitution, was not obliged to consult the Regional Governments from a strict legal point of view. But in a Federation like Nigeria, in order to assure harmony and co-operation, such consultation is incumbent upon whoever holds executive authority at the Centre. The fact that there was consultation between the various governments in the first census and none in the second would lead one to the conclusion that there was some fishy business over the second Census.

74. See the Northern House of Assembly Debate, March 4, 1964. Author's italics.

75. Northern House of Assembly Debate, March 17, 1964.

76. See Chapter 3.

77. See the *Nigerian Tribune* of December 28, 1964. *Note*: the *Nigerian Tribune* is an Action Group-owned newspaper.

78. *The Problem of Nigerian Unity: The Case of Eastern Nigeria*, International Press, Aba, p. 18. *The Daily Sketch* was the official newspaper of the NNDP-controlled Government of Western Nigeria.

79. The Elliot Commission of 1945, whose recommendation led to the establishment of a University College at Ibadan as Nigeria's first University, could not recommend the establishment of a university in the Federal capital of Lagos.

80. See White Paper *Educational Development*, pp. 169–70 (Sessional Paper No. 3 of 1961, Federation of Nigeria, Lagos, 1961). The White Paper, in addition, made provision for a Faculty of Law and a Medical School for the University.

81. Professor Eni Njoku, BA, M SC, PH D, was one of the first members of staff of the University College, Ibadan. He has been lecturer, senior lecturer, professor and dean, and has also served Nigeria as a cabinet minister (Mines and Power) in 1952. After brief experience of politics, he went back to the University. Between 1956 and 1962 he was Chairman of the Electricity Corporation of Nigeria. Professor Njoku was a member of the Council of the University of Ibadan from 1954 till he took up his new appointment in Lagos.

82. See UNESCO, Draft Report of Advisory Commission for the Establishment of the University of Lagos, September 1961.

83. See an Open Letter to the Nigerian People – by 50 members of the University of Lagos academic staff who were either dismissed, or had given notice of resignation, Lagos, 1965.

84. Professor Njoku's replacement was published in the various Lagos national newspapers on March 1 as front-page news.

85. Council Paper No. 119.

86. He secured this appointment through the recommendation of Professor Njoku who, as a member of the Provisional Council of the University of Zambia, had recommended him.

87. See protest letter to the Prime Minister by Professor Eni Njoku against the prostitution by the Provisional Council of the procedure for appointment of a vice-chancellor, 1965.

88. Professor L. C. B. Gower resigned from the Council in protest against the decision to replace Njoku with Biobaku.

89. Biobaku's credentials were never submitted to the Senate for consideration and report. See *The Crisis at the University of Lagos* (Implications and Way Out), Ribway Printers, Lagos p. 5.

90. See advertised statement by the Senate on the University of Lagos Crisis, *Nigerian Morning Post*, Monday, April 5, 1965, p. 11. As Davidson Nicol pointed out, 'African Universities should hesitate to appoint political nominees as Heads of Institutions or an African of poor academic standing . . . the best of them [university academic staff] . . . will not serve for long under a Vice-Chancellor with no academic reputation'. See Nicol, Davidson, 'Our Universities', *Africa: A Subjective View*, Longmans and Ghana Universities Press, 1964, p. 37. Dr. Nicol has served in various commissions connected with university affairs – such as the Ghana Universities Commission; the UNESCO Commission on University curricula; the Committee on Needs of Priorities of the University of East Africa, etc. He is therefore eminently qualified to speak on the matter.

91. On this, Dr. Nicol has this to say: 'The heavy dependence of universities on government for their finance is utterly unhealthy. It involves the risk that the staffing of the university may eventually become political. This by itself may not be dangerous if the men at the helm of State have clear ideas of the functions of a university, or themselves have had successful university careers. . . .' Ibid., p. 42.

92. Ibid., p. 40.

93. See 'The Nationalist', *West African Pilot*, March 15, 1965, p. 1.

94. For the same reason, in the Lagos University, Dr. Biobaku could not get reputable and renowned academics to work with him. Mass promotion of remaining academic staff followed, while students who graduated ultimately in that university by the end of the year 1965 were made lecturers.

95. This resolution was signed by Mr. M. O. Afolabi-Oloja (a Yoruba student), Speaker of the Students' Union Congress.

96. This protest letter was supported by fifty-nine in favour of Njoku, six against, and five abstentions.

97. See post.

98. This offer was, of course, rejected outright by Professor Njoku.

99. See Parliamentary debates of April 10 and 23, 1965. Mr. Akinjide was then the General Secretary of the NNDP. In his maiden speech in Parliment in April 10, he accused 'one of the Deans from overseas' of inspiring the crisis.

100. See post.

101. See post.

102. See post.

103. Circulated at a Press Conference called at Bristol Hotel, Lagos, about end of June 1965.

104. See Ashby Commission Report on Higher Education in Nigeria.

105. 151 students signed to withdraw from the University. This was published in the Lagos newspapers about the end of June 1965.
106. Professor Eni Njoku later became the Vice-Chancellor of the University of Biafra (formerly University of Nigeria), at Nsukka.
107. Professor Dike resigned in December 1966.

CHAPTER 3

108. The way in which Sir Abubakar was appointed to the premiership was suspected by Southern politicians as evidence of intrigue by the colonial régime to perpetuate its dominance over Nigeria. Sir Abubakar was appointed Prime Minister even before all the results of the elections were out. This led to a protest by Dr. Azikiwe to Sir James Robertson who was then the Governor-General of Nigeria.
109. *President Azikiwe: Selected Speeches 1960–64*, op. cit., p. 10.
110. Okpara, Dr. M. I., 'Pragmatic African Socialism' (lecture delivered to undergraduates of the University of Ife), Ibadan, 1965.
111. *President Azikiwe: Selected Speeches 1960–64*, op. cit., p. 13.
112. For instance, Nwachukwu Abengowe, an UPGA lawyer, was sentenced to six months imprisonment with hard labour: B. D. O. Anyaegbunam was sought for internment with a warrant of arrest.
113. *Drum* Magazine (Nigeria Edition), March 1965.
114. *Nigerian Outlook*, October 31, 1964, p. 3.
115. The Governor of the North, Sir Kashim Ibrahim, did not attend.
116. Note that Ahmadu Bello and Chief Akintola were the leaders of the NPC and NNDP – two Parties which had entered into an alliance called the NNA for the purpose of contesting the Federal Eelections.
117. This phrase is vague and no definition of what was actually meant was given to the nation. Apparently the President felt that he had struck a compromise between the contending Parties.
118. *Nigerian Outlook*, January 5, 1965, p. 3.
119. Odegard and Rosenblum (ed.), op. cit., (first semester) p. 171.
120. Ibid, p. 174. Authors' italics.
121. Mr. Justice Brett, of the Supreme Court of Nigeria, once stated that 'the courts throughout the British Commonwealth have traditionally regarded questions of policy as outside their scope'. Chief Justice Dixon, expressing similar views, asserted that 'there is no other safe guide to judicial decisions in great conflicts than a strict and complete legalism'. The sovereignty of the British Parliament has forced the English courts into a narrow view of their constitutional role, and the Commonwealth courts have tended to follow English decisions and precedents blindly. It is submitted that Nigeria should not have followed this approach, especially after 1963, when it ceased sending appeals to the Privy Council and being bound by the Privy Council decisions. In the United States, which is a Federation with a written consitution like Nigeria, the tendency is to adopt the liberal rather than the literal approach for, according to Frankfurter: 'It is a Constitution we are interpreting, not an insurance clause in small type', and it is inadmissibly a narrow conception to 'disregard the gloss which life has written upon them'. The United States Constitution is relatively brief and therefore leaves much room for judicial interpretation. Like the US Constitution, the Nigerian Constitution is not exhaustive, and therefore it cannot be said that the framers of the Nigerian Constitution excluded the courts from policy making.

122. *Drum* (Nigeria edition), March 1965.

123. See Niebuhr, Reinhold, *Moral Man and Immoral Society*, Charles Scribner's Sons, New York, 1960, p. 53.

124. Crowder, op. cit., p. 92.

125. Before this, the Yorubas had successfully warded off attempts by the Muslims to carry their holy war southward across the Niger, which thus became the natural boundary between the Yoruba and Muslim kingdoms.

126. Crowder, op. cit., p. 92.

127. An Oba's salary was cut to the humiliating sum of one penny per annum for opposing Chief Akintola's policies.

128. Ikejiani, op. cit., p. 118.

129. Ibid., p. 120.

130. *Nigerian Outlook*, October 19, 1965, p. 8.

131. Ijebu Province is the home province of Chief Obafemi Awolowo, the jailed AG leader, whose imprisonment increased rather than diminished his popularity. Understandably, this province had been seething with anti-NNDP feelings and was naturally the first place where the mass discontent exploded.

132. *Nigerian Outlook*, November 22, 1965, p. 4.

133. The Commissioner of Police in Western Nigeria, Odofin Bello, was later charged in court with corruption in high places when certain evidences of his complicity with the NNDP were uncovered.

134. *Nigerian Outlook*, op. cit., p. 11.

135. *Nigerian Outlook*, October 19, 1965, p. 3.

136. See post, Chapter 5.

CHAPTER 4

137. Nduka, Otonti, *Western Education and the Nigerian Cultural Background*. Oxford University Press, Ibadan, 1964, p. 26.

138. This was the Government school for teachers at Nassarawa, near Kano, in 1909.

139. Bello, Ahmadu, *My Life*, Cambridge University Press, 1962, p. 135.

140. Ahmadu Bello used the phrase 'native foreigners'. Ibid., p. 136.

141. Coleman, op. cit., p. 360.

142. Ibid., p. 322.

143. Ibid., p. 359.

146. Ibid., p. 358.

145. 'The North and Constitutional Developments in Nigeria', (*Nigerian Crisis*, 1966,) Vol. 5, 2nd. Imp. 1967, p. 3.

146. Contained in a statement by Sir Ahmadu accepting the results of the Nigerian census of 1963. Authors' italics.

147. Ahmadu Bello's Statement was a rejoinder to Dr. Okpara's statement refusing the census figures.

148. Authors' italics. The Minister's concluding statement offers some clue to the subsequent pogrom that took place in Nigeria.

149. *Nigeria Disunity: The Guilty Ones* (published by the Ibo State Union), Enugu, p. 14. Authors' italics.

150. p. 97.

151. Sections 23 (2), 24 (4), 25 (2) and 27 (2) of the Nigerian Republican Constitution.

CHAPTER 5

152. This power was not specifically provided for in the Nigerian Constitution, but scattered provisions of the Constitution, and the way the courts acted in the past supply ample evidence for this conclusion, based on logic. See SS. I, 69 (4), 115, 117 (2) (c) and 125 (1) (c) of the Republican Constitution. See also *Balewa v. Doherty* (1961), all NLR, Part IV; (1963) WLR 949.

153. Here the article published in the law journal, '*The Law Student*' (1965–6 issue), by Samuel U. Ifejika, is adapted with the permission of the Law Students' Association, University of Nigeria, Nsukka. The article in question was entitled 'The Judiciary and Human Freedom in a Democracy'.

154. See Preamble to the 1963 Republican Constitution of Nigeria.

155. I Cranch, 137 (1803).

156. See *Balewa v. Doherty* (1961).

157. (1960). NRNLR, p. 24.

158. S. 114. See *Government of Eastern Nigeria v. The Federal Government* on the census (unreported).

159. S. 115.

160. S. 117 (2), (c) and (d).

161. See Jefferson's letter to Judge Spencer Roane of the Virginia Supreme Court, September 6, 1819; letter to Madison dated Paris, December 20, 1787; letter to W. H. Torrance, June 11, 1815, etc. Thomas Jefferson represents the 'con' side of the debate that broke out over the *Marbury v. Madison* case, although no other law was declared unconstitutional until half a century later. Interestingly, Jefferson, at the time of the framing of the US Constitution, favoured some type of judicial control, although he later disagreed with how John Marshall expounded it. However, Hamilton, another of the Founding Fathers, in No. 78 of *The Federalist*, categorically stated that judicial review was meant to form part of the US Constitution. See post.

162. *Daily Express*, May 4, 1962.

163. See also Hamilton in No. 78 of *The Federalist*, where he stated that 'it would require an uncommon portion of fortitude in judges to do their duty as faithful guardians of the Constitution, where legislative invasions of it had been instigated by the major voice of the community'.

164. See Ford, P. L., *The Writings of Thomas Jefferson*, G. P. Putnam's Sons, New York, 1897, Vols. IX and X.

165. 261, US 525, at p. 544 (1923).

166. See also Dicey, A. V., *The Law of the Constitution*, Macmillan, London, pp. 143–70. Dicey, holding that the Bench can and must determine the limits of both the Government and the Legislature, asserted that judges are not only guardians but masters of the Constitution. The Supreme Court and like institutions are protectors of the federal compact. Hicks, U.K., 'Political Implications of Federalism', *Federalism and Economic Growth in Underdeveloped Countries*, George Allen and Unwin, 1963, pp. 38–44; Jennings, Sir Ivor, *The Law and the Constitution*, University of London Press, 1963, pp. 62–3; Laski, Harold J., *A Grammar of Politics*, George Allen and Unwin, London, 1960, pp. 541–50.

167. Pp. 182–3, Butterworth's African Law Series, 1963.

168. Ibid., pp. 182–3.

169. Ibid, p. 181 – Publius.

170. In the case of Nigeria, the governments of the Regions which were not in control of the central government as well, and therefore in opposition at the centre through the political parties under which they held power in the Regions.

171. S. 112.
172. S. 113.
173. S. 113 (1).
174. S. 113 (2).
175. SS. 129 and 133 (1) and (4).
176. S. 133 (3).
177. See supra.
178. *Daily Express*, May 4, 1962.
179. Ibid.
180. *Williams v. Majekodunmi*, FSC 166/1962.
181. Dr. M. A. Majekodunmi, a Federal minister.
182. Vol. 41, No. 1 of October 1962.
183. (1962) F.S.C. 187/1962. Akintola sought a declaration that he had been wrongly removed from the office of Premier of the Western Region.
184. This method was resorted to because Akintola, as Premier, would not advise the Speaker to convene Parliament to determine his popularity on the floor of the House.
185. See supra.
186. Awolowo had also, while Premier of W. Nigeria, earned the hostility of some highly-placed officials in his Region.
187. See supra.
188. See supra, Chapter 2.
189. *A. Eleye Datubo and Theodore A. Ezeobi vs. Provisional Council of the University of Lagos, Dr. E. N. O. Sodeinde and Chief A. Y. Eke*, Suit No. LD/100/65, per Justice Taylor at the Lagos High Court.
190. The costs awarded against the Provisional Council exceeded those awarded against the Students by £15 15s.
191. *DPP v. Adams* (1965).
192. See supra, p. 69.
193. *Inspector-General of Police v. Samuel Ifejika*, case No. D/232/65.
194. See supra p. 69.
195. Presumably, the NNDP-Controlled Government of Western Nigeria.
196. At the Ijebu Ode High Court, July 27, 1965 (unreported). Authors' Italics.
197. 'Brief for a Better Court System', New York Times Magazine, May 5, 1957, pp. 67ff.
198. Authors' italics.

CHAPTER 6

199. March 16, 1966.
200. About this time, soldiers were ruthlessly slaughtering the Tivs in an attempt to quell the many-months-old disturbances there. Three thousand lives are estimated to have been claimed in the riots. (The official figure was 300.)
201. Boro carried out his assignment. In February 1966, he declared the secession of the Delta area from Nigeria. He was sentenced to death for treason but was later released when Ironsi was overthrown. He later became a senior officer in the Nigerian Army.
202. When Chief Fani-Kayode, the NNDP Deputy Premier, was arrested by the patriots of the Revolution, he exclaimed: 'I knew that the Army was going to come but I did not know that was the way they would come.' See *January 15: Before and After*. Enugu, 1967, p. 14.

203. There had been a slight Cabinet reshuffle on the 14th. Mr. Okafor had been promoted to the position of a Minister of State. Another NCNC member, Mbazulike Amechi, was given Cabinet rank. Chief T. O. S. Benson (NNDP) was also made a Minister of State.

204. The President, Dr. Azikiwe, was absent in London.

205. Katsina, later a Lt.-Col. and Military Governor of the North under the Ironsi regime. When Lt.-Col.-Gowon created his twelve states, Katsina became Chairman of the Northern Council of States.

206. *Nigeria's Military Government: First 100 Days*, Daily Times of Nigeria Ltd., Apapa, Nigeria, p. 5, column 2.

207. *The Economist*, March 5, 1966.

208. Legum, Colin, 'Can Nigeria Escape Her Past?' *The Observer*, January 30, 1966.

209. Jones, J. D. F., 'When will the Army begin to Govern?' *The Financial Times*, May 5, 1966.

210. 'Nigeria is born again', *Drum*, May 1966.

211. *The Economist*, February 12, 1966.

212. *Daily Times*, February 17, 1966.

213. Schwarz, Walter, 'Basic Mistrust of South's intentions in Northern Nigeria', *The Economist*, June 3, 1966.

214. *Nigeria's Military Government: First 100 Days*, p. 7.

215. *West Africa*, June 4, 1966.

216. *The Economist*, June 18, 1966.

217. Garrison, Lloyd, 'Nigeria: A crisis with deep roots', *The New York Times* (International edition) June 2, 1966.

218. *West Africa*, June 4, 1966. Authors' italics.

219. *January 15*, p. 37. For full details of this and subsequent massacres, see the Reports of the Atrocities Tribunal of Enquiry set up by the Government of Eastern Nigeria to investigate the 1966 pogrom.

220. He directed his Chief of Staff, Lt.-Col. Gowon, who was later to lead the mutiny which overthrew him, to investigate the events of January 15. The report of this investigation was never released until he was murdered by Gowon's men on July 29.

CHAPTER 7

221. Bello, Ahmadu, op. cit., pp. 133 ff. See also *The North and Constitutional Development in Nigeria*, pp. 6–21.

222. *January 15: Before and After*, op. cit., p. 41. This letter portrays a Northern attitude to the régime of Major-General Aguiyi-Ironsi. Authors' italics.

223. Ibid pp. 43 and 44.

224. Ibid., p. 41.

225. Ibid., p. 42.

226. Ibid., p. 42.

227. For a more detailed account of this operation, see *January 15*, pp. 41–60, which agrees so well with our private and independent notes that we find it unnecessary to reproduce them here.

228. See *Nigerian Pogrom: The Organised Massacre of Eastern Nigerians*, Eastern Nigerian Ministry of Information.

229. *Nigerian Crisis 1966: Eastern Nigeria Viewpoint* (Crisis Series, Vol. 1), Government Printer, Enugu, 1966, p. 22.

230. *Daily Times*, August 2, 1966, pp. 1–2.

231. *Crisis 1966*, op. cit., p. 8.
232. Ibid., pp. 3–9.
233. *Daily Times*, August 2, 1966, p. 2.
234. Ibid., p. 2.
235. *Nigeria, 1966*, p. 57.
236. *Daily Times*, August 2, 1966, pp. 1–2.
237. See post.
238. The hand-over of government to Ironsi by the Council of Ministers has a semblance of legality but is of no legal significance. There is no provision in the Nigerian Constitution authorising anybody to hand over the government of the country to the Army or, for that matter, to anyone.
239. Among such officers and members were Brigadier Ogundipe, Chief of Staff, Supreme Headquarters, who, in fact, was the next senior officer to General Ironsi. Another was Lt.-Col. C. Odumegwu Ojukwu, then Military Governor of Eastern Nigeria. It will be recalled that the Eastern Military Governor had, in the course of the revolt, tried to persuade Brigadier Ogundipe to assume leadership in the Centre in the absence of General Ironsi.
240. See post, pp. 207 ff.
241. See *Aburi Report: Nigeria, 1967*, Daily Times Press Ltd., Lagos, 1967, column 3, p. 4.

CHAPTER 8

242. *Daily Times*, August 3, 1966, p. 16. See also *Crisis 1966*, op. cit., pp. 22–3.
243. Ibid., p. 23.
244. Northerners had earlier expressed their own views, as contained in their terms for a ceasefire.
245. On May 29, following the disturbances in Northern Nigeria, in which thousands of Biafrans lost their lives and property at the hands of Northerners, the Eastern Governor appealed for restraint and calm. In his absolute belief in the oneness of Nigeria, he appealed to Easterners returning home in flight to go back to the North and continue their business in the assurance that the Government had the situation well in hand.
246. *Daily Times*, August 9, 1966, p. 2, contd. p. 4.
247. This was endorsed later in the meeting of August 9, 1966.
248. *Daily Times*, August 9., 1966, p. 16.
249. 2, Gowon never consulted anybody with regard to maintenance of peace and security in Lagos, which he decided to rule as a conquered territory. It was envisaged that the Police and not the Army should take charge. 3, The *Ad Hoc* Constitutional Conference was not convened until September 12, about three weeks behind the recommended date. 4, Rather than decentralise the country, he ultimately applied an even tighter and more extreme type of centralisation than Nigeria had ever known, reducing his administration to something very akin to dictatorship. 5, The Supreme Military Council could not meet because Gowon did not make conditions in Lagos suitable for such a meeting by the removal of Northern troops from the West and Lagos.
250. See *Nigerian Outlook*, May 2, 1967. During the Ad Hoc Conference on the Nigerian Constitution, and after five days of meeting, Chief Obafemi Awolowo, irritated by the delay tactics adopted by the North over most urgent and important issues, had to remind the Northern delegation that 'most people are tired with the present army occupation in the country'. Furthermore, at a conference of Yoruba leaders of thought held at Ibadan, Western Nigeria, on

May 1, 1967, the same Awolowo, as 'leader of the Yorubas', warned that, unless the West and Lagos had become conquered and occupied territories, Northern troops in these areas should be repatriated to the North immediately, in accordance with the decisions of August 9, 1966, and the wishes of the people themselves. And among the reasons which Chief Awolowo gave to the Western Military Governor during May 1967 for his resignation from the Ad Hoc Constitutional Committee, just before its meeting scheduled to take place in Benin on May 5, was that, in spite of the call in November and December 1966 by the Western leaders of thought for the removal of Northern soldiers from the West, nothing had been done to meet this demand. Even the National Conciliation Committee, appointed by Gowon himself in a communiqué issued in Lagos on May 18, 1967, and signed by its secretary, Dr. Lawrence Fabunmi, recommended that, as a matter of urgency, immediate steps should be taken to post military personnel back to barracks within their respective regions of origin. See *Nigerian Daily Sketch*, May 19, 1967.

251. *Daily Times*, August 30, 1966, p. 2.

252. This was a broadcast over Radio Television Kaduna and the Nigerian Broadcasting Corporation. His troops still believed that secession was the proper thing for the North to do, and that they could achieve this objective only by violence. They therefore did everything within their power to make the work of the Ad Hoc Conference impossible, thus showing their lack of faith in one Nigeria and in a negotiated settlement. The Northern leaders had in fact assured them that they could secure for them at the Conference table a separate Republic. As a result the North, in its first memorandum at the Conference, advocated a Common Services Organisation in which every region would have the right to secede unilaterally. When at a later stage the Northern delegates were persuaded that secession would not be in the best interest of the North, and they therefore had to reverse their earlier stand, fresh violence erupted in the North and Lagos – about September 29, while the Ad Hoc Conference was still in session in Lagos.

253. See *Sunday Times*, September 25, 1966, p. 16.

254. *Daily Times*, September 28, 1966.

255. *New Nigerian*, September 26, 1966.

256. *Nigerian Outlook*, September 26, 1966. Title: 'Safety First.'

257. *Daily Times*, August 30, 1966, p. 2.

258. Ibid., p. 2.

259. Quoted from '*The Ad Hoc Conference on the Nigerian Constitution*' (*Nigerian Crisis Series*, Vol. 4, 1966), Government Printer, Enugu, p. ii.

260. *Crisis '66*, op. cit., pp. 29–30.

261. The Conference of September 12, 1966, was scheduled to begin at 11 a.m. Because of the late arrival of the Eastern Delegation, it could not start until about 1 p.m.

262. One of the reasons for adjourning the Conference of August 9 for one week was to allow Western Nigeria time to make a full selection of its delegation, since Col. Robert Adebayo, recently appointed Acting Military Governor for the West, was still holding consultations with the leaders of thought there. The West had only two representatives at the August talks, Professor Akin Mabogunje, of the University of Ibadan, and Dr. F. A. Ajayi (Solicitor-General).

263. See *Daily Times*, September 8, 1966, p. 16.

264. *Crisis 1966*, op. cit., p. 31.

265. Ibid., pp. 53–5.

266. *Daily Times*, September 13, 1966, p. 1, contd. p. 5.

267. It has to be observed here that Gowon later rejected a confederal system

of government. When it seemed clear that the Ad Hoc Conference would recommend this kind of government for Nigeria, Gowon unilaterally dismissed the Conference.

268. *The Ad Hoc Conference on the Nigerian Constitution*, op. cit., p. 1.

269. Ibid., p. 2.

270. Ibid., p. 1.

271. Ibid., p. 2. Authors' italics.

272. Ibid., p. 2.

273. Ibid., p. 3.

274. See *The Ad Hoc Conference*, op. cit., p. 15.

275. The West and Lagos, however, presented an alternative proposal for the establishment of a 'true Federalism'. It is their proposals in respect of a 'Commonwealth of Nigeria' that we are concerned with here, as the first Ad Hoc Conference eventually veered towards a loose form of association.

276. See supra.

277. See *Sunday Times*, September 18, 1966, p. 16. Authors' italics. When Gowon ultimately created 12 states on paper for Nigeria, he did not ascertain whether 'the majority of the people directly concerned' wanted it or not' Even among the minorities that demanded states, there was no agreement, as pointed out earlier. Only a referendum or plebiscite could have been used to ascertain the true wish of 'the people directly concerned'. The situation in the country would not allow this. But Gowon was in a hurry to score political points.

278. Ibid., p. 1, contd. p. 16. See also *The Ad Hoc Conference*, op. cit., p. 20, for the full statement.

279. Ibid., p. 20.

280. B. J. D. and J. O. C., 'Real Issues at the Lagos Conference', *Nigerian Opinion*, Vol. 2, No. 10 of October 1966, p. 113.

281. Mr. Mbu was once a Federal Minister of State in charge of the Navy. After the parting of the ways with Nigeria, he served Ojukwu's administration first as Chairman, Biafra Public Service Commission, and later as Commissioner for Foreign Affairs. He is the chief spokesman for Ogoja (one of the so-called minority areas in Biafra), and all his actions and utterances during the Biafran struggle with Nigeria were directed towards the solidarity of the Biafran people.

282. See *West Africa*, No. 2605, May 6, 1967, p. 579.

283. For full report, see *Minority Commission Report*, (HMSO), London, 1958.

284. Ibid., Part VI, cap. 14, p. 87, para. 1.

285. Ibid., p. 87, para. 2.

286. Ibid., p. 87, para, 3.

287. See *The Ad Hoc Conference*, op. cit., p. iii.

288. Cecil King was then Chairman of the (Nigerian) Times Group of newspapers and Chairman of the International Publishing Corporation of Britain and Japan in Nigeria. He was also a Director of the Bank of England. All through the Nigerian crisis and the Biafra–Nigerian conflict, he showed interested concern about these events. His utterances leave no one in doubt that he was worried about the fate of his newspaper in Nigeria. He wanted Nigeria to remain as one united country, no matter what the Biafran case might be. In a statement once credited to him by Radio Nigeria (NBC news 7 a.m.) on December 15, 1967, and by Radio Television Kaduna (6 p.m. news, December 14, 1967,) he had expressed concern about the press in Nigeria because of the Nigerian Government attitude. Lt.-Col. Gowon assured him that he would not dictate policy to the press, but that 'a good press should strive to bring Nigeria together'.

289. *Daily Times*, September 14, 1966.

290. *The Ad Hoc Conference*, op. cit., pp. iv and v.

291. An account of this pogrom is given in Chapter 5.

292. The interim report was, in fact, largely the report of the Ad Hoc Sub-Committee.

293. See supra. pp. 190ff.

294. *Ad Hoc Conference*, op. cit., p. x. For a further exposition of the Eastern position on the state issue, see address by the Military Governor of the East to the second meeting of the Consultative Assembly on October 4, 1966 – just a day after the Ad Hoc Conference adjourned in Lagos. In fact, the State question was the central theme of that meeting of the Consultative Assembly. A meeting held by the Eastern Consultative Assembly between August 31 and September 2 appointed a special Committee to go into the matter. That Committee, chaired by Dr. Okoi Arikpo, who also served as its secretary, eventually agreed that the fears of the minorities could be allayed and their rights safeguarded in some other ways than the creation of autonomous States. It was agreed that the solidarity of Eastern Nigeria must be maintained against her adversaries, and that further fragmentation of the Region should not be encouraged, the Eastern Region having already lost the Southern Cameroons. They recommended in place of states a new system of provincial administration, in which certain legislative and executive functions and powers would devolve upon provincial units. Such units would be guaranteed a reasonable degree of autonomy. This recommendation has since been implemented by the splitting up of Eastern Nigeria (now Biafra) into twenty Provinces, with one administrator in charge of each.

295. *Sunday Times*, October 2, 1966, p. 1.

296. See Ojukwu's broadcast to the nation (per ENBC Network) October 22, 1966.

297. These numbered about 100.

CHAPTER 9

298. *Daily Times*, December 27, 1966, p. 1.

299. '*On Aburi We Stand*' (a broadcast by His Excellency, Lt.-Col. Odumegwu Ojukwu, on Saturday, February 25, 1967). Government Printer, Enugu, p. 2.

300. *The Meeting of the Nigerian Military Leaders* (Official Document No. 5 of 1967), Government Printer, Enugu, p. 4.

301. Also present in the meeting were Secretaries of the various Regional Governments and of Lagos – viz.: S. I. A. Akenzua, Permanent Secretary, Federal Cabinet Office; P. T. Odumosu, Secretary to the Military Government, West; N. U. Akpan, Secretary to the Military Government, East; D. P. Lawani, Under-Secretary, Military Governor's Office, Mid-West; Alhaji Ali Akilu, Secretary to the Military Government, North.

302. *Aburi Report: Nigeria 1967*, Daily Times Publications, Lagos, 1967, column 1, p. 2.

304. Ibid., column 1, p. 2.

305. Lt.-Col. Gowon declared that there was no chairman, but that 'we are all joint-chairmen'.

306. *The Meeting of the Nigerian Military Leaders*, op. cit., pp. 3–4.

307. See Appendix I.

308. The suggestion to embody this resolution in the communiqué came from Lt.-Col. Ojukwu also, as an alternative to his proposal that a copy of the declaration be deposited with the secretariat of the Organisation of African Unity.

309. See post.

L

310. On January 15, 1967, the Lagos Government gave the first indication that all was not well by releasing a publication entitled *Nigeria 1966* which, among other acts of disaffection, attacked and libelled the Military Governor of the East. This publication, whose draft was completed after the Aburi accord, was formally launched in many foreign capitals, including London and Washington.

311. See Appendix III.

312. Authors' italics.

313. Ojukwu explained that Aburi decided that the Regions should move slightly apart.

CHAPTER 10

314. *Nigerian Outlook*, March 9, 1967, p. 1.

315. *The Economist*, March 5, 1966.

316. *Nigerian Outlook*, March, 31 1967.

317. Enahoro, Peter, 'Before the Darkness Falls' (2), *Nigerian Outlook*, April 1, 1967, p. 3.

318. Enahoro, Peter, 'Before the Darkness Falls' (1), *Nigerian Outlook*, ibid.

319. *Nigerian Outlook*, April 20, 1967, p. 1.

320. It is pertinent here to ask how constitutional and legal was Gowon himself and what constitution he was talking about.

321. The Ad Hoc Committee had been unilaterally dismissed in September 1966 by Lt.-Gol. Gowon. See supra., pp. 203–4.

322. Chief Awolowo had been convicted on a charge of treasonable felony against the Federation. See supra., p. 115.

323. *Nigerian Outlook*, April 26, 1967, p. 8.

324. Authors' italics.

325. *Nigerian Daily Sketch*, May 2, 1967, pp. 1 and 8.

326. Lagos was divided on this issue. Jakande headed the faction for a loose federation while the Oba of Lagos and Major Johnson (the Military Administrator of Lagos) headed the opposing faction. It is believed that Major Johnson's group was backed by the few but powerful 'naturalised Lagosians' who feared that a loose federation would reduce the importance of the Central Government, to which they owed their positions of influence and affluence. Another point of dissention was the position of Lagos in the event of a break of the Federation. While the Jakande faction preferred a merger with Western Nigeria, the Johnson group understandably wanted a sovereign Lagos State.

327. *Nigerian Daily Sketch*, May 5, 1967, p. 1.

328. *Nigerian Daily Sketch*, May 6, 1967, p. 1.

329. *Nigerian Daily Sketch*, May 8, 1967, p. 8.

330. *Advance*, May 7–13, 1963, p. 1.

331. Dr. Ibiam and Justice Mbanefo later renounced their British knighthoods in protest against Britain's massive military aid to Nigeria in the Biafra–Nigeria war.

332. *Advance*, May 21–7, 1963, p. 1.

333. See *Nigerian Outlook*, May 22, 24, 25 and 26, 1967.

334. *Nigerian Outlook*, May 26, 1967.

335. *Daily Sketch*, May 29, 1967, p. 1.

336. See Appendix IV.

337. See *Nigerian Outlook*, May 31, 1967, p. 1. Gowon's reaction to Biafra's Declaration of Independence was to declare war on her on July 6, 1967.

CHAPTER 11

338. Named after Oliver Lyttelton (later Lord Chandos), the then Colonial Secretary, who chaired the Conferences that formulated that Constitution.

339. Jennings, *Some Characteristics of the Indian Constitution*, Madras, 1953, p. 55.

340. International experts had recommended that the project should, for economic reasons, be sited in Eastern Nigeria, but the NPC-dominated Federal Government decided to site the major part of it at Idah, Northern Nigeria.

341. See *Nigerian Crisis 1966: Pogrom*, op. cit., p. 27.

342. *Nigeria and Biafra: The Parting of the Ways*, Government Printer, Enugu, 1967, p. 3.

343. The Central African Federation composed of Southern and Northern Rhodesia and Nyasaland provides a good comparison. A federation was created on September 1, 1953, out of negotiations between the Colonial Office and the European political leaders. The African leaders, who had boycotted the discussions, rejected the new political arrangements. When Roy Welensky, the Federal Prime Minister, called a Federal Election in April 1962, mainly on the question of the Federation, Africans who were allowed to vote boycotted it. After 1962, the British Government could no longer support the views of the European minority on the Federation. After the creation of an African majority in the Northern Rhodesia Legislative Council, African leaders seized the opportunity to destroy the Federation. Since Britain here acknowledged the right of the component parts to secede, Banda and Kaunda pulled their countries out of the Federation. The federal experiment ended on December 31, 1963. But these three countries are today still co-operating economically. See Cowan, L. Gray, 'The European in Independent Africa', *The Dilemmas Of African Independence*, op. cit., pp. 43–52.

APPENDICES

I

AGENDA FOR MEETING OF NIGERIAN MILITARY LEADERS AT ABURI, GHANA, JANUARY 4–5, 1967

1. Opening address by the Head of State of host country.
2. Response by Head of the Federal Republic of Nigeria and Supreme Commander of the Nigerian Armed Forces.
3. Review of the current situation in Nigeria, with particular reference to:
   (a) Organisation of the Nigerian Army;
   (b) Implementation of the agreement reached on August 9, 1966, in regard to the disposition of Army personnel.
4. Resumption of talks by the Ad Hoc Constitutional Committee. Acceptance of unanimous recommendations in September, 1966.
5. Problems of displaced persons, with particular reference to:
   (a) Rehabilitation;
   (b) Employment;
   (c) Property.
6. Arrangements for future meetings of the Supreme Military Council and the Federal Executive Council.
7. Communiqué.

ANNEX A:

COMMENTS BY MILITARY GOVERNOR, EASTERN NIGERIA

1. Better be deleted. If host wishes to make opening address this should entirely be his decision.
2. Not acceptable.
4. Should read 'Acceptance and implementation of unanimous recommendations of Ad Hoc Constitutional Committee in September'. This, along with 3(b) of draft agenda, would inspire confidence and reassure public of good intentions.
6. Should read 'Arrangements for future meetings'.
7. New item 7 should be – 'Government information media'.

II

A

MINUTES OF THE MEETING OF NIGERIAN MILITARY LEADERS HELD IN GHANA ON JANUARY 4–5, 1967

(These Official Minutes were to have been adopted by the Supreme Military Council at its next meeting.)

The Supreme Military Council held its meeting in Ghana on January 4–5.

Those present were:

Lt.-Col. Yakubu Gowon
Colonel Robert Adebayo
Lt.-Col. C. Odumegwu Ojukwu
Lt.-Col. David Ejoor
Lt.-Col. Hassan Katsina
Commodore J. E. A. Wey
Major Mobolaji Johnson
Alhaji Kam Selem
Mr. T. Omo-Bare

Secretaries: Mr. S. I. A. Akenzua, Permanent Under-Secretary, Federal Cabinet Office; Mr. P. T. Odumosu, Sectetary to the Military Government, West; Mr. N. U. Akpan, Secretary to the Military Government, East; Mr. D. P. Lawani, Under-Secretary, Military Governor's Office, Mid-West; Alhaji Ali Akilu, Secretary to the Military Government, North.

OPENING

1. The Chairman of the Ghana National Liberation Council, Lt.-General J. A. Ankrah, declaring the meeting open, welcomed the visitors to Ghana and expressed delight that Ghana had been agreed upon by the Nigerian military leaders as the venue for this crucial meeting. He considered the whole matter to be the domestic affair of Nigeria and, as such, he refrained from dwelling on any specific points. The General, however, expressed the belief that the Nigerian problems were not such that cannot be easily resolved through patience, understanding and mutual respect. Throughout history, he said, there has been no failure of military statesmen, and the eyes of the whole world were on the Nigerian Army. He advised that

soldiers are purely statesmen and not politicians, and the Nigerian military leaders owe it as a responsibility to the 56 million people of Nigeria successfully to carry through their task of nation-building. Concluding, the General urged the Nigerian leaders to bury their differences, forget the past and discuss their matter frankly but patiently.

2. Lt.-Col. Gowon invited the Nigerian leaders to say a 'joint thank you' to their host, and all said thank you in unison in response to Lt.-General Ankrah's address.

3. At this point the General vacated the Conference table.

IMPORTATION OF ARMS AND RESOLUTION RENOUNCING THE USE OF FORCE

4. Lt.-Col. Ojukwu spoke next. He said that the Agenda was accept-able to him subject to the comments he had made on some of the items. (See Appendix 1.) Lt.-Col. Ojukwu said that no useful purpose would be served by using the meeting as a cover for arms build-up, and accused the Federal Military Government of having engaged in large-scale arms deals by sending Major Apolo to negotiate for arms abroad. He alleged that the Federal Military Government re-cently paid £1 million for some arms bought from Italy and now stored up in Kaduna. Lt.-Col. Ojukwu was reminded by the Military Governor, North, and other members, that the East was indulging in an arms build-up and that the plane carrying arms which recently crashed on the Cameroons border was destined for Enugu. Lt.-Col. Ojukwu denied both allegations. Concluding his remarks on arms build-up, Lt.-Col. Ojukwu proposed that if the meeting was to make any progress, all the members must at the outset adopt a resolution to renounce the use of force in the settlement of the Nigeria dispute.

5. Lt.-Col. Gowon explained that, as a former Chief of Staff, Army, he was aware of the deficiency in the country's arms and am-munition, which needed replacement. Since the Defence Industries Corporation could not produce these, the only choice was to order from overseas and an order was accordingly placed to the tune of £1 million. He said that to the best of his knowledge the actual amount that had been paid out was only £80,000, for which he signed a cheque on behalf of the General Officer Commanding. The £80 million about which so much noise has been made was nothing but a typographical error in the Customs in recording the payment of £80,000. As to why these arms were sent up to the North, Lt.-Col. Gowon referred to lack of storage facilities in Lagos and re-minded his Military Colleagues of the number of times arms and ammunition had been dumped in the sea. This was why, he said, it

became necessary to use the better storage facilities in Kaduna. The arms and ammunition had not been distributed because they arrived only two weeks previously and have not yet been taken on charge. After exhaustive discussion, to which all members contributed, and during which Lt.-Col. Ejoor pointed out that it would be necessary to determine what arms and ammunition had arrived and what each unit of the Army had before any further distribution would take place, the Supreme Military Council unanimously adopted a Declaration proposed by Lt.-Col. Ojukwu, that all members:

(a) renounce the use of force as a means of settling the Nigerian crisis;
(b) reaffirm their faith in discussions and negotiation as the only peaceful way of resolving the Nigerian crisis; and
(c) agree to exchange information on the quantity of arms and ammunition available in each unit of the Army in each Region and in the unallocated stores, and to share out such arms equitably to the various Commands;
(d) agree that there should be no more importation of arms and ammunition until normalcy was restored.

The full text of the Declaration which was signed by all members is attached as Annex B to these minutes.

REORGANISATION OF THE ARMY

6. The Supreme Military Council, having acknowledged the fact that the series of disturbances since January 15, 1966, have caused disunity in the Army, resulting in lack of discipline and loss of public confidence, turned their attention to the question of how best the Army should be reorganised in order to restore that discipline and confidence. There was a lengthy discussion of the subject, and when the arguments became involved, members retired into secret session. On their return they announced that agreement had been reached by them on the reorganisation, administration and control of the Army on the following lines:

(a) Army to be governed by the Supreme Military Council under a chairman to be known as Commander-in-Chief of the Armed Forces and Head of the Federal Military Government;
(b) establishment of a Military Headquarters comprising equal representation from the Regions and headed by a Chief of Staff;
(c) creation of Area Commands corresponding to existing Regions and under the charge of Area Commanders;

(d) matters of policy, including appointments and promotion to top executive posts in the Armed Forces and the Police to be dealt with by the Supreme Military Council;

(e) during the period of the Military Government, Military Governors will have control over Area Commands for internal security;

(f) creation of a Lagos Garrison including Ikeja Barracks.

7. In connection with the reorganisation of the Army, the Council discussed the distribution of Military personnel with particular reference to the present recruitment drive. The view was held that general recruitment throughout the country in the present situation would cause great imbalance in the distribution of soldiers. After lengthy discussion of the subject, the Council agreed to set up a Military Committee, on which each Region will be represented, to prepare statistics which will show:

(a) present strength of Nigerian Army;
(b) deficiency in each sector of each unit;
(c) the size appropriate for the country and each Area Command;
(d) additional requirement for the country and each Area Command.

The Committee is to meet and report to Council within two weeks from the date of receipt of instructions.

8. The Council agreed that pending completion of the exercise in paragraph 7 further recruitment of soldiers should cease.

9. In respect of item 3 (b) of the Agenda, (implementation of the agreement reached on August 9, 1966), it was agreed, after a lengthy discussion, that it was necessary for the agreement reached on August 9 by the delegates of the Regional Governments to be fully implemented. In particular, it was accepted in principle that army personnel of Northern origin should return to the North from the West. It was therefore felt that a crash programme of recruitment and training, the details of which would be further examined after the Committee to look into the strength and distribution of army personnel had reported, would be necessary to constitute indigenous army personnel in the West to a majority there quickly.

NON-RECOGNITION BY THE EAST OF LT.-COL GOWON AS SUPREME COMMANDER

10. The question of the non-recognition by the East of Lt.-Col. Gowon as Supreme Commander and Head of the Federal Military Government was also exhaustively discussed. Lt.-Col. Ojukwu

based his objection on the fact, *inter alia,* that no one could properly assume the position of Supreme Commander until the whereabouts of the former Supreme Commander, Major-General Aguiyi-Ironsi, was known. He therefore asked that the country be informed of the whereabouts of the Major-General and added that in his view it was impossible, in the present circumstances, for any one person to assume any effective central command of the Nigerian Army. Lt.-Col. Ejoor enunciated four principles to guide the meeting in formulating an answer to the question of who should be Supreme Commander. These were the:

(a) problem of effective leadership;
(b) crisis of confidence in the Army;
(c) disruption in the present chain of command;
(d) inability of any soldier to serve effectively in any unit anywhere in the country.

Lt.-Col. Gowon replied that he was quite prepared to make an announcement on the matter, and regretted that a formal announcement had been delayed for so long, but the delay was originally intended to allow time for tempers to cool down. He reminded his colleagues that they already had the information in confidence. After further discussion, and following the insistence by Lt.-Col. Ojukwu that Lt.-Col. Gowon should inform members of what happened to the former Supreme Commander, members retired into secret session and subsequently returned to continue with the meeting after having reached an agreement among themselves.

11. At this point, the meeting adjourned until Thursday January 5. The Communiqué issued at the end of the first day's sitting is attached as Annex D.

THE POWER OF THE FEDERAL MILITARY GOVERNMENT, VIS-À-VIS THE REGIONAL GOVERNMENTS

12. When the meeting resumed on January 5, it proceeded to consider the form of government best suited to Nigeria in view of what the country has experienced in the past year (1966). Members agreed that the legislative and executive authority of the Federal Military Government should remain in the Supreme Military Council, to which any decision affecting the whole country should be referred for determination provided that, where it is not possible for a meeting to be held, the matter requiring determination must be referred to Military Governors for their comment and concurrence. Specifically, the Council agreed that appointments to senior ranks in the Police, Diplomatic and Consular Services, as well as appoint-

ments to super-scale posts in the Federal Civil Service and the equivalent posts in Statutory Corporations, must be approved by the Supreme Military Council. The Regional members felt that all the Decrees or provisions of Decrees passed since January 15, 1966, and which detracted from the previous powers and positions of Regional Governments, should be repealed if mutual confidence was to be restored. After this issue had been discussed at some length the Council took the following decisions.

The Council decided that:

(a) *On the reorganisation of the Army*

   (i) the Army to be governed by the Supreme Military Council under a chairman to be known as Commander-in-Chief of the Armed Forces and Head of the Federal Military Government;

   (ii) establishment of a Military Headquarters comprising equal representation from the Regions and headed by a Chief of Staff;

   (iii) creation of Area Commands corresponding to existing Regions and under the charge of Area Commanders;

   (iv) matters of policy, including appointments and promotion to top executive posts in the Armed Forces and the Police to be dealt with by the Supreme Military Council;

   (v) during the period of the Military Government, Military Governors will have control over Area Commands for internal security;

   (vi) creation of a Lagos Garrison including Ikeja Barracks.

(b) *On appointment to certain posts:*

The following appointments must be approved by Supreme Military Council:

   (i) Diplomatic and Consular posts.

   (ii) Senior posts in the Armed Forces and the Police.

   (iii) Super-scale Federal Civil Service and Federal Corporation posts.

(c) *On the functioning of the Supreme Military Council.* Decisions affecting the whole country must be determined by the Supreme Military Council. Where a meeting is not possible such a matter must be referred to Military Governors for comment and concurrence.

(d) That all the Law Officers of the Federation should meet in Benin on the January 14 and list out all the Decrees and provisions of Decrees concerned so that they may be repealed not later than January 21 if possible;

(e) That for at least the next six months, there should be a purely Military Government, having nothing whatever to do with politicians.

A statement on the Supreme Military Council is attached as Annex C.

SOLDIERS INVOLVED IN DISTURBANCES ON JANUARY 15, 1966, AND THEREAFTER

13. Members expressed views about the future of those who have been detained in connection with all the disturbances since January 15, 1966, and agreed that the fate of soldiers in detention should be determined not later than end of January 1967.

AD HOC CONSTITUTIONAL CONFERENCE

14. The Council next considered the question of the resumption of the Ad Hoc Constitutional Committee and the acceptance of that Committee's recommendations of September 1966. After some exchange of views, it was agreed that the Ad Hoc Committee should resume sitting as soon as practicable, to begin from where they left off, and that the question of accepting the unanimous recommendations of September 1966 be considered at a later meeting of the Supreme Military Council.

THE PROBLEMS OF DISPLACED PERSONS

15. The Council considered exhaustively the problems of displaced persons, with particular reference to their rehabilitation, employment and property. The view was expressed and generally accepted that the Federal Government ought to take the lead in establishing a National Body which would be responsible for raising and making appeal for funds. Lt.-Col. Ojukwu made the point, which was accepted by Lt.-Col. Katsina, that, in the present situation, the intermingling of Easterners and Northerners was not feasible. After each Military Governor had discussed these problems as they affected his area, the Council agreed:

(a) on rehabilitation, that Finance Permanent Secretaries should resume their meeting within two weeks and submit recommendations and that each Region should send three representatives to the meeting;

(b) on employment and recovery of property, that civil servants and Corporation staff (including daily-paid employees) who have not been absorbed should continue to be paid their full salaries until March 31, 1967, provided they have not got alternative employment, and that the Military Governors of the East, West and Mid-West should send representatives (Police Commissioners) to meet and discuss the problem of recovery of property left behind by displaced persons. Lt.-Col. Ejoor disclosed that the employment situation in his Region was so acute that he had no alternative but to ask non-Mid-Westerners working in the private sector in his Region to quit and make room for Mid-Westerners repatriated from elsewhere. Lt.-Col. Ojukwu stated that he fully appreciated the problem faced by both the Military Governor, West, and the Military Governor, Mid-West, in this matter and that, if in the last resort either of them had to send the Easterners concerned back to the East, he would understand, much as the action would further complicate the resettlement problem in the East. He assured the Council that his order that non-Easterners should leave the Eastern Region would be kept under constant review with a view to its being lifted as soon as practicable.

16. On the question of future meetings of the Supreme Military Council, members agreed that future meetings would be held in Nigeria at a venue to be mutually agreed.

17. On the question of Government information media, the Council agreed that all Government information media should be restrained from making inflammatory statements and causing embarrassment to various Governments in the Federation.

18. There were other matters not on the Agenda which were also considered, among which were the form of Government for Nigeria (reported in paragraph 12 above) and the disruption of the country's economy by the lack of movement of rail and road transport, which the Regional Governors agreed to look into.

19. The meeting began and ended in a most cordial atmosphere, and members unanimously issued a second and final communiqué, a copy of which is attached to these minutes as Annex E.

20. In his closing remarks the Chairman of the Ghana National Liberation Council expressed his pleasure at the successful outcome of the meeting and commended the decision taken to the Nigerian leaders for their implementation. Lt.-Col. Gowon, on behalf of his colleagues, thanked the Ghanaian leader for the excellent part he had played in helping to resolve the issues. The successful outcome of the meeting was then toasted with champagne, and the Nigerians took leave of the Ghanaians.

21. The proceedings of the meeting were reported verbatim for each Regional Government and the Federal Government by their re-

spective official reporters, and tape-recorded versions were distributed to each Government.

B

DECLARATION ON USE OF FORCE

WE, the members of the Supreme Military Council of Nigeria meeting at Aburi on 4th day of January, 1967, hereby solemnly and unequivocally:

(i) DECLARE that we renounce the use of force as a means of settling the present crisis in Nigeria, and hold ourselves in honour bound by this declaration;
(ii) REAFFIRM our faith in discussions and negotiation as the only peaceful way of resolving the Nigerian crisis;
(iii) AGREE to exchange information on the quantity of arms and ammunition in each unit of the Army in each Region, and also on the quantity of new arms and ammunition in stock.

The signatories to this declaration were:
Lt.-Col. Yakubu Gowon, Col. Robert Adebayo, Lt.-Col. Odumegwu Ojukwu, Lt.-Col. David Ejoor, Lt.-Col. Hassan Katsina, Commodore J. E. A. Wey, Major Mobolaji Johnson, Alhaji Kam Selem, and Mr. T. Omo-Bare.

C

STATEMENT OF THE SUPREME MILITARY COUNCIL

The Supreme Military Council now meeting in Ghana has agreed on the following reorganisation of the Army:

(a) The Army is to be governed by the Supreme Military Council the Chairman of which will be known as Commander-in-Chief and Head of the Federal Military Government.
(b) There will be a Military Headquarters on which the Regions will be equally represented and which will be headed by a Chief of Staff.
(c) In each Region there shall be an Area Command under the charge of an Area Commander and corresponding with the existing Regions.

(d) All matters of policy including appointments and promotions of persons in executive posts in the Armed Forces and Police shall be dealt with by the Supreme Military Council.

(e) During the period of the Military Government, Military Governors will have control over their Area Commands in in matters of internal security.

APPOINTMENTS

2. The following appointments must be approved by the Supreme Military Council:

(a) Diplomatic and Consular posts.
(b) Senior posts in the Armed Forces and the Police.
(c) Super-scale Federal Civil Service and Federal Corporation posts.

3. Any decision affecting the whole country must be determined by the Supreme Military Council. Where a meeting is not possible such a matter must be referred to Military Governors for comment and concurrence.

D

MEETING OF THE SUPREME MILITARY COUNCIL OF NIGERIA HELD IN GHANA, JANUARY 4, 1967

COMMUNIQUÉ

A meeting of the Supreme Military Council of Nigeria was held in Ghana on January 4, 1967. Present were:

Lt.-Colonel Yakubu Gowon,
Colonel Robert Adebayo,
Lt.-Colonel Odumegwu Ojukwu,
Lt.-Colonel David Ejoor,
Lt.-Colonel Hassan Katsina,
Commodore J. E. A. Wey,
Alhaji Kam Selem,
Mr. T. Omo-Bare.

The meeting which was held in a most cordial atmosphere was opened with an address by the Chairman of the National Liberation Council of Ghana, Lt.-General J. A. Ankrah.

The meeting discussed a number of issues and took decisions.

These included a declaration renouncing the use of force as a means of settling the present crisis in Nigeria and holding themselves in honour bound by the declaration. They also reaffirmed their faith in discussions and negotiation as the only peaceful way of resolving the Nigerian crisis.

The meeting has adjourned to resume in the same venue to morrow, January 5, 1967.

E

MEETING OF THE SUPREME MILITARY COUNCIL OF NIGERIA HELD IN GHANA, JANUARY 5, 1967

SECOND AND FINAL COMMUNIQUÉ

The Supreme Military Council of Nigeria resumed its meeting in Ghana on January 5, and continued and concluded discussion of the remaining subjects on the Agenda. The Council reached agreement on all the items.

On the powers and functions of the Federal Military Government the Council reaffirmed its belief in the workability of the existing institutions subject to necessary safeguards.

Other matters on which agreements were reached included the following:

(i) Reorganisation, administration and control of the Army.
(ii) Appointments and promotions to the senior ranks in the Armed Forces, the Police, Diplomatic and Consular Services, as well as appointments to super-scale posts in the Federal Civil Service and the equivalent posts in the Federal Statutory Corporations.

On the question of displaced persons the Supreme Military Council agreed to set up a committee to look into the problems of rehabilitation and recovery of property. In this connection the Military Governor of the East assured the Council that the order that non-Easterners should leave the Eastern Region would be reviewed with a view to its being lifted as soon as practicable. Agreement was also reached that the staff and employees of Governments and Statutory Corporations who have had to leave their posts as a result of recent disturbances in the country should continue to be paid their full salaries up to the end of March 31, 1967, provided they have not found alternative employment.

The Council agreed that the Ad Hoc Committee on the constitutional future of the country should be resumed as soon as practicable and that the unanimous recommendations of the committee in September 1966 will be considered by the Supreme Military Council at a later meeting.

The Council unanimously agreed that future meetings of the Council should be held in Nigeria at a venue to be announced later.

The entire members of the Supreme Military Council express profound regret for the bloodshed which has engulfed the country in the past year and avow to do all in their power to ensure there is no recurrence of the unhappy situation.

The Members of the Supreme Military Council place on record their profound appreciation and gratitude for the constructive initiative and assistance rendered by the Chairman of the National Liberation Council, the Government and people of Ghana.

Peduase Lodge, Aburi,
January 5, 1967

III

FEDERAL PERMANENT SECRETARIES' RECOMMENDATIONS ON ABURI

INTRODUCTION

1 The implications of the decisions of the Supreme Military Council meeting held in Aburi recently are commented upon *seriatim* in this paper.

2 Reorganisation of the Army:

a. *The Title 'Commander-in-Chief'.* Objections are raised to the use of 'Commander-in-Chief' which the Aburi meeting agreed should be the new title for the Chairman of the Supreme Military Council and Head of the Federal Military Government on the grounds that:

(i) it would be a subtle way of either abolishing the post of Supreme Commander or declaring it vacant, to be filled by the unanimous decision of the Supreme Military Council; if the latter, there would be considerable instability caused by political and military manoeuvres to fill the post;

(ii) the Aburi decision transfers the Executive Authority of the Federal Military Government from the Head of Federal Military Government and Supreme Commander (in accordance with Decree No. 1) to the Supreme Military Council. The implication of this is that the Commander-in-Chief would have no powers of control or dismissal over the Military Governors; a situation which is incompatible with military administration.

b. *Establishment of Military Headquarters.* It is considered:

(i) that the establishment of Military Headquarters with equal representation from the Regions headed by a Chief of Staff amounts to confederation;

(ii) that there is a need for clarification on the term 'Military Headquarters' as distinct from 'Supreme Headquarters'.

c. *Creation of Area Commands.* It is considered that the creation of Area Commands has the following implications:

(i) dividing up the Nigerian Army into regional ones, without links with or effective unified control over the Army by the 'Supreme Commander';

(ii) since area command would be under the control of Military Governors who can use the Army for internal security, there is the serious political implication in respect of the creation of states in which the status of minorities cannot be guaranteed by the Supreme Commander;

(iii) since under the constitution the operational control of the army is vested in the Prime Minister (and after January 15, 1967, in the Supreme Commander), the acceptance of the Aburi decision would require the amendments to the Armed Forces Acts and the Constitution;

(iv) no authority is vested with the power for the use of the Army, for external attacks on Nigeria.

d. *Matters of Policy*, etc., in the Armed Forces and Police vested in Supreme Military Council.

It is considered that the acceptance of this decision dispenses with the Army and Police Councils.

e. *Creation of Lagos Garrison*. If the Lagos Garrison is intended to be the same status as 'Area Commands', it would imply that Lagos is regarded as another 'Area Command'. The Commander-in-Chief might not have direct control over any group of soldiers in any 'area' – a very vulnerable situation. Otherwise, the Lagos Garrison can only be interpreted as the Commander-in-Chief's 'Body Guard'.

f. *Preparation of Statistics by Military Committee*. This can be regarded as a useful exercise as long as there is unfettered and free inspection of all military operations in the regions.

3) *'Appointments to Certain Posts'*. There appears to be need for clarification as to the specific categories of officers for the appointment of whom the Supreme Military Council will like to be responsible. It is observed that:

a. whichever category of officers is meant, the effect of this decision will tend to paralyse the functions of the Federal Public Service and the Police Service Commissions;

b. if Regional Governors leave power to appointments, the loyalty of Federal Officers would be to their regions of origin – meaning in effect that there will be no Federal Civil Service;

c. the acceptance of this decision would also require, as the law officers have reported, amendments to those sections in the Constitution dealing with appointment to Nigeria Police, the

Federal Public Service Commission and sections of various acts dealing with appointment in Federal Statutory Corporations;

d. furthermore, it is observed that while Military Governors will have power to appoint, or approve appointments of Federal Government servants, there is no corresponding power of the Supreme Military Council to even influence the appointments to senior posts in the Regional Public Services. This clearly makes the Federal Military Government subordinate to the Regional Governments.

4 *Powers of the Federal Military Government.* It is considered that the vesting of the legislative and executive powers in the Supreme Military Council and the introduction of the element of Regional Military Governors' consent in the Federal Legislation will leave the Federal Executive Council with virtually no functions, and the powers of the Federal Military Government *vis-à-vis* the Regional Military Governments will no longer exist. This view has been expressed in the Report of the Law Officers' meeting held recently in Benin; the relevant sections of which report are quoted as follows:

Section 69. As regards the powers of the Federal Military Government *vis-à-vis* the Regional Governments, all the Law Officers, excepting those from the East, are of the view that effect would be fully given to the Aburi decision in this regard by repealing the provisions of the suspended Section 69 with necessary modifications whereby the Federal Military Government will now have power to make Decrees to the following extent:

a. With respect to the Federal Territory of Lagos . . . on matters included in the Exclusive Legislative List and the Concurrent Legislative List; provided that, where there is an inconsistency between a Federal Decree on a Concurrent matter and a Regional Edict on the same matter, the Federal Decree will prevail.

Under this arrangement the Military Governors will have no power to make Edicts on matters on the Exclusive Legislative List but will have powers to make Edicts on matters in the Concurrent Legislative List on residual matters.

The view of the Eastern Law Officers is that the introduction of the element of Regional consent in Federal Legislation must necessarily modify the position as it was before January 17 in the sense that there will be a lacuna in the legislative activities of both the Supreme Military Council and the Regions where consent is not given. It appears therefore to be the intention of the Aburi decision that such a lacuna should be filled by the Regions. With respect to matters on the Concurrent Legislative List, it is their view that the Region can legislate without Federal consent and without any fear of repugnancy in relation to Federal law. With respect to matters in the Exclusive Legislative List, they have proposed that the Supreme Military Council be asked to elucidate the position. They have adopted this approach because the Aburi decision does not appear to have made any distinction between both the Exclusive and the Concurrent Legislative Lists.

Section 8 of Decree No. 1

(a) This section deals with the composition of the Supreme Military Council and the Federal Executive Council. . . .

(b) Sub-section (v) of the section at present provides, *inter alia*, that the Supreme Military Council and the Federal Executive Council may act notwithstanding any vacancy in their membership or the absence of any member. . . .

(c) It is understood that one of the Aburi agreements is to the effect that all legislative and executive authority is now to be vested in the Supreme Military Council. It is not known, however, whether in the light of this decision it is still the intention to retain the Federal Executive Council as a body separate and distinct from the Supreme Military Council. If, however, the intention is to retain the Federal Executive Council, then in regard to that body, some answers for the purpose of clarity and the avoidance of any doubts or argument in the future will have to be provided to questions similar to those already raised. . . .

The questions raised are quoted:

(i) Whether it is the intention of the Aburi agreement that a meeting of the Supreme Military Council will not be properly constituted and so cannot properly be held unless all the Military Governors are present.

(ii) Whether where all the Military Governors are present at a meeting of the Military Council decisions of the Council can properly be taken only with the concurrence or unanimity of all the Military Governors or by a majority of the Military Governors, or else by a majority of all the members present.

(iii) Whether where one or more military Governors are present at any meeting of the Supreme Military Council their concurrence in decisions taken at such a meeting will still be necessary before such decision can be implemented.

(iv) Whether all Decrees (whether affecting the whole country or not) are to be formally approved by the Supreme Military Council before they are signed by the Head of the Federal Military Government.

(v) In what manner should the concurrence of the Military Governors in the making of Decrees (in their capacity as members of the Supreme Military Council) be signified, that is, for instance, whether it will be enough for this to be signified orally in the course of a meeting of the Supreme Military Council or by writing under their respective hands or whether there should be a column in the Decree for the appending of signature.

In the light of the implications of the Aburi decisions as quoted above:

(a) the recommendations of the law officers should be adopted, i.e. the powers and functions of the Federal Government as contained in the Exclusive and Concurrent Legislative Lists should be restored;

(b) the law officers should confine themselves to only those decrees which tend to over-centralise the administration.

5 *Composition of the Federal Military Government.* The decision that the civilians should not be associated with the Federal Military Government for the next six months is incompatible with the various promises which the Supreme Commander has made to the Nation in this regard. Civilians, including ex-politicians, are closely associated with Military Governors in the running of the Regional Military Government. There is, therefore, a clear need to associate reputable Nigerians with the Federal Executive Council as previously recommended in the summary:

(a) A provisional Federal Government should be established immediately comprising:

(i) the Supreme Commander of the Armed Forces (Chairman);

(ii) the Head of the Navy, Army, Air Force, Police;

(iii) three civilian members each from the East, Mid-West, North, West and one from Lagos;

(iv) Attorney-General of the Federation.

(b) The civilians must be people who were not actively involved in

politics in the past five years, of undoubted integrity and independent character.

(c) They will, on oath and by their instrument of appointment,
be debarred from seeking political office for at least five years.

(d) They will be appointed by the Supreme Commander and the
Head of the Federal Military Government himself.

(e) The civilian members will be assigned portfolios as Commissioners.

6 *Soldiers in detention.* It is considered that the determination of
the fate of the soldiers in detention should be done after assessing
the possible reactions of the rank and file in the Army. This is necessary to avert any adverse repercussions.

7 *Ad Hoc Constitutional Conference.* It is considered that the
'Aburi Decisions' – in so far as they tend towards strengthening the
Regions at the expense of the Federal Government and hence towards the setting up of a confederal system of Government – are
incompatible with the unanimous decisions of the Ad Hoc Constitutional Conference. It seems more advisable, therefore, to stick to
previous recommendations and advice to the Supreme Commander,
viz.:

(a) that the Ad Hoc Constitutional Conference should stand adjourned indefinitely;

(b) that the immediate political programme announced to the
nation on November 30, 1966 by the Supreme Commander
should be implemented and the country must be so informed.

8 *Problems of displaced persons.* It is suggested that:

(a) when the meeting of Permanent Secretaries of the Ministries
of Finance resumes, the principle of revenue allocation should
not be discussed as it was not mentioned in the minutes of the
Aburi Meeting;

(b) the decision to continue to pay salaries till the end of March
1967 does not take into consideration economic factors which
are linked with it. For instance, the railways are not fully
running and cannot earn enough revenue with which to pay
their servants who are not working. The P & T is in the same
plight and the Federal Ministry of Finance has indicated its
inability to make additional financial provision for this purpose. Secondly, it does not make sense to include daily paid
workers among those whose salaries should continue to be
paid. The decision should therefore be reconsidered.

(c) that there is no reason to leave out the Military Governor of the North from sending representatives to discuss the problem of the recovery of property because Northerners who left the East also left their property behind.

(ix) *Summary of Conclusions and Recommendations:*

(a) If the adoption of the title Commander-in-Chief declares the post of Supreme Commander vacant, serious instability would result from political and military manoeuvres to fill the post.

(b) The creation of Area Commands without any unified and effective central control of the Nigerian Army has serious political implications: internally, because of the vulnerable position of the Commander-in-Chief or Supreme Commander and the status of minorities; externally, because no single authority is vested with the power to use the Army for defence against external aggression. Acceptance of the Aburi meeting's decision would require amendments to the Armed Forces Acts and the Constitution.

(c) To avert possible repercussions, the determination of the fate of soldiers in detention should be done after assessing the possible reactions of the rank and file of the Army.

(d) The decision to appoint or approve appointments of Federal public servants will not only paralyse the Federal Public and Police Service Commissions but will also create Regional loyalties among Federal public servants.

(e) The decision that displaced persons should continue to receive their salaries till the end of March 1967 should be reconsidered for economic reasons.

(f) The vesting of executive powers of the Federal Military Government on the Supreme Military Council with the introduction of the element of consent of the Regional Military Governors makes the Federal Military Government subordinate to the Regional Military Governments, and this amounts to accepting confederation. The powers of the Federal Government as contained in the Exclusive and Concurrent Lists should be restored as recommended by the law officers.

(g) The Ad Hoc Constitutional Conference should stand adjourned indefinitely and the immediate political programme announced by the Supreme Commander to the nation on November 30, 1966, should be implemented.

(h) There is a clear need to associate reputable civilians with the Federal Executive Council as previously recommended and the nation should be so informed.

(i) If the intention of the Aburi decision is to restore to the Regions the Constitutional powers which were taken from them before January, 1966, the Supreme Commander should instruct the law officers to list the relevant decrees for repeal.

Cabinet Office, Lagos.
January 20, 1967.

IV

PROCLAMATION OF THE REPUBLIC OF BIAFRA
(*Enugu, May 30, 1967*)

IT IS RIGHT and just that we of this generation of Eastern Nigerians should record for the benefit of posterity some of the reasons for the momentous decision we have taken at this crucial time in the history of our people.

The Military Government of Eastern Nigeria has, in a series of publications, traced the evils and injustices of the Nigerian political association through the decades, stating also the case and standpoint of Eastern Nigeria in the recent crisis.

Throughout the period of Nigeria's precarious existence as a single political entity Eastern Nigerians have always believed in fundamental human rights and principles as they are accepted and enjoyed in civilised communities. Impelled by their belief in these rights and principles and in their common citizenship with other Nigerians after Amalgamation, Eastern Nigerians employed their ideas and skills, their resourcefulness and dynamism in the development of areas of Nigeria outside the East. Eastern Nigerians opened up avenues of trade and industry throughout the country; overlooked the neglect of their homeland in the disposition of national institutions, projects and utilities; made available their own natural resources to the rest of the country; and confidently invested in the general economic and social development of Nigeria. Politically Eastern Nigerians advocated a strong, united Nigeria; for ONE COUNTRY, ONE CONSTITUTION, ONE DESTINY. Eastern Nigerians were in the vanguard of the struggle for national independence and made sacrifices and concessions for the cause of national unity. They conceded the inauguration of a Federal instead of a Unitary system of Government in Nigeria.

Leaders of Northern Nigeria have told us several times that what our former colonial masters made into 'Nigeria' consisted of an agglomeration of people, distinct in every way except in the colour of their skins, and organised as a unit for their own commercial interests and administrative convenience. The name 'Nigeria' was regarded by many as a mere 'geographical expression'.

In course of time, the peoples of the other parts of Southern Nigeria found that they possessed many things in common with those of Eastern Nigeria, and while the colonial master made adjustments to accommodate these common ties between the Southern inhabitants, the peoples of the North insisted on maintaining their separateness.

On October 1, 1960, independence was granted to the peoples of Nigeria in a form of 'Federation', based on artificially made units. The Nigerian Constitution installed the North in perpetual dominance over Nigeria. The Federation was predicated on the perpetual rule by one unit over the others. The Constitution itself contained provisions which negatived the fundamental human freedoms which it purported to guarantee for the citizens. Thus were sown, by design or by default, the seeds of factionalism and hate, of struggle for power at the Centre, and of the worst types of political chicanery and abuse of power. One of two situations was bound to result from that arrangement: either perpetual domination of the rest of the country by the North, not by consent, but by force and fraud, or a dissolution of the federating bond. National independence was followed by successive crises each leading to near disintegration of the country. Some of the major events which are directly attributable to the defective and inadequate Constitution may here be mentioned.

In 1962 an emergency was imposed on Western Nigeria. Jurists agree that the imposition was unconstitutional; it was a ruse to remove certain elements in Western Nigeria known to have taken a firm stand against the misuse of political power. A puppet of the North was manoeuvred into power in Western Nigeria.

Also in 1962, and again in 1963, Nigerians tried for the first time to count themselves. What should ordinarily be a statistical and dull exercise was, because of the nature of the Constitution, turned into a fierce political struggle. The official figures established by these censuses have been discredited.

Federal elections followed in December 1964 – elections which have been described as the most farcical in our history. Candidates were either kidnapped, killed or forced to withdraw from the elections. Results announced were in direct opposition to the actual facts. The Southern parties had boycotted the election, and the deadlock which followed brought the country near to dissolution. The situation was patched up; the conflagration was brought under control, but its embers lay smouldering.

On October 11, 1965, elections were held to the Western House of Assembly. The puppet Government of that Region existed, not by the will of the people of Western Nigeria, but because of the combined power of the Federal Government and the Northern Nigeria Government which installed it. The electorate of Western Nigeria was not permitted to declare its will in the elections. Fraud, foul play and murder were committed with impunity. The smouldering embers of the recent past erupted with unquenchable virulence. The irate electorate showed its resentment in its own way. Complete disorder followed. Yet the Federal Government, dominated by the North, fiddled with the issue and even refused to recognise what the whole world had known, namely that Nigeria was on the brink of disaster.

Only the Armed Forces remained politically uncommitted and non-partisan. Some of their officers and men revolted against the injustices which were perpetrated before their very eyes and attempted to overthrow the Federal Government and Regional Governments. In desperation, the Ministers of the Federal Government handed over power to the Armed Forces under the supreme command of Major-General J.T.U. Aguiyi-Ironsi.

The Military administration under Major-General Aguiyi-Ironsi made the first real attempt to unite the country and its peoples. The Northerners saw in his efforts the possibility of losing their control of the affairs of the country. So while its leaders paid lip-service to unity they laid plans for making sure that it could never be achieved. Major-General Aguiyi-Ironsi was, of course, an Easterner, but the majority of the individuals at the head of affairs were not. At no time under the civilian rule did Eastern Nigerians hold a dominating position in the Government of the Federation.

On May 24, 1966, the Military Government issued a decree designed to provide a more unified administration in keeping with the military command. The people of Northern Nigeria protested against the decree and on May 29, 1966, thousands of Easterners residing in the North were massacred by Northern civilians. They looted their property. The Supreme Military Council set up a tribunal to look into the causes of those unprovoked acts of murder and pillage and determine what compensations might be paid to the victims. The Northern Emirs declared their intention to pull Northern Nigeria out of the Federation rather than face the tribunal. But the Supreme Military Council justly decided that the tribunal must do its duty.

Then on July 29, 1966, two months after the May murders and despoliation, and four days before the tribunal was due to commence its sitting, the real pogrom against Eastern Nigerians residing in the Federation began. Major-General Aguiyi-Ironsi and his host, Lt.-Col. Francis Fajuyi, were kidnapped at Ibadan and murdered. This time Northern soldiers acted in concert with Northern civilians. Defenceless men, women and children were shot down or hacked to death; some were burnt, and some buried alive. Women and young girls were ravished with unprecedented bestiality; unborn children were torn out of the wombs of their mothers.

Again on September 29, 1966, the pogrom was resumed. Thirty

thousand Eastern Nigerians are known to have been killed by Northerners. They were killed in the North, in Western Nigeria, in Lagos; some Eastern soldiers in detention at Benin were forcibly removed from prison by Northern soldiers and murdered.

At the time of the incident, millions of Eastern Nigerians resided outside the East and persons from other parts of the country lived in this Region. While Eastern Nigerians who assembled at Northern airports, railway stations and motor parks were set upon by Northern soldiers and civilians armed with machine guns, rifles, daggers and poisoned arrows, the Army and Police in the East were specifically instructed to shoot at sight any Eastern Nigerian found molesting non-Easterners living in the Region. By early October the sight of mutilated refugees, orphaned children, widowed mothers and decapitated corpses of Eastern Nigerians arriving at our airports and railway stations inflamed passions to such an extent that it was found necessary to ask all non-Easterners to leave the Region in their own interest. Since the events of July 1966 there has been a mass movement of population in this country. Nigerian society has undergone a fundamental change; it is no longer possible for Eastern Nigerians to live outside the Region without fear of loss of life or of property.

Two facts emerge from the events described above. The widespread nature of the massacre and its periodicity – May 29, July 29, and September 29 – show firstly that they were premeditated and planned, and secondly that Eastern Nigerians are no longer wanted as equal partners in the Federation of Nigeria. It must be recalled that this was the fourth in a series of massacres of Eastern Nigerians in the last two decades.

At the early stages of the crisis, the world was told that it was a conflict between the North and the East. That pretence collapsed when it became clear that Northern soldiers move into Western Nigeria and Lagos as another step in Northern Nigeria's bid to continue her so-called conquest to the sea. Belatedly, it was generally accepted that the fundamental issue was not a struggle between the East and the North, but one involving the very existence of Nigeria as one political entity.

Throughout the Nigerian crises, some of the indigenous judges have been found quite unequal to their calling by reason of their involvement in partisan politics. People soon lost faith in them, and would not go to their courts for redress. In some measure, they were responsible for the collapse of the rule of law in certain parts of Nigeria. Providence has spared us in the East from this terrible calamity.

It is now necessary to summarise the attempts of the Government and people of Eastern Nigeria to solve the crisis, and of the bad faith with which these attempts have been received.

On August 9, 1966, representatives of the Military Governors meeting in Lagos made decisions for restoring peace and for clearing the way for constitutional talks notably the decision that troops be all repatriated to their region of origin. These decisions were not fully implemented.

On September 12 the Ad Hoc Constitutional Conference consisting of delegates representing all the Governments of the Federation met in Lagos, and for three weeks sought to discover a form of association best suited to Nigeria, having regard to the prevailing circumstances and their causes and future possibilities. This Conference was unilaterally dismissed by Lt.-Col. Gowon, the Head of the Lagos Government.

It had then become impossible for the Supreme Military Council, the highest governing body in the Federation, to meet on Nigerian soil. As long as Northern troops were in Lagos and the West, no venue could be found acceptable to all the Military Governors for a meeting of the Supreme Council in Nigeria. It met at Aburi in Ghana on January 4 and 5, 1967, on the basis of an agenda previously determined by officials of Governments of the country and adopted by the Supreme Military Council. Decisions reached at the meeting were ignored by Lt.-Col. Gowon and the North. In the interest of this Region and of the whole country, the East stood firmly by those decisions, and warned that they would be applied to Eastern Nigeria if steps were not taken by the Lagos Government to apply them generally. The East rejected all measures which did not reflect the decisions at Aburi.

The Aburi accord was not implemented by the Lagos Government. All the meetings of Military Leaders held since Aburi were held without the East. All the decisions taken by Lagos were taken without comment and concurrence from the East.

It became evident that each time Nigerians came close to a realistic solution to the current crisis by moving towards a loose form of association or confederation, Lt.-Col. Gowon unilaterally frustrated their efforts. When the representatives of the Military Governors decided on August 9 that troops be repatriated to their Regions of origin, and it appeared to him that this would lead to confederation, he unilaterally refused to fully implement that decision. When in September the Ad Hoc Constitutional Conference appeared near to agreement on a loose Federation, he unilaterally dismissed them indefinitely. When in January 1967 the Military Leaders agreed at Aburi on what the Federal Permanent Secretaries correctly interpreted as confederation, he unilaterally rejected the Agreement to which he had voluntarily subscribed. When in May 1967 all the Southern Military Governors and the Leaders of Thought of their Regions spoke out in favour of Confederation, he dismissed the Supreme Military Council and proclaimed himself the dictator of Nigeria – an act which, to say the least, is treasonable.

Following the pogrom of 1966, some two million Eastern Nigerians have returned from other Regions, refugees in their own country. Money was needed to care for them – not to give them mere relief but to rehabilitate them and, in time, restore their outraged feelings. The Lagos Government was urged to give the Eastern Nigeria Government its share of the statutory revenues; Lt.-Col. Gowon refused to do so in the hope that the weight of the burden would lead to the economic collapse of Eastern Nigeria.

Ultimately, and beginning from April 1, 1967, steps were taken to recover what was due to Eastern Nigeria and to enable this Region and her people to survive. These are the 'Survival Edicts': the Revenue Collection Edict, the Legal Education (Eastern Nigeria) Edict, the Statutory Bodies Edict and the Court of Appeal Edict.

At each stage during the crisis, in accordance with the democratic and republican spirit of Eastern Nigerians, the people were fully consulted for their advice and guidance.

On August 31, 1966, the First Consultative Assembly and the Advisory Committee of Chief and Elders consisting of four representatives from each administrative division and other interests were summoned and the facts relating to the crisis put before them. Their advice was as follows:

Be it resolved as follows:
1. We, the representatives of the various communities in Eastern Nigeria gathered in this Consultative Assembly, hereby declare our implicit confidence in the Military Governor for Eastern Nigeria, Lt.-Col. Odumegwu Ojukwu, in all the actions he has so far taken to deal with the situation which has arisen in Nigeria since May 29, 1966.
2. In view of the grave threat to our survival as a unit in the Republic of Nigeria, we hereby urge and empower/advise him to take all such actions that might be necessary to protect the integrity of Eastern Nigeria and the lives and property of its inhabitants.
3. We advise constant consultation by His Excellency with the Consultative Assembly.
4. In view of the gravity of the present situation we affirm complete faith in and urge the need for solidarity of Eastern Nigeria as a unit.

M

5. In view of the present situation of things no delegates be sent to Lagos for any constitutional talks unless the safety of the delegates is guaranteed.

After the adjournment of the Ad Hoc Constitutional Conference, these bodies, now enlarged to consist of ten representatives from each administrative division in Eastern Nigeria, and other sectors of the community, were summoned. The delegates to the Ad Hoc Constitutional Conference placed a full report before them, and by a resolution dated October 7, 1966, the Consultative Assembly and the Advisory Committee of Chiefs and Elders advised as follows:

1. PLACES on record its deep gratitude to the Eastern Nigeria Delegation to the Constitutional Conference in Lagos for the diligent and faithful way in which, under conditions of severe strain, tension and fear, they carried out the mandate given to them by the Consultative Assembly and the Chiefs and Elders of Eastern Nigeria.

2. ENDORSES the stand of the Eastern Delegation at the Lagos Constitutional Conference.

3. URGES that, as an interim measure, a beginning be made to implement those aspects of the recommendations as relate to the Armed Forces at least to the extent of returning them to their Regions of origin and vesting the operational control of the regional contingents in the respective Military Governors.

4. REAFFIRMS its acceptance of the Report of the Committee on the Pattern of Constitution for Eastern Nigeria within the Federation of Nigeria and the additional suggestions proposed by the Graham-Douglas Constitutional Committee regarding the legislative and executive functions to be devolved upon the Provincial Units, and urges that the Constitutional Committee should forthwith study the details of the scheme, with particular reference to the number and size of provinces, the distribution of functions between the Provinces and the Regional Government, financial arrangements and the method and timing of implementation.

5. ENDORSES both the principle of the creation of more states in Nigeria and the statement of the Eastern Delegation to the Lagos Constitutional Conference to the effect that the splitting up of the country at this stage is not what is needed to normalise conditions of life in the country and provide a sense of security for its inhabitants, and that immediate constitutional arrangements for the country as a whole should be made on the basis of the existing Regions in order to save the country from impending disintegration.

6. SINCE the issue of the creation of more states is a vital and in-

evitable item on the Agenda of the Lagos Constitutional Conference, RECOMMENDS the following as the conditions upon which the creation of states should proceed:

(a) The basis for the creation of states must be mutually agreed upon beforehand and must be uniformly and consistently applied throughout the country.
(b) The creation of states must take place simultaneously throughout the country.
(c) The creation of any new state must be based upon the consent of the people of the area which is to be included in the proposed state and where two or more distinct tribal groupings are comprised within such area the wishes of each such grouping must be separately ascertained and respected.
(d) The population, area and economic resources of any new state which it is proposed to create must be reasonably commensurate to the enormous functions which the states will be expected to perform under the new constitutional arrangements envisaged for Nigeria.

7. IN VIEW of the fact that the desire on the part of the minority groups for self-determination is the active force behind the demand for the creation of more states, and since in the context of present-day Nigeria minorities are defined by reference to tribe, AFFIRMS its belief that the best hope for a satisfactory solution to the problems of Nigeria lies in the recognition and preservation of the separate identity of the various tribal or linguistic groupings and their right to develop each along its own line and at its own pace; accordingly RECOMMENDS that the creation of states throughout Nigeria should be on the basis of tribal or linguistic groupings or mutual consent between the linguistic groupings.

8. ADVISES that, until the agreements reached by the personal representatives of the Military Governors on August 8 and 9 are fully implemented, and until immediate compensation is paid by the Federal Military Government for the lives and property of Easterners lost in the disturbed areas of Nigeria, the Eastern Nigeria Delegation should no longer participate in future Constitutional Conference.

9. SATISFIED that the interim report of the Constitutional Conference has been completely overtaken by the most recent events in the country, ADVISES that the only possible and logical solution

to the problem of political association for Nigeria lies in the organisation and running of common services.

A. IKOKU,
Chairman.

DATED October 7, 1966.

On November 23, 1966, they met again to consider the progress of the crisis. They resolved as follows:

RECALLING the atrocious murders of persons of Eastern Nigeria origin and other acts of barbarism and inhumanity committed against us in other parts of Nigeria by fellow countrymen among whom they lawfully resided;

AWARE of the planned and determined effort to exclude Eastern Nigeria and her people from the public affairs and public offices of the Federal Republic of Nigeria;

CONSCIOUS of the attempt made and being made, by the Government and people of Eastern Nigeria, in spite of the wrongs done to Eastern Nigerians, to promote peace and salvage what is left of Nigeria and her honour;

DETERMINED to protect and defend the integrity of Eastern Nigeria and the dignity of her people;

CONFIRMING the mandate given by us to our Delegates to the Ad Hoc Constitutional Conference, and our confidence in them, and, having noted with regret the indefinite adjournment of the meeting of the Ad Hoc Constitutional Conference by Lt.-Col. Yakubu Gowon for alleged inability to agree upon the venue of the meeting as well as, according to him, because of other difficulties which he has not named;

OBSERVING that, even though the decision to appoint the Ad Hoc Constitutional Conference was a unanimous agreement of the Governments of the Federation, yet the adjournment was made without consultation with or consent by the Eastern Nigeria Government;

HAVING also noted the many acts of bad faith on the part of the Gowon Government and its inability to fulfil promises or implement agreements unanimously reached;

FINDING now that there is a plot hatched up by certain civil servants and other officials with the active involvement of Lt.-Col. Yakubu Gowon to impose a constitution and certain other measures on Nigeria;

REAFFIRMING the implicit confidence of the people of Eastern Nigeria in His Excellency, Lt.-Col. Odumegwu Ojukwu, and assuring him of the solidarity of Eastern Nigeria and their support and admiration for the way he has handled the present crisis facing Nigeria;

ALSO ASSURING His Excellency of the admiration of the people of Eastern Nigeria in the Military Government of Eastern Nigeria and their desire for its continued administration until it has achieved its objective of creating a new society in Eastern Nigeria;

WE DO HEREBY RESOLVE that our Military Governor be advised as follows:

1. To take any measures he considers appropriate for the defence and protection of the integrity of Eastern Nigeria, the lives and property of its inhabitants.
2. To maintain utmost vigilance against subversion of the Government of Eastern Nigeria not only from outside the Region, but also from within and to deal ruthlessly with anybody, high or low, engaged in subversion.
3. To resist the imposition on the people of Eastern Nigeria of any constitutional, administrative or legislative measures taken without prior consultation and agreement.
4. To reject any solution which will undermine the economic and industrial progress and prosperity of Eastern Nigeria or which will tend to sow the seeds of future friction among the Regions of this country.
5. To continue with the good progress made so far in the rehabilitation of refugees.
6. To speed up the implementation of Provincial Administration with legislative and executive powers, and the re-establishment of Customary Courts.
7. To spare no efforts at the right time to purge former holders of public offices of corrupt practices so as to set a shining example for the youths of this Region, and inculcate into the people the spirit of honesty, integrity, fair play, mutual trust and a feeling of oneness which will provide the basis for our future progress.
8. To continue Your Excellency's efforts to bring about a meeting of Military Leaders and the reconvening of the Ad Hoc Constitutional Conference under conditions of adequate security satisfactory to Your Excellency.
9. To ensure that only men and women of integrity and merit are appointed to public offices in the Region and that a code of conduct for public officers be drawn up for Eastern Nigeria.

LASTLY, we assure Your Excellency that no Eastern Nigerian, whether living inside or outside this Region, has the mandate or support of the people of this Region to speak for or represent them UNLESS appointed with the recommendation and approval of Your Excellency acting on behalf of Eastern Nigeria.

A. IKOKU,
Chairman.

DATED November, 23, 1966.

Since that date matters had become worse; sanctions had been imposed on Eastern Nigeria, war-like preparations made against her; her isolation was complete. Men and women in the Region, incensed by the treatment meted out to them by an unrepentant Lagos and the North, called for the declaration of Eastern Nigeria as a sovereign independent state.

In these circumstances, the joint meeting of the Consultative Assembly and the Advisory Committee of Chiefs and Elders was reconvened for a clear statement on the future course of action. After an appraisal of the development in the Nigerian crises past and present had been presented to the joint session, a telegram just received from the Lagos Government was read. The full text is as follows:

FURTHER MY TELEX OF TWENTIETH MAY X I HAVE JUST RECEIVED YOUR LETTER PG/0897/11 OF MAY 16, 1967 X AS YOU ARE AWARE ECONOMIC MEASURES COMPLAINED OF WERE LIFTED IN RESPONSE TO RECOMMENDATIONS OF NATIONAL CONCILIATION COMMITTEE WITH EFFECT FROM MAY 23 X THEREFORE DEEPLY DISAPPOINTED THAT YOU HAVE NOT RESPONDED POSITIVELY X IT IS NOT TOO LATE TO COMMENCE MEASURES TO RESOLVE CRISIS WITHOUT BLOODSHED AND KEEP THE COUNTRY TOGETHER X

IT IS DESIRABLE YOU DECLARE YOUR AGREEMENT WITH POLITICAL AND ADMINISTRATIVE PROGRAMME RECENTLY PROCLAIMED BY THE SUPREME MILITARY COUNCIL X THIS YOU WILL RECALL REQUIRES THE URGENT CREATION OF STATES SIMULTANEOUSLY ALL OVER THE COUNTRY TO REMOVE THREAT OF DOMINATION, PREPARATION OF NEW CONSTITUTION ON THEIR BASIS X NEW CONSTITUTION CAN PROVIDE ALL SAFEGUARDS CONSIDERED NECESSARY FOR STATE GOVERNMENTS X ALSO PROGRAMME ENVISAGES IMMEDIATE APPOINTMENT OF A REVENUE ALLOCATION COMMISSION TO FIND NEW FORMULA ON BASIS OF PRINCIPLE OF DERIVATION AND NEED TO PROVIDE ADEQUATE FUNDS FOR ESSENTIAL CENTRAL GOVERNMENT FUNCTIONS X PROGRAMME WILL ENSURE FAIR PLAY AND JUSTICE FOR ALL SECTIONS OF THE COUNTRY X

THEREFORE I EARNESTLY APPEAL TO YOU TO COOPERATE TO ARREST
FURTHER DRIFT INTO DISINTEGRATION X ON THE BASIS OF THE FORE-
GOING REPRESENTATIVES OF ALL GOVERNMENTS CAN MEET WITHOUT
FURTHER DELAY TO PLAN FOR SMOOTH IMPLEMENTATION OF THE
POLITICAL AND ADMINISTRATIVE PROGRAMME ADOPTED BY ALL YOUR
COLLEAGUES OF THE SUPREME MILITARY COUNCIL X
MOST IMMEDIATE

On the evening of Saturday, May 27, 1967, the joint session of the
enlarged Consultative Assembly and the Advisory Committee of
Chiefs and Elders, after full deliberation, passed a resolution the
text of which is as follows:

WE, THE CHIEFS, Elders and Representatives of Eastern Nigeria,
gathered at this Joint Meeting of the Advisory Committee of
Chiefs and Elders and the Consultative Assembly do solemnly
declare as follows:

WHEREAS we have been in the vanguard of the national movement for the building of a strong, united and prosperous Nigeria
where no man will be oppressed and have devoted our efforts,
talents and resources to this end;

WHEREAS we cherish certain inalienable human rights and state
obligations such as the right to life, liberty and pursuit of happiness; the right to acquire, possess and defend property; the
provision of security; and the establishment of good and just
government based on the consent of the governed;

WHEREAS in practical demonstration of these beliefs, our people
settled in other parts of Nigeria served their country in many
capacities, and contributed immensely to the growth and development of Nigeria;

WHEREAS we are living witnesses of injustices and atrocities
committed against Eastern Nigeria, among which are the premeditated murder of over 30,000 of our innocent men, women and children by Northern Nigerians, the calculated destruction of the
property of our sons and daughters, the shameless conversion of
two million Eastern Nigerians into refugees in their own country
all this without remorse;

WHEREAS in consequence of these and other acts of discrimination and injustice, we have painfully realised that the Federation
of Nigeria has failed, and has given us no protection;

WHEREAS in spite of these facts, the Government and people of
Eastern Nigeria have persisted in their efforts to find a practical
and just solution that would preserve the continued existence of
Nigeria as one corporate unit and restore peace and confidence

as demonstrated by the initiative of our Military Governor in getting all the military leaders together at Aburi, Ghana;

WHEREAS the hopes which the Aburi Agreement engendered have proved to be misplaced and have been destroyed by a series of acts of bad faith and distortions and finally by a refusal on the part of the 'Lagos Government' to implement these and other Agreements, notwithstanding the fact that they were freely and voluntarily entered into;

WHEREAS the Federation of Nigeria has forfeited any claim to our allegiance by these acts and by the economic, political and diplomatic sanctions imposed against us by the so-called Federal Government;

AND WHEREAS the object of government is the good of the governed and the will of the people its ultimate sanction;

NOW, THEREFORE, in consideration of these and other facts and injustices, we, the Chiefs, Elders and Representatives of all the Twenty Provinces of Eastern Nigeria, assembled in this Joint Meeting of the Advisory Committee of Chiefs and Elders and the Consultative Assembly, at Enugu this 27th day of May, 1967, we hereby solemnly:

(a) MANDATE His Excellency Lt.-Col. Chukwuemeka Odumegwu Ojukwu, Military Governor of Eastern Nigeria, to declare at the earliest practicable date Eastern Nigeria a free, sovereign and independent state by the name and title of the REPUBLIC OF BIAFRA.

(b) RESOLVE that the new REPUBLIC OF BIAFRA shall have the full and absolute powers of a sovereign state, and shall establish commerce, levy war, conclude peace, enter into diplomatic relations, and carry out, as of right, other sovereign responsibilities.

(c) DIRECT that the REPUBLIC OF BIAFRA may enter into arrangement with any sovereign unit or units in what remains of Nigeria or in any part of Africa desirous of association with us for the purpose of running a common services organization and for the establishment of economic ties.

(d) RECOMMEND that the REPUBLIC OF BIAFRA should become a member of the Commonwealth of Nations, the Organisation of African Unity and the United Nations Organisation.

(e) RECOMMEND the adoption of a Federal Constitution based on the new provincial units.

(f) REAFFIRM His Excellency's assurance of protection for the persons, properties and businesses of foreign nationals in our territory.

(g) DECLARE our unqualified confidence in the Military Governor of Eastern Nigeria, Lt.-Col. Chukwuemeka Odumegwu Ojukwu, and assure him of our unreserved support for the way and manner he has handled the crisis in the country.

So help us God.

THE DECLARATION

Fellow countrymen and women, YOU, the people of Eastern Nigeria:

CONSCIOUS of the supreme authority of Almighty God over all mankind, of your duty to yourselves and posterity;

AWARE that you can no longer be protected in your lives and in your property by any Government based outside Eastern Nigeria;

BELIEVING that you are born free and have certain inalienable rights which can best be preserved by yourselves;

UNWILLING to be unfree partners in any association of a political or economic nature;

REJECTING the authority of any person or persons other than the Military Government of Eastern Nigeria to make any imposition of whatever kind or nature upon you;

DETERMINED to dissolve all political and other ties between you and the former Federal Republic of Nigeria;

PREPARED to enter into such association, treaty or alliance with any sovereign state within the former Federal Republic of Nigeria and elsewhere on such terms and conditions as best to subserve your common good;

AFFIRMING your trust and confidence in ME;

HAVING mandated ME to proclaim on your behalf, and in your name, that Eastern Nigeria be a sovereign independent Republic,

NOW THEREFORE I, LIEUTENANT-COLONEL CHUKWUEMEKA ODU-MEGWU OJUKWU, MILITARY GOVERNOR OF EASTERN NIGERIA, BY VIRTUE OF THE AUTHORITIY, AND PURSUANT TO THE PRINCIPLES, RECITED ABOVE, DO HEREBY SOLEMNLY PROCLAIM THAT THE TERRI-TORY AND REGION KNOWN AS AND CALLED EASTERN NIGERIA TO-GETHER WITH HER CONTINENTAL SHELF AND TERRITORIAL WATERS SHALL HENCEFORTH BE AN INDEPENDENT SOVEREIGN STATE OF THE NAME AND TITLE OF 'THE REPUBLIC OF BIAFRA'.

AND I DO DECLARE THAT:

(i) all political ties between us and the Federal Republic of Nigeria are hereby totally dissolved;

N

   (ii) all subsisting contractual obligations entered into by the Government of the Federal Republic of Nigeria or by any person, authority, organisation or government acting on its behalf, with any person, authority or organisation operating, or relating to any matter or thing, within the Republic of Biafra, shall henceforth be deemed to be entered into with the Military Governor of the Republic of Biafra for and on behalf of the Government and people of the Republic of Biafra, and the covenants thereof shall, subject to this Declaration, be performed by the parties according to their tenor;

  (iii) all subsisting international treaties and obligations made on behalf of Eastern Nigeria by the Government of the Federal Republic of Nigeria shall be honoured and respected;

  (iv) Eastern Nigeria's due share of all subsisting international debts and obligations entered into by the Government of the Federal Republic of Nigeria on behalf of the Federation of Nigeria shall be honoured and respected;

   (v) steps will be taken to open discussions on the question of Eastern Nigeria's due share of the assets of the Federation of Nigeria and personal properties of the citizens of Biafra throughout the Federation of Nigeria;

  (vi) the rights, privileges, pensions, etc., of all personnel of the Public Services, the Armed Forces and the Police now serving in any capacity within the Republic of Biafra are hereby guaranteed;

 (vii) we shall keep the door open for association with, and would welcome, any sovereign unit or units in the former Federation of Nigeria or in any other parts of Africa desirous of association with us for the purposes of running a common services organisation and for the establishment of economic ties;

(viii) we shall protect the lives and property of all foreigners residing in Biafra, we shall extend the hand of friendship to those nations who respect our sovereignty, and shall repel any interference in our internal affairs;

  (ix) we shall faithfully adhere to the charter of the Organisation of African Unity and of the United Nations Organisation;

   (x) it is our intention to remain a member of the British Commonwealth of Nations in our right as a sovereign, independent nation.

LONG LIVE THE REPUBLIC OF BIAFRA!
AND MAY GOD PROTECT ALL WHO LIVE IN HER!

V

THE BIAFRAN NATIONAL ANTHEM
Land of the Rising Sun

Land of the rising sun, we love and cherish,
    Beloved homeland of our brave heroes;
We must defend our lives or we shall perish,
    We shall protect our hearths from all our foes;
But if the price is death for all we hold dear,
    Then let us die without a shred of fear.

Hail to Biafra, consecrated nation,
    Oh fatherland, this be our solemn pledge:
Defending thee shall be a dedication,
    Spilling our blood we'll count a privilege;
The waving standard which emboldens the free
    Shall always be our flag of liberty.

We shall emerge triumphant from this ordeal,
    And through the crucible unscathed we'll pass;
When we are poised the wounds of battle to heal,
    We shall remember those who died in mass;
Then shall our trumpets peal the glorious song
    Of victory we scored o'er might and wrong.

Oh God, protect us from the hidden pitfall,
    Guide all our movements lest we go astray;
Give us the strength to heed the humanist call:
    'To give and not to count the cost', each day;
Bless those who rule to serve with resoluteness,
    To make this clime a land of righteousness.

NNAMDI AZIKIWE

INDEX

ABA, 233, 297
Abajue, G., 118
Abakilike, 233, 247
Abdul, Alhaji M. Kokori, 54
Abdussalami, 90
Abengowe, Nwachukwu, 301
Abeokuta, 15–16, 297; Garrison, 129, 130, 131, 132, 157–8
Aberdare, Lord, 19
Aburi, meeting of Nigerian Supreme Military Council at, and 'Aburi Accord', 5–6, 167, 207 ff., 245–6, 263, 267; decisions reached, 213 ff.; different interpretations, 218–19, 230 ff., 270; agenda, 315; minutes, 316 ff., Communiqués following, 325–6; Federal Permanent Secretaries' recommendations on, 320 ff., 328; Federal Government's non-implementation of, 220 ff., 340
Accra, 18
Action Group party, 35, 37, 40, 42, 43–4, 73, 93, 113, 115, 142
Ad Hoc Constitutional Conference 1966, 31, 177 ff., 263, 306, 307, 322, 340, 342, 344; Committee, 239
Adaji, Alhaji Hashim, 142
Adams, T. K., 69, 116–18, 304
Adderley, Sir Charles, 296
Addis Ababa, as venue for Nigerian Conferences, 203, 209
Adebajo, Ayo, 43
Adebayo, Col. Robert, 168, 212, 232, 238, 240, 307, 315, 324, 325
Adebiyi, Sgt. Y., 129
Adegbenro, Alhaji Dauda, 93, 142
Adegbenro v. *Akintola*, 113
Ademola, Sir Adetokumbo, 115
Ademolegun, Brigadier, 128, 130, 138, 139
Ademoyega, Major, 127, 129, 132, 139
Aderemi, Sir Adesoji, 41, 114
Aderemi v. *Akintola*, 113
Aderigbo (Clerk of Federal Parliament), 88
Adeyemo, Michael, 118
Adkins v. *Children's Hospital*, 110
Ado Ekiti, 93

Afolabi-Oloja, M. O., 300
Agricultural Research, Federal Dept. of, 259; institute of, Samaru, 258
Air Force Headquarters, 258
Airports: Kano, 258; Ikeja, 259
Ajayi, Dr. Festus A., 175, 182, 307
Akenzua, S. A., 179, 309, 316
Akifu, Alhaji Ali, 135, 316
Akinfosile, Chief Obu, 182
Akinjide, R. A., 67, 117, 300
Akinsanya, Oba Samuel, 182
Akintola, Chief Samuel (Prime Minister, Western Nigeria), 40–1, 43, 44, 52, 73, 74, 76, 82, 89 ff., 99, 113 ff., 127, 128, 139, 299, 301, 304
Akitoye, King, 13–15, 297
Akpan, N. U., 175, 269, 309, 316
Akran, Oba C. D., 145, 156
Akure, 93
Alexander, Major-Gen. H. T., 279, 280
Alexandra, Princess, 34
Alimi, Mallam, 89–90
Allagoa, Chief, 182
Aluko, James, 43
Aluko, Dr. Samuel A., 55, 64, 243
Amachree, G. K., 243
Amaigbo, 17
Ameche, Mbazulike, 304
Amogu, Oji, 118
Amuwo, Tunde, 43
Ankrah, Lt.-Gen. J. A., 212, 316–17, 323, 325
Apapa, 159
Apolo, Major, 317
Archives, National, 259
Ardo, Alhaji Buba, 174, 182
Arikpo, Dr. O., 243, 309
Arinze, Bishop, 269
Armaments, Importation of, 213, 233, 317
Army, Nigerian: in politics, 127 ff., 141 ff.; effect of coups on morale, 172; leadership of, discussed at Ad Hoc Conference, 200; — discussed at Aburi Conference, 212, 214–15, 318–19; — federal decree on after Aburi, 221; Aburi decisions on, 321, 324–5, 328–30, 334;